West Midlands Vol I

Edited by Steve Twelvetree

First published in Great Britain in 2003 by
YOUNG WRITERS
Remus House,
Coltsfoot Drive,
Peterborough, PE2 9JX
Telephone (01733) 890066

HB ISBN 1 84460 162 5
SB ISBN 1 84460 163 3

FOREWORD

Young Writers was established in 1991 as a foundation for promoting the reading and writing of poetry amongst children and young adults. Today it continues this quest and proceeds to nurture and guide the writing talents of today's youth.

From this year's competition Young Writers is proud to present a showcase of the best poetic talent from across the UK. Each hand-picked poem has been carefully chosen from over 66,000 'Hullabaloo!' entries to be published in this, our eleventh primary school series.

This year in particular we have been wholeheartedly impressed with the quality of entries received. The thought, effort, imagination and hard work put into each poem impressed us all and once again the task of editing was a difficult but enjoyable experience.

We hope you are as pleased as we are with the final selection and that you and your family will continue to be entertained with *Hullabaloo! West Midlands Vol I* for many years to come.

CONTENTS

The Poems

Please Help Me!

Please help me stop this disaster!
Because if you help me it will be faster!
I hope you realise;
The extraordinary size,
Of some of the animals dying!
Please help me stop this disaster.

There is the huge hungry lion,
The slippery slimy seal,
The gigantic bellowing bear!
The dog that's eating a pear.
These are all going to say bye-bye.

This isn't fair, the rabbit, guinea pig and hare.
They are all going to evacuate,
If we're lucky, it might just be 8.
This just is not fair.

Do you know
That I can show
What life is like
Doing business on your bike.
It is hard to get along,
If you are not strong.
It is unbelievable
It is really unhealable

We could use some help sometimes!
Did you notice, this poem rhymes?
Whether you are old or young
Your life will not be sold,
To anyone that gets in the way
Not even if they offer to pay,
We could use some help sometime.

Samantha James (10)
Amblecote Primary School

Excuses, Excuses

'Late again Beth, what's the excuse this time?'
'The baby rolled down the hill.'
'Well why couldn't you pick him up?'
'Because I fell in the largest puddle.'
'Well why couldn't you run to school
And dry yourself off there?'
'Because the baby wailed and Mom had to change him.'
'Oh why don't you just sit down and pass me your homework?'
'Haven't got it.'
'Why not Beth?'
'Fell down the loo.'
'Why couldn't you do it again?'
'Baby screwed the paper up and played ball.'
'Surely there was some spare?'
'No, Mom chucked it all in the bin
Thinking it was used foil.'
'Well you will have to do it again at breaktime.'
'I can't.'
'Why this time Beth?'
'My pen will run out and it cost a thousand pounds.'
'Well why can't you use a pencil?'
'Because I can see the future and I will be sick.'
'Why can't you do it when you are better?'
'Because dinosaurs will come and invade the school.'
'Oh no the future is now, I am going to be sick.'
'Beth come back at once!'

Emily Langridge (10)
Amblecote Primary School

Guess What?

It's your worst nightmare,
It's in the air,
You breathe it in,
It sends shivers down your skin.

It's in your dreams,
It makes you scream,
I don't know what it means,
It hasn't been seen.

Juliet Lamb (11)
Amblecote Primary School

Graffiti

Colour, colour everywhere,
Nobody seems to care!
Colour, colour everywhere,
Nobody seems to care!

Conquering the environment,
Contaminating buildings.
Spray cans everywhere,
Beware, beware, beware!

Water spraying like a jet,
It still leaves faint marks.
Council workers scrubbing walls,
Working in our parks!

Everything is clean,
No graffiti to be seen.
But come back next day,
Sprayed again the same old way!

Colour, colour everywhere,
Nobody seems to care!
Colour, colour everywhere,
Nobody seems to care!

James Thornton (11)
Amblecote Primary School

Is It Enough?

Cans and bottles,
Plastic bags,
Christmas cards,
Grotty rags.

It's great for the environment,
A terrific thing to do,
The Earth's a better place if we . . .

Papers and books,
Oil and glass,
Shoes and clothes,
Our rubbish and trash.

It's great for the environment,
A terrific thing to do,
The Earth's a better place if we . . .
Recycle,
Recycle,
Recycle.

Amanda Millward (11)
Amblecote Primary School

Pollution

In the water,
In the air,
Even in the ground,
It makes no sound.

Now you know it's everywhere,
Your planet's dying out,
Don't sit watching your TV,
Come and tidy up with me.

In the atmosphere,
A trail of thrilling horror,
Lurks in the ocean,
Destruction in motion.

Please help me clear it up,
For the sake of mankind,
It's a fantasy to come true,
I'll hope for you.

Tomas Buckby (10)
Amblecote Primary School

POLLUTION

Blowing in the icy wind,
Dumped onto the streets,
Empty, deserted, confused bins,
Cluttering all the streets.

Colourful splashes everywhere,
Revealing huge bold words,
Does anybody care about
The rude disgusting words?

Thick coal, black ooze,
Seeping into seas,
Harmless fish are dying,
The oily thick black seas.

Why don't we walk or run?
Instead we take the car.
Lush green plants choking,
The deadly poisonous car.

Laura Power (10)
Amblecote Primary School

Extinction Tick-Tock

Elephants are ending
Foxes are fleeing
Dodos already dead
Animals have already fled
Seals are skinned
Man has sinned
Sharks sinking
Man not thinking
Wolves whine
Thieves lost
Tigers trapped
They've collapsed
Man is dangerous
We are furious
Man is greedy
Animals are bleeding
We are killing.

Michael Wood (10)
Amblecote Primary School

Sticky Mess

Oil pollutes the water,
Looks slimy, thick and black,
Sand gets covered,
Animals scuttling back.

Sits like a blanket,
A thick black lake,
Smells like a factory machine,
A fateful mistake.

Oil, an oozing substance,
Black as a panther's sheen,
Floating to the seashore,
Waiting to be seen.

Oil, oil gets everywhere,
Nobody seems to care.
Oil, oil gets everywhere,
Nobody seems to care.

Sam Fletcher (11)
Amblecote Primary School

EXTINCTION (THEIR TIME'S UP)

The humans are hunting
Pigs are grunting.
Sharks are sinking
Men are winking.
Cheetahs are trapped
Men have clapped.

Frogs are frying
Men are enjoying.
Kangaroos are clinging
Men are singing.
Whales are wailing
Men are still sailing.
Seals are slipping
Men are clipping.
Extinction is coming!

Martin Fletcher (10)
Amblecote Primary School

EXCUSES, EXCUSES

'Late again Amy, what's the excuse this time?'
'My mom forgot to wash our clothes.'
'What happened after your mom washed them?'
'We lost the car keys.'
'What did you do once you found them?'
'Gravity broke and the car floated into space.'
'Right sit down and hand in your homework.'
'Can't Miss.'
'Why not?'
'The baby scribbled on it.'
'Why couldn't you rub it out then?'
'Because it was colour.'
'What happened after that?'
'Dad washed it to clean the car with.'
'Then what?'
'Mom thought it was scrap and threw it in the bin.'
'Right you will have to do it at play time then.'
'Can't Miss.'
'Why not now?'
'Mom shredded my pen.'
'Why can't you buy a new one?'
'It costs too much.'
'You will have to borrow one from school.'
'Can't!'
'Why not now?'
'Dad said I can't borrow ones from school.'

Rosie Pritchard (10)
Amblecote Primary School

HELP THEM

Because of us . . .
Pandas are parting!
Because of us . . .
Snakes are snookered!
Because of us . . .
Fish are frying!
Because of us . . .
Sharks are shocked!
So help them!

Because of us . . .
Otters are off!
Because of us . . .
Tigers are trapped!
Because of us . . .
Lynx are losing!
Because of us . . .
Rabbits are running!
Please help them!

Because of us . . .
Seals are slipping away!
Because of us . . .
Foxes are fleeing!
Because of us . . .
Hippos are hungry!
Because of us . . .
Dolphins are dying!
Save them for us.

Yvette Sedgley (10)
Amblecote Primary School

Impossible Dream

Bubblegum,
Chocolate bars,
Newspapers,
Magazines.
Sweet wrappers,
Crisp packets,
Blowing in the breeze!

By the door,
On the floor,
In the street,
In a heap.
In the park,
While it's dark,
Blowing in the breeze!

Bubblegum,
Chocolate bars,
Newspapers,
Magazines.
Sweet wrappers,
Crisp packets,

. . . Gone!

Lucy Millward (11)
Amblecote Primary School

Rubbish

Put that litter in the bin!
Dropping litter is a sin.
A rusty old can, can kill a bird
To drop litter is so absurd.

Remember some litter does not rot
Plastics and nylon and whatnot.
Metal too may not decay
So put it in the bin today.

Ben Jackson (10)
Amblecote Primary School

Excuses, Excuses

'Late again, what's the excuse this time Simon?'
'Aliens tested on me for an hour Miss.'
'Couldn't you run away?'
'But my brother shot my dad Miss.'
'Couldn't you phone the ambulance?'
'No, I had to come to school.'
'OK, everyone sit down and give in your homework.'
'Dog ate it Miss.'
'Why couldn't you do it again?'
'I did do it again Miss.'
'Where is it then?'
'Potty Miss.'
'OK go to the corridor.'
'I can't, my mom said don't let people boss me around.'
'Do it now!'
'Have not got a pen Miss.'
'Use one of mine.'
'I am allergic.'
'I'll phone your dad.'
'Shot Miss.'
'I'll phone your mum then.'

Cheryl Bloomfield (10)
Amblecote Primary School

It's Here

They all know it's there,
Animals are being killed,
Hurry don't stare,
Tips are being filled.

They just don't want to know,
Because they're not prepared,
They're not recycling, oh no!
Recycle, recycle I declare!

The trees are toppling down,
'Timber!' the beast shouts,
Trees are replaced by the town,
No trees left we will soon count.

Why on earth are you standing there?
The monkeys are in fear!
It's not just a nightmare,
It's really happening here.

Emily Weaver (11)
Amblecote Primary School

Help!

Litter's deadly,
Never in the bin,
Always in your way,
Killing, killing, killing.

People always dropping it
And never pick it up,
Help the animals survive this crime,
Please clear up all the muck!

Kirsty Owen (11)
Amblecote Primary School

Round And Round

In the bin, in the air,
Nobody seems to care!
It just stays there,
Nobody seems to care!

In the water, in the air,
Nobody seems to care!
It just stays there,
Nobody seems to care!

In the ground round and round,
Nobody seems to care!
It just stays there,
Nobody seems to care!

Richard Hanson (11)
Amblecote Primary School

Recycle Glass

Recycle glass
And you will be class,
You can cycle,
To the recycling point,
Don't pollute with your car,
Jog instead it's not too far,
When you get to the recycle bin,
Don't forget to drop them in,
Crashing, smashing, bashing as they drop,
Don't forget to recycle next time
You drink some pop.

Kieran Parish (10)
Amblecote Primary School

The Magical Dream

First eternal darkness
Then a light as bright as sapphire appears in front of you
And fills the space with multicoloured light.
Mystical clouds come over your fragile head while you sleep.
Characters pop out of nowhere
Some familiar, some stranger.
The magical dream takes you on an adventure
To places you have never been to before,
With strange smells and different sights.
Chattering whispers, traffic noises and babies crying
Fade into the distance as the bells ring out.
The bells are still ringing
What could it mean?
The picture is fading
What could it mean?
It's time to wake up and finish your dream.

Kristian Lehmann (9)
Amblecote Primary School

Deadly Mist

The mist creeps through the town,
With its fearful claw.
Oozing through your windows,
It's knocking at your door.

Roaming through your town,
Pollution is everywhere.
Can we stop this vile mist,
Because it's always there?

The mist creeps out of town,
It's got no fearful claw.
Oozing out of windows,
Stopped knocking at your door.

We have stopped pollution,
But for how long?
We found the right solution,
Pollution has all gone.

Holly Timperley (10)
Amblecote Primary School

COLOUR

Sabotage your neighbourhood,
Smothering the wall,
Scraped on your garbage cans,
Sprayed on the wall.

The council come and clear it up,
With their jet machine.
They scrub and scrub to wash it away,
Bright and new and clean.

Sabotage your neighbourhood,
Smothering the wall,
Scraped on the garbage cans,
Sprayed on the floor.

Green, yellow, red, white,
Big, bold coloured streaks,
Green, yellow, red, white,
Vandalise the streets.

Jarnal Shinji (11)
Amblecote Primary School

Pollution

Pollution is worldwide
And it always stands at your side.

Wherever you go
Whatever you do
Pollution is all around you.

It's in the litter
It's in our rubbish
And even in our human waste.

It's in our cars
And our lorries
And you can almost feel the taste . . .

Sam Grosvenor (10)
Amblecote Primary School

Smelly, Stinky, Slimy

Smelly, stinky, slimy!
Thousands every day,
They are everywhere,
Bin men take them all away.

Smelly, stinky, slimy!
The smell is getting worse,
The bins are getting fuller,
It is a horrid curse.

Smelly, stinky, slimy!
When they have been used.
They can't take it any more,
They expand and start to ooze!

Lucie Hadlington (11)
Amblecote Primary School

Litter Bug

Put it in the bin,
Clear it up,
They don't care,
They just stare.

Put it in the bin,
Clear it up,
Don't be lazy,
It makes you crazy!

Put it in the bin,
Clear it up,
Make it clean
And keep it green.

James Grosvenor (10)
Amblecote Primary School

Pollution

Getting hotter,
Ice melting,
Oceans rising,
Suffocating planet.

Beware! Beware!

Ice shrinking,
No one cares,
Drowning world
Cities destroyed.

Beware! Beware!

Anthony Bullock (11)
Amblecote Primary School

Dolphins Are Going To Be Extinct

D is for in danger
O is for ocean, so dirty; not clean
L is for losing their home
P is for parting with their family
H is for their habitat
I s it true that dolphins rescue people?
N o one has ever killed dolphins except for the French
S hort-snouted spinner dolphins have never been spotted
in the Atlantic because of *us killing them!*

Stacey Dowler (10)
Amblecote Primary School

My Pet Hamster

My pet Mo,
She is so mad,
She is always climbing on the silver, sparkling bars,
She is so funny,
She looks like lots of brown leaves,
The sound that she makes is eating all the time,
She smells of food because she is always eating,
She is as soft as a feather,
My pet Mo.

Naomi Stroyde (9)
Amblecote Primary School

A Cockatiel

I am a cockatiel
You're a human.
Rather my home
Or your comfort?
Rather my friend the wallaby
Or your fur coat?
Rather see a kiwi bird free
Or see a kiwi bird caged up?
Be as dumb as a dodo and destroy trees
Or be smart as a fox
And recycle rubbish.
    The choice is yours . . .

Adam Watkins (10)
Amblecote Primary School

Recycling?

Hey everyone!
. . . start recycling specs.
And *help* them in poorer lands.

Hey everyone!
. . . start recycling specs.
And *help* them in poorer lands to see.

Send your specs to opticians
Just like me!

Sarah Smith (11)
Amblecote Primary School

I Love Dogs

A beautiful little Labrador
Was crossing the bridge to explore
When he saw a sly cat
He followed it
It had gone behind a shed
And the Labrador twitched his nose
When the dog went behind the shed
The cat had gone
The dog went home to dig for his bone.

Sara Dakin (9)
Amblecote Primary School

All About Bedtime For Me

I can feel a bed squeaking,
I can hear birds singing,
Cars beeping, people talking.
I can smell chips cooking.
Dreams come,
Stars floating, designs dancing.
I'm alone in the darkness, wanting to go to sleep,
I am so comfy.

Emma Goodall (9)
Amblecote Primary School

The Picker

My dad picks his scabs, pick, pick.
That's how it sounds when he picks,
He squeezes his arm which makes blood come up,
It sounds like a squelch.
It smells a bit like smelly feet
Which makes it more disgusting.
I call him The Picker.

Mark Clement (9)
Amblecote Primary School

Bogeyman

My brother picks his nose.
It's really, really horrible.
It's squelchy bogies.
It smells like revolting mushy peas
And it tastes like rough beans.
It feels like green, soft bananas
And we also call him *Bogeyman!*

Lauren Baggs (9)
Amblecote Primary School

Ice

Ice, ice everywhere, it's like a white blanket on the floor
And it's sparkly and glistens like diamonds on the floor.
It's white as clouds in the sky.
Before it turns to ice it trickles like a tap.
It stays and stays till the sun comes out.

Natalie Poole (9)
Amblecote Primary School

My Cousin

I love my cousin,
My cousin is really nice.
I play games with her every night.
Whenever we play we always play nice.
When I go home and get ready for bed
I never go to sleep,
I just sit there thinking about her instead.

Emily White (9)
Amblecote Primary School

Water

The sea is blue and very deep.
The waves crash upon the shore.
There are many shells that you can keep.
Amongst the rocks you will find jellyfish
Cockles, mussels and shrimps
To pick up by hand.

Jessica Houghton (9)
Amblecote Primary School

My Mom

My mom is kind
My mom is mad
My mom hates dogs like me,
I don't know why she dyes her hair
I think it's because of me,
But I like my mom like she is now.

Louise Redman (9)
Amblecote Primary School

CHEETAH

Never trust a cheetah
They always get their prey
Fast and furious at night and deadly in the day
They travel as fast as a speeding train
They're as swift as a bird
And have a clever and quick brain.

Laura Green (9)
Amblecote Primary School

HULLABALOO!

Galoos go bing
Balloos go bong
In the land of Hullabaloo!

Monkeyoos scream and shout
They're angry, they're mean, they're all full of steam,
In the land of Hullabaloo!

Cheerioos are always cheery
Watch out, they'll give you a right whopping meany
Their eyes pop out, they'll give you a shout
In the land of Hullabaloo!

This land is quite a mean place
I'm warning you, you better watch out
In the land of Hullabaloo!

Kirsty Thomas (10)
Blackheath Primary School

GHOST

I was climbing on the stair;
I felt something scary present.
Then I found a ball of hair;
I wish it was more pleasant!

It feels like a ghost
Here to scare
But there's a problem
No one knows it's there.

As I was sleeping in my bed,
Something blared out of the TV.
As I turned to run away I felt a hand upon my head
I thought it was my hamster Bee-Vee.

I think it's a ghost
Here to scare!
But there's a problem
No one knows it's there!

Oh, once today at school
When the clock struck 2,
I felt a ghoul
Floating around me.

It must be a ghost
Here to scare,
But there's just one problem,
No one knows it's there.

Anthony Aldridge (10)
Blackheath Primary School

SLIPPERY SAM

Slippery Sam slid out of bed,
Under the door
And over the stairs.

Down in the kitchen,
Round a bowl
And he filled it with
Big black coal.

Black and white
All colourful and bright.

He left the bowl
That was full of coal.

Over the stairs
And under the door.

He got dressed in his thermal vest
He went to school
With his mate called Paul.

His mate called Paul
Is very cool.
After school he plays pool
With his mate until it's very late.

Sam slid round his mom,
Over the stairs
And under the door
Into bed with his ted.

Rebecca Rees (8)
Blackheath Primary School

HULLABALOO

Red as a mad clown's nose,
Orange as a blazing fire, oh no, it's been put out by a hose,
Yellow as a baby's blanket, soft and warm, *shh!*
As turquoise as the deep sea in Hawaii, *whoosh!*
Green as the fungus on your toes.
Blue as the roaring dragon comodos.
Crystal as the diamonds waiting to be found . . . I'm rich!
Gold as my sister's heart - before she spits out milk
(occasionally sick!) *Eeecch!*
Purple like my mommy's hug all soft and warm,
Black like a wasp's stripes (if you get to see them before . . . *oouch!')*

These are the colours of the hullabaloo
And if you didn't know better
They might be the colours of you!

Alice Cope (9)
Blackheath Primary School

HIKI THE AFRICAN ELEPHANT

Hiki the African elephant is a very small elephant,
Other elephants tease him here and there,
Jump from behind bushes to give him a scare
Each day he measures his height
Before he gets his daily fright,
Every month Hiki must grow an inch or so
Otherwise he will be teased and pinched,
One day later Hiki will grow,
Better luck next time because his friends don't know.

Christopher Hamblett-Jones (8)
Blackheath Primary School

Hullabaloo

You join us here on news tonight
With a fabulous story about a food fight
Strangely enough it happened at a wedding
I got so excited I had to change my bedding
A lot of racket and hullabaloo
Better get dodging, here comes a shoe
It started out perfect, then it all went wrong
The wedding singer won't sing his song.
He's too busy getting stuck in
Hey what's this, he's throwing a bin?
The bride and groom now hate each other
So now they're not friends, obviously not lovers
Now everyone's gone home, oh what a sight
That was the story about the food fight.

Sarah Banner (11)
Blackheath Primary School

Hullabaloo

Banging, shouting, stamping, screaming
It's got to be hullabaloo
Drums banging steel twanging
It's got to be hullabaloo
Singers singing, dancers dancing
It's got to be hullabaloo.

Windows smashing, metal clanging
It's got to be hullabaloo
Kids talking, people walking
It's got to be hullabaloo
Music beating, DJs swinging
It's got to be hullabaloo.

Nicole Redfern (10)
Blackheath Primary School

THE OTHER WAY AROUND

I eat with a pencil
And write with a spoon.
I listen with my mouth
And talk with my ears.

I love my mum
But not my dad.
I love my dad
But not my mum.

I cut with a fork
And I eat with a knife.
I drink from a plate
And eat from a cup.

I love my sister
But not my brother.
I love my brother
But not my sister.

Aden Griffiths (10)
Blackheath Primary School

A RAINY DAY TURNS INTO SNOW

Raindrops falling from the sky,
Glistening as they go,
How fast they fly, how fast they fly,
Going to and fro.

I hear silent patters on my window,
Settling down the door,
I have no real fear to show,
It's only half-past four.

Peeping out I have a look,
Wondering what I'll find,
It's like a cover of a book
Where the white pages combined.

Danielle Harrison (10)
Blackheath Primary School

I'D LIKE TO PAINT

I'd like to paint
A duck yodelling
To Humpty Dumpty.

I'd like to paint
A pink star
Walking down town.

I'd like to paint
A thin elephant
Kissing a mouse.

I'd like to paint
An ice lolly
Selling frozen men.

I'd like to paint
A purple house
Driving a car.

I'd like to paint
A multicoloured tree
Playing football.

I'd like to paint . . .

Kylie Jarvis (9)
Blackheath Primary School

All About Me

Hi, my name is Chi
And this poem is all about me.

I'm choco crazy
And I'm also mega lazy.

I may be fat
But I'm certainly not a rat.

I'm half Chinese
And half Vietnamese.

I'm quite clever,
Some say I'm the best ever.

I'm a clumsy little boy,
Whose best friend I call Foy Boy.

I'm 10 years old
And I used to be bold.

Vincent Bang (10)
Blackheath Primary School

Hullabaloo

There once was a hullabaloo
As the football flew down the loo
It landed in style
After flying a mile
And was joined by the goal scorer's shoe!

Christopher Smith (11)
Blackheath Primary School

My Dog

My dog plays with a ball.
When she sees a cat she puts her ears up.
She chases the cats away
When you play with her you wind her up.
She bites me by accident but not on purpose.
She is black all over.
She yowls in the night.
She keeps me awake.
She is a German shepherd.
I like her very much.
I bought her when she was a puppy.
She has another dog to comfort her.
She is a good dog.
She can run as fast as she can.
    She is called Sukie.

Samantha Sidebottom (8)
Blackheath Primary School

Hullabaloo

There once was a hullabaloo,
When the hamster fell down the loo,
He jumped around
And fell below ground
And now he lives in a shoe.

Peter Lynch (10)
Blackheath Primary School

My Cat

My cat plays with a piece of paper.
He eats biscuits and crisps.
Runs around the garden like someone silly.
Chases the birds.
He is black and white.
He has green eyes and a little black tail.
He sits on the back of the chair.
He is only a kitten.
He has got a little black spot on his back.
He is very, very silly.
He eats anything.
He can run very fast.
When he is cold he sits by the fire.
He is called Sooty.

Rosie Holland (8)
Blackheath Primary School

Final Day

It is the day,
We all rejoice,
It is the day,
The day we all leave school.
Everybody runnin',
Everybody screamin',
Cos this is da day
We all leave school.
All da teachers sighin'
At the racket we are makin'.
Cos this is the day we all leave . . .
School!

Michael Wilkinson (9)
Blackheath Primary School

Christmas Treats

Christmas treats here and there
Little trees like spiky hair
Christmas treats here and there
Christmas treats everywhere.
Christmas treats here and there
These are the treats that we share
Christmas treats here and there
Nice and sweet, lovely too
Christmas treats here and there
Tasty and sugary, shiny too.
Christmas treats here and there
We love treats anywhere
Christmas treats dancing around like funny clowns
Christmas treats here and there
Christmas treats everywhere.

Josh Billingham (8)
Blackheath Primary School

Untitled

One day the bells rang in the church
The birds were standing on a perch
The cat was chasing a mouse
In the big round house
The fish was swimming in a bowl
The dog was digging a hole
For the black and white mole.

Luke Farrington (8)
Blackheath Primary School

HULLABALOO!

You join us here at Up Town Rock,
Where an alien's landed in Sistan Mock.
He's come from the planet Goballdy Goo,
This creature is making a hullabaloo!

He's making a racket, stamping around,
The buildings are shaking and so is the ground.
All the town's people don't know what to do,
This monster has created a hullabaloo!

The alien is moving, he's come out the cave,
He's chasing the people to their early grave.
Reporting from Town Rock, I'm Diddly Doo,
The creature has caught me, hullabaloo!

Stacey Bissell (10)
Blackheath Primary School

CHRISTMAS

C hristmas is the best time of year
H appy time on Christmas Eve
R ip presents open on Christmas
I ce on cakes and food
S anta brings presents under trees
T oys to play with
M oms bring presents to you
A family party at Christmas
S anta brings presents when you are good.

James Martin (8)
Blackheath Primary School

Dragons

Dragons round the light bulb.
Dragons out the window.
Dragons in my bedroom.
Dragons everywhere!
Dragons in Fairy Land.
Dragons in the sky.
Dragons in my house.
They're eating all my pie!
Dragons, dragons everywhere.
Dragons in the park.
Dragons in a Sainsbury's trolley.
Riding down a slide.
You never know they could be anywhere.

Leah Hampton (8)
Blackheath Primary School

Christmas

C hristmas is brill and fine
H ands tearing all the time
R udolph with his red nose
I ce could even freeze your toes
S nowflakes falling swift and slow
T insel has a lovely glow
M e and mom make a pompom
A t the Christmas tree I hang the pompom on
S uper presents come each year.

Joe Davidson (9)
Blackheath Primary School

GHOSTS

Under the bed,
In the wardrobe
And spinning around on the globe!
Some nights
Bring frights
Might even wear your mum's tights
They creep at nights
Send out bites
I think they have a secret den
Well guess what?
I don't care
Because I see right through them!

Elisa Danks (9)
Blackheath Primary School

HALLOWE'EN

People going to trick or treat,
Ghosts and monsters come to meet.
Witches flying in the air,
Giving people quite a scare.
If you think you will escape,
Well think again my matey mate.
Tonight is the night the dead will rise,
Ghosts will come, each a different size.
Please be careful, it's not a pretty sight,
Please beware on Hallowe'en Night.

Natasha Phillips (7)
Blackheath Primary School

My Holidays

Holidays are fun and very good
The children are off school and playing about
In the green grass fields
The apples are juicy and red
You can see rabbits and hares jumping around
We see a horse in the field
People go on holiday when we are off school
Children going round other children's houses
I can see my friend Sarah eating an apple.

Laura Palmer (8)
Blackheath Primary School

The Haunted House

I went to the haunted house
I saw a grey lady
Was it a ghost?
Were there more grey ladies?
I felt very, very scared.
There was only me and my sister there.

Hayley Dellicott (8)
Blackheath Primary School

Hullabaloo!

I like hullabaloo, hullabaloo, hullabaloo,
What I like also, it's big, it's small, it's hullabaloo,
And I like something else too, it's pretty, it's ugly, it's hullabaloo,
I like one more thing too, it's fab, it's thin, it's hullabaloo,
So what I like is big, small, pretty, ugly, fat, thin . . .
It's hullabaloo, hullabaloo, hullabaloo!

Rhys Bennett (9)
Blackheath Primary School

CHRISTMAS

C hristmas is a happy time,
'H appy Christmas,' people say,
R ice pudding with chocolate chips,
I cing on the chocolate cake,
S anta comes in the middle of the night,
T insel wrapped around the tree,
M essages from people around the world,
A happy new year from me,
S anta has brought the presents.

Danielle Perigo (8)
Blackheath Primary School

CHRISTMAS

C hristmas is a time of the year,
H appiness comes once a year,
R obins under the holly trees,
I cicles glow in the night.
S anta arrives with presents,
T insel on the tree,
M agic in the air,
A happy new year,
S anta on his way.

Jason Bodycote (8)
Blackheath Primary School

Birthdays

B irthday's today, let's celebrate
I n and out the town
R eceive presents and treats from you
T oday it is my birthday
'H appy birthday!' sang my friends
D ear friends you're invited to a party.
A very special party
Y ou people, let's have fun!

Sarah Ann Carpenter (9)
Blackheath Primary School

Trucks

T rucks are fab
R eally shiny
U ntil they get dirty
C all the boss!
K ind to use
S urfing down the motorway.

Ashley Clements (10)
Blackheath Primary School

Valentine's Day

People sending cards and letters,
Love is in the air
People are in love today.

Getting cards and chocolate hearts
People are opening cards today
It's a special day for everyone!

Amy Baker (9)
Blackheath Primary School

FOOTBALL

F ootball is crazy,
O n the pitch is where I score,
O n the pitch is where I play,
T eams are coming,
B aggies are scoring,
A ll people shouting,
L ong football matches,
L ots of people going to matches.

Andrew Baker (8)
Blackheath Primary School

FOOTBALL

F ootball is good,
O h, I think it's a goal,
O h, it's a miss,
T oo much talent,
B ang it in the net,
A ston Villa score again,
L ucky Aston Villa,
L iverpool lose.

Thomas Oakes (8)
Blackheath Primary School

BIRTHDAYS

B ritney's music,
I cing on the cake,
R ed bright ribbons in little girl's hair,
T hinking of balloons popping,
H appy birthday music song everywhere.
D addy's travelling in the car,
A great big present waiting for me,
Y ippee! Yippee! A great big present for me.

Lauren Poole (8)
Blackheath Primary School

SPIDERS

S piders are creepy and scary,
P eople say they are hairy,
I 've never had a spider as a pet,
D ear Dad, can I have a set?
E ating spiders, people do,
R iding on spiders I never knew.
S uper spider, they are not very super,
Do you think so too?

Jake Aldridge (8)
Blackheath Primary School

Christmas

Christmas snow floating in the breeze
Robins singing very loudly
Santa flying over them
People having Christmas pudding
It's nearly dark
It's snowing outside
Christmas is nearly over.

Jamie Smith (9)
Blackheath Primary School

My Best Friend

My best friend, Thomas W,
Is very, very nice and cute.
He likes football, just like me,
He kicks the ball anywhere,
But I bet he does not care
And he sometimes plays with me.
I just really, really, really like him,
Indeed I do.

Jack Davies (8)
Blackheath Primary School

Easter

E aster eggs we eat at Easter time,
A little egg, that's all you need.
S unny skies, bright as can be,
T he children having a load of fun,
E veryone enjoying Easter fun,
R eally, Easter is my favourite time of year.

Hannah Stokes (7)
Blackheath Primary School

SMILES

S miles are really clever
M any last forever,
I love smiles, they're full of glee
L ike buttercups, I can see.
E very smile makes me glad
S miles are like hugs from Dad!

S mile, smile it makes you feel good;
M y heart is like a silver bud.
I 'm always happy, can't you see,
L ovely smiles belong to me.
E very smile can be free
S mile and sing, you will soon see!

Laura Pike (10)
Blanford Mere Primary School

A TASTY MATHS LESSON

Brainless children in,
smart teacher like a pin.
Times, divide, add, subtract,
twelve children divided by eight.
When I'm using my head,
I think that I'm in bed,
homework books at the ready,
I have to take it steady,
and that's my maths lesson.

Olivia Rathbone
Blanford Mere Primary School

Animal Addition

One wild worm wriggling on a rock,
Two terrible tribal tortoises tickling,
Three toucans teaching tribal tricks,
Four foul fennec foxes fighting for food,
Five falling frogs filling five frying pans,
Six stupid salmon smelling six skunks,
Seven super sea lions sailing the seven seas,
Eight electric eels eating eight eggs,
Nine nattering newts nipping northern ninjas,
Ten Tasmanian tigers tripping over turtles,
Eleven elegant echidnas expecting eight more,
Twelve triceratops tricking three toucans,
Thirteen thrushes thrilling thirteen toads,
Fourteen flaming fireflies flying around,
Fifteen fantastic falcons flying famously.

Robert Mason (10)
Blanford Mere Primary School

Counting Dinosaurs

One little dinosaur lost in the forest,
Two hungry raptors chasing after it,
Three massive dinosaurs smashing down big trees,
Four happy herds walking all together,
Five strong stegosaurus with their big strong spikes,
Six pterodactyls fighting over their midnight snack,
Seven gigantic brontosaurus playing in the lake,
Eight enormous dinosaurs walking in a pack,
Nine peckish dinosaurs looking for their food,
Ten hungry T-rexes chasing after me!

Sean Claridge (11)
Blanford Mere Primary School

Zany Zoo

Two turtles teething in terrible tornadoes
Four fighting falcons, flapping fiercely
Six selfish slugs, singing
Eight elephants eating eggs for energy
Ten pterodactyls treating terrible toucans
Twelve turtles torturing terrible
Pterodactyls
Fourteen frightened foxes fleeing from frogs
Sixteen silly servants shouting short songs
Eighteen evil eagles eating elephants
Twenty tigers in a trance turning
and twisting

All crazy animals doing crazy things,
Eagles eat, falcons fight and the slugs sing
That's two times two in my zany zoo.

Emily Burton (11)
Blanford Mere Primary School

How Many Animals?

One frightened falcon flying from danger,
Two buzzing bumblebees buzzing around,
Three tigers trashing a tumbling tree,
Four diving dolphins dozing in the sun,
Five crazy cats chasing mice.
Six sensible seals following orders,
Seven slithering snakes, slipping across a surface,
Eight hilarious hyenas giggling for good,
Nine bouncing bunnies jumping up and down,
Ten huge hares hopping about.

Lauren Saint (11)
Blanford Mere Primary School

Numeracy Poem

What is 2x6?
I count all the sticks.
I'm counting the number line,
1, 2, 3, I'm doing fine.
I can count,
What amount?
'What time is it, Clair?'
'It's time to share.'
I've got one lizard
And add a wizard.
My brain has power
And I work in maths for an hour.
I like maths,
I count the paths.
How many children are having fun?
Now maths has begun.

Kristy Redmond (8)
Blanford Mere Primary School

Underwater Madness

One flying fish frying more fish,
Two terrible toads teaching tiny toads,
Three tiny tadpoles trying to tidy the sea,
Four flying frogs staring at me,
Five perky penguins pecking at me,
Six stirring salmon steering on stones,
Seven sly sharks swimming slowly,
Eight electric eels eating meat,
Nine naughty dolphins swimming in cycles,
Ten tamed whales sounding for their food.

Sioned Williams (10)
Blanford Mere Primary School

Maths

Number lines on time,
everyone's doing fine.
Add and take away,
halving, doubling,
everyone's bubbling,
maths is really fun,
we've only just begun.

Numbers one, two and three,
counting on - whoopee!
Sharpen pencil all the time,
teacher says, 'Divide by nine.'
Now it's almost the end,
time to go round the bend.
'Goodbye maths teacher, we've done very well.'
Now it's time to say farewell.

Charlotte Richards (8)
Blanford Mere Primary School

Under The Water Number Poem

One wild whale whining like mad,
Two tired turtles as lazy as can be,
Three troublesome terrapins terrorising the two tired turtles,
Four funny fish swimming upside down,
Five fierce frogs flying through the water,
Six sneaky sharks seeking for their lunch,
Seven sly swordfish stabbing at the rocks,
Eight eating eels munching at the seaweed,
Nine nosy newts knowing nothing at all,
Ten hammerhead sharks hammering other fish.

Rosie Whitehouse (11)
Blanford Mere Primary School

Animal Alliteration

One angry ant annoyed with another ant,
Two slippery snakes slithering sideways
in the sun.
Three pecking pigeons pecking at people,
Four big bouncing bunnies
bouncing backwards.
Five naughty gnats nipping
at new neighbours.
Six conniving cats carelessly scratching chairs.
Seven leaping leopards lying lazily
in the shade.
Eight whining whales, wading wildly.
Nine dark dogs doing dangerous things,
Ten terrible tigers with tails that are ticklish.

Natalie Hughes (10)
Blanford Mere Primary School

Ace Animal Alliteration!

Ten terrapins teasing tedious turtles,
Twenty terrified toucans twirping time away.
Thirty foul fish flicking fins frightfully,
Forty flying flamingos flapping fiercely.
Fifty flattering foxes flipping over finches,
Sixty slippery seals surfing stupidly.
Seventy silly sheep sitting on straw,
Eighty elegant elephants eating electric eggs.
Ninety nasty newts knitting nine nighties,
One hundred horrifying humans hoping
for holidays!

Kathryn Hales (11)
Blanford Mere Primary School

The Recipe For Maths Pie

For a brill maths lesson
You will need:
One smart maths teacher.
Stir in some interested pupils,
Next, add a pinch of maths assessments,
Break a few times tables
on the side of the chair,
Mix then sieve the mixture
to remove the lumps of table legs.
Cook for five minutes then cover with sugar.
When cooled, decorate with maths books.
Last of all, cut off any excess chair legs and start.

Grace Massey (8)
Blanford Mere Primary School

Cheeky Little Animals!

One fishy fish flipping in the tank
Two cunning cats conniving to catch them
Three mini mice munching at the cheese
Four funny ferrets fighting the cunning cats
Five more mini mice start to crawl in
Six slimy water snails slithering towards the fish
Seven more cunning cats creep into the house
Eight of the mice start to count
Nine naughty newts watching the snails
Ten terrible children scare them all away!

Nicholas Bates (10)
Blanford Mere Primary School

MATHS!

Numbers on the
number line,
children learning
all the time.
Having numbers
anywhere.
Oh no!
It's past nine!

Maths is really,
really fun
because we have
just begun.
Nine and nine
is always fine.

Numbers on the
dancing line,
while the children
have story time.

Lauren Beddall (8)
Blanford Mere Primary School

MATHS IS FUN

M aths is fun
A nd nothing else is,
T en times five is fifty.
H exagons are shapes,
S hapes are so much fun.

Harry Jackson
Blanford Mere Primary School

THE NUMBER POEM

First of all get a smart teacher
and add some peppers,
Then some children
also some frogs' legs.
Count the toes first -
get a child that is thirsty
and start cooking.

When it's ready, a counting stick
starts to take the mick.
Also a blackboard
with some chalk of course,
A maths book with squares
and four pears.
2, 4, 6, 8 - who do we appreciate?
Not the King!
Not the Queen -
But the mighty maths team.

Stephanie Charman (9)
Blanford Mere Primary School

MATHS

M athematics is a great subject,
A dding and dividing.
T aking away is such good fun,
H exagons are shapes,
S hapes are to do with maths.

Hollie Portch (8)
Blanford Mere Primary School

The Best Recipe Ever

You first start by adding a mathematics teacher
Plus some interested children,
Then stir some times tables,
Start cooking!

Use some adding and some subtracting sticks,
Start mixing in,
Stir about three dice
And several number lines.
You will end up with a superb mathematical maths lesson.

After you have done all of the instructions,
Get a clean blackboard and start learning some times tables,
Then do some counting and then start simmering it
In with numbers.

Victoria Mason (8)
Blanford Mere Primary School

Maths Cake

For a brill maths lesson
you need one smart teacher.
Then mix in some interested pupils.
Next add in times tables.
The add sign and the take away,
the multiply and times,
all the numbers, even minus.
After that, add a pinch of maths books,
start to sieve the mixture to get out all the lumps.
Finally, cook for 10 minutes.
When you take it out, take any excess maths books.
Now eat, eat, eat!

Megan Burda (8)
Blanford Mere Primary School

2, 4, 6, 8

2, 4, 6, 8, what do we appreciate?
Addition, subtractions, division, times tables and maths,
2, 4, 6, 8, what do we appreciate?

2, 4, 6, 8, what do we appreciate?
2 and 2 are 4, 3 and 3 are 6,
4 and 4 are eight, so
What do we appreciate?

2, 4, 6, 8, what do we appreciate?
8 and 40 are 48,
60 and 60 are 120,
20 and 8 are 28,
So what do we appreciate?

Rhys Williams (8)
Blanford Mere Primary School

Maths

I am nearly nine,
I think nine is fine,
I am eight,
That's great.
I remember when I was seven,
My cousin was eleven,
I remember when I was six,
I made pictures with sticks,
I remember when I was five,
I looked in a hive,
I remember when I was four,
I still crawled on the floor!

Rachel Green (8)
Blanford Mere Primary School

Mind-Boggling Maths!

Frances fears fractions,
Callie can't count,
Time isn't Tom's thing
Brett says, 'Block graphs are bad!'
Co-ordinates confuse Chloe,
Alison asks about axis,
Henry hates hexagons
Barry's bored of bar charts.
Angles aren't Anna's best,
Triangles are Tina's test,
Isabel isn't interested in inverse operations,
Semi-circles scare Sarah,
Tim tries to do translation.
No one knows negative numbers,
Mind-boggling maths!

Alison Bissell (11)
Blanford Mere Primary School

The Maths Poem

Five times one equals five,
The number five is alive,
Ten counting sticks to count,
But I don't know the amount.
And a smart teacher to teach,
Who likes to see the beach,
Get a blackbird to write,
I think about numbers day and night.

Ruby Davies
Blanford Mere Primary School

Animal Counting Poem

One orange octopus eating an orange
Two terrifying tigers tickling three Tunisian tarantulas
Three tiny termites trying to trap tongues
Four flexible foxes fleeing from frogs
Five fearsome fleas fighting for fish
Six strong snakes with a scent of sugar
Seven small snails slide slowly down a slope
Eight eels ate eleven eggs
Nine newts never eat nectar
Ten tall turtles trying to talk
Eleven elephants always eat everything
Twelve terrapins turning around to eat
Thirteen Tasmanian devils talking to tarantulas
Fourteen frogs fighting for glory
Fifteen fearsome fish frightened of ferrets.

Christopher Gerrard
Blanford Mere Primary School

S-H-A-P-E-S

*S*hapes are super and spectacular, so they satisfy
S*h*apes are helpful and handy - they heal hopeless heads
Sh*a*pes aid adults to aim a little higher
Sha*p*es please people for perfect peace
Shap*e*s ease everything for everybody and everyone
Shape*s* save souls so *use them!*

Jodie Franks (10)
Blanford Mere Primary School

NUMBER POEM

1,760 yards in a mile,
63 muscles to make you smile.
8 pints make a gallon
4 wheels on my wagon!

6 eggs in a box,
10 pairs of smelly school socks!
12 months in a year
Wigan's only got one pier!

1000cm in a metre
500mls in half a litre,
24 hours in a day
31 days in the month of May.

Numbers big and also small
We have to learn to use them all.

Alex Hargrove (9)
Blanford Mere Primary School

ANIMAL NUMBER POEM

One old orange octopus wanted an orange,
Two tigers talked about teachers,
Three tiny tigers talked about turtles,
Four fabulous friends fighting about food,
Five frightened fish fretting about sharks,
Six slippery, shimmering, sticky snakes slipped under the door,
Seven stubborn snails having a race,
Eight enormous elephants enjoying a bath,
Nine nattering natterers nattering away on the phone,
Ten terrible tarantulas tidying up.

Louise Southall (10)
Blanford Mere Primary School

Counting Animals

One rich rhino wriggling in the dirt
Two twisted tigers twiddling their paws
Three wiggling worms wading through the mud
Four fearless frogs eating all the fish
Five foul foxes fighting for food
Six super fine snakes sucking on some bones
Seven stupid snails eating some worms
Eight enormous elephants eating some leaves
Nine naughty newts swimming in the pond
Ten terrible teasing turtles eating everything!

Richard Brown (11)
Blanford Mere Primary School

Counting With Animals

One old octopus with O's on him
Two terrible tigers fighting in a tree
Three tongue-tickling tarantulas
Four foul fish fighting for food
Five frightened frogs fleeing from a fox
Six sly snakes sliding around
Seven seagulls squabbling over a sea horse
Eight earwigs eating earthworms
Nine naughty newts nibbling at a nut
Ten Tasmanian devils twirling wildly.

Paul Malyon (11)
Blanford Mere Primary School

Numbers Up To Ten

I like numbers, big and small,
soon we will start to know them all.
We can start at number 1
then we can go on and on . . .
I couldn't believe it, if it was true
if we didn't have number 2!
I wonder what life would be
if we didn't have number 3?
There would be no number on my door
if we didn't have number 4.
Oh how could I survive,
if we didn't have number 5?
I couldn't do any tricks,
if I didn't have number 6.
There wouldn't be David Beckham
if we didn't have number 7.
It would always mean that I was late,
if the clock had no number 8.
If there wasn't number 9
I wouldn't get to school on time.
If we didn't have number 10,
I would be zero years old and then
where would we be?

Georgia Davis (10)
Blanford Mere Primary School

Road Code

4,123 to go past Dudley!
Take the 449 to get to Wolverhampton on time
On the 4,176 it's either Telford or Quitz!
Take the 458 to Bridgenorth - you won't be late!
For Shrewsbury to arrive, take the A5.

Passed Oxford on the M40 - can't stop, I'm in a hurry,
I'll take the M23, Gatwick for me.
For the channel, under the sea, use the M20!
Nana's on the 487, well it must be Heaven!
So when you're on the road,
Follow, follow, follow the code.

Jenny Armstrong (9)
Blanford Mere Primary School

NUMBERS

There's 13 in a baker's dozen,
How confusing!
But at school it's 12;
That's the dozen we are using.

5, 4, 3, 2, 1
Counting goes on and on.

Life begins at 40
The key at 21.
But even when you're not here
Numbers count on and on.

5, 4, 3, 2, 1
Counting goes on and on.

How many numbers can you see?
Numbers big and small -
100 grams, 12 o'clock,
Just try and count them all!

5, 4, 3, 2, 1
Counting goes on and on!

Helena Forrest (10)
Blanford Mere Primary School

Ten Little Animals

One outstanding octopus obstructed
outrageous sharks

Two talkative tigers terrified
treacherous termites

Three threatening tarantulas think to
trash the treasure

Four fidgety falcons fly from
fertile fields

Six slithering snakes snigger
past skilful shrews

Seven slow snails sparkle in the sun

Eight elaborate elephants are eager to elect

Nine naughty newts neglecting noise

Ten teasing termites terrorising timid toads.

Myles Bennett (10)
Blanford Mere Primary School

Alliteration Numeracy Poem

M athematical men may make many methods for
A nyone adding arithmetic numbers
T ime to times, tens and thousands
H undreds upon hundreds . . .
S ums see shapes straight and strict, so solve them if you dare!

Joanne Slater (11)
Blanford Mere Primary School

A MATHEMATICAL CAKE

For a juicy mathematical recipe for a lesson
First find a brainy teacher,
Add some interested children,
Mix in a maths board and start cooking.
Take as many hard tests and sprinkle them on top,
Addition and division taste the best but you could use
subtraction or multiplication if you want.
This recipe is intelligent and smart
because you'll know it off by heart.

You could use number lines,
for a bit of decoration if you like, but I'd use number bonds.
Hope you enjoy your mathematical cake,
just try not to fry the tens, they burst into five's!

2, 4, 6, 8 who do we appreciate?
Not the King, not the Queen
But the tasty mathematical recipe!

Alexandra Hill (8)
Blanford Mere Primary School

SHAPES

S ums are really easy, like half of eighteen is nine
H ow easy is this? Don't stop, you're doing fine!
A right angle is 90°, that is a fact
P erhaps now we should move on to minus - subtract!
E asy now, don't go too fast. Stick with the rest
of the children in the class.
S hapes are fun, so stay by their side.
What a cool number ride!

Nicola Barlow (10)
Blanford Mere Primary School

Numbers

Numbers are really great!
They tell you how long you have to wait.
They tell you which station you are watching,
They tell you how many times to sing something.
They tell you how long your lessons are,
And how many points are on a star.
They tell you how many people there are,
And how many sweets are in a jam jar.
They tell you the number of cars on the street,
They tell you how many things there are to eat.
They teach you to count in different ways,
And teach you the number of weeks and days.
They tell you what the date is and how many
Letters are in whizz,
Without numbers, I wouldn't know what to do,
I wouldn't even know how many laces are in my shoe!

Laura Fellows (10)
Blanford Mere Primary School

The Three Times Table Trouble!

Three terrible termites terrified the teachers,
Six stubborn snakes slipped under the doors.
Nine naughty newts nattering about food,
Twelve tigers tried to twist out of the cage.
Fifteen falcons fled over the school,
Eighteen enormous elephants eat all the food.
Twenty-one terrible tiny school children, having a food fight!

How will the teachers cope?

Rebecca Haydon (11)
Blanford Mere Primary School

Delving Into Numbers

One squared is one
Two squared is more,
Three squared is nine
Don't stop, you're doing fine!

Four squared is sixteen,
Five squared is twenty-five,
Six squared is thirty-six
That ends with the digit six!

Half of seven is three point five,
Half of eight is four.
Half of nine is four point five,
Half of ten is also more!

Double five point five, is eleven,
We're all in counting heaven!
Double six that makes twelve,
Into numbers we can delve!

Alex Munkley (9)
Blanford Mere Primary School

Hullabaloo

Hullabaloo is a strange noise,
It's enough to send you anticlockwise!
Hullabaloo is such a commotion
It's enough to make you go in slow motion.
Hullabaloo can break your eardrum;
It's enough to make your ear numb.
Watch out!
Hullabaloo is on the run.

Patrick James (9)
Blanford Mere Primary School

SNOWMAN

Here alone in the garden am I
Standing here watching the sky
Nothing to measure, only a fly
I'm a very lonely snowman.

Here alone in the garden am I
Standing here watching the sky
Nothing to do, so I start to sing
I've got a friend called Lou and
9 x 8 is 72!

Here alone in the garden am I
Standing here watching the sky
I wouldn't believe it even if it was true
9 x 8 is 72, would you?

Here alone in the garden am I
Standing here watching the sky
Then the sun comes out, so I have to melt
All that's left is 15ml of water and my belt!

Charlotte Gordon (10)
Blanford Mere Primary School

SHAPES

S quares have four sides, they really do
H alf 6 is 3, take away 1 is 2
A ngles can be different or alike;
P erimeter is the outside, like riding my bike.
E stimation is a very close guess,
S ymmetry is fun, I love shapes Oh yes! Oh yes!

Sarah Whitehouse (10)
Blanford Mere Primary School

NUMBERS

Some are big and some are small,
We've got to use them all!
There's one, two and three and four,
But don't forget there's even more!

They go to a million
Or even a zillion,
You could count the leaves of grass
Believe me, there's a great big mass!

Some are big and some are small,
We've got to use them all!
There's one, two and three and four
But don't forget there's even more!

Ben Edwards (9)
Blanford Mere Primary School

NUMBERS

Small numbers make me glad,
big numbers make me mad!
Just because you can't work them out -
don't just go and pout or shout.
Numbers, numbers, can't you see;
you all belong to me!

Numbers are our friends,
their friendship never ends.
Without them our life wouldn't be complete
they are the things you love to meet.

Sharnie Whitehouse (9)
Blanford Mere Primary School

Numbers Of The World

I think number one
Is one more than none.

Number two
I think birds flew.

Number three,
It gives people a flea.

Number four
A couple of pounds more.

Number five
You don't halve it with a knife.

Number six
What's the percentage of liking tricks?

Number seven
Is four less that eleven.

Number eight
You're coming up to a huge gate.

Number nine
You're doing fine.

Number ten,
Tony's den.

Jack Burton (9)
Blanford Mere Primary School

Christmas Feelings

It was a day to go
I had broken my toe!
I was glad, but also mad,
My sister was excited
My brother was delighted.

Presents on the floor,
Hiding behind the door.
What a hullabaloo!
Are you feeling happy too?

Christmas feelings, they are flowing!

Heather Proudler (9)
Blanford Mere Primary School

Christmas

C hristmas makes me feel happy
H olly hanging down,
R inging bells and singing carols
I n the church and in the town.
S now falling on my face
T winkling of the leaves,
M aking footprints in the snow
A nd the rustling of the trees!
S now makes me feel happy at
this celebration time.

Amy Lane (10)
Blanford Mere Primary School

Number Poem

Take a teacher that can mix
Three numbers that kick,
Put them in a big bowl
Then mix them up, so it looks whole.
Put it in a pan, then push it in the oven,
Get it out to let it cool
And then take it to school.

Anna Holyoake (9)
Blanford Mere Primary School

Daisies

D elicate, delightful daisies,
A midst the verdant grass.
I lluminating the meadow walk,
S tanding tall and straight as I pass.
I magine, imagine a field full of beauty -
E ndless carpets of yellow and white,
S o bright and so pretty, what a beautiful sight!

Amy Cresswell (8)
Blanford Mere Primary School

Mathematical Maths

Mathematical maths, many methods,
Numeracy numbers nobody knows,
Memorise all methods
Double! Divide!
Take away! Times!
Remember, revise!

Jonathan Bridgewater (10)
Blanford Mere Primary School

SUNFLOWERS

S tanding, waving in the breeze
U nable to speak or walk,
N ever jealous of other flowers
F lowing sideways, twice too many,
L owering its petals on the ground.
O ver sea, the petals fly,
W herever, whenever
E ver still, always calm.
R olling down the waterfall.
S eeds settle and make even more.

Bethany Fisher (9)
Blanford Mere Primary School

FLOWERS

F lowers make my heart sing
L ike a miniature diamond ring,
O h who could be happier than me?
W hat I notice makes me full of glee.
E very flower has its own special colour,
R ed, yellow and getting duller.
S ome flowers are tall, taller than me,
flowers are locked up but I set them free!

Allanah Hickman (10)
Blanford Mere Primary School

ALEX

Alex quite enjoyed school,
He thought that it should rule!
Alex had colour in his cheeks,
Alex had a small mouth to speak.

Alex had never said this in his mind,
But now he was seeing another side.
Alex was feeling neglected,
He looked in the mirror and it reflected
A sad lonely face, full of pain,
He didn't think he could go on, he'd go insane!

Alex's dad was putting on his coat
Alex asked what he was doing and he said,
'I'm going on the beat!'
Alex asked if he could go
And Dad replied, 'I suppose so, come along son.'
Alex came back, not so sad
And his mom, not knowing this said,
'Oh come on, it's not so bad.'
Alex explained he was quite happy,
His mom kissed him and he said,
'Don't be soppy!'

Alex's mom led him through
And he saw a tablecloth, all brand new.
'Oh Mum, you shouldn't have!'
And she replied, 'Oh I should.
You're my son, my love!'

So Alex was welcomed back to his house,
By his mum, his dad, his dog and his mouse.
So Alex realised the only thing that was,
Was him, his family, his mouse and his dog!

Jennifer Anne Bywater (9)
Brandhall Primary School

The Stars That Live Beyond

Starlight
Star bright,
Won't you shine for me tonight?
In the night,
In the light,
Won't you shine for me tonight?

In the sky,
The stars fly by.
Tonight they'll shine,
The stars, they are there, rather fine.

I want to ride the stars,
On a rocket to Mars.
I love the stars,
And I did *see* Mars!

The stars are cool,
They are so small.
I wish they were mine,
Because they're so fine.

Starlight,
Star bright.
Won't you shine for me tonight?
In the night,
In the light,
Won't you shine for me tonight?

Jade Robson (10)
Brandhall Primary School

A Runaway Trial

There lived a princess who had long brown hair and blue eyes,
Her Prince Charming had a photo of her with him eating pies.
This is the sound of romance!

Her Prince Charming had asked her to dance
And on this very day, the prince made a vow
Then he found the princess talking to an owl.
'Oh Princess,' he said, 'marry me and we will sail away.
Oh just for a penny and a lovely day.
We will sail away for years and many will shed tears.'

Then a bad king tried to stop them with all his lies,
The prince came and grabbed him and said he would die.
So they ran away and never turned back
And when they did, the king made a *quack!*
At last they were finally married,
For how long before this, they had tarried!
The prince gave his princess a ring
Then the wedding bells rang, *ding-ding-a-ling!*

Raquel Brown (10)
Brandhall Primary School

Fire

Fire, furnaces burning
Flames, flickering, churning
Orange, yellow, red
Flames licking the bed.

Water spurting out
But flames flicker about
'Helps' growing louder
As the flames regain their power

Babies screaming in bed
Children laying there, dead
Parents looking about worriedly
Firemen rushing in, hurriedly.

Mary Johnston (10)
Brandhall Primary School

High School

This year I'm going to high school
I'm excited, but I'm scared
I hope I'm going to like it there
I need to get prepared!

I'll get a nice new uniform
A blazer and a tie
I will feel all dressed up
But also rather shy!

The school is such a big place
My whole routine will change
Although I'm feeling quite grown up
It's still a little strange!

When the teacher is talking
I must pay attention
If I don't and I get caught
I will get detention!

This year I'm going to high school
I hope I don't lose my way
I suppose I'll soon get used to it
I'll be there every day!

Elizabeth Neale (11)
Brandhall Primary School

Mystery Of The Ocean

Dancing through the soft green waves,
Leaping and diving almost as one,
Through the depths of the Atlantic Ocean
High above the Pacific Ocean.

Their sleek grey skin
And warm brown eyes,
Part the rivers and the seas
Working as one, in harmony.

Dodging, flipping, jumping high
They spin through walls of salt spray water,
Flipping their tails, batting their fins,
Sounding so sweet, so far under the sea.

Inside their packs of complete safety,
They spin and mate to carry on their kind,
They're beautiful in full paradise,
They're dolphins.

Isabel Cope (10)
Brandhall Primary School

Happiness And Hate

Happiness

Happiness is yellow, like a shining sun,
It tastes like vanilla ice cream.
It smells lovely and fresh like vanilla.
It looks like people enjoying themselves,
It sounds like children playing.
It feels like joyful laughter and fun.

Hate

Hate is black, like red-hot flames,
It tastes like hot peppers.
It smells terrible and bad,
It looks like the flames in Hell.
It sounds like you're alone in the dark.
It feels like somebody is hitting you.

Winnie Lam (10)
Brandhall Primary School

COLA BOTTLES

Fizzy, wizzy, cola bottles
Really fizzy, fuzzy.
They are really sitty sottle,
Or sizzy, sizzy, suzzy.

Sizzy, wizzy cola bottles
Really sizzy, suzzy.
They are really fitty fottle,
Or fizzy, fizzy, fuzzy.

Buzzy, wizzy, cola bottles
Really buzzy, buzzy,
They are really witty wottle,
Or wizzy, wizzy, wuzzy.

Wizzy, buzzy cola bottles,
Really wizzy, wuzzy,
They are really bitty bottle,
Or buzzy, buzzy, buzzy.

Jaber Ahmed (9)
Brandhall Primary School

It's All About Me

Once, a long time ago, in a large house,
A girl who lived there was Cindy and
she had a mouse.
In fact she had everything
And she loved to sing.

'I want everything Mummy, oh Mummy, I do!'
'No, you can't have everything, that's selfish of you!'
Cindy's mum went upstairs, and came down again
with some money.
She said, 'Quickly go and get us some honey!'
So Cindy, she moaned, but go shopping she did.
'Yuck! It has honey on the lid.'
Cindy's mum had fallen asleep, she didn't hear a peep.
Cindy ran past her house, 'I've lost her!' cried Mum,
'Just like the sheep.'
That was the end of Cindy and Mother Bo Peep.

Komal Chauhan (10)
Brandhall Primary School

Love And Fear

Love

Love is red like a big red heart,
It tastes like a sweet fruit.
It smells like a red rose in a pot,
It looks like a blossom in the sky.
It sounds like twenty birds tweeting,
It feels like Heaven.

Fear

Fear is black, like fire,
It tastes like a big red flame,
It smells like burnt rubber,
It looks like people dying.
It sounds like trembles,
It feels like a heavy rock.

Gemma Firstbrook (10)
Brandhall Primary School

The Secret Love

The castle stood on top of a big steep hill,
There lived a princess, a queen, a king and a dog named Bill.
One day they did some gardening, it was hot in the shining sun
And when they had finished doing the garden, they had coffee
and a bun.

They were chatting a while and then started more talking,
They stopped and put things away, then started walking.
'We're going for a meeting with the guard and to ring your nan.'
That's not much trouble - someone called a policeman.
'Why?' asked the princess, going into the garden with the dog
And she met the policeman, who bought her a frog.
They spoke and decided to run away together -
Because they wanted to be in love forever.
Now quickly the lovers and pet ran out of the door,
They eventually got married and were happy for evermore.

Catherine Moseley (9)
Brandhall Primary School

MAD FOR FOOTBALL MATCHES

We played football
The goals were small
I scored two goals
The pitch was full of holes.

We were winning 2-0
Whilst going up, up the hill
They got one back
Because our defence was slack
Our defence cleared the ball
When I gave out a call.

They scored again
It flew in like a ten foot train
The whistle went
And the car didn't have a dent.

Christopher Davis (9)
Brandhall Primary School

COLOUR PENCILS

We come from the big apple, New York,
With lots of bright yellow chalk
Meet the red rest
We think they're one of the best.

We meet the enormous neighbourhood,
There is danger that it might flood,
But I always should
Do my best
In the long, tiresome test.

We will all be together,
No matter what the weather.
As my grand-aunt is Heather
And she is as light as a feather.

Sukhjit Hayer (10)
Brandhall Primary School

In The Park

Aaron and Simon are in the park,
Listening carefully to the dogs bark,
They have got a big round ball
They got it from the shopping mall.

Their mom and dad were walking down,
Walking past the dancing clown.
They rambled past the very small pond,
But not for really very long.

Their friend came along
Singing a gangsta' song
He asked if he could play,
What else could we say
But, 'Yes, you can play
For the rest of the day!'
Michael lost the ball
The one from the shopping mall.

They had a small fight
He had a big fright.
After which he lost his sight.

Aaron Pamma (9)
Brandhall Primary School

Love And Fear

Love

Love is red, like a cherry
It tastes like a sweet strawberry
It smells like a big red rose
It looks like a big red heart
It sounds like people enjoying it
It feels like a dream.

Fear

Fear is black, like a stormy night
It tastes like a big black stone
It smells like something burning
It looks like a puff of black smoke
It sounds like a thunderstorm
It feels like a person kicking you.

Rebecca McCluskey (9)
Brandhall Primary School

The Witches' Spell

1, 2, 3 ugly witches were dancing round the football pitches
Dropping bombs, singing songs, poking people with their prongs.
Chanting spells, ringing bells, making pots of dirty smells,
Using dogs to make frogs, sitting on the waiting logs,
Chanting spells, ringing bells, making pots of dirty smells.

Elizabeth Holland (11)
Brandhall Primary School

Sadness And Joy

Sadness

Sadness is red like Hell
Sadness is bitter and spicy
It smells like a battlefield
It looks like flames and dead bodies
It feels painful and deadly

Joy

Joy is red, like a heart
Joy is sweet and nice
Joy smells like Heaven
It looks like a red rose
It sounds like angels singing
It feels like having a massage.

Simon Nicholson (10)
Brandhall Primary School

Love

Love is like a rose
It tastes like a pineapple,
It smells like peaches,
It looks like a cuddly kitten.
It sounds like a song,
It feels like a soft blanket.

Jack Fleet (10)
Brandhall Primary School

HAPPINESS

Happiness:

Happiness is joyful
Happiness is yellow
Happiness tastes like oranges
Happiness smells like Calvin Klein
Happiness looks like trees and games
Happiness sounds like music
Happiness smells like videos.

Fear:

Fear is sadness
Fear is a red flame
Fear tastes like chillies
Fear smells like onions
Fear looks like a devil
Fear sounds like horror
Fear feels like blood.

Ben Greenhouse
Brandhall Primary School

LOVE AND FEAR

Love:

Love is red, like a sweet strawberry
It tastes like shiny cherry ice cream,
It smells like a big red rose
It looks like a wonderland.
It sounds like a waterfall
It feels like fun.

Fear:

Fear is black, like the flames in Hell
It tastes like red-hot peppers in your mouth,
It smells like something is burning
It looks like a stormy night.
It sounds like thunder
It feels like you're going to die.

Karry Blakeway (10)
Brandhall Primary School

GIRLS' FOOTBALL

I play in a girls' team - football
It is really cool
I scored a goal
It was a side-pass goal.

I missed the ball
In the sports hall.
Every Thursday I go and train,
Another girl scored again!
We are winning this time
But the ball went past the line.

It's time to end the match,
We need the ball to catch
The whistle was blown
And it's time to go.

Katie Peasley (10)
Brandhall Primary School

Love And Fear

Love

Love is the colour of shiny red roses,
It tastes like berries from a berry bush.
It smells like a rose from Heaven,
It looks like the red sun from above.
It sounds like the golden ocean down below.
It feels like I'm floating in the sky.

Fear

Fear is a black cloudy sky
It tastes like rotten fruit,
It smells like a musty, cold, damp place,
It looks like a shadow in a dark street.
It sounds like horror running down the corridor.
It feels like being in Hell.

Hannah Withey (10)
Brandhall Primary School

Happiness And Fear

Happiness

Happiness is green, like frogs,
It tastes like hot chocolate.
It smells lovely and tasty,
It looks like a lovely flower garden.
It sounds like the birds singing
It feels like being together.

Fear

Fear is brown, like dogs,
It tastes like rotten eggs.
It smells nasty and damp,
It looks like a big dark house.
It sounds like guns,
It feels like being chased.

Rhiannon Toy (9)
Brandhall Primary School

Love And Hate

Love

Love is red like a loving couple,
Love tastes like Heaven.
Love smells so fresh and sweet,
Love looks like red roses all around you,
Love sounds like humming bees.
Love feels like a dream.

Hate

Hate is black like black ink,
Hate tastes horrible.
Hate smells like rotten bins,
Hate looks like friends splitting up.
Hate sounds like people fighting,
Hate feels like painful punches.

Shaunnie Dudley (10)
Brandhall Primary School

Noises At Night

I sometimes hear
A noise that is near
It's not very clear
And I'm full of fear.

My heart jumps into my head
And I leap out of my bed.
I have nothing to wear
But I don't want to be bare.

I grab my gear
And tear down the stairs.
There is nobody near
It's the night of New Year.

Oh my dear
I listen with my ear
My brother is downstairs
Dressed, holding a spear.

I am now feeling weary
It's dark and it's eerie
I tear up to bed
To rest my tired head.

Tomorrow is school in the morning
Although it is boring
But there's lots more I have to learn
So the more I will earn.

Daniel Humpherson (10)
Coppice Primary School

The Boy Who Cried Wolf

The boy who cried wolf all began
With a shepherd boy, a little man
Guarding the sheep, he was really bored,
Fun around the corner, is what he thought.

'A wolf, a wolf!' the shepherd boy cried.
No one knew that he really lied.
When the men came, from the shepherd's shout
No wolf was found crawling about.

When a wolf really, actually came,
The boy shouted, the sheep were in pain.
The men thought he was playing a game,
Like every day, when he did the same.

The sheep were going fast, one by one,
Until they disappeared and had gone.
The little boy learned not to lie
When his boss was looking in his eyes.

Philip Griggs (10)
Coppice Primary School

Homophonic Poem

I went to the beach and what did I see?
A beech, a beech, a big old beech tree.
I climbed *old beech,* from the top I could see
The sea, the sea, the deep blue sea.

I looked the other way and in my sight
Oh delight, an ice cream van on this site.
I ran down to meet him and said, 'I'll have two!'
Then my friend shouted, 'I'll have one too!'

Patrick Ball (10)
Coppice Primary School

GHOSTS

Ghosts are scary, ghosts are mad,
Ghosts are clever, so is Emma.
Ghosts are mean, and oh so lean.
Ghosts never sleep, they earn their keep,
Ghosts everywhere, including your sleep.
Ghosts show emotions, they drink potions.

Ghosts can fly just like flies
Ghosts can creep just like birds cheep,
Ghosts can sing, just like dances swing
Ghosts can kill but can also get ill
Ghosts can sail through the air like a snail
Ghosts don't eat whilst sitting on a seat.

Emma Freeman (9)
Coppice Primary School

SUMMER

On the hills, summer flowers grow
Golden boats on streams, gently row.
In the fields and orchards, farmers sow,
In the forest, at play, is a doe.
In a nest in the trees, here sits a crow,
In the garden, Grandma sits to sew
And in the house, Dad stubs his toe.

Hayley Dobson (10)
Coppice Primary School

K-Pax

The sun is dim
The Earth is pure
The world is peaceful even without laws,
The trees are beautiful, like no other plant
And the skies are just the same.
Everyone knows right from wrong
And they're friends with every planet.
K-Paxians, one is named Prote.
They help mankind very well, if you ask me
K-Pax is the place where everyone's free!

Max Spare (9)
Coppice Primary School

Summer

S unbathing on the beach and relaxing in the shade
U nderneath umbrellas, drinking cocktails.
M ums can't get off the sand to swim in the sea
M inds of children are thinking of ice creams.
E arly mornings are bright and sunny
R eturn back to the hotel for a good night's sleep.

Kshoni Gunputh (9)
Coppice Primary School

VOLCANO

A room is colourful, overflowing with life,
Dying to be seen and bursting into action.
A world to explore, like an unknown land,
Waiting to be found like a volcano ready to blow.
An inferno, a confined space explodes.
There's a desolate plain, nothing comes near.

A whirlwind in the back of its head.
A burst, a spread of colour,
Vibrant yellow spurts of lava shoot out of a gaping gap.
Mourning. Wiped out space. Lonely.
Never being used like miles near treacherous dangers.
It's alone.
Bursts of anger follow like this, then eruptions take place.
People would much rather be outside
Than worrying about burials.

Elliot Partridge (10)
Gig Mill Primary School

BIRD'S LIFE

The baby crawls in and out of its welcoming nest.
It cries for its mother.
The mother goes and hunts,
She swoops and sways over treetops and leaves.
Her glistening wings glide as the wind blows west.

The baby bird starts to fly,
Through the bright blue open sky.
She's not a very steady bird,
Her wings try to flap but it's too hard she says,
The mother tries to help.

But now her bird has grown up
She flew away and built her nest
And when the wind blows west
She looks back where she once grew up.

Amy-Louise Cole (9)
Gig Mill Primary School

THE JOURNEY THROUGH THE HOSPITAL

Beds colliding from place to place,
Antiseptic smell fights for your face.
Sweetly scented flowers stand upon a desk,
Set out neatly in a vase,
Everything else is a mess!
Children panicking every step you go,
Nurses dashing,
To and fro.
Watches and clocks constantly being checked,
Children's play area completely wrecked!
Cafe crumbs littering the floor,
All you can hear is the slam of the door,
Signs pointing in different directions,
Man screams while having injections.
Corridors as long as a midsummer day,
All treatment is free so no need to pay.
Staff dressed in green, blue and white,
The nurses ask if you are alright?
Ambulances arrive all day and night,
The sight of blood is quite a fright.
The lights go down, everyone's asleep,
Every so often, a nurse has a little peep!

Kirstie Thorley (10)
Gig Mill Primary School

THE CITY

Cars are jammed, they're stuck in the mud,
To get through animals trudge,
Stereos play loudly in the trees,
The pavements are littered with golden brown leaves,
The chirping of planes as they take off,
The engines are loud, the chirping is soft,
Trees tower as high as can be,
In the city there are lots of great things to see.

The burrows so firm, made out of brick,
The roads of mud, so soft and thick,
Streets are congested with busy ants,
As the leaves fall, they swirl and dance,
The peace of the forest like the noise of the city,
The weeds of the town and the plants of the forest so pretty,
Cars race like dogs on walks,
People stop as they talk.

The rosy red berries are shared around,
The litter like leaves blowing across the ground,
People are rushing quickly for food,
Animals fight and squabble for food,
Noises echo around the town,
Cars zoom, people frown,
The forest and city are quite the same,
The animals hibernated as winter came.

Tim Browning (9)
Gig Mill Primary School

THE FOREST

The great city is like a great forest,
Prominent in the midst.
Busy people rushing around
Like ants looking for food.
The owls screech, protesting,
As the cars cough their way to work.
The waterfalls crash
Like the cockerel of the forest.
Towering buildings like tall trees,
Perched above the clouds.
The leaves blow through branches
Like newspapers through the crowd.
Where on earth did this all begin?

A great forest, prominent in the midst
Like a great city,
Ants rummaging for food
Like busy people rushing around.
The cars cough their way to work
As the owls screech, protesting.
Like the cockerel of the forest,
The waterfalls crash.
Tall trees like towering buildings,
Perched above the clouds.
Newspapers blow through the crowd
Like leaves blowing through branches.
Where on earth did this all begin?

Megan Davies (9)
Gig Mill Primary School

The Beach

The sun reflects on the shiny sand,
Lots of wild fish below the ocean,
Plenty of flares under the sea,
Floating and twisting all around.
The beach gets busy as people come to play,
Children's holes get bigger and larger,
The dolphins jump like the sun moving across the sky
As it gets dark people leave,
Today has been a busy day,
The sleepy sun creeps behind the horizon -
After its wash, the next day,
It's smooth, hot and sparkly like it was before.
The sun creeps up slowly after its sleep,
Like the children building vast sandcastles.
The sun sits lazily in its deckchair,
As people read their newspapers.
All the sunglasses on people's faces,
The caps and the bathing suits,
Are being sold at the nearby shop,
People go home as the sun dies down.

Rosie Packham (10)
Gig Mill Primary School

The Storm

The sea roars
As it reaches higher and higher.
Forming a peak of sprouting bubbles,
The sea crashes its side
With a shattering roar,
Against the mountain's side.
The mountain's echo
Fills the salty air.

The dolphins leap
Out of the protecting waves.
Birds swoop from the echoing mountain
Escaping the crashing sea,
The echoes of the fighting mountain
And the roar from the protesting sea
Composes music of the storm,
That drifts off with the salty air,
Into the atmosphere.

Beth Townsend (9)
Gig Mill Primary School

The Desert Of Stars

The sheets of stars glittering and
Shimmering in the sky like an
Amazing curtain of sand.
The two humped satellites trudge
Painstakingly.
Moving through space's maze.
Asteroid showers rain on planets
Like a sandstorm on a bewildered traveller.
Tiny lizards scurrying around
Hunting like an astronaut for glory and elation.
Huge planets eccentric and extravagant
Towering like massive mountains,
Gigantic black holes gaping,
Intimidating like sinking sandpits,
The marvels of the constellations
Wonderfully dawning in the desert twilight,
Oh the shimmering wonders -
Space, how it pales in comparison
To the desert's face.

Duncan Smith (10)
Gig Mill Primary School

The Dentist

Ancient needle-shaped doors slam shut,
The only place left is the minute wooden hut,
The deserted old castle, or maybe not quite,
A man wanders around at exactly midnight.
Faded windows too full of dust to see,
If there is even one tiny lonely bee,
The top turret crumbles down, becomes mouldy stone,
Crash, crash, crashing along with a moan.

A friendly dentist you might think,
He waits until you take a blink
And there he is in front of you
With a needle and a pot of glue.
You cry and cry,
Because you may die
And then you run with all your might,
You hope that he is out of sight,
Next you turn around, he's still there
And then you stop and stare,
He's fading away, the sun's coming up
And then phew . . . he's just disappeared.

Megan Terry (9)
Gig Mill Primary School

Candles

The running of the wax like fish being chased,
The burning smell of the candle like a surfaced-
Smelling fish lying still,
A fish's gills flapping about like the flicker of the candle,
The shortening of the candle like a fish being eaten bit by bit,
The still candle holder like a dead fish,
A long, straightened out fish like a tall, tall candlestick.

The tropical fish swim as the colourful flames blend together,
The sharp fins like the tip of the flame,
The flickering candles bulge out as a pufferfish blows itself up,
The tail of the fish sways swiftly as a flame sways
Swiftly to the left and to the right.
Its tail fins are pushing back like a gust of wind
Blows it out and the darkness falls like the end of the day.

Gabrielle Walley (9)
Gig Mill Primary School

Sounds And Sights Of The Ocean Floor

A whistle sweeps between the walk,
The pitter-patter in the distance,
Dolphins towering high, then jump.
Danger of the grab, the catch of juicy food,
Hidden underneath with a pool of shade.
Seaweed shaking with a wild whiff,
Lions pounce with a rumble and crash,
Dancing wildlife swinging and twisting,
Clouds of sand in thc air blowing.
Green rushes in with blue with a tropical feel.
The morning is lush and full of dormant animals.
Soon creatures are rising, it's full of life,
Afternoon, collecting bunches of food,
Hide in shade waiting for more.

Evening comes, mist above,
Full of sounds, creep about,
The track of nature, what a dangerous place.

Vicky Wittin (10)
Gig Mill Primary School

LIFE

Sea is very cold and watery,
Flooding over the thirsty land,
Taking all the shells and stones,
As it passes the beady sand.

People walk by the seas,
Listening to the buzzing bees.
Fishes swimming round and round,
Like kids playing in the playground.

Palm trees wave all day and night,
Dolphins jump about in sight.
Octopuses with eight legs,
Spider plants and smelly eggs.

Girls and boys run round the rocks,
Taking off their shoes and socks.
Building sandcastles really tall,
Putting shells on that are small.

Dogs paddle in the salty water,
Nan's playing with their granddaughter,
The waves curl up and crash back down,
As if it is the tricks of a clown,
I wonder why everything seems fresh
And why do we call it life?

Charlotte Lake (10)
Gig Mill Primary School

IMPRISONED

Solid walls like an inflexible back,
People trudging around on dark, damp pavements,
Freezing cold beds with wind storming through,
The cracks in the wall.

Rest hour comes,
People putting tough exercise into
Stiff aching muscles,
All of a sudden it's all over.

Jack White (9)
Gig Mill Primary School

My Shadow

I've got this person that follows me around,
I don't know how but she doesn't make a sound,
She's really quite special, exclusive to me,
She's always there, wherever I may be.

When I'm happy, she's happy too,
When I'm feeling sad, she feels blue,
I've got a friend that's not always there,
But when she is she's ready to care.

She comes out in sunshine, in in the rain,
I never know when I'll see her again,
Don't know where she'll be, she's quite hard to find,
Sometimes in front, sometimes behind.

When the sun is low, she is tall,
When the sun is high, she is small,
So who is this person? I think that you know
It has to be my special shadow.

Sophie Waring (10)
Gig Mill Primary School

SUMMER

The sun comes up,
You think you're in luck,
You go to get ready,
But there's none,
It's all gone.

You wonder in shock,
But you've been knocked.

The suncream is all gone.

You're burning up,
You're turning red,
But you survive.

Now it's day two
And your cream is in hand,
Time to go and explore
And search for the sand,
But the clouds come out and
Summer is no more.

You almost faint in shock,
This is just marvellous.

Beautiful flowering buds,
Yellow, pink, orange and red,
The worms, spiders and slugs are
Ruining my flowerbeds.

Summer's pretty leaves on trees,
Unlike autumn's crinkling leaves
All ripped and trampled on,
But after a while summer is all gone.

Kelly Marie McCutcheon (10)
Gig Mill Primary School

Prison

The silence of prison,
Is softened by
The serenading cry,
Of a bird nearby.

The jangle of keys,
Brings fear to the heart
If only they'd known how to be smart,
Now knowing theft isn't a good art.

The prisoners huddle together,
Like birds in a nest,
Not allowed life which is best,
Smelling the spring zest.

The birds are free,
Prisoners are sad,
Once bad,
Now driven mad.

Fran Wright (9)
Gig Mill Primary School

Sea Life

Its mouth is as vast as a church,
It gobbles up anything that hurts,
If a boat comes by, it stretches up high,
Its dinner is here!
Along comes the boat's fear,
As it tries to turn away,
It's lucky to survive,
That rough tormenting sea.

Amy Law (9)
Gig Mill Primary School

THE URBAN FOREST

Crippled leaves blow around a forest glade like
newspapers in an alley.
Squirrels scurrying, collecting nuts, resembling busy
workmen piling bricks.

Wind blowing, trees swaying, children in the street playing.
Forest giants, leaves so green, skyscrapers' windows that gleam.

Traffic roaring, horns hooting, akin with birdsong echoing
through the trees.

Signs pointing in all directions, this way, that way, move along.
While in the woodland, green shoots, showing very soon
spring will have sprung.

Douglas Partridge (10)
Gig Mill Primary School

THE FOREST

Forests of structures
Paved with tarmac and concrete leaves,
The sly foxes like salesmen
Burrow effortlessly into people's minds.

Cities of mud,
Paved with wood and dung.
Buskers like baby birds
Busking for food,
Out of the mother's throat.

Guy Bartle (10)
Gig Mill Primary School

A Brilliant Summer

It is summer, hip hooray
I love to play at the beach every day,
The sun wakes up to the morning,
It's a sunny day so let me play.

The smoothness of the sand,
The seashells are like a band,
When the morning appears,
A major miracle may be near.

It's getting to the end of my favourite season,
Maybe you can tell me why that might be the reason,
I will remember about this season,
About all the summer we have made.

Samantha Sheen (9)
Gig Mill Primary School

Contrasts

Tall, man-made concrete blocks,
Just standing there,
Tall, natural plants,
Growing and changing.

Cars vrooming, horns tooting,
The noisy music of the city,
Birds singing, wind whistling,
The peaceful music of the forest.

Michael Cooper (9)
Gig Mill Primary School

The City Life

Towering buildings flooded by steep
Streams of oozing mud.

Immense layers of litter like fruits on
The forest floor.

Traffic caused by fallen trees,
Roaring engines like bears' hungry stomachs.

Streams of people in the city streets,
The noise of the massive busy city echoes
In the silence of the forest.

The massive layers of mess are left,
As the city slowly falls asleep.

Amy Pritchard (9)
Gig Mill Primary School

I Wonder

I wonder what a cross between
A museum and a leopard would be like?
It must have loads of spots
And can run at the speed of light!

It must be very interesting
With a shop with things for sale,
It must look very impressive,
Standing there wagging its tail.

Matthew Wooldridge (9)
Gig Mill Primary School

City Life

Campers walk through thick pavements of mud,
The noise of feet hitting the boggy ground,
Buildings swarming with bugs,
Rivers of flowing people,
Fires of burning work.

Cars racing as fast as lightning,
Traffic building like storms,
Streets with animals rummaging through trash,
Factory smoke discharges into the clean air,
Animals run the city.

Thomas Griffiths (9)
Gig Mill Primary School

Sea And Land

S eashells strewn upon the shore
E choing like voices in a cave
A mazing creatures flying through the water.

L ike birds soaring up in the sky
A uthors come here to compose their words
N othing compares to these beautiful worlds
D o not destroy the sea and the land.

There is nowhere on Earth quite like it.

Olivia Emerson (10)
Gig Mill Primary School

THE CITY

Shoppers dragged their bags through rustling leaves,
Overtowering buildings bending over like trees.
Trains running over tracks, like the sound of animals scavenging.

The soft humming of cars like the whistle of baby birds,
Heavy lorries crunching over big and little pine cones,
Accidents on the road and tourists trekking over bugs.

Charlotte Hudson (10)
Gig Mill Primary School

SUMMER SPELL

This is our winter place,
But the trees are full
And all the leaves are fresh and green
And the river that we skated on
Is flowing quick and fast,
Our voices are clear,
Everything is green.

In the winter we had snow fights,
I smashed the ice,
A dog jumped over the river,
Dad fell in the snow,
I made my first snowman.

Ryan Deasley (9)
Haslucks Green Junior School

The Owl

She hoots all day
And hoots all night,
She looks all bright,
She's such a delight.

She has big eyes,
She makes me cry,
She is a baby,
She's growing up to be a lady.

She swoops from branches,
Going past the crunchy leaves,
She does not notice that she has flown past her food.

Katie Victoria Gladwin (8)
Haslucks Green Junior School

The Jaguar

The jaguar is big, spotty and brown,
With his huge pounce
And one big bounce,
He catches his prey for the night,
With his sparkling teeth,
Ripping meat,
His teeth are soon red but
He'll soon be dead because of the eyes of man,
For the lovely coat he wears on his back.

Olivia Jane Stevens (9)
Haslucks Green Junior School

AUTUMN

Autumn is wet
Autumn is sunny
Autumn leaves are unusually funny
Colours of yellow
Colours of orange
Leaves falling everywhere
Until the trees are bare.

Weather hot
Weather cold
Sometimes rains
Sometimes not
Sometimes you get a cold
And your nose is dripping with snot.

Trees, trees
Leaves, leaves
The trees are losing these every day
Leaves, leaves,
Trees, trees
Soon they'll be bare
Trees, trees,

There's no leaves there.

James Healy (8)
Haslucks Green Junior School

AUTUMN

Conkers hard,
Conkers soft,
Conkers of different sizes,
Conkers big,
Conkers small,
Full of random surprises.

Rain coming down,
Pattering on the ground,
Wind gale force,
Taking you off course,
Autumn!

Joshua Currier (8)
Haslucks Green Junior School

THE BUSH DOG

Swimming, diving,
In and out,
Eating rodents,
Yuck.

Bush dogs,
Meeting in the rainforest,
So the cubs can play,
Wanting to play forever,
But now it's the end of the day.

Bush dogs,
In the morning, hunting,
Hunting for their food,
Find their prey and kill it,
Ate and ate and chewed.

The family go to sleep,
To have a little snore,
Wake up in the morning,
To start the day once more.

They're bush dogs.

Laura Dunnion (9)
Haslucks Green Junior School

AUTUMN

It is autumn, the colours
Red, brown and yellow,
Autumn has colours everywhere,
The leaves are beautiful,
They are like crisps, crunchy crisps.

Squirrels scamper for nuts,
They collect food for their young,
The squirrels live in trees,
In thick branches.

The acorns are shiny,
From the wind and rain,
Fall from the trees,
Come from leaves again.

The weather is cold,
Wind and rain,
The leaves are falling,
From the trees once more again.

Sophie Rose Green (8)
Haslucks Green Junior School

SNAKE

S lithering through the branches
N ot stopping, searching for food
A constrictor will wrap you
K illing you instantly
E nd.

Alec Higgins (9)
Haslucks Green Junior School

AUTUMN

Autumn leaves are crisp and crunchy,
Red, yellow, orange and brown,
Bare branches, leaves of the trees are falling,
The clock goes back.

It's cold and wet,
It's foggy and windy,
The wind whipping up leaves,
Very, very slippy.

Scampering squirrels,
Looking for nuts,
Sliding on the slippery ice,
There are puddles everywhere.

Matthew Allison (8)
Haslucks Green Junior School

AUTUMN

Crunchy leaves falling,
Off the trees everywhere,
You look, there is
Always leaves, red
And orange leaves,
Brown leaves turn yellow.

Time's going back
And it's getting darker
And darker
And there are loads of puddles.

Dipesh Parmar (9)
Haslucks Green School

Summer Spell

This is our winter place

The trees are full of leaves
And all the trees are lovely and green
The river that we skated on
Is flowing quick and fast
The air is warm and blowing
And our voices can't be heard
And everything is alive under the sun.

In the winter we used to make snowmen
But now we build damns,
My snowball though was great until
The sun had melted it away.

Laura Steeley (9)
Haslucks Green Junior School

The Toucan

The toucan's body,
As black as night sky,
The toucan's beak,
As bright as the sun,
The toucan's breast,
As white as a page,
The toucan's voice,
As loud as children playing,
The toucan's tail,
As long as a winding road.

Emily Hale (8)
Haslucks Green Junior School

AUTUMN

Leaves are
Crunchy and wet
And are big and yellow
And all kinds of autumn colours.

Branches are bare
With leaves on the floor
And wind is whipping the leaves.

The clocks go back
And I am late for school
And conkers fall on my head
And I don't want to get out of my bed.

Alexandra Capewell (8)
Haslucks Green Junior School

ANACONDA

A long and winding snake
N ever to be trusted
A s it can eat an alligator
C rocodiles hunt it
O ver 5 metres long
N ever over 10 metres
D eath in its wake
A nd it's not poisonous.

John Bristow (8)
Haslucks Green Junior School

Jaguars

A jaguar runs fast,
They run like the wind,
Eat flesh on the way,
They have black spots and yellow fur,
The jaguar is the most powerful animal,
They climb trees and lie on the branches,
To go to sleep.

Jake Williams (9)
Haslucks Green Junior School

Jaguar

J ungle animal lives
A nimals that include jaguars
G ood for challenge
U p in the treetop all of the jaguars
A nd down they go
R ainforest animals are endangered.

Faye Beecham (9)
Haslucks Green Junior School

The Squirrel

He has a giant tail,
He is small and not very tall,
He has got big front teeth to chew on nuts,
He's got a pink nose,
He wiggles his whiskers wherever he goes.

Thomas Myles Butterly (9)
Haslucks Green Junior School

The Mole

They have digging front claws,
That come out of their paws,
Moles eat worms,
Which would give us germs,
They eat lumps of mud
Which they have for their pud.

They have a soft little nose
And very sharp toes,
Moles have small eyes
But are still very wise.

Alex Weir (9)
Haslucks Green Junior School

Guess Who?

Hard-worker
Heavy-thinker
My-waiter
Meal-maker
House-keeper
Late-moaner
Shopping-loner
Money-spender
Pony-lender
Food-mixer
Clothes-fixer
Chocolate-eater
Heavy-seater.

My mum.

Lisa Young (11)
Henley-in-Arden Primary School

The Dolphin And The Monkey

(Inspired by 'The Owl And The Pussy-Cat' by Edward Lear)

The dolphin and the monkey
Went to the jungle
In a tiny hot air balloon,
They took their sink
And the local ice rink
Wrapped up in a purple cocoon.

The monkey looked down
To the world below
And sang to a piccolo,
'Oh amazing dolphin!
Oh, dolphin my sweetheart
What a gorgeous dolphin, you know,
You know,
You know,
What a gorgeous dolphin, you know!'

Dolphin said to the monkey,
'You're very hunky,
You know how to treat a lady!
Oh, let us be together
For now and forever,
But how shall we show our love?'

They glided along
For 3 months and 4 days,
To the island where the sheep are green
And there in a house was a little mouse,
Holding 2 heart-shaped rings,
Heart-shaped rings,
Heart-shaped rings,
Holding 2 heart-shaped rings.

'Dear mouse are you able
To swap for a table, your rings?'
Said the mousey, 'Of course.'
They took them away, but broke up the next day,
Because of a hair on a horse.

They fought each other,
Monkey got help
From his brother,
Who screamed at the sight of blood,
Along they would battle,
Through herd and through cattle.

They fought for evermore,
Evermore,
Evermore,
They fought for evermore.

Brooke Maddison (10)
Henley-in-Arden Primary School

Pain

Pain is as red as blood,
It smells like rubber burning,
Pain tastes dirty and disgusting,
Pain sounds like glass smashing,
It feels like a cut on your leg,
Pain lives in the heart of a raging storm.

Nicholas Mitchell (9)
Henley-in-Arden Primary School

I Wish I Was . . .

I wish I was a TV doing nothing all day,
I could watch the telly,
I could turn the picture upside down,
I would mess with the controller and
Turn the volume up!

I wish I was an astronaut in my shining shuttle,
I could float in my room all day,
There is no gravity,
Discovering new life forms on distant planets,
I hope I don't get chased and fall down a cavity.

I wish I was a bed, all cuddly and warm,
People lying on me and I keep them warm,
I hope I'm not dumped,
I wonder how old I am, am I from the war?

I wish I was a frog having a dip in my pond,
I wouldn't have to use a comb,
I would eat the flies and nobody would mind,
People coming, taking me from my home.

Matthew Norrington (11)
Henley-in-Arden Primary School

I Am Rudolph

I am Rudolph flying in the air,
Delivering presents throughout everywhere.

Pitch-black sky,
Sparkling silver stars,
Pluto, Saturn, Jupiter and Mars.

Pulling the sleigh full of toys,
Giving presents to girls and boys,
Making them happy everywhere.

Landing now on the houses,
Santa's watching the houses,
By now I'm going home.

Richard Millar (10)
Henley-in-Arden Primary School

Crackle, Crackle, Pop

I am a cracker,
Covered in glitter,
That sparkles under the
Dimming lights.

I stretch and I break
With a thundering crackle,
I make people smile
With the prize I give them.

Screaming and gleaming faces,
They shine as bright as a star.

Now all the faces have gone,
I'm back in the box like I was before.

Going to be recycled,
For next year,
So I can make people smile
And I can crackle again,
I can . . .
Crack!

Ellie Isom (10)
Henley-in-Arden Primary School

I Wish

I wish I was a ladybird
Flying through the air,
Everyone looking at me
But am I really there?

I wish I was a pop star
Singing all day,
Eating all the sweets and stuffing myself
Having no time to play!

I wish I was a tree
Standing tall and grand,
In the dark forest
And there I will still stand.

I wish I was a lion
Cuddly and invited to tea,
Running through the land
Because they're special to me.

I wish I was an artist
Art, brushes, paint and paper,
Would you like to see my work?
Well maybe later!

I wish I was a teacher
Drinking coffee all day,
Working out answers to maths
And taking the kiddies out to play!

I wish I was . . .

Julianna Fossett
Henley-in-Arden Primary School

I Wish I Was A . . .

I wish I was a rabbit,
Bouncing through the wood,
But Mum would say, 'Now don't be silly!'
I murmured, 'Yes I could!'

I wish I was a vet,
Helping animals that are sick,
If I could take one home with me,
I would not know who to pick.

I wish I was a ballerina,
To point my toes and skip,
Mum says, 'I wouldn't do that
You'll probably fall or trip.'

I wish I was a lion,
To roar and roam the plain,
But Mum would say, 'Don't be daft
You would end up a real pain.'

I wish I was a leopard
And leap on my prey,
But Mum would say, 'Keep on dreaming,'
I thought it might happen one day.

I wish I was a teddy bear,
To be cuddled with love,
Mum would say, 'I don't think so,
Now find your odd glove!'

Victoria Iggo (10)
Henley-in-Arden Primary School

ABSTRACT NOUNS

Sadness,
Sadness is dark black,
Sadness smells like burnt roast chicken,
Sadness tastes like charcoal,
Sadness sounds like babies crying,
Sadness feels like a rough stone,
Sadness lives in a grave.

Anger,
Anger is grey,
It smells like hot iron burning,
Anger tastes like bitter sherbet,
It sounds like hot lava running down a hill,
It feels like a knife going down your throat,
Anger lives in the heart of a bear.

Happiness,
Happiness is bright orange,
It smells like chocolate cake,
It tastes like roast chicken,
Happiness sounds like beautiful harp music,
It feels like a teddy all soft and cuddly,
I live in the beautiful flower.

Chloé Bradford (10)
Henley-in-Arden Primary School

I AM THE PRESENT

I am the present under the Christmas tree,
I am the present waiting to be opened,
I am the present opened with glee,
I am the present that gets played with happily,
I am the present given to Dad,
I am the present very sad,

I am the present that somebody once had,
I am the present you wish you had,
I am the present that people like,
I am the present better than a bike,
I am the present much, much better than a bike
And I hope I'm the present you really like.

Darren Eborall (11)
Henley-in-Arden Primary School

FEELINGS

Pain,
Pain is sour red,
Pain smells like scolding ash,
Pain tastes like boiling hot water on fire,
It sounds like someone screaming in pain,
It feels rough and sharp,
It lives in your feelings.

Love,
Love is pink and lilac,
It smells of roses and oranges,
It tastes like chocolate and fruits,
It sounds like angels singing,
It feels smooth and silky,
Love lives in your heart.

Hunger,
Hunger is purple and rough,
It smells of food and drink,
It tastes of chocolate and sweets,
It sounds like a thunderstorm and an earthquake,
It feels sharp,
Hunger lives in your stomach.

Alex Pritchard (10)
Henley-in-Arden Primary School

NONSENSE POETRY

(Inspired by - 'The Owl and the Pussy Cat' by Edward Lear)

The lion and the unicorn went to France
In a gorgeous jet-black jet,
They took some CDs, mainly from the Bee Gees,
Wrapped up in an old debt,
The unicorn looked down to the city below
And sang to a big cello.
'Oh lovely lion, oh lion, my love,
What a furry lion you are,
You are,
You are,
What a furry lion you are!'

'Unicorn,' said the lion, 'oh where were you born?
You must have been born in a choir.
Oh let us be married, how long we have tarried,
But what shall we do for a ring?'

They flew away for a year and a month
To a country where the ding bush grows
And there in a field, a piggy wig kneeled,
With a ring at the end of his nose,
His nose,
His nose,
With a ring at the
End of his nose.

'Dear pig are you dying to sell for a farthing
Your ring?'
Said the piggy, 'I will'
So they took it away and were married next day
By the owl who lives in the barn,
They dined on dips and oven chips,
Which they ate with their hooves and claws
And hand in hand on the hay bales,
They danced by the light of the sun,
The sun,
The sun,
They danced by the light of the sun.

Joseph Sheridan (10)
Henley-in-Arden Primary School

I Am The Angel

I am the angel waiting in the box,
When I'm out I'm free!
I am the angel on the top of the tree,
Everyone's happy that I glisten and
They look up at me.

I am the angel silent and still,
I am the boss, I have the power.

I am the angel, I glisten brightly,
I rule, I am mighty.

I am the angel, I shine at the top,
Looking down at the little ants.

I am the angel, I look over people,
I love Christmas time!

Rosina Ayling (10)
Henley-in-Arden Primary School

Christmas Tree

I am a Christmas tree sitting in a shop,
I am waiting for a fairy on top.

I am a Christmas tree finding my home,
I am now away and alone.

I am a Christmas tree still in a house,
I am asleep quiet as a mouse.

I am a Christmas tree ready to decorate,
I am watching a family debate.

I am a Christmas tree shining quite bright,
I am thinking the tinsel's too tight.

I am a Christmas tree guarding the gifts,
I am watching their minds drift.

I am a Christmas tree being packed away,
I now have to go, I wish I could stay.

Olivia Beaumont (11)
Henley-in-Arden Primary School

I Am The Reindeer

I am the reindeer
Who helps pull Santa
Around the world
We twist and steer.

I am the reindeer
That leads the way
The morning is going as fast as the day
I went shopping and had to pay.

I am the reindeer
That takes the sleigh
Around the world
To Jupiter and Mars.

Jonathan Russell (11)
Henley-in-Arden Primary School

I Wish I Was A . . .

I wish I was a parrot,
So I could fly above the tropical island sea,
But Mum would say, 'It's too hot there!'
And call me in for tea.

I wish I was a cat,
I'd kick up lots of sand,
I'd play with all the other cats
'Eat your lunch!' Mum just demands.

I wish I was a dinosaur
And make a great big nest,
But Mum would say, 'It's too dangerous!
You wouldn't be able to fit in your vest!'

I wish I was a tiger,
With a terrifying stripy head,
But Dad would say,
'I hate cats and roaring animals,'
And send me up to bed!

Jordan Eborall (9)
Henley-in-Arden Primary School

I Wish I Was A . . .

I wish I was a popstar,
In a bright pink spangly vest,
But Mum would say you don't suit pink
And tell me to get dressed.

I wish I was a princess,
With lots of garden land
But Mum would say our garden's small
'Eat your lunch,' she would demand.

I wish I was a mermaid,
I would swim through all the sea
But my mum would say we have no sea
And call me in for tea.

I wish I was an adult
I would fill my child with dread
I would shout and scream at her all day
And send her up to bed.

Laura Reaper (9)
Henley-in-Arden Primary School

I Wish . . .

I wish I was a star,
To twinkle for the moon,
My mother said, 'That's a silly dream,
Now go and tidy your room!'

I wish I was a policeman,
To fight all the baddies,
My father said, 'Don't be stupid,'
And made me have a paddy.

I wish I was a cat,
To lazily lie around,
My brother said, 'That would be bad,
To hear that awful miaow sound.'

I wish I was a popstar,
To hear my fans shout 'Woo'
My family said, 'We'd really hate that
Because we like you as you.'

Imogen Frost (10)
Henley-in-Arden Primary School

I Wish I Was A . . .

I wish I was a dolphin,
I'd never ever rest,
But Mum would say I'd get too tired
And tell me to get dressed.

I wish I was the sea,
I'd splash onto the sand,
But Mum would say I'd have no friends,
'Eat your lunch!' she would demand.

I wish I was an actress,
The crowd would watch with glee,
But Mum would say I'd get stage fright
And call me in for tea.

I wish I was a maze,
I'd make people grow red,
But Mum would say that I'm too mean
And send me up to bed.

Rosanna Levy (9)
Henley-in-Arden Primary School

The Bird And The Fox

(Inspired by 'The Owl And The Pussy-Cat' by Edward Lear)

The bird and the fox, they went to France,
In a tatty, rain-grey train,
They took some peach and their pet leach
And also their pet Great Dane.
The bird looked up at the starry sky
And hummed to a small banjo,
'Oh darling fox, oh fox my darling,
What a sweet fox you are oh!
You are oh!
You are oh!
What a sweet fox you are oh!'

Fox said to the bird, 'You're better than curd!
How beautifully nice you hum,
Please let us be wedded, how long we have dreaded,
But what shall we do for our tums?'

They choo-chooed away for two years and four days,
To the place where the pip pans grow
And there in a lake, a fish swam fat to his face,
Where a smell of McDonald's goes,
It goes!
It goes!
Where a smell of McDonald's goes.

'Dear fish are you able to sell for a table
A dish?'
Said the fish, 'I will!'
So they took it away and were wedded the next day,
By the crab that lived on a hill,
They dined on chips and ice cream whips
Which they ate with a rickety fork
And paw in wing, on the edge of the hill,

They danced all the way to York,
To York,
To York,
They danced all the way to York!

When they got to York, mile after mile
Not in the tatty train,
They bought some pork and a silver fork
And ate while sitting in a lane.
The fox looked at the bird and said,
'Dear bird, how absurd!'
'Why thank you fox, why thank you!
Thank you,
Thank you,
Why thank you fox, why thank you.'

The fox and the bird finished the meal
And got in the rain-grey train,
They took home their peach and their pet leach
And also their pet Great Dane.
The bird looked up at the darkening sky
And hugged the fox and said,
'Oh darling fox, oh fox my darling,
What a sweet fox you are!' he said,
'You are!' he said,
'You are!' he said,
'What a sweet fox you are!' he said.

Mollie Allen (9)
Henley-in-Arden Primary School

ABSTRACT NOUNS

Terror,
Terror is fiery, hot burning red,
Terror is the smell of fire gushing out of a
Dragon's throat,
It tastes burnt and hot,
It sounds like melting iron grinding together,
Terror feels hard and sharp like an axe's blade,
Terror lives in the dark dungeons.

War,
War is blood-red,
It smells like the smoke from a cannon,
Ready to shoot,
War tastes like a burnt piece of metal,
It sounds like screaming and dying,
It feels hot and ruthless,
War lives in a threatened fortress.

Evil,
Evil is darkened red,
It smells like a heart of a volcano,
It tastes like burnt ashes,
Evil sounds like demons screaming in Hell,
It feels like rough tombstones,
Evil lives in the dark shadows.

Bradley Rice (9)
Henley-in-Arden Primary School

Stressful Christmas

This is a poem that will blow your mind,
Some stressful Christmas facts you might find,

C is for crowds that gather the streets,
H is for hurrying with your aching feet,
R is for ruining that special surprise,
I is for irritating children's cries,
S is for snow in your face,
T is for trauma when you're late,
M is for moans that you can't stand,
A is for agony when she's around,
S is for sighs when the shop's closed.

Christmas is a lovely delight,
When you're not having a fight.

Chloe Harrison (9)
Henley-in-Arden Primary School

Great White Shark Poem For Vegetarians

When I am lying in the dark
I think about the great white shark,
He won't come in, no scary stuff,
My bedroom isn't wet enough.

That poor shark can't share my dinner,
If he did he'd get much thinner,
Being veggie isn't good for him,
Cos sprouts don't grow where
Great
Whites
Swim . . .

Jake Brookes (10)
Henley-in-Arden Primary School

I Wish I Was A . . .

I wish I was a dolphin,
With a golden treasure chest,
But Mum would say, 'Don't be daft!'
And tell me to get dressed.

I wish I was a tiger,
In the jungle I would stand,
But Dad would say, 'Don't be daft!'
'Eat your lunch,' Mum would demand.

I wish I was a canary,
The whole world I would see,
But Mum would say, 'Don't be daft!'
And call me in for tea.

I wish I was a bat,
Filling people with fear and dread,
But Dad would say it's nonsense
And send me up to bed.

Katie Brinkworth (10)
Henley-in-Arden Primary School

Boisterous Blizzard

I am a whirling blizzard,
A powerful mystic wizard,
Accidentally causing trouble,
Always getting into muddles.
Soon there will come a day,
When I will slowly die away,
The summer has nearly come
And I'll disappear gone, gone.

Adam Beech (11)
Henley-in-Arden Primary School

Guess Who?

Hard-snorer,
Work-poorer,
Hard-sleeper,
Football-keeper,
Not-cool,
Likes-pool,
Loves-chilli,
Hates-me,
Hard-eater,
Dirty-keeper,
Meat-eater,
Goal-keeper.

My brother.

Luke Brackstone (11)
Henley-in-Arden Primary School

What's My Pet?

Mad-barker
Rubber-chewer
Fast-runner
Good-swimmer
Great-catcher
Fast-eater
Bone-lover
Meat-lover
Soft-fur
Cute-face
Fast-brinker.

Tia-Rose Varney (7)
Lady Katherine Leveson CE Primary School

Hullabaloo Is His Name

A weird water dragon,
That makes an awful racket
It screams baloo! Baloo!
Hullabaloo is its name.

Shining blue scales,
Protect it from swords and spears,
His skin as tough as leather
Hullabaloo is its name.

He lives in a great underwater cave,
As dark as dark can be,
His yellow eyes glowing like fire
Hullabaloo is its name.

Rising out of the water,
He claps his great silver wings,
Shaking his head like a wet dog,
Hullabaloo is its name.

Leanne Greatrex (9)
Lady Katherine Leveson CE Primary School

Love

The colour of love is red roses,
The smell of love is a wedding cake as
sweet as icing sugar.
Love tastes like a romantic dinner out.
Love sounds like two married people
on holiday, listening to a lovely sound of singing.
Love feels like two people kissing.
Love lives with two people.

Benjamin Price (9)
Lady Katherine Leveson CE Primary School

Images Of The Moon

The moon flashes
Like the lamp posts glistening down the street
The moon sparkles
Like an expensive diamond shimmering in the starlight
The moon twinkles
Like a star nursery glittering beautifully
The moon glares
Like a trapped animal in a cage

The moon is
A round cheddar cheese
The moon is
A stunning diamond necklace
The moon is a
Football waiting for a goal
The moon is
An eye glaring through the darkness.

Laurelle Stewart (9)
Lady Katherine Leveson CE Primary School

Peace

Peace is white
It smells like Heaven, full of sweets
Peace tastes like a cream
and lemon lollipop
It sounds like a choir singing
It feels like clouds
as fluffy as snow
Peace lives in a church.

Jaydeep Singh Marwaha (9)
Lady Katherine Leveson CE Primary School

Guess Who?

Floor-scratcher
Rat-eater
Fish-lover
Tuna-scoffer
Mouse-chaser
Bird-catcher
Tree-climber
Pole-scrapper
Quick-sleeper
Good-jumper
Fast-runner
Food-muncher
Milk-drinker
Fast-eater
Vet-hater.

Zeynab Hafeez (8)
Lady Katherine Leveson CE Primary School

My Pet

Floor-scratcher
Mouse-chaser
Bird-eater
Fish-lover
Tree-climber
Food-scoffer
Good-sleeper
Fast-runner
Good-fighter
Fast-eater
Fancy-colour
Lovely-purrer.

Natasha Fox (8)
Lady Katherine Leveson CE Primary School

My Gran

Bingo-winner
Good-singer
Car-driver
Roller coaster-rider
Embarrassing-person
Something-certain
Skirt-wearer
People-carer
Funny-dancer
Goalie-prancer
House-cleaner
Getting-meaner.

Lydia Bennett (8)
Lady Katherine Leveson CE Primary School

Nana's Pet

Food-gobbler
Flea-scratcher
Cat-chaser
Pill-hater
Hole-digger
Bone-chomper
Loud-mouther
Walk-lover
Waste-bin.

Rebekah Flint (9)
Lady Katherine Leveson CE Primary School

Extinction

Where have all the dinosaurs gone?
There used to be lots,
But now there are none.

Where did the dodo go?
Some say it died, they don't know,
When Admiral and his sailors came,
They ate them all up and skeletons
They became.

The mammoth became extinct as well,
Got eaten up my man,
It's not fair, indeed the mammoth was my pal.

There we have it, the story of three
Creatures of the land, of all the
Creatures you would think it should
Have been man who died.

Julia Harbidge (10)
Lady Katherine Leveson CE Primary School

Who Is It? (Kenning)

Dog-hater
Fish-lover
Mice-chaser
Fussy-pussy
Tree-climber
Who am I?

Amie Harrison (9)
Lady Katherine Leveson CE Primary School

HULLABALOO

He glides through the water like a dolphin
Upon the waves
He makes a splash like a whale flipping its tail
He's a hullabaloo

His wet scaly skin
Shimmers in the sunlit water
He nudges the boats like a sea monster at play
He's a hullabaloo

He eats the fish
That get in his way
He eats the kelp at the bottom of the bay
He's a hullabaloo

Kayleigh Cowen (9)
Lady Katherine Leveson CE Primary School

MY PET KENNING

Fast-wheeler
Small-drinker
Face-cuter
Nut-eater
Snow-liver
Easy-loser
Furniture-chewer
Funny-lover
Mad-adventurer
Is-clever
Great-climber.

Lucy Fenn (8)
Lady Katherine Leveson CE Primary School

Christmas Poem

Christmas pud,
Tastes so good,
Christmas dinner,
Is a winner.

The holly,
Is just so jolly,
I saw my tree
And it shines with glee.

Christmas is celebrations
And lots of decorations,
The children tell no lies
And for Santa they leave mince pies.

Rebeca Joan Prichard (11)
Lady Katherine Leveson CE Primary School

Peace

Peace is white,
It smells like doves flying in the air,
Peace tastes light and white,
It sounds like flapping wings from a dove,
It feels like white fluffy wool,
Peace lives in the heart of you.

Kiran Didially (9)
Lady Katherine Leveson CE Primary School

Anger

Anger is crimson
It smells of hot fire.
Anger tastes burnt and bitter
It sounds like losing your voice,
It feels hard.
Anger lives on hatred.

Megan Currie (9)
Lady Katherine Leveson CE Primary School

What Not To Tell Your Teacher

Never tell your teacher
What you think about her hair
You'd be brave if you say it
Most pupils do not dare

Never tell your teacher
Why your homework's by your bed
Because if you tell your teacher
The consequences you will dread

Never tell your teacher
Why you don't want to do PE
Your teacher will not like this
So take this tip from me

Never tell your teacher
That her lessons are a bore
Always tell your teacher
That she just should teach some more.

Afua Acquah (10)
Our Lady & St Kenelm RC Primary School

WHAT A HULLABALOO!

It's Bonfire Night

Fireworks are:
Loading, exploding, whizzing and sizzling.
Banging, clanging, shining and twining,
Smashing, clashing, sparkling and sparking.
Flashing, dashing, twirling and whirling,
What a wonderful sight!

Children start:
Saying, playing, talking and walking,
Eating, drinking, daring and scaring,
Screaming, dreaming, hopping and dropping,
Crying, lying, jumping and bumping,
What a din!

Bonfire is:
Flashing, bashing, burning and turning,
Glowing, showing, spitting and hissing,
Raging, changing, storming and warming,
What beautiful flames!

Grown-ups are:
Lighting, fighting, singing and embarrassing,
Kissing, missing, cunning and running,
Crying, spying, moving and grooving,
How humiliating!

Now we end:
Leaving, grieving, slowing and going,
Wondering, thundering, falling and calling,
Crying, sighing, hopping and stopping,
What a hullabaloo!

Leah Olive (11)
Our Lady & St Kenelm RC Primary School

The Swan

He cries like the lonely whirl of the wind,
He awakens the whole lake at night.
He opens his beak
And squawks across the water.

His feathers are white as snow,
As he glides across the silent water,
By kicking his legs
In a flowing pattern.

The swan is as smooth as silk
As well as satin ballet shoes,
He cleans himself every night
By rubbing plants all over him.

He makes me feel sad, he does,
His lonely face is always there,
I don't know how he manages
To be so sad and glum!

Elegant and mature he is,
His neck is always up straight,
He is very proud of himself
He always shows off.

He dives like a fish in the sea,
Not very excitedly,
He does it for the fun of it,
Not very willingly.

His beak is as gold as the sand,
Brighter than the sun,
This is how he was born,
Afar in the lonely sea.

Ailsa Suleman (10)
Our Lady & St Kenelm RC Primary School

WHAT AM I?

These animals are slithery and shiny
Some are large and some are tiny.
Some are big and some are not
Some have noses full of snot.
Some are long with rattly tails
And some are short and fat, with scales.
Some are black or red or green
So they are camouflaged and
Can't be seen!
They live in grass and trees and sand,
They live in water and on the land.
Some are nice and some are nasty
Some taste horrid and some are tasty.
Most are thin and have no legs,
They don't have babies, but they lay eggs.

Lydia-Alice Humphries (8)
Our Lady & St Kenelm RC Primary School

THE DOLPHIN

When I saw the dolphin it was
Splashing and crashing,
Moving and grooving,
Playing.

When I swam with the dolphin I was
Laughing and giggling,
Sinking and floating,
Prancing and dancing,
Playing.

At the end of the day, I had to say bye, but I'm glad
Because I've got a new best friend.

Clare Corcoran (9)
Our Lady & St Kenelm RC Primary School

THE SEA

The sea is a famished dog
Giant and grey,
He rolls on the beach all day
With clashing teeth and saliva jaws
For hours and hours he gnaws
Like a dinosaur, roaring at its prey.

The sea is like war,
Clashing against the beach,
With waves as its army
Slashing out of reach.

As dawn approaches all is quiet,
The silent sea recedes,
The tragic life soon to come.

Charlotte Collins & Kerry Basterfield (10)
Our Lady & St Kenelm RC Primary School

WHY SHOULD WE LIVE THE LIFE?

Why should we live the life where buildings are thrown
Into places which are now cold and unknown?
Where snow is so dirty and grey
When it used to be as clear as day.
Where the air is polluted and kills living things,
When it used to be as golden as diamond rings,
Where the ground is covered with concrete and tar,
When it used to be grass as bright as a star,
Where rubbish litters the ground,
When it used to be unknown and unfound.
Why should we live in the life where buildings are thrown
Into places which are now cold and unknown?

Miranda Jones (9)
Our Lady & St Kenelm RC Primary School

Silly Old Baboon

There was a baboon, who one afternoon said,
'I think I will fly to the sun.'
So with two great palms
Strapped to his arms,
He started his take-off run.

Mile after mile
He galloped in style,
But never once left the ground.
'You're running too slow.'
Said a passing crow
'Try reaching the speed of sound.'

So he put on a spurt,
By God, how it hurt!
The soles of his feet caught fire,
There were great clouds of steam
As he raced through the stream.
But he still didn't get any higher.

Racing on through the night
Both his feet caught alight,
And smoke billowed out from his rear.
Quick to his aid
Came a Fire Brigade,
Who chased him for over a year.

Many moons passed by,
Did baboons ever fly?
Did he ever get to the sun?
I've just heard today
That he's well on his way!
He'll be passing through Brussels at one.

PS: Well what do you expect from a baboon?

Jennifer Amanda Owen (10)
Our Lady & St Kenelm RC Primary School

My Teachers

They're mean and strict
They're naughty and nasty.
They're fat but tall
They're the teachers at my school.

They shout, they ball
They holler and haul,
They never listen at all,
They're the teachers at my school.

They smack, they hit
They whack and spit,
They beat and maul,
They're teachers at my school.

Stay away, keep out!
Move house, move town!
You won't like them all
Cos they're the teachers at my school.

Jessica Willetts (9)
Our Lady & St Kenelm RC Primary School

Under The Sea

Under the sea is a very bright place
Everyone smiling, there's no time to waste.
They're laughing and joking
Playing and soaking.
The sun is down, it's time to rest
The sun is up, they're dressing in their best.
I bet you want to know more about
Life under the sea -
Come back with the magic key!

Isabel Feeney (8)
Our Lady & St Kenelm RC Primary School

The Big House

Here is the house,
the doors are open wide
so step this way,
come right inside!

This is the hall
full of potted plants,
umbrellas, boots
and elephants!

Here is the maid
her name is Mabel,
giving a shine
to the dining table.

Here is the kitchen,
here is the cook,
baking bread
and reading a book.

Up the stairs
mind how you go!
There's a man coming down
with a buffalo.

George Madden (7)
Our Lady & St Kenelm RC Primary School

A Winter Poem

Snowflakes falling
Winds tender, calling,
Up in blue, soothing skies.

Winter's coming,
Let's celebrate.
Cheers of laughter are so great.

Light the candle
Come outside,
It's dark, but don't worry, we have light to guide.

Snowflakes falling
Winds tender, calling,
Up in blue, soothing skies.

Catherine Higgins (9) & Esther Woakes (8)
Our Lady & St Kenelm RC Primary School

WAR

War is looming
Leaders are discussing, arguing
and *disagreeing!*

War is starting, fighting and thumping,
Yelling and shooting,
Killing and suffering,
Blasting and crashing,
Battling and bombing,
Shouting and screaming,
Ducking and running,
Roaring and banging,
Burning and hurting,
Throwing and exploding,
Flashing and bashing.

Families hugging and kissing,
Cheering and clapping,
Crying and laughing.
Leaders discussing, arguing
and *agreeing!*

Natalie Kelleher & Charlotte Collins (10)
Our Lady & St Kenelm RC Primary School

CHOCOLATE ISLAND

Why do we live in a world so wet and windy?
Bungalows, houses, terraced and detached.
We go to school
For no reason at all
Chocolate once a week. *No way!*
Why don't we have some every day!

Hey! We can!

My chocolate island has:
Bounty trees
Milky Way houses
Minty and orange Aero skies
Chocolate animals roaming around
No teachers or parents to boss me about
White chocolate snow
And sea as well

I'll invite my friends for tea today
And for breakfast we'll have croissants with chocolate spread
That is . . .

Until we wake up!

Rebecca Davies & Rachael Robertson (10)
Our Lady & St Kenelm RC Primary School

MY FAMILY AND FRIENDS

My dad is big and strong
He likes to sing The Simpsons theme song
He thinks Homer is the best
Because he walks around in a vest.

My mum loves me,
She always makes me my favourite tea,
She is very nice,
But she doesn't like mice.

Francesca, my friend, is a star
She lives in Romsley which isn't far
She likes to dance - she is so great
We are the best of friends - what a mate!

Saskia, my friend, lives far away
I'll see her soon, in fact in May
She is very kind
I think about her in my mind.

Fae Doherty (8)
Our Lady & St Kenelm RC Primary School

MR UNDER-THE-BED

Dear Mr Under-the-bed,

I am writing to complain about my bed,
and to ask you to stop putting nightmares in my head.
I really get quite worried with you lurking under there,
with your long green fingernails and bright purple hair.
There is another thing which you don't do -
whilst I am searching high and low, looking for you.
You don't cough very loudly or even sneeze,
or breathe out so deeply or scratch away your fleas.
There is another thing that I want to ask you
about all of the rumours that my mum thinks are true.
Do you ever actually come out -
and make me scream and kick and shout?
But you're not that scary, there is another,
you'll never guess that it's my brother!
So next time you come, please stay for tea,
and you can both contest to see who scares me!

Anna Toner (10)
Our Lady & St Kenelm RC Primary School

Croco Keith

There once lived a crocodile,
Who had white and glistening teeth,
He swam a mile, had some style,
And his name was Croco Keith!

Now Croco Keith,
He came from Blackheath,
He stole some jewels,
What a horrible thief!

At Croco Keith's funeral,
Everyone turned up,
Except his mother and father,
And his little doggy - Pup!

Lily Miriam Elshaktori & Lauren-Cole Doswell (8)
Our Lady & St Kenelm RC Primary School

The Football Match

Players running
Police watching
Crowd cheering
Referee looking.
One team scores in the last minute,
The referee blows his whistle -
The match is over.

Alexander Birch (8)
Our Lady & St Kenelm RC Primary School

THE MONSTER

There's a monster in the front room,
Eating the vacuum, *voom, voom, voom!*
Now he's watching TV,
Drinking a cup of home-made tea
Now he's having a feast
Oh what an ugly beast!
He's eating almost everything,
There goes a fork, *clink, clink, clink!*
He's gone outside,
What's he doing now?
Oh no! He's eaten a cow!
He likes cabbage, carrots too
What's next on the menu?
The answer is *you!*

Daniel Webb (8)
Ruckleigh School

HALLOWE'EN

Vampires dance with their ghoul friends,
Witches date wizards.
It's cold with snowy, icy blizzards.
Owls are hooting,
Trolls are snooting.
Monsters are creepy, slimy and hairy,
Children are very, very scary.
Dracular wants blood!
The monsters need some slime and mud,
The creeps are sleeping all through the night,
Ready for another scary fright.

Jacob Dworkin (8)
Ruckleigh School

My Teacher Thinks

My teacher thinks
I'm working
But I'm not!
I'm battling a ruby-eyed tiger at the Colosseum,
I'm flying over London on a sparrow's back
And winning the balloon race.

My teacher thinks
I'm writing
But I'm not
I'm watching an emerald-green dragon's egg hatch
I'm becoming a jester at an ice palace
Then I'm surfing the Pacific on a stingray.

My teacher thinks
I'm watching
But no!
Instead I'm venturing into a deserted city
Riding a swan
And swinging on a vine through
Space, the universe, and eternity . . .

Beth Jellicoe (10)
Ruckleigh School

A Recipe For Winter

Take the robin redbreast whistling on a branch
One cold winter's morning.
Silver frost like lace on my window,
And the sparkling icicles hanging from the roof.

Stir together the carol singers standing at the door,
Children dancing merrily around the Christmas tree,
And thick snow crunching under my feet.

Add the pine trees with tinsel and lights,
The skaters wrapped up warm on the frozen lakes,
And the snowman with his hat and carrot nose.

Decorate with stars twinkling on dark nights,
Animals going into hibernation for the long winter days,
And Santa Claus rushing past on his sleigh.

Zoë Reynolds (10)
Ruckleigh School

The Haunted House

In the bedroom, the broken door creaks open,
The candlelight shades away.
There is a shadowy reflection in the mirror
And the only sound was the wind, howling
through the cracked window.

In the hall, the pictures are talking and following me,
The stairs are broken and shattered.
The armour is rattling, almost falling on me,
The chandelier is moving left to right
And the only sound heard was someone
creeping down the stairs.

In the attic the chest of drawers are covered in cobwebs,
The old toys are all broken and the teddies are rough.
The boxes are open with skeletons' heads in them.
The suitcases are crushed and shattered
And the only sound heard was the chest of drawers
being pushed along.

Neelam Ali (11)
Ruckleigh School

My Teacher Thinks

I am working
But I am not
I am being chased by Zao in Iceland over a frozen lake
Now I am speeding around the Thames chasing Cigar Girl
In the Q boat
Now I am in the ice palace drinking beer
Now I am hand gliding off a cliff
Now I am back at M16 all scarred and bruised.

My teacher thinks
I am reading but I am not
I am exploring Wai Lin's secret armoury
Now I am being chased by a helicopter in Vietnam
Now I am flying a plane with Pussy Galore
Now I am playing golf with Goldfinger
Now I am exploring Crab Key with Honey Ryder.

My teacher thinks
I am listening but I am not
I am para-surfing on a dog, eating a melon, watching the news.

Callum Waddell (9)
Ruckleigh School

Winter Is Here

The snow was shimmering
White was the ice on the lake.
Snowmen, all sparkling in the sun,
Icicles on the water fountain, sparkling like crystal.
Fluffy glistening white stuff drifted to the ground.
Snow turns to slush and night falls.

James Coombes (8)
Ruckleigh School

My Teacher Thinks

My teacher thinks I'm working
But I'm not
I'm swimming with dolphins
In the Caribbean.
Now I'm watching telly with my mum.

My teacher thinks I'm thinking
But I'm not
I'm stewing sprouts with Jamie Oliver
Now I'm on a hovercraft
With James Bond
Now I'm in a world with *no boys.*

My teacher thinks I'm listening
But I'm not
I'm listening to someone call my name
Rosie! Rosie!
It's Mrs Whelam, I'm back at school
Boring that's what Rosie thinks.

Rosanna Wilkinson (9)
Ruckleigh School

Mrs Peel

There once was a teacher called Mrs Peel
Who couldn't stop eating meals,
She got so fat
That she went splat!
And that was the end of Mrs Peel.

Mimi Leung (10)
Ruckleigh School

My Teacher Thinks

My teacher thinks
I am working
But I'm not
I'm driving a Ferrari in the mountains
Now I'm making evil plans to take over the world
And even playing for Aston Villa and beating
Manchester United.

My teacher thinks
I am writing
But I'm not
I'm going to every museum in the world with my nanny
Now I'm winning a million on 'Who Wants To Be A Millionaire?'
And even landing on the moon.

My teacher thinks
I'm reading
But I'm not
I'm gambling money in Las Vegas
Now I'm swimming in the sea with sharks
And flying on the clouds in the blue sky.

My teacher thinks she knows everything - but she doesn't!

Darryl Thomas Grogan (9)
Ruckleigh School

Limerick

There was a lady called Sue,
She wanted her hair to turn blue,
She dipped it in ink,
But her hair turned pink,
That unlucky lady called Sue.

Christopher Peel (11)
Ruckleigh School

BEHIND THE STAFFROOM DOOR

I stand outside the staffroom door
Wondering now what lies in store.

Do they have jacuzzis and an Olympic-sized pool
Or a short fat manicurist, who sits on a stool?
Do they have movies with a widescreen TV
Or maybe a film set, which I just can't see?
Are they feasting with wine and steak
Or having a boring potato bake?
Do they have computers with Internet shopping
Or maybe a butler to do all their mopping?
I wonder if they have chocolate cake,
If they do, I'll have them burned at the stake!

Now I have made up my mind,
I'll be a teacher to know what's inside.
Until then I'll wait behind this door,
Dreaming of what lies in store.

Sondos Ibrahim (10)
Ruckleigh School

SNOWFLAKES

Snowflakes are flakes of slushy soft snow,
Ponds twinkle and glisten.
Some people throw snowballs whilst
I catch snowflakes,
Drifting down to the ground.
Snowflakes dance whilst they
Twirl around.

Nathan Tomlinson (7)
Ruckleigh School

My Teacher Thinks

My teacher thinks
I am reading
But I am not
I am flying on a swallow's back
I am sleeping on a cloud of silk
I am flying on a broomstick upside down
I am climbing in the sky.

My teacher thinks
I am listening
But I am not
I am riding on a polar bear
I am having dinner with a zombie
I am going back in time
I am being haunted by a ghost
I am having a fight with some sharks.

My teacher thinks
But I hear a voice
'Catherine! Catherine!
Please pay attention!'

Oh no! I'm back in the normal world.

Catherine MacNamara (9)
Ruckleigh School

Snow

Snow is soft and woolly
And it's very slippery too.
The sky is as pale as snow,
Colours white, grey and blue.

Snow is gentle and peaceful
When I walk, I can hear a crunchy sound.
The snow floats down to Earth,
A sheet of white, covering the ground.

Florentina Harris (8)
Ruckleigh School

My Teacher Thinks

My teacher thinks
I am working,
But I'm not
I'm playing football with David Beckham,
I'm jumping out of an aeroplane,
I'm living in a house made of chocolate.

My teacher thinks
I am listening,
But I'm not
I'm fighting a killer whale,
I'm a car going round the world
I'm walking on the sun.

My teacher thinks
I am reading
But I'm not.
I'm climbing up Mount Asama,
I'm racing a leopard,
I'm flying in the air.

But Mrs Whelan shouldn't be the teacher, I should!

Philip Todd (9)
Ruckleigh School

My Teacher Thinks

My teacher thinks
I am working
But I'm not!
I'm catching a billionaire burglar
Or climbing with a koala bear
Now I'm eating a huge burger

My teacher thinks
I am interested
But I'm not!
I'm riding on an elephant's back
Or wrestling Jaws the shark
Now I'm going up in a space rocket

My teacher thinks
I am listening
But I'm not!
I'm running a marathon
Or swimming with turtles
Now I'm on safari playing with monkeys

I think
My teacher's working
But she's not!

Edward Reynolds (9)
Ruckleigh School

Snow Time

Snowflakes dancing all around,
Wind whirling down the town,
Icicles falling from a tree,
Crashing on the ground.

Snow looks like icing,
Cold, cold as can be,
Then in the morning,
It's gone as I can see.

Francesca Dunn (7)
Ruckleigh School

MY TEACHER THINKS

My teacher thinks
I am writing
but I'm not.
I'm swimming with dolphins
Riding on the best roller coasters
I am the richest man in the world
I am cutting the biggest birthday cake in the world.

My teacher thinks
I am calculating
but I'm not.
I am a great white shark
I am a Formula One driver, winning every race
I am in Las Vegas winning a lot of money
I am a famous cricket player
I am better than David Beckham at football
I am better than Venus Williams at tennis

My teacher thinks I'm the best
Am I?

Jack Jaeger (10)
Ruckleigh School

My Teacher Thinks

My teacher thinks

I'm working
But I'm not
I'm about to start the London Marathon
I'm very popular like *David Beckham*
I'm playing for *Manchester United* and winning against *Liverpool*

My teacher thinks

I'm working
But I'm not
I'm climbing Mount Everest for the tenth time
I can speak every language in the world
I'm driving a Formula One car
And now I'm the richest kid in the world

My teacher thinks

I'm working
But I'm not
I'm the king of the world
I own every single game and game console in the world

My teacher thinks

I'm the smartest child in the class, but I'm not!

Kalpesh Prajapat (10)
Ruckleigh School

Winter

Winter is here, cold as ever,
Snow falls on the ground.
As the snow falls, it shines upon us,
The people shiver every time.

The sky is pale and grey
People crunch their feet in the snow.
Snowflakes dancing down to Earth
Covering all the world.

Hamza Rafiq (8)
Ruckleigh School

My Teacher Thinks

My teacher thinks
I'm working
But I'm not
I'm running through a golden cornfield, ready to jump and fly,
I'm soaring through the air.
I'm whooshig past aeroplanes and I'm plummeting into the ocean.
Splash! I'm breathing underwater,
I'm seeing colossal whales and deadly sharks.
A dolphin throws me high into the air to glide with birds.

My teacher thinks
I'm learning
But I'm not
I'm trekking through a jungle and climbing high trees,
I'm swinging with monkeys and I come across the almighty Angel Falls
Holding my breath, I take a dive, deeper and deeper I fall and splash
I'm at the bottom of the cascading Falls.

My teacher thinks
I'm a star
Am I?

Pratteek Srinivas Bathula (9)
Ruckleigh School

My Teacher Thinks

Mrs Whelan thinks
I am working
But I'm not!
I'm beating someone to the top of Mount Everest
Now I'm strangling an octopus
And now I'm flying to the moon on a spaceship.

Mrs Whelan thinks
I am writing
But I'm not
I'm swimming across the English Channel
Now I'm king of the world.

Mrs Whelan thinks
I am watching
But I'm not!
I'm throwing someone off of an aeroplane
Now I'm dropping someone into shark-infested waters
And now I'm pushing someone off the top of the
Empire State Building.

Mrs Whelan thinks a lot of things
But she's never right!

Christopher Smith (9)
Ruckleigh School

Snowflakes

Little, round, pointed, tiny snowflakes
They are twirling, turning.
A new day and there is more snow,
But by the time they hit Earth
They turn into a puddle.

William McGovern (7)
Ruckleigh School

My Teacher Thinks

My teacher thinks
I am watching
But I'm not!
I'm wrestling tigers in a Roman Colosseum,
I'm on safari in the Amazon jungle,
I'm having a party in the White House.

My teacher thinks
I am interested
But I'm not!
I'm riding hyenas in the Sahara desert,
I'm fighting Mohammed Ali on the top of K2
I'm scuba-diving with sharks.

My teacher thinks
I am reading
But I'm not!
I'm flying a Harrier jet for the Royal Air Force,
I'm lifting Big Ben up with my bare hands
I'm in a submarine - the Red October!

My teacher thinks I'm a star in class
Am I?

George Droulias (9)
Ruckleigh School

Limerick

There was a young man from Peru,
Who dreamed of eating his shoe,
He awoke with a fright
In the middle of the night
And found that his dream had come true!

Vincent Cheung (10)
Ruckleigh School

My Teacher Thinks

My teacher thinks
I am working
But I'm not
I'm in the jungle fighting lions, tigers and snakes.
Now I'm in an extremely old house hearing things
and feeling cold breaths of air on my back.
Now I'm in a field, riding a tornado
Suddenly I'm on a cliff, about to jump 300 feet into the water.

My teacher thinks
I am thinking
But I'm not
I'm the owner of a huge chocolate factory.
Now I've got a clock that can stop time.
I'm in a cartoon world and if you are not careful,
you will fall off the page.
I'm as thin as paper and when I jump I can glide
like a paper aeroplane.

My teacher thinks
I am writing
But I'm not
I'm in Egypt, exploring a pyramid
I'm swimming in the Atlantic Ocean and a great
white shark is swimming right under me.
I'm riding on a giraffe's head.

Ben Bennett (9)
Ruckleigh School

My Teacher Thinks

My teacher thinks
I'm working
But I'm not.
I'm riding a kangaroo in the Australian bush
I'm flying a spitfire in World War II
I'm climbing K2
I'm riding an ostrich in the Grand National.

My teacher thinks
I'm reading
But I'm not.
I'm talking to an alien from space,
I'm flying with a golden eagle.
I'm fighting a huge lion,
I'm journeying into space with a gorilla.

My teacher thinks
I'm interested
But I'm not.
I'm racing a cheetah
I'm singing to Queen Elizabeth II
I'm swimming with a hammerhead shark,
I'm rally driving with Colin McRae.

My teacher thinks
I'm daydreaming
But am I?

James Fletcher (10)
Ruckleigh School

What Is Yellow?

Yellow are the daffodils moving in the gentle breeze
Yellow is the sun, shining through the trees.
Yellow are the lions, prowling in the jungle,
Yellow are the buttercups in a cute bundle,
Yellow are the fruits like a lemon and banana.
Yellow is like small Labrador puppies,
Yellow is the colour of busy little bees,
Yellow is the sparkle of stars in the night,
Yellow is the twinkle of a small fairy light.
Yellow is the wind on a lovely summer day,
Yellow is the sound of children going out to play,
Yellow makes me feel happy.

Rebecca Westwood (11)
Ruckleigh School

Winter

Winter is when snow comes down,
The trees are white and I see the children
Play in the snow.
I came to play in the snow
I go to make a snowman.
I put a hat on it and a scarf,
I have a snowball in my hand
I then throw it at my friend.
I roll in the snow and I get colder and
Colder but I don't care.
My mum tells me to come inside.

Eleanor Carr-Smith (7)
Ruckleigh School

What Is Blue?

Blue is the water swishing and washing,
Blue are the bluebells, blowing in the wind.
Blue are people's eyes, shining in the sun
Blue are the cars whizzing down the road,
Blue are the blue tits, flying all around,
Blue are the whales, splashing all around.
Blue is the ink flowing out of pens,
Blue are the gloves, keeping my hands warm,
Blue is something out of the ordinary,
Blue is the sky on a sunny day.
Blue are the clothes that we love to wear,
Blue is Pluto hanging in the sky.

Ben Coleman (11)
Ruckleigh School

Winter

Snow drifting its way to the ground
Snowflakes dancing merrily outside,
Looking like twinkly stars glowing in the night.
A snowman peacefully standing there,
Covered with snow.
A carrot for his nose, four chocolate buttons
For his big, jolly smile,
The snow drifts, the snowman just stands there
With a big jolly smile.
Snow drifts again.

Mark Jaeger (7)
Ruckleigh School

Snowflakes

Snowflakes are dancing round and round,
Making shapes upon the ground
Like little raindrops.
Falling on the pond, making
Ripples on the icy water.
Ducks are flying away, to go to
another lake to stay.
The snowflakes run down my nose
making me giggle.
But now it's time to go,
The sun sets and glows.

Katie Cogley (7)
Ruckleigh School

The Day Was Brilliant

I asked my mum if I could go outside to play,
The snow was very soft and smooth.
I thought that with snow, I was going to have a brilliant day.

There were lots and lots of icicles,
We played in loads of snow.
Then my brother and I went to get our bicycles.

The lake was covered with ice and snow,
The trees were covered with icicles and snow.

Nancy Foote (8)
Ruckleigh School

Snow

The snow is freezing cold
It is shining brightly in the sun.
The snow is twirling gently
It is falling peacefully and quietly.
It's slushy and crunchy,
Like a crisp in my hand.
It's like a sheet falling to the ground
Floating slowly down.
And then the snow just melts from the sun
And leaves puddles on the ground.

Ashton Greig (8)
Ruckleigh School

Winter Is Here

As I got up, the little, white, cold snowflake
I saw yesterday, gave me a clue what happened.
A little snowman wouldn't hurt, I built a snowman
Eyes were made of coal and the nose was made from a carrot
And even as I shivered from head to toe,
Snowflakes drifted like leaves.
I went back in to watch the snowflakes,
The icicles were like diamonds.

Ruchira Sharma (8)
Ruckleigh School

If You Were . . .

If you were an ant
you would be small
striding through the
long grass worrying
about nothing at all.

If you were a bee
buzzing through the sky.
You'd pick up pollen
as you went by

If you were a fly
irritating people you
would have to say
bye-bye.

Splat! Squash!

Alice McElholm (9)
Ruckleigh School

Snowballs

Snowballs are falling from the air
And they don't make a sound,
When I pick it up it makes a crisp sound.
The ice is shining like silver rings,
I throw my snowball at it but it never breaks.
The air is so pale that I cannot see the clouds,
But snowballs are falling.

Duncan Wigley (7)
Ruckleigh School

WINTER IS HERE

All icy crystals fresh in the sun and the snow glittering.
All trees frosty wet.
Everything clean like snow,
Slippery, gathering wet snowflakes all falling down.
Crumbly, slushy, icy cold,
Snowmen, soft, freezing white, like wet icicles.
Mountains, smooth and white.
Shimmering ice, glittering in the sun.
Cold white houses, covered with snow.

Shyam Kotecha (8)
Ruckleigh School

A SNOWY DAY

Snow is soft and woolly
Catching snowflakes floating down,
Silver snow, buried high
It's slippery on the ground.
The sky is as pale as snow,
Snowmen dancing, twisting, twirling,
Turning, drifting in the air.
White snow crunching underfoot.
Snow is everywhere!

Daniel Younan (7)
Ruckleigh School

Winter Is Here

The lake is full of ice and snow, sparkling in the light,
The smooth and lean frosty white, looks like wool lying there tonight.
Icicles hanging down from the roofs of houses
Slippery ice makes me slip.
The freezing cold makes you shake and shiver in the snow
The sun rises and all the snow is melting.
All the snow crumbles when I make footprints,
The snow falls on your tongue.

Samuel Maguire (7)
Ruckleigh School

Winter Is Here

The icicles are cold, the snow is white,
Look at the snow gathering,
The icicles are like crystals and very fresh.
The snow is icy, cold and clean,
What fun it is to play in the smooth snow,
Look at the glistening icicles and sparkling snow.
Slushy, smooth, white frost hanging down
Look at the snow melting and sparkling.

Andrew Dillon (7)
Ruckleigh School

WHAT IS BLUE?

Blue is the sea smacking against the rocks,
Blue are the whales squirting water.
Blue are eyes staring at me,
Blue is a blue tit hopping by,
Blue are cars whizzing past.
Blue are bluebells dancing in the wind,
Blue is ink splattered on my page.
Blue is the sky on a hot summer's day.
Blue are blueberries, juicy and ripe.
Blue makes me feel sad and miserable.

Katie Jacks (11)
Ruckleigh School

SNOWFLAKES

A snowflake drifts down while dancing,
It falls down twinkling to the ground.
Sparkling like silver jewels
It covers the Earth with a huge white blanket
Dropping from the sky.
Everything is white,
Not a colour to be seen,
Not a sound to be heard.

Katy Smith (7)
Ruckleigh School

SNOWFLAKES

White, icy snowman,
Standing still and quiet
In my cold woolly garden.
Snowflakes dropping on the ground
Snowflakes dancing all around.
Roads are icy,
Streets are cold.
Slippery, as I have ever known.

Sophie Burrows (7)
Ruckleigh School

WINTER IS HERE

Winter has come
Snow is slushy and soft,
We all go and play outside,
Snow is shimmering, sparkling too.
Icicles hanging from the roof,
The lovely shining bright sun has come out,
All the snow is melting
We all go back inside!

Karina Gahir (7)
Ruckleigh School

Winter Is Here

Snow is very cold and icy
Especially white and wet
And it's slushy, smooth and fresh.
It's very crunchy when you move your feet
And it sparkles in the light.
Some icicles hanging down from houses
And snow on the trees
And snow blowing in the breeze.

Charlotte Greig (8)
Ruckleigh School

Winter Is Here

One day I made a snowman
It was cold, fresh, white and frosty.
I used a carrot for his nose
I used two stones for his eyes.
I used a banana for his mouth.
I went to go on my sleigh outside
I went ice skating on the pond,
Afterwards, I went in for my tea.

Harvey Jennings (7)
Ruckleigh School

WINTER IS HERE

Some fluffy crumbling white snowballs appear,
As white and as fresh as can be.
The roads are white and glistening as can be
All houses have white roofs.
All trees have snow on them that looks like cotton wool.
All children are having snowball fights
And getting as snowy as can be.

Lucy Winter (7)
Ruckleigh School

WINTER IS HERE

When the slushy, glittering snow starts to fall
I go outside on the slippery snow
And I would like to build a frosty snowman.
So I get my clean hands in the fresh snow
I get a pile of snow with sparkling bits in it,
And get a pile of snow,
I put it all together
And it makes a cheerful, cold snowman.

Victoria Beech (7)
Ruckleigh School

SNOW

This morning in the white, cold, frosty air,
Snowflakes were falling softly, slowly.
Footsteps sounded like crisps crunching
Catching delicate snowflakes,
Dancing in the air.
Sparkling and smiling on my tongue.

Sumeet Virdee (7)
Ruckleigh School

Winter Is Here

Crystal flakes are falling from the sky,
The snow looks clean and smooth.
I held some snow and it was cold
Then it became night.
The snow was glittering in the dark
Then I was shivering to death.
When I woke up in the morning -
The snow had all melted on the ground.

Yasmin Ella Webb (7)
Ruckleigh School

Winter Is Here

One winter's morning, snow was falling,
Glittering in the sunlight.
We had snowball fights.
Snow is cold,
Snow is icy,
Icicles hanging from the treetops.
Snow is white,
Snow is fluffy like cotton wool.

Rebecca Jacks (8)
Ruckleigh School

Winter Is Here

Slushy snow is falling down
Harder than you would expect.
Twinkling, gleaming snow, nicer than you would expect.
Nice day to build a snowman,
Sparkling icicles hanging down.
I hear the snow whispering through the trees,
When the snow is glittering, I love snow.

Laura Newboult (7)
Ruckleigh School

My Red Colour

The red blood of a cut
The red flame of fire
The red rose that shines bright
The red heart that pumps like mad
The red sunset that glows in the sky
The red devils that kill at night
The red face that is shy
The red flag that waves around
The red ant that is poisonous
The red jumper that keeps you warm
The red blood when you die
The red beautiful feathers of a parrot
The red boat that floats on water
The red car that zooms past shops and houses
The red football team that wins the match
The red of a clown's nose
The red of a juicy cherry.

Nishal Bhavik Magdani (9)
St Alphege CE Junior School, Solihull

Nonsense Is Nonsense

My mum speaks nonsense
My dad speaks nonsense
My brother speaks nonsense
My pet speaks nonsense

And how many times have I told you . . .
Nonsense is nonsense.

Anything my aunt speaks
Anything my uncle speaks
Anything my gran speaks
Anything my grandpa speaks is . . .
Nonsense

And how many times have I told you . . .
Nonsense is nonsense.

Georgina Buck (8)
St Alphege CE Junior School, Solihull

Christmas Day

It's snowing on Christmas Day,
It's time to rejoice and play.

The wind is whistling through my fingers,
I can hear the beautiful choir singers.

The wise men travel up and down,
Trying to find the holy town.

I'm on my sledge whizzing to and fro,
Onto flat ground, *oh,* it's going slow.

Ashley Fraser (9)
St Alphege CE Junior School, Solihull

TIGER

Hiding, hiding right away, taken from his home.
Eating easy food, no need to pounce, scared,
Trapped, surrounded by bars made of chrome,
Through which the people stared.

Walking, walking, always walking.
Never different, always the same,
Driven by instinct to keep stalking.
When he was a cub this is where he came.

Wondering, wondering where his family is,
Dreaming about freedom.
He does not know the cage is his,
Nor that it is his kingdom.

Staring, staring always at him,
Wondering who he is,
Until the light goes dim,
Thinking what is this?

Hiding, hiding right away, taken from his home.
Eating easy food, no need to pounce, scared,
Trapped, surrounded by bars made of chrome,
Through which the people stared.

Neil Marshall (9)
St Alphege CE Junior School, Solihull

DOLPHIN

Swiftly it swims around,
gracefully it dives up and down,
smoothly it zooms through the water,
how beautiful is the sight.

Its beautiful body,
its smooth soft skin,
do you know what I'm talking about?
A dolphin.

Lucy Stoddart (8)
St Alphege CE Junior School, Solihull

My Sister

My little sister was born so small
It is such a wonder she's grown so tall.

As a baby she was pretty and cute and would open her mouth and mime
Giggled a lot and then slept most of the time.

She would squeal when she saw me and almost cheer
Squeeze my finger to keep me near.

When she began to move she shuffled around at an amazing speed
Oh when will she walk it will be fun indeed!

Now she can count and sing and dance about
She laughs and hugs and has silly sulks.

She is such a character she plays the fool
Soon she will be going to St Alphege School.

She is my sister so precious I love her lots
She even pinches and hides my socks.

Her dimples she has two and bright eyes and smile too
I cannot stay cross for long. Oh I do love you!

Rebecca Leonard (10)
St Alphege CE Junior School, Solihull

A CHRISTMAS ALPHABET

A is for the angel on the Christmas tree
B is for the baby smiling radiantly
C is for a candle with a glow so bright
D is for the donkey walking through the night
E is for Emmanuel who will never leave us
F is for the frankincense given to Jesus
G is for gold which glistens like the sun
H is for happiness given by my mum
I is for ivy that climbs up the wall
J is for Jesus who started it all
K is for the kings, wise men three
L is for light guiding us to thee
M is for myrrh the wise men brought along
N is for noel we hear in the song
O is for oranges, a big bowl in the hall
P is for presents, some big, some small
Q is for our Queen who speaks to us all
R is for robin with his special call
S is for snow that falls on the ground
T is for tinsel that hangs all around
U is for unity which we would applaud
V is for the virgin Mary who gave us our Lord
W is for worship in the church where we go
X is for kisses under the mistletoe
Y is for Yuletide, log fires roaring
Z is for zzzzzz . . . Christmas afternoon, Daddy's asleep snoring.

Emily Pillinger (9)
St Alphege CE Junior School, Solihull

The Magic Box

(Based on 'Magic Box' by Kit Wright)

I will put in my box . . .

The touch of morning breeze,
The dew from the fresh grass,
A colourful touch from a rainbow.

I will put in my box . . .

The sound of a sizzling sausage,
The sun burning its flame.

I will put in my box . . .

A taste of Heaven's gate,
The taste of the North Star,
The taste of golden honey from a bee.

I will put in my box . . .

The smell of a flying cloud,
A smell of a flame burning in the air,
The smell of sand from the Sahara desert.

I will put in my box . . .

A sight of the moon,
A sight of snow in the frost,
A sight of my family.

My box is fashioned

With Saturn's ring,
The most expensive jewels,
Thunder from the mist and the air
And a dragon's eye.

Jayant Pancholi (9)
St Alphege CE Junior School, Solihull

Colours

White is like a dove sailing off over the sea
Colours
Red is like blood trickling down my skin
Colours
Blue is like the sky gliding around the world
Colours
Green is like fresh spring grass
Colours
Yellow is like the shining sun over the world
Colours
Black is like the atmosphere covering all the world
Colours.

Oliver Mitchell (9)
St Alphege CE Junior School, Solihull

Football Crazy, Soccer Mad

I'm football crazy,
Soccer mad.
My mother thinks I'm mental,
A crazy little lad.
Football is the name of the game
And I'm the one to play it
It really is the beautiful game
And that's why I always
Display it!
Football.

Jared Bentsi-Enchill (8)
St Alphege CE Junior School, Solihull

Friends

You are the friend I like to please,
Someone with whom I feel at ease.
You are the friend who with me shares
All my pleasure, all my cares.
You are the friend I like to meet,
To talk with, eat with, laugh with, and weep
And you are the one to whom I send
Love and thanks from a special friend.

Natalie Lewis (10)
St Alphege CE Junior School, Solihull

Colour

The red of blood,
The petal of a rose,
The bright red of a clown's nose.

The red of a cherry,
The red of a devil,
The red of a heart.

Oliver Sleeman (9)
St Alphege CE Junior School, Solihull

The Sea

The sea is like a bear growling
And the waves are dancing ladies swirling.
The sea is calm, calm as the clouds
That curl along the shore.
The sea is like a peaceful chair folding itself up.
The sea is the poem that's going to sing you to sleep.

Katie Ambridge (7)
St Alphege CE Junior School, Solihull

SPRING

Sound the flute!
Now it's mute,
Birds delight,
Day and night;
Nightingale,
In the dale,
Dark in sky,
Merrily, merrily to welcome in the year.

Little boy,
Full of joy;
Little girl,
Sweet and small;
Cock does crow,
So do you;
Nervy voice,
Instant noise,
Merrily, merrily welcome in joy.

Little lamb,
Here I am;
Come and lick
My white neck so thick;
Let me pull
Your soft wool;
Let me kiss
Your soft face;
Merrily, merrily we welcome in newborn.

Emily Heartfield (8)
St Alphege CE Junior School, Solihull

Touch And Feel

Touch!
What can you feel?
The smooth petal
Of a pretty flower,
A buzzing bee
Using power.

Touch!
What can you feel?
The fluffy fur
Of a kitten's fluff.
Have you ever felt
Something like that stuff?

Touch!
What can you feel?
The slimy snake's scales
That are rough and cold.
A fish that's slimier
That's really bold.

Alexandra Holder (7)
St Alphege CE Junior School, Solihull

Winter At School

W rite, write, write all day
I nk may spill all the way
N o one is allowed out to play
T eachers may have a cold
E veryone may get the day off
R ight everyone work, work, work.

Olivia Sheppard (8)
St Alphege CE Junior School, Solihull

Best Friends

B est friends are fun to play with
E verybody needs a friend
S hare secrets with friends
T here are lots of games to play with friends.

F riends live forever
R idiculous jokes with friends
I n friendship you have bracelets
E very day we play
N aughty friends never keep secrets
D o dreamy games with friends.

Wendy Norman (8)
St Alphege CE Junior School, Solihull

Topsy-Turvy

Mum's going crazy,
Dad's going lazy,
Brother's being cool,
Sister's playing netball,
Granny's doing cooking,
Grandad's going sightseeing,
Uncle's off to the leaning tower,
Auntie's picking flowers.
The world's going
Topsy-turvy.

James Whitfield (9)
St Alphege CE Junior School, Solihull

S

S
is it a snake slithering through the long grass?
S
is it a swirl neatly written on a clean page?
S
is it an eel swirling through the weedy water?
S
is it a river running through a rocky mountain?
S
is it the tail of a dog or a big horse?
S
is it a rope whirling round a pole?
What is it?

Luke Boswell (8)
St Alphege CE Junior School, Solihull

TOUCH (WHAT CAN YOU FEEL?)

Touch!
What can you feel?
The scaled snake it feels so rough
Slithering through the grass to catch the mouse
The mouse's blood floats down deep in the ground.

Touch!
What can you feel?
The scattered cat, all of its fur
It rolls down the grass right to the ground.

Judith Kefas (8)
St Alphege CE Junior School, Solihull

My Magic Box

(Based on 'Magic Box' by Kit Wright)

I will put in my box . . .
A huge page of intricate road maps,
The smell of crunchy and crispy fish cakes,
The sea crashing on the rocks,
A blanket of delicious melted chocolate,
The congested motorway, stretching for miles.

My box is fashioned out of
The bark of a golden tree, encrusted with autumn leaves,
With a rich crimson, velvet lining.
Its hinges are steely icicles.
A picture of me, set in jewels, is on the lid.

I will put in my box . . .
The feathery touch of an angel's wing,
A world where nobody has anything bad happen to them.
The smell of heavenly flowers
And the starry end of the universe.

Benjamin Coupland (9)
St Alphege CE Junior School, Solihull

Clown On The Mantelpiece

There's a clown on the mantelpiece
And he plays the fiddle,
He has a white face,
With a red nose in the middle.

On his head is a bowler hat,
On top of a mass of blue hair,
On his face is a look of contentment,
His thoughts I wish he would share.

He faces the television,
With his fiddle still under his chin,
I know he's watching it really,
You can tell by his cheeky grin.

His eyes are slightly open,
Just enough to see,
I'm sure I saw his smile waver
And I'm sure he's watching me!

Hannah Boswell (11)
St Alphege CE Junior School, Solihull

Mythological Madness

The unicorn, the one-horned horse,
Has wings that glow so bright.
With shining gold and silver coat
He soars through the moonlight.

The Minotaur, half-man, half-bull,
Takes his axe wherever he goes.
With sharp and dangerous pointed horns
And a glinting ring in his nose.

The slimy fire-breathing dragon
Has scales all the way round,
Nostrils the size of saucers
And a terrible roaring sound.

The terrifying Cyclops
Who looks as tall as the sky.
He eats men for his breakfast
And has one evil eye.

George Spann (9)
St Alphege CE Junior School, Solihull

My Pet Cat

My pet is a playful cat
He is quite furry and kind of fat
His food he always will eat
And every day he looks for a treat.

Oh how bright he is
And it's quite a sight
When he jumps at a certain height
Or plays with his feet so white.

He is really grey and brown
But looks black and white
And on his face and paws
There is a splash of white.

I named him Little Rascal
Because that's what he is
I know that I'll love him
As long as he lives.

Karisa Tavassoli (8)
St Alphege CE Junior School, Solihull

My Secret Poem

S ecrets are kept forever,
E verybody keeps them quiet,
C an you tell I'm keeping one,
R idiculous if you can tell,
E verybody has one,
T o the end of your life.

Rosie Holland (8)
St Alphege CE Junior School, Solihull

LONELINESS

I call but no one answers
I look but no one's there
A tiny light in a dark room
I fight off anyone who tries to come near
I whisper things that only you can hear
I make you feel unsure and frightened
I am sincere my friend is fear
I am as solitary as a huge black bear
I hide among the mist around me
You cannot see me but I'm always waiting
A moment of life in a vast, lonely world
I am loneliness.

Emily Clarke (10)
St Alphege CE Junior School, Solihull

TOUCH (WHAT CAN YOU FEEL?)

Touch (what can you feel?)
The chick, soft and fluffy it still has to grow a mass
The spikes of a hedgehog sniffing the grass
The scaly scales of a snake
The hard, edible cheese squashing in a cake.

Touch (what can you feel?)
A cat with fluffy fur
Soft and sweet stones on a beach
Waiting to meet
A leaf on the ground
Flowers all around.

Rebecca Adams (7)
St Alphege CE Junior School, Solihull

THE KEY

The stormy sea was clashing below the battling clouds,
The grey night sky was blackening, above the wind crying loud,
The towering cliff was standing, with triumph over the sea.
Though a person in a brown tunic, walked over the cliff in the
moonlight to the edge where it could see.

It walked upon the cliff edge, watching stones tumbling down,
To the barren sea that was wailing, a look, a mourning frown,
To the half full moon, the wolves were giving an angry roar.
Though that person in the brown tunic, was standing no more.

Sitting at the cliff, the stranger sat and hung,
On the edge for hours, it listened to what the wind sung,
Then out of its pockets the stranger revealed a shining key.
But that person in the brown tunic fed the golden light to the sea.

As the night-time brightened, as dawn was coming soon,
The stranger fled as its notion was of the going moon,
The wind was puffing stronger and blew off the chestnut hood.
That person in the brown tunic, hid a woman, there she stood.

The sea bellowed in anger, or in pain, that I couldn't tell,
The wind was even stronger; it knocked over a tower bell!
This key disturbed the village and made the wind and sea roar.
Look! That person in the brown tunic, could be seen no more.

This key was drifting downwards, into the shell-crusted sand,
And was buried in the ocean, touched by only one hand,
But that person was a stranger above it. It could note,
That strange thing glittering golden, hiding from nets of ships nor boat.

The sea was still a-tremble; the villagers said a curse,
Then out of the salty waters, the strange key came and burst,
Out of the misty ocean, flew up through air then down,
That strange thing glittering golden, to the bedside of someone in town.

Emma-Niamh Wilson (11)
St Alphege CE Junior School, Solihull

Homework's Very Fat

Boring books and piles of paper stuffed inside my bag,
I'd rather walk a hundred miles with a dirty hag.
The door swings open and my bag falls on the floor,
Instead of doing homework I'd rather eat meat raw.
I stomp up the winding stairs and sit at my desk,
I rip my bag wide open and pick up the first little test.
Homework's very fat.

It's now Sunday and homework's squashing Sunday flat,
I'd rather go in a dark gloomy cave and be bitten by a bat.
I pick up my ink pen and scribble my seven times table
on a piece of scrap,
I'd rather be banned from all my CDs - rock, pop and rap.
I really don't want to do that homework.
Homework's very fat!

Victoria Hodgkisson (9)
St Alphege CE Junior School, Solihull

Touch, What Can You Feel?

Touch, what can you feel?
The soft, furry, fluffy coat of a playful kitten
The smooth, hissing, tough-scaled snake.

Touch, what can you feel?
The spiky, prickly, sharp hedgehog
The fluffy fur of a newborn chick.

Megan Astley (7)
St Alphege CE Junior School, Solihull

TOUCH

Touch
What can you feel?
The crunch of leaves
Of an acorn tree
The fluffy feathers
Of a newborn chick.

Touch
What can you feel?
The silky and wet
Spider's web
The fins of a very wet fish.

Touch
What can you feel?
The smooth and heavy stone
That came from the beach.

Touch
What can you feel?

Albert Davis (7)
St Alphege CE Junior School, Solihull

TOUCH

Touch
What can you feel?
The sharp spikes of a hedgehog,
The dancing evening grass, slimy under your fingers.

Touch
What can you feel?
The smooth surface of a gleaming conker,
The furry surface of a chestnut fox slinking by.

Touch
What can you feel?
The silky surface of a dolphin leaping in the air,
The sharp surface of a shark's teeth.

Jessica Cuttriss (7)
St Alphege CE Junior School, Solihull

Up In The Attic

Up in the attic
Where nobody goes
Is an old bag of rusty coins
An old broken up wardrobe
An old pair of boots
A stuffed owl without a hoot
Past comics
A box of tonics

And . . . something's creeping

And . . . down in the cellar

Where nobody goes
Is a smelly pile of coal
A rat caught in a trap
An ancient cricket bat
A battered old hat
A blood-smeared cue
Blood spots

And . . . something's breathing.

Jamie Woolley (10)
St Alphege CE Junior School, Solihull

TOUCH, WHAT CAN YOU FEEL?

Touch!
What can you feel?
I can feel a furry cat
Wearing a summer hat.

Touch!
What can you feel?
I can feel a wooden chair
As I feel a teddy bear.

Touch!
What can you feel?
The soft, brown, furry coating of a cat
A cat lying on a mat.

Touch!
What can you feel?
The silky, brown, crumpled leaves
Sticking to my sleeves.

Emily Petch (8)
St Alphege CE Junior School, Solihull

TOUCH, WHAT CAN YOU FEEL?

Touch, what can you feel?
I can feel the fur of a soft, happy cat,
The scaly, slimy, slippy, spitting snake.

Touch, what can you feel?
A furry chick chirping with glee,
A spiky, prickly hedgehog
Scuttling in the leaves.

Sophie Brown (7)
St Alphege CE Junior School, Solihull

TOUCH, WHAT CAN YOU FEEL?

Touch!
What can you feel?
The water crashing down on me,
The scaly snake in my hand.

Touch!
What can you feel?
The soft wind blowing through my fingers,
The grass on my finger.

Touch!
What can you feel?
The money that is in my pocket,
The furry, playing cat,
The leaves on my feet,
The prickly hedgehog.

Maddy Abrams (7)
St Alphege CE Junior School, Solihull

TOUCH, WHAT CAN YOU FEEL?

Touch, what can you feel?
The smooth rattle of leaves,
A storm of nasty thieves.

Touch, what can you feel?
A silky thread of a spider's web,
A tree that can be soft.

Amy Garner (7)
St Alphege CE Junior School, Solihull

ASTRONAUT

I wish I was an astronaut,
With my head spinning round in space.
I'd fly to all the planets,
Have suns and moons upon my face.
I'd take my best friend Jenny,
We would take some midnight feasts.
We would go to the red planet,
And watch the alien beasts.
We would go to the moon,
Let's hope it would be sunny.
I would dare Jenny to jump in a crater,
We would hire our own moon buggy.
We would play golf with asteroids,
Trees from Jupiter too.
We would use craters for holes,
We would see some Star Wars' droids.
If I were an astronaut up in space,
I'd miss all these things on Earth.
But what I'd miss most of all,
Is my mum's friendly smiling face.

Katie Dobson (9)
St Alphege CE Junior School, Solihull

TOUCH, WHAT CAN YOU FEEL?

Touch,
What can you feel?
The soft, warm fur of a newborn chick
A leaf falling down on me.

Touch,
What can you feel?
The web brushing on me
The sliver of a snake hissing at me
The cat miaowing at the foot of me.

Joshua Melvin (8)
St Alphege CE Junior School, Solihull

DANCE OF THE DOLPHINS

Slow, slow, quick, quick, slow,
Ride the waves
And here we go.

Quick, quick, leap up high,
Arch your back,
It's time to fly!

Fly, fly, puff and blow,
Blow some bubbles
In a row.

Puff, puff, waltz and spin,
Shake your tail,
Flick your fin.

Slow, slow, quick, quick, slow,
Take a partner,
Dive down low.

Quick, quick, slow, slow, quick,
Listen carefully,
That's the trick!

Rebecca Scott (8)
St Alphege CE Junior School, Solihull

Colours

Red is the sign of danger,
Red is the colour of flames,
Red is the colour of blood,
Red takes all the blame.
Blue is the colour of the sea,
Blue is the colour of rivers,
Blue is the colour of Birmingham City,
Blue is the colour of the sky.
Yellow is the colour of the flowers,
Yellow is the colour of the sun,
Yellow is the colour of someone's hair.
White is the colour of clouds,
White is the colour of paper,
White is the colour of school shirts.

Callum Walker (8)
St Alphege CE Junior School, Solihull

Candle, Candle

Candle, candle in the night,
You give off a bright light.
Candle, candle you shed no harm,
In the light you are calm.
Candle, candle flickering like a flame,
You show us no shame.
Candle, candle Jesus you show,
Never will you be our foe.

Joshua Brampton (10)
St Alphege CE Junior School, Solihull

SEASONS

Seasons come around every year
Spring, autumn and Christmas cheer.

Spring stands for a gentle breeze
But hay fever makes me sneeze.

Summer stands for seaside sights
I'll make a sandcastle with all my might.

Autumn leaves are falling down
Orange, yellow, even brown.

Winter stands for a big white rug,
Everybody wants a Christmas hug.

Sophie Thompson (8)
St Alphege CE Junior School, Solihull

TOUCH

Touch,
What can you feel?
The soft and smooth fur of the cats
Running up a tree.
I could feel a person
Running about with glee.

Touch,
What can you feel?
The rough scales of a snake in the grass.
I felt a kangaroo
When it was leaping its way up the pass.

Charlotte E Branson (8)
St Alphege CE Junior School, Solihull

In The Pyramid

And something's . . . moving

A shark's fin
An old bin
A hole in a pan
A photo of a man
A wrecked and horrible box
A scary, blooded fox

And . . . something's breathing

A wrapped and walking mummy
A bandage from his tummy
A rusty coffin
Some wet comics
A dead bug
And a slimy slug

But all is quiet.

Mark Stanion (10)
St Alphege CE Junior School, Solihull

Sisters

Sisters are such big pests,
Even if you're in the middle of a test.
Such big pains, oh they are,
But make sure they don't go too far.
But they still are the best,
So don't be mean,
Or they might get keen.

Chloe Mitchell (8)
St Alphege CE Junior School, Solihull

The Aliens Are Here

The aliens are here,
the spacecraft is a-humming.
Hovering over the house,
ever nearer coming.
Above this house they hover,
silence the only sound.
Coming ever nearer,
all our heartbeats pound.
The sound is coming closer
as we near our fate,
now the roof's collapsing
under all that weight!

Rachel Parker (10)
St Alphege CE Junior School, Solihull

Light

Light is powerful
Light is light
Light is strong
And can burn your eyes

Light is good
Light is kind
Light is my mind

Light makes you see
Light makes you smile
Light comes in the dawn
Light values our time.

Kathryn Heather (10)
St Alphege CE Junior School, Solihull

WINTER

Winter with sparkling frost and shimmering snow
you are cold and hard and fall from the clouds
swallowing the land in white, frosting trees.
The animals hibernate away from you
if they do not hibernate they are frozen cold.

You are cold and come in winter
you are hail in huge loads.
You beat on our heads rebounding off coats
whacking into our eyes, blinding us
and hurting winter animals
making huge gouges in their backs
through fur and skin.

Nathaniel Hughes (8)
St Alphege CE Junior School, Solihull

I LOOK THROUGH MY TELESCOPE

I look through my telescope and gaze at all the stars
I look through my telescope, I can see as far as Mars.

I look through my telescope, it's the middle of the night
I look through my telescope at the bright moonlight.

I look through my telescope, the rooster is singing
I look through my telescope and listen to church bells ringing.

I can't look through my telescope, it's time to go to school
Why is it that life can sometimes be so cruel?

Stephanie Biddle (9)
St Alphege CE Junior School, Solihull

The Grandfather Clock

I look and I stare at the grandfather clock,
as it bangs against its sides with a tick-tock.
It ticks and it tocks and it tells the time
and as it does it makes a wallop of a chime.

I think what it would be like to be a grandfather clock,
working all day and not able to stop,
as time goes by its hands get tired,
but it's always getting admired.

I hear the mighty grandfather clock,
the bang it makes gives me a shock.
When I hear the noise it makes from my bed,
it keeps on going on in my head.

Millie Duck (8)
St Alphege CE Junior School, Solihull

Diamond

Inside the tiger's tail, the swishing axe.
Inside the swishing axe, the tiger's eye.
Inside the tiger's eye, the starry sky.
Inside the starry sky, the tiger's paw.
Inside the tiger's paw, the grassy plain.
Inside the grassy plain, the tiger's claws.
Inside the tiger's claws, the deer's cry.
Inside the deer's cry, the black rose.
Inside the black rose, the tiger's reflection.
Inside the tiger's reflection, the blazing sun.
Inside the blazing sun, the tiger's laugh.
Inside the tiger's laugh, the babbling brook.
Inside the babbling brook, the tiger's tail.

Andrew Turner (11)
St Alphege CE Junior School, Solihull

School Dinners

School dinners at my school
Are as crazy as can be.
Ice cream topped with custard,
Deary, deary me!

School dinners at my school
Are as gruesome as you could think.
Fish fingers topped with custard
I want to puke in the sink!

School dinners at my school
Are as yucky as can be.
Chocolate topped with mustard
Deary, deary me!

So that's why I swapped
To packed lunch!

Naomi Rose Harryman (9)
St Alphege CE Junior School, Solihull

Poppy

Poppy is our puppy,
We love her very much.
She comes dashing when we call her,
She is beautiful to touch.
Her velvet pads, her pointed ears,
She is so very, very dear.
Her coat is sleek and shiny,
Her nose is cold and black
And when we throw her special toy,
She runs and brings it back!

Eliot Davis (9)
St Alphege CE Junior School, Solihull

A Smart Poem

Here is the smart car gleaming and new,
Carrying a couple to the front church pew.

The jolly husband and quick-witted wife,
Opening the windows to bring in life.

Tearing up the A41,
Watching children having fun.

Flashing past markets and stalls,
Listening with interest to the bargain calls.

So now here they stop with a great big lurch,
Ready to enter the old Baptist church.

Gabrielle Chan (10)
St Alphege CE Junior School, Solihull

Inside the Unicorn's Horn

Inside the unicorn's horn, a bolt of lightning,
Inside the bolt of lightning, the glistening mane,
Inside the glistening mane, the streaks of sunlight,
Inside the streaks of sunlight, the shining eyes,
Inside the shining eyes, the magical meadow,
Inside the magical meadow, a golden hoof,
Inside the golden hoof, the emerald grass,
Inside the emerald grass, the snowy teeth,
Inside the snowy teeth, a swirling tornado,
Inside the swirling tornado, the unicorn's horn.

Sarah Adcock (10)
St Alphege CE Junior School, Solihull

I Was Being Watched

I couldn't help thinking,
That I was being watched,
By the dreaded, strict teacher,
Master Melbotched.

My heart was beating faster,
Almost every sec,
If my fear fell into his hands,
I'd be beaten round the neck.

I'm sure I don't know the reason,
My vowels are all correct
And my spelling was totally perfect,
I checked and checked and checked.

Jonathon Webb (11)
St Alphege CE Junior School, Solihull

Inside A Horse's Eye

Inside a horse's eye, a mountain range.
Inside a mountain range, a horse's ear.
Inside a horse's ear, a grey, foggy mist.
Inside a grey, foggy mist, a horse's mane.
Inside a horse's mane, a rocky beach.
Inside a rocky beach, a horse's hoof.
Inside a horse's hoof, a large blue sea.
Inside a large blue sea, a horse's tail.
Inside a horse's tail, a gravelly path.
Inside a gravelly path, a glistening mane.
Inside a glistening mane, a blizzard.
Inside a blizzard, a horse's eye.

Gemma Tighe (11)
St Alphege CE Junior School, Solihull

Candle

Candle, candle fill the night
With your overwhelming light,
Candle, candle burn our shame
Using a small lick of flame,
Candle, candle bright as a bulb
Glowing yellow, orange and gold,
Candle, candle help us remember,
That shining star from December.

Josh Petch (10)
St Alphege CE Junior School, Solihull

Red

The red blood from a slash
The flame of a fire
The red of a rash.

The red of a berry freshly picked
The red of a wonder flower
The red of rosy cheeks.

Douglas Griffiths (8)
St Alphege CE Junior School, Solihull

The Sea

The sea is beautiful
as it ripples in the wind,
as the sun streams on the bright blue sea
but is as cold as can be.
I walk into the sea
as a waves comes over me.
I love the sea.

Alice Fennell (7)
St Alphege CE Junior School, Solihull

Dolphin

The beautiful blue sea, a beautiful rainbowfish.
Oh look a dolphin, he is coming closer
and he is after the rainbowfish.

Oh isn't he graceful!
Do you wish you could see a dolphin
swimming in the ocean?

Mary Montgomery (7)
St Alphege CE Junior School, Solihull

Roses

R oses, roses, red and tall,
O n thick long stems that tower up tall,
S ome are pink, some are red, at night they go to bed,
E ven grow up the garden wall,
S o every day they wake up and smile.

Alice Claronino (7)
St Alphege CE Junior School, Solihull

Flowers

Flowers big, flowers small,
Flowers as big as a ball!
Flowers are sweet, flowers smell
Flowers are a shape of a jingle bell.
Flowers are short, flowers are tall
Some flowers are as tall as a garden wall.

Beatrice Freeman (7)
St Alphege CE Junior School, Solihull

Light

I race around the corners
Making darkness go
With you I always will be
Moving as the fastest thing
In the night and day
Darkness dies before me
I will never leave you
Without me you would be dead
For I am *light.*

Peter Bailey (11)
St Alphege CE Junior School, Solihull

Are You?

Are you a techno junkie?
Are you a console king?
Are you computer crazy?
Is that your favourite thing?
Because it's mine!

Oliver T Griffin (8)
St Alphege CE Junior School, Solihull

Down In The Cellar

Down in the cellar
Where nobody goes,
There is the tiger,
Painting his toes.

Down in the cellar
Where nobody looks,
There is the giraffe
Reading big books.

Down in the cellar,
Where nobody sees,
There is the big bear
Cooking his fleas.

Down in the cellar
Where nobody meets,
There is the hippo
Washing his feet.

Down in the cellar,
Where nobody hears,
There is the baboon
Drinking Dad's beers.

Down in the cellar,
They're all having fun,
Feasting on ice cream,
Cakes and sticky buns!

Jenny Abrams (10)
St Alphege CE Junior School, Solihull

The Door!

The door big and bold,
The door silver and gold,
The door very creepy,
The door old and creaky.

The door what's behind?
The door what could I find?
The door does my key fit?
The door should I open it?

Jyoti Pancholi (9)
St Alphege CE Junior School, Solihull

Moon

Slowly, silently creeps the moon
in her sparkling, silver lagoon.
Shining brightly in the sky
while owls hoot and wolves cry.

Planets, Jupiter, Venus and Mars
circle the world, the moon and the stars.

Brittany Fisher (11)
St Alphege CE Junior School, Solihull

DEATH

The colour is burgundy,
It smells like mouldy cheese,
It tastes like bright blood mixed with sour soup.
Do you think it sounds like bombs exploding?
Death feels all sharp and painful, like sharks' teeth.
Death lives in the heart of the underground
With wriggly worms, scary, hairy spiders and slimy slugs.

Josie Humphries (9)
St James's CE Primary School, Stourbridge

DEATH

Death is black blood,
It smells like rotten eggs.
Death tastes like grubby spiders *eerrgghh.*
Death sounds like a pause . . .
It feels like hot air,
Death lives in the soul of every person.

Katie Smith (9)
St James's CE Primary School, Stourbridge

HOPE

Hope is red and pink.
Hope smells like freshly picked roses.
Hope tastes like sweet chocolate.
Hope sounds like birds singing.
Hope lives in your heart of hearts.

Ryan Astley (9)
St James's CE Primary School, Stourbridge

Old Age

Old age is a deep cruel lilac, like a bruise.
It smells like a wet dog,
It tastes like mouldy fruit.
Old age sounds like eerie music and ancient doors creaking.
It feels spine-chilling, like having an icy shower.
Old age lives on the gloomy side of everyone's heart.

Thomas Greensill (9)
St James's CE Primary School, Stourbridge

Happiness

Happiness is lilac.
It smells like freshly picked roses,
It tastes like melted chocolate.
Happiness sounds like beautiful birds tweeting in the trees.
It feels soft and furry like the fur of a cat,
Happiness lives in the heart of a playful child.

Lydia Willetts (9)
St James's CE Primary School, Stourbridge

Evil

Evil is blood-red.
It smells like a rotting animal.
Evil tastes as hot as a chilli pepper.
It sounds like creepy cackling laughter.
Evil feels hard and bumpy like a crocodile's coat.
It lives in the very core of the Earth.

Stephanie Homer (10)
St James's CE Primary School, Stourbridge

Peace

Peace is a forget-me-not-blue,
It smells like a white lily opening.
Peace tastes like the sweetest apple.
It sounds like a joyful butterfly, fluttering.
It feels warm and smooth like a kitten
sleeping in front of the fire.
Peace lives in the heart of a rainbow reaching above
the clouds, sprinkling its colours around.

Robyn Bullingham (9)
St James's CE Primary School, Stourbridge

Happiness

Happiness is a light navy blue sky,
It smells like a hot doughnut with sugar on the top.
It tastes like a warm winter's soup with vegetables in it.
Happiness sounds like peace and quiet all around the world.
It feels like a cold ice pudding.
Happiness lives in the house of hope.

Joshua Burden (10)
St James's CE Primary School, Stourbridge

War

War is a brutal black.
War smells of gruesome, red, revolting blood.
War tastes of sweaty hands in your mouth.
War is loud with tearing bangs crackling in the air.
You feel quivery and hurt with fear trembling in your feet.
War lives in the heart of death and cruelty.

Gareth Reynolds (10)
St James's CE Primary School, Stourbridge

Joy

Joy is golden grass swaying gently in the breeze,
It smells like freshly picked red roses.
It tastes like hot, melted chocolate.
Joy sounds like laughter and girls giggling.
It feels soft and warm like a fluffy towel.
Joy lives in the heart and soul of every person.

Bethany Gilburt (10)
St James's CE Primary School, Stourbridge

Anger

Anger is burgundy blood flowing through a body.
It smells like mouldy blue cheese.
Anger tastes like fiery red chilli peppers.
It sounds like a bomb exploding.
Anger feels like a rough potato sack.
It lives in an enormous pool of lava.

Sam Footman (9)
St James's CE Primary School, Stourbridge

Death

Death is flesh-running blood.
It smells like rotten cheese.
The taste of death is burning dynamite.
It sounds like a volcano erupting.
It feels like Flubber.
Death lives in a grave in a dirty old cemetery.

Adam Holmes (10)
St James's CE Primary School, Stourbridge

PEACE

Peace is a calm, wondrous white,
It smells like sweet fragrant flowers.
Peace tastes like cool, red, refreshing strawberries.
It sounds like green trees gently swaying in the
blowing wind, *whoosh!*
Peace feels soft and relaxing.
It lives in the centre of the hopeful Heaven above.

Richard Perks (10)
St James's CE Primary School, Stourbridge

HAPPINESS

Happiness is forget-me-not-blue.
It smells like light bluebells in the deep dawn air.
Happiness tastes all flowery and sweet.
It sounds like a lovely draught coming by.
Happiness feels all peaceful and happy.
It lives in a beautiful garden with just one other friend.

Danielle Parry (9)
St James's CE Primary School, Stourbridge

DEATH

Death is a deep gory red.
It smells like old smelly socks.
It tastes like salty sea water.
It sounds like a gun firing.
Death feels coarse and rough.
Death lives in a dark and gloomy cave.

Jonathan Wheeler (9)
St James's CE Primary School, Stourbridge

Disease

Disease is an evil jet-black.
It smells like rats crawling about in the sewers
And tastes like old mouldy apples
which have been rotting away.
It sounds like people screaming in pain
And feels like a sharp stabbing pain.
Disease lives in the heart of all evil.

Stephen Willows (10)
St James's CE Primary School, Stourbridge

Death

Death is like jet-black lightning striking you.
It smells like mouldy bread.
It tastes like rotten apples.
Death sounds like deep dark laughter.
It feels like a dish of spiders.
Death lives at the foot of the graveyard.

Jay Hatton (9)
St James's CE Primary School, Stourbridge

Joy

Joy is yellow,
It smells like roses.
Joy tastes like sweet candy,
It sounds like happy children playing.
Joy feels like a warm bed,
It lives in your heart.

Alex Rock (10)
St James's CE Primary School, Stourbridge

HATE

Hate is black,
It smells like cigarette smoke.
Hate tastes like hot wood burning.
It sounds like breaking glass crashing to the ground.
It feels rough like tree bark.
Hate lives inside a robber stealing a purse.

James McPhee (10)
St James's CE Primary School, Stourbridge

LOVE

Love is shining red,
It smells like ripe red strawberries growing on a bush.
Love tastes like a box of sweet chocolates.
It sounds like a pair of golden bells.
Love feels like silk,
Love is in the heart of children.

Thomas Hillman (9)
St James's CE Primary School, Stourbridge

LOVE

Love is brilliant red,
Love smells like fresh roses.
It tastes like sweet sugar,
It sounds like the gentle rippling of the calm sea.
Love feels gentle,
Love lives in the middle of your heart.

Kathryn Cope (9)
St James's CE Primary School, Stourbridge

Death

Death is a dark, deadly black,
It smells like stale smoke wafting through the fresh air.
Death tastes like deep red blood,
It sounds like gigantic black bombs dropping.
Death feels like shooting pains,
It lives in the dark underworld.

Charlotte Cope (9)
St James's CE Primary School, Stourbridge

Death

Death is solid black,
It smells like fear,
Death tastes like bitter revenge,
It's like a fierce volcano erupting,
It feels like a dagger shooting painfully through your hands.
Death lives inside a murderous mind.

Daniel Padmore (9)
St James's CE Primary School, Stourbridge

Love

Love is sparkling pink,
It smells like fresh poppies swaying in the sun.
Love tastes like mouth-watering white chocolate,
It sounds like rain gently trickling down.
Love is like a warm cushion cuddling up next to me,
Love is inside you forever.

Kate Shillingford (9)
St James's CE Primary School, Stourbridge

Happiness

Happiness is yellow,
It smells like fragrant golden roses.
It tastes like lovely hot pizza.
Happiness sounds like birds singing in the morning,
It feels like a warm blanket wrapped round you.
Happiness lives in everyone's heart.

Carl Whitfield (10)
St James's CE Primary School, Stourbridge

Old Age

Old age is grey,
It smells like cheese.
It tastes like rotten potatoes,
It sounds like a little church mouse.
Old age feels like bumpy paper,
Old age lives in night and day.

Sophie Smith (9)
St James's CE Primary School, Stourbridge

Old Age

Old age is the colour grey,
It smells like burnt toast.
Old age tastes like sweet honey in a pot,
It sounds like creaky floorboards,
It feels very dry.
Old age lives in a warm cosy cottage.

Bethan Skelding (9)
St James's CE Primary School, Stourbridge

Ugliness

Ugliness is mucky, murky brown,
It smells like a dead skunk.
Ugliness tastes like sour lemons,
It sounds like a dentist's drill digging in a tooth,
It feels like a rough and bumpy road.
Ugliness lives in the underworld.

Jordan Cooper (9)
St James's CE Primary School, Stourbridge

Laziness

Laziness is violet,
It smells like rubbish in an American alley.
Laziness tastes like flat lemonade,
It sounds like a dog panting like a steam train,
It makes you feel sleepy.
Laziness lives in the heart of the sofa.

Rachelle Smith (9)
St James's CE Primary School, Stourbridge

Joy

Joy is a pure, glorious green,
It smells like a delicate rose on a summer's day.
Joy tastes like icing on a cake.
Joy sounds like the song of a blackbird,
It feels soft and cuddly.
Joy lives in a spring garden.

Amy Walker (9)
St James's CE Primary School, Stourbridge

HATRED

Hatred is coloured dark navy.
Hatred smells of a dead body,
It tastes like a rotten super-sour lemon,
It sounds like a screaming spirit tortured by chains.
Hatred feels like a squishy porcupine,
It lives in the body of a person unable to love.

Matthew Owen (9)
St James's CE Primary School, Stourbridge

FUN

Fun is the colour of a shiny rainbow,
It smells like a delicious cake.
Fun tastes lovely and sweet,
It sounds like children playing in the park,
It feels smooth and fluffy.
Fun lives in the centre of our hearts.

Thomas Brown (9)
St James's CE Primary School, Stourbridge

WAR

War is multicoloured,
It smells like smoke.
War tastes like hot, burning fire,
It sounds like fireworks exploding in mid-air.
War feels like blood pouring through your hands.
War lives in the Middle East.

Julian Edwards (9)
St James's CE Primary School, Stourbridge

Death

Death is black,
It smells like a vast empty space.
Death tastes like air and dust,
It sounds like echoes from cries of the dead,
It feels sharp and shivery.
Death lives in Hell.

David Miles (9)
St James's CE Primary School, Stourbridge

Happiness

Happiness is baby blue,
It smells like big bulging bluebells.
Happiness tastes like succulent sweets,
It sounds like a sweet song,
It feels like a cushion, soft and squishy.
Happiness lives in a park full of children.

Jak Batchelor (10)
St James's CE Primary School, Stourbridge

Joy

Joy is a grape-green,
It smells like freshly picked flowers.
Joy tastes of sweet sugar,
It sounds like birds singing songs in the morning.
It feels like a breath of fresh air.
Joy lives in a field of flowers.

Robyn Pope (9)
St James's CE Primary School, Stourbridge

DISEASE

Disease is brown,
It smells like sweltering metal.
Disease tastes like rotten milk,
It sounds like a spraying aerosol,
It feels like cold clammy shivers.
Disease lives in rats.

Tomas Alma (9)
St James's CE Primary School, Stourbridge

PEACE

Peace is optimistic orange,
it smells like incense.
Peace tastes like chocolate,
It sounds like groovy music.
Peace feels like a soft feather,
It lives in a dove.

Samantha Rafferty (10)
St James's CE Primary School, Stourbridge

DEATH

Death is black as black,
it smells empty like a small sack.
Death tastes like stone,
it sounds like an echo,
it feels sharp and cold.
Death is all around us.

Jack Aaron (9)
St James's CE Primary School, Stourbridge

Hullabaloo

The football ground, people noisily crazy!
When the players make a goal they all shout extremely loudly.
The people are very noisy
When the footballers come out to play.
When it's their football day.
The players come out to have some fun,
The people are extremely, viciously noisy.
So when it is a football match, just cheer! Don't shout!

Vishal Rai (9)
Victoria Park Primary School

Party

It's the wave of the underground
The rave is like a pound
It is insane
The people in da neighbourhood
Think they are a pain
The presents are pumping
People are jumping.

James Newton (9)
Victoria Park Primary School

My Party Cinquain

Parties
Parties are great
You can have them all night
There is music you can dance to
Parties.

Abigail Townsend (10)
Victoria Park Primary School

CHRISTMAS

When snowflakes are dropping
And icicles are hanging,
The carollers are singing
And Christmas trees are standing.
It's Christmas.

When snowmen are standing
And the turkeys are roasting.
When children are slipping
And the Christmas lights are twinkling.
It's Christmas.

When tinsel is sparkling
And the crackers are cracking.
When everyone is laughing
And isn't it exciting?
It's Christmas.

When nothing is stirring
And mince pies are lying.
When reindeer are landing
And Santa is climbing.
It's Christmas.

Ramandeep Kaur Tiwana (10)
Victoria Park Primary School

PARTY

Parties are fun
Children are eating
Delicious food
Dads are drunk
Mums are dancing
By the flashing lights
People are talking

Some people are coming
To the party
The party is great
Music's on
Bossy children are making mess
Under the tables
The party is finished.

Mandip Shergill (9)
Victoria Park Primary School

The Stormy Night

The crashing rocks
The tumbling box
Hullabaloo! Hullabaloo!
The dark dull sky
As the birds fly by
Hullabaloo! Hullabaloo!
The wind is whistling
The squirrels are tickling
Hullabaloo! Hullabaloo!
The white sparkling snow
The river goes flow, flow, flow
The river is crashing and splashing
Hullabaloo! Hullabaloo!
The rain tapping on the doors
You never know it might be yours
Hullabaloo! Hullabaloo!
The lightning is striking
Hullabaloo! Hullabaloo!
The thunder is under
Hullabaloo!

Jordan Savell-Boss (9)
Victoria Park Primary School

My Bedroom

M y favourite thing is my bedroom
Y eah, I like my bedroom because it's great

F unctional it is
A gain it's really great
V arious things are under my bed
O ver the other side there's my desk
U nder my bed it's dark and creepy
R un, run
I t is dark
T he bed is very creaky
E veryone likes my bedroom, oh what a hullabaloo!

T he party is such a hullabaloo in my bedroom
H ide, hide, it's creepy under the bed again
I s that you in that cupboard
N ever, I'm not going to hide
G reat because I don't care said my friend
S o I'm not scared anymore, yeah!

Manpreet Kaur Malhi (9)
Victoria Park Primary School

Hullabaloo Cinquain

Chaos
Everywhere
There is hullabaloo
I hate it when there's noise about
Chaos.

Jordon Ellis (9)
Victoria Park Primary School

MAN U VS VILLA

At the footie shout, shout, shout
Drunk fans without no doubt

People from Peckham
Shouting for Beckham

Giggs legs it on the left
Shouting heads off because he dazzles the rest

Ball! Ball! he crosses the ball
Swearing, bad mouthing because the goalie had a great fall

The referee doesn't blow the whistle
So the Villa fans thought of killing the ref with a missile

Van Nistelrooy has scored
Fans cheer, 'More, more, more!'

Villa fans have shut their mouths
And they feel like an elf
Embarrassed hiding behind a shelf.

Simran Bhopal (10)
Victoria Park Primary School

ANIMALS OF THE WORLD

A ntelopes prance
N ewts dance
I nsects stalk
M ankind talk
A lsatians howl
L ions prowl
S nakes slither, hither and thither.

Laura Cann (10)
Victoria Park Primary School

HULLABALOO!

H orrible noises across the street
U seful noises like a beat
L oud noises, quiet noises
L ittle noises, soft noises
A car or a bus tooting its horn
B ig noises, little noises
A mbulances rushing - sirens blaring
L ots of people shouting and rushing
O r dogs and cats barking and screaming
O r is it me just dreaming?

Muhammad Abid (10)
Victoria Park Primary School

MY FAMILY

My family is very popular,
Yowling and howling in and out the house.

Father is shouting,
Auntie is screaming.

Mum is cooking,
I am playing.

Little kids are crying,
Your house is like this?
What a state!

Zulaikha Faatima (9)
Victoria Park Primary School

Happy The Dog

M iserable all the time
Y et I miss him

P ets are fun
E specially in different places
T he end of his life

D eath of a perfect pet
O verall I am sad
G rowing without my faithful dog.

Ineel Kler (9)
Victoria Park Primary School

The World

T he world is very round
H elp it to stay healthy
E veryone sees the sun, moon and Earth.

W ith people getting dead
O range and blue is the sky
R ound the world people go
L ord, Lord help us
D on't tell lies.

Saschelle Jonas (10)
Victoria Park Primary School

SHIPWRECK

A ship was sailing peacefully one night
When it hit the rocks and disappeared out of sight
Lightning flashed across the sky
The crew didn't know how the ship crashed or why
Anyway the crew didn't want to die
They wanted to climb out
But the captain was full of doubt
Thunder was rumbling across the sky
When they heard it they had quite a scare
Then the captain told them to set off the flare
But nobody saw it so they were stranded there
They climbed out of the ship with a rope
Then the captain saw a car through his telescope
So in they climbed and drove back home.

Ibrahim Abbass (10)
Victoria Park Primary School

SEASONS

When it is windy the leaves are rustling
Every day it is quiet
All day people stay indoors
The weather is turning in summer
Happy people are putting on their swimsuits
Every year it is hot
Rustling leaves and windy weather are something of the past.

Reneè Hussey (10)
Victoria Park Primary School

Hullabaloo

Noisy, nasty children
The kids from next door
They're in big trouble
Now their window is on the floor
Stinky, sticky eggs
Pouring out my hair
My mom's shouting with flashing eyes
Those kids are making up lies
Then my teacher's to the rescue
He grabs them by the ear
'You've copied all your homework!'
It's their turn for a smacked rear
My mom comes and shoos me away
Boy was that a day!

Charlotte Bromwich (9)
Victoria Park Primary School

Oh No! Great Big Party

It is Kelly's birthday today
We'd better get things ready
Before she comes from school
So I've made a plan
The things were all ready
When Kelly came from school
She saw all the things
That her sister, brothers, Mum and Dad
Worked hard to do.

Liridona Hasani
Victoria Park Primary School

THE WONDERFUL WORLD

T he world is rough
H ere you can see the sun
E arly in the daytime

W onderful
O ne world there is
R ound and soft
L ovely to see
D ay time, night-time.

Kerry Wilding (10)
Victoria Park Primary School

THE WORLD

T he world is great
H ere people live
E arthquakes shake the ground

W ith people getting scared
O ther animals getting worried
R ound the world people go
L earning about the environment
D reaming about it.

Sarah Carter (9)
Victoria Park Primary School

HULLABALOO

In the town centre it is hullabaloo!

Babies crying
Teenagers sighing
People shouting
Dogs barking
Homeless are lurking
There is noise coming from the clubs and pubs
Let's go home, I have got a headache
Cause the town centre is such a hullabaloo!

Shelby Crooks (9)
Victoria Park Primary School

THE CROWD

The park, the park is full of people
People are talking, people are walking
People in the crowd are having fun
Chatting together and having a run.

Sandeep Khera (10)
Victoria Park Primary School

Mundo Macho

Autores Españoles e Iberoamericanos

Terenci Moix

Mundo Macho

(Novela salvaje)

Edición a cargo de
Pedro Manuel Víllora

Prólogo de
Pere Gimferrer
de la Real Academia Española

PLANETA

Córcega, 273-279, 08008 Barcelona (España)

Ilustración de la sobrecubierta: *anterior*, Sabú en «La reina de Cobra», 1944 (foto © Universal Pictures, coloreada por el autor); *posterior*, foto © Colita

Primera edición: diciembre de 1998

Depósito Legal: B. 48.722-1998

ISBN 84-08-02849-9

Composición: Foto Informática, S. A.

Impresión y encuadernación: Printer Industria Gráfica, S. A.

Printed in Spain - Impreso en España

PRÓLOGO

—

TERENCI MOIX Y LA NOVELA DE LA CRUELDAD

Recién aparecida, Mundo Macho *enlaza, en la producción de Terenci Moix, antes con algunos aspectos de* Olas sobre una roca desierta *y, sobre todo, de* La torre de los vicios capitales, *que con* El día que murió Marilyn, *su novela de más reciente publicación.* La paradoja es sólo aparente. Por una parte, la gestación de* El día que murió Marilyn *es anterior a la de* Olas sobre una roca desierta *y aun a la de* La torre de los vicios capitales; *por otra, Moix es claramente un escritor*

* Atendiendo a un deseo personal del autor, he reproducido, a guisa de prólogo a la presente traducción castellana, la reseña que de la edición original catalana de este libro publiqué en *Destino,* en el número correspondiente al 1.º de mayo de 1971. Pensé al principio en reelaborarla; luego he caído en la cuenta de que, por una parte, alterar sustancialmente el planteamiento sería tanto como escribir otro artículo, no necesariamente mejor, y, por otra, el hecho de que con posterioridad a *Món mascle* hayan aparecido otras importantes novelas de Moix, si bien introduciría aquí nuevos elementos de referencia, no vendría, en fin de cuentas, a modificar nada de cuanto esencialmente digo sobre *Món mascle.* Quede, pues, el artículo tal como apareció, y yo con la esperanza —no sé si ilusoria— de que pueda ser de alguna utilidad.

bifurcado, bipolar, que alterna el relato propiamente realista con el de libre invención y fantasía (y aun puede fusionar uno y otro, como en Olas sobre una roca desierta*). Así, si la tan esperada* El sexe dels àngels *se anuncia como una obra de carácter realista, en* Mundo Macho *Moix da rienda suelta a la imaginación, tan parcamente representada en las letras catalanas en el momento en que* La torre de los vicios capitales *señaló la tumultuosa irrupción de nuestro autor en la escena pública. Sabemos que, tras* El día que murió Marilyn, *Moix —resuelto, por una parte, a ser un escritor profesional y profesionalizado y, por otra, a no arriesgar su patrimonio literario en publicaciones precipitadas— había dado preferencia a producciones de carácter más bien periodístico, a fin de obtener el respiro económico necesario para una elaboración cuidadosa de su obra novelesca (y, todo hay que decirlo, para una vida personal que ha procurado adquirir los visos de mito o leyenda doméstica que permite el país). Podía temerse que, perdido en trabajos marginales, y llevado, además, de su temperamento de caudaloso grafómano, Moix se dispersara como escritor. Los resultados —excelentes, a mi juicio— obtenidos en* Mundo Macho *bastan para disipar tales temores.*

Sin duda, Mundo Macho *puede sorprender —y, en algunos sectores, irritar— tanto como las otras obras del autor. Tiene más a su favor inicialmente: en pocos años de intenso trabajo, Moix ha aprendido considerablemente acerca de su oficio, y puede decirse que la estructura novelesca de* Mundo Macho *es la más madura y equilibrada de cuantas hasta hoy nos ha ofrecido. Ahora bien: Moix, al mismo tiempo, no ha vacilado —aquí, como en las ocasiones anteriores— en jugar fuerte y arriesgar el todo por el todo, hasta el punto de que* Mundo Macho *debe considerarse una auténtica rareza, no sólo en la historia de la novela catalana, sino pura y simplemente en la actual novela europea. Se tiene de Moix —y ello es hasta cierto punto exacto— la imagen de un escritor «literario», de un escritor de segundo grado, es decir, de un escritor cuya materia es antes cultural que vital; del prototipo, en suma, de escritor refinado, elaborado y esnob. Si ello fuera la única verdad, el éxito de público de Moix sería inexplicable. Se olvida con demasiada frecuencia otra faceta, decisiva ésta: si Moix utiliza los datos culturales, lo hace casi con la directa espontaneidad de un* naïf *—y precisamente por ello puede utilizarlos impunemente—. Moix es capaz de la mayor elaboración, pero su principal arma es la sinceridad.* Mundo Macho *hubiera sido un fracaso en manos de otro escritor; se hubiera convertido en una exhibición de escenas de sadismo verbenero sobre el exotismo de un decorado de bazar. Ciertamente se me dirá que, a determinado nivel,* Mundo Macho *no es, en fin de cuentas, otra cosa. Pero la extraordinaria convicción de Moix hace posible que de ello nazca la poesía, un poco al modo de la que emana de las escenas de la selva virgen pintadas por el aduanero Rousseau. Existe, con todo, una diferencia capital: Moix no es, en último término, un* naïf*; sabe perfectamente con qué material está trabajando y, lo que es más, utiliza a sabiendas lo que de barato —empleo este término para eludir los de* camp *o* kitsch*— pueda haber en este material; convierte, así, las limitaciones de dicho material en un dato estético más.*

A primera vista, el argumento de Mundo Macho *es notoriamente un pretexto. Un ídolo de la canción es arrebatado a un reino imaginario en sus rituales. La técnica empleada —que, de modo muy discreto, introduce aquí y allá una posibilidad de dis-*

tanciamiento reduciendo los actos a proyecciones sobre una pantalla cinematográfica— sugiere que el relato puede ser simplemente una metáfora: el mimetismo decorativo del reino del «Mundo Macho» puede hallar en la vida real —como más de una vez insinúa el propio narrador— una correspondencia en el fervor histérico de los fans *del cantante. Pero esta dimensión —como lo que, muy ocasionalmente, pueda haber de apólogo político: así en la aparición de la cruz gamada— es, a todas luces, lo que menos puede importarle a Moix, y diríase que cumple en su novela la misma función de encubrimiento que en la de Sade desempeña el aparente propósito moralizador. No he nombrado a Sade en vano:* Mundo Macho *es ante todo y por encima de todo la descripción de un universo regido por la crueldad, de una sociedad utópica feroz —a modo de utopía negativa— como las descritas por Sade en* Aline et Valcour *o la* Histoire de Juliette. *Al igual que en Sade, existe un cierto margen de ambigüedad, y también, verosímilmente, un cierto margen de cautela o autocensura, pero las intenciones del autor no pueden ser más claras. Por lo demás, la similitud en el funcionamiento de la imaginación, e incluso frecuentemente en el vocabulario y los procedimientos, no puede resultar más sorprendente. Existe, sin embargo —y aquí se hace visible la personalidad peculiar de Moix—, una importante diferencia: Sade es, ante todo, un moralista (aunque sea un moralista «à l'envers») y en la elegante sequedad de su prosa jansenista no hay apenas lugar —si se exceptúa algún pasaje italiano de la* Historie de Juliette— *para digresiones decorativas; en Moix, en cambio, el propósito decorativo es central, y los mismos elementos de erotismo o crueldad serán subrayados ante todo como parte de un decorado. Lo cual diferencia también la intención central de los autores: Sade nos propone una ascesis negativa encaminada a erigir la contrafigura de la moral aceptada, en tanto que Moix, si utiliza elementos sádicos, los subordina a una finalidad estética y no a una subversión moral.*

Mundo Macho *es, así, una gigantesca cabalgata decorativa que utiliza profusamente el* collage *de estilos artísticos, el* pastiche *de lenguajes sagrados de religiones primitivas, el technicolor de las películas de romanos rodadas en Hollywood o Cinecittà, toda la imaginería, en fin, que había poblado los sueños de los protagonistas de* El día que murió Marilyn *u* Olas sobre una roca desierta. *La narrativa de imaginación de Moix no desmiente, por tanto, su narrativa realista; son, simplemente, el haz y el envés de un mismo universo, la cara visible y la oculta, o, si se prefiere, la luminosa y la sombría. Probablemente,* Mundo Macho *esté llamado a suscitar opiniones contrapuestas; su coherencia con la anterior obra del autor resulta tan patente como su singularidad. La audacia de Moix, una vez más, no ha sido en vano. La vitalidad de una literatura puede medirse, en cierto sentido, por su capacidad de acoger obras susceptibles de suscitar escándalo o polémica. En esta línea —que fue la de Moix desde sus comienzos—,* Mundo Macho *dará nuevamente fe de vida del sector más inquieto de la novela hispana.*

PERE GIMFERRER
de la Real Academia Española

NOTA DEL AUTOR

—

Esta edición de *Mundo Macho*, que considero definitiva, guarda muy notables diferencias con la que apareció en su día. Si por un lado la nueva situación española me ha permitido incluir elementos que la censura franquista obligó a eliminar, por otro lado he tendido a un importante proceso de sintetización, eliminando fragmentos que, vistos con la debida perspectiva, sobrecargaban la estructura narrativa.

Un último detalle, importantísimo a nivel estilístico: la versión castellana apareció en una mediocre traducción que he revisado repetidas veces, hasta el aburrimiento. La edición que el lector tiene en las manos es el resultado de muchas horas intentando que la traducción inicial, ajena a mí, se parezca en algo al castellano que escribo actualmente, o al castellano *tout court*. A pesar de las innumerables correcciones, todavía conviene que ruegue al lector la lectura de este *Mundo Macho* como un libro traducido de otro idioma, lo cual no lo invalida, por supuesto, pero sí explica diferencias de estilo con mis más recientes libros, escritos directamente en castellano.

TERENCI MOIX

A Joaquim Molas,
una novela que no es lo que parece,
ni lo que no puede parecer

Non temere nuotare contro il torrente; è d'un'ànima sordida pensare comme il volgo perchè il volgo è in maggioranza.

GIORDANO BRUNO

Desde tiempo inmemorial, el hombre ha encontrado placer derramando la sangre de sus hermanos, y para contentarse ha disfrazado su pasión criminal bajo la máscara de la justicia o la religión. Pero su finalidad siempre fue el insólito placer que le produce matar.

DE SADE, *Juliette o las prosperidades del vicio*

IGNORO SI DEBERÍA CONTAR cómo llegué o, por el contrario, cómo conseguí escapar. Era el Mundo Macho. Y esta inquietud pavorosa, que el viento del desierto se lleva consigo, me hace regresar, me devuelve la idea, rotunda, inconfundible, de que sigo prisionero. De hecho, durante los tres meses que permanecí encerrado en la clínica, con tantos paseos entre parques y estanques; durante este período de letargo absoluto, he tenido el tiempo suficiente para descubrir que lo más importante de esta historia, de esta obsesión, no reside tanto en la forma en que fui atrapado o me ayudaron a huir, como en la etapa intermedia, alucinante, durante la cual aquel universo fue real, aquella pesadilla.

Era el Mundo Macho. Ditjma Nau. Ditjma Nau.

Pero, contra la opinión de los médicos, a pesar de las amenazas de mi representante y las exigencias de la casa discográfica, he regresado a Egipto y, al adentrarme hacia Minia, bordeando siempre el Padre Nilo, he podido comprobar que la obsesión no ha desaparecido. La obsesión no se cura ni siquiera con la placidez de todos los bosques de Suiza, que rodean a esas clínicas, cuidadas como un juguete de niño rico y emplazadas a orillas de los lagos más adecuados. Hoy, de nuevo en Egipto, mientras busco a los dos misteriosos raptores que podrían devolverme a aquel mundo, la obsesión se materializa en el hundimiento total de mis nervios y en el alejamiento de cualquier forma de razón. La fuerza de la pesadilla rompe mi resistencia de antaño, y las callejas del suburbio se llenan de sombras que van a hacerse palpables de un momento a otro, mientras la pobre realidad de esta ciudad de provincias irá transformándose en las intrincadas selvas del Mundo Macho, en la compacta cadena de rocas que se pierden entre las nubes, y de la cual, si Batsá no mentía, yo he sido el único que logró salir. Del mismo modo que soy el único en poderlo contar ahora, mientras busco la entrada de aquel país que seguramente no he de volver a hallar. El único en contarlo, en haberlo visto; en saber, no sin espanto, que el Mundo Macho existe. Y, finalmente, el único que jamás será creído.

Este pobre loco. Yo.

QUISIERA ADVERTIR AL MUNDO; quisiera revelar el peligro que amenaza a los jóvenes más fuertes y bellos. Imbuido de esta obligación, deambulo por los laberintos de la ciudad donde fui raptado, y sólo encuentro las miradas desconfiadas de los adolescentes cuya complicidad pretendo ganar. ¡A saber qué pensarán! La razón de mi estancia en una ciudad que, turísticamente, sólo es un puente de enlace entre lo que consideramos la civilización y las olvidadas ruinas de Tell-el-Amarna, se ha convertido en un enigma público: una curiosidad motivo de conversación en los cafés. Sé que soy la amenaza de lo inexplicable (un policía vino anoche al hotel para pedir información sobre el joven extranjero que, desde hace dos meses, se pasea por la noche de Minia y se eterniza en los callejones siempre enlodados por el agua de los riegos públicos y la arena que el viento arrastra del desierto; el joven que, sin escupir este polvo tan incómodo para cualquier europeo, deambula de mostrador en mostrador, se detiene, tembloroso, vacila y se decide, finalmente, a abordar a los nativos para formularles las preguntas más peregrinas).

¡Siempre la misma duda! Los adolescentes, que me miran con expresión equívoca, apoyados en los porches de las calles principales, o bien fumando su narguila en la plaza, ¿cómo reaccionarían, por quién me tomarían si me decidiera a descubrirles que las rocas de la cordillera ignorada, en cuyas simas gobierna Epsamón, les están aguardando implacables? ¿Me creerían si les pronosticara que esta misma noche pueden desaparecer para siempre, engullidos por las montañas que marcan la frontera entre el desierto de los herejes y las selvas del Mundo Macho? ¿No se burlarían de mí si les gritase que corren el riesgo de ser arrastrados a los confines del Imperio, allí donde persona alguna podrá jamás localizarles? Sin duda me arriesgaría a más de una burla, y estos ojos que ahora se limitan a mirarme con picardía y acaso a suponer que mi interés es el de un comprador de cuerpos, me acusarían de loco y, en el remoto supuesto de un mínimo de piedad, insinuarían que, cuando uno es incapaz de aguantar una borrachera, es mejor no beber. Ni tampoco drogarse, aunque mi obsesión, mi pesadilla, nada tengan que ver con el alcohol ni la droga, y sin embargo no dejen de ser alcohol y droga a la vez.

¿Por qué extraña fatalidad tuve que ser el único en conocer el Mundo Macho, el único en padecerlo y en lograr el regreso? Uno cualquiera de los días, años o siglos que pasé en el palacio real de Lur, Astor me dijo que yo era hermoso, incluso mucho; pero no tanto como para creerme imprescindible en las ceremonias sagradas de la Perpetuidad de la Raza que se celebran cada primavera, cuando yo, Nebjeperura Nofretere, el que es Co-Divino, regreso victorioso de las tierras de la Nada y hago revivir sobre el Mundo Macho las fuentes genuinas de la vida. No, no sé de razón alguna que me convierta en imprescindible. Rellos, el de los ojos verdes como el agua del río subterráneo que atraviesa el Mundo Macho; Gitón, de cuerpo esbelto como las palmeras de los Jardines de Homo Demeter; y el mismo Avitachí, cuyo pecho adolescente traspasarían las flechas en la primera ejecución que presidí como exige la ley de Cobra, tenían muchos más atributos físicos que yo, no sólo indigno de contribuir a la procreación de titanes que desea el Mundo Macho, sino, incluso, de ocupar el altísimo lugar que Epsamón me reserva en su palacio, a la cabeza de sus ejércitos aniquiladores, en la admiración y obediencia de sus súbditos.

¿Por qué yo?

Intuyo que empiezo a razonar según la religión del

Mundo Macho, y que la idea de raza y perfección se va apoderando de mí, como otra obsesión. En mi deambular por las callejas donde hace tiempo empezó mi aventura, los rostros de los adolescentes a quienes hace sólo una semana me obstinaba en advertir del gran peligro, se van convirtiendo en elementos del machismo; de sangre apropiada o inadecuada a la perfección de la raza. Dejan de ser individuos amenazados a quienes urge salvar, y se convierten en rostros y cuerpos útiles a las intenciones de Epsamón, o bien inútiles para lo que su Iglesia quiere perpetuar. Y la idea de la raza bella, poderosa y superior, genuina invención del Mundo Macho, se apodera de mí con una fuerza que ya me siento incapaz de rechazar; gran espanto, pero, también, locura no exenta de una fascinación que me corroe el alma...

ANOCHE, el viento del desierto soplaba furiosamente contra las montañas de la orilla izquierda del Nilo; bramaba con un ímpetu idéntico al de aquella Navidad del pasado año o del anterior (ni siquiera eso puedo precisar), después que Charlie Walsh, Dennis Branden y Morgan Willard me dejasen solo en la Corniche, enfrentado al misterio del río bajo la noche y a tantos muertos antiguos entrevistos en las profundidades de las necrópolis faraónicas. Anoche, el silbo del desierto transportaba una arena parecida; las ratas corrían entre la rocalla próxima al río; la luna empalidecía las montañas. El mismo hedor del año pasado; los mismos aguazales eternos en las polvorientas calles; idénticos rostros miserables, siempre extenuados, siempre en busca de la propina de los escasos turistas.

Anoche, sí, decidí visitar a Spiros Markopoulos, crucé la calle que separa el antiguo convento francés y el café Al-Hashik, sin dejar de observar un solo instante a los grupos de adolescentes minieses que, por ser la flor de su raza, también son víctimas potenciales de la cacería del Mundo Macho.

Markopoulos se extrañó de que, llevando yo un mes y medio en Minia, no me hubiese decidido hasta entonces a corresponder a la visita que él nos había ofrecido tan gentilmente, la otra vez.

—*Any time you come back, do get here for some opium...*

Pero le bastaron cuatro o cinco frases mías, por supuesto inconexas, para comprender que estaba pasando por una grave depresión; y tal vez esto justificase con creces, no ya la falta de cortesía implícita en el olvido de su invitación, sino incluso una estancia tan larga como inexplicable en la ciudad. Así pues, sus ojos indicaron que sospechaba, y acto seguido me rogaron que empezase a aclararle misterios.

Con todo, me parece más justo introducir el enigma particular de Spiros Markopoulos; es decir, por qué un personaje tan valioso, erudito singular, experto en los problemas menos divulgados de la era amárnica, hombre destinado a brillar por sus virtudes en una sociedad más refinada, acepta renunciar al puesto que por derecho le corresponde y se resigna a vivir, desde hacía más de treinta años, en una ciudad que, aparentemente, sólo puede ofrecer un interés mediocre, y aun reservado a quienes se dedican a la poco agradecida tarea del pequeño comercio. Y es que Minia, para decirlo de una vez, es un simple centro comercial, situado a 157 millas de El Cairo y, para un europeo, cita anónima en medio de esta distancia; sólo que, dentro del *nomen* del que es capital, puede representar una especie de avanzadilla de cierto grado de civilización.

Aquí dejaron los europeos la huella de un vano intento por reproducir la añorada comodidad del bulevar Saint-Germain o del barrio de Grosvenor. El efecto no puede ser más deprimente: en plena tierra de los faraones, rodeados por el profundo misterio de un paisaje muy abrupto, que el tiempo aceptó respetar, surge el anacronismo brutal de las fachadas europeas orientadas hacia el Nilo; sobresale una cabalgata de motivos claramente modernistas: ninfas, hadas, pastorcillas románticas, pétreas florestas de jardinería inglesa, tirabuzones de *madama* parisina, desgastándose bajo el polvo y la suciedad. Momias de nuestro siglo, de nuestra cultura inmediata, depositadas hace sólo cincuenta años en un país de momias seculares.

El desierto otorga a Egipto la inmensa fascinación de una tumba cerrada; el desierto se convierte en el más cautivador de cuantos fenómenos pudiera presentir un alma obsesa. Sus ruinas lo son en una dimensión sobrenatural; sólo sus vientos pueden sugerir una idea exacta de la Furia divina. Dulce conmiseración de lo eterno, ampárame y vela por mí ahora, mañana y siempre. Mundo Macho, Mundo Macho: ¿quiénes serán tus nuevas víctimas?

Pero, a pesar del comercio, Minia es una ciudad llena de mediocridad, donde la triste certeza de la vida provinciana se muestra sin tapujos; no habría ofrecido ningún atractivo a mis compañeros yanquis de no constituir el punto de enlace más directo para una visita a la necrópolis de Beni-Hassan y a las ruinas de la ciudad de Akenatón. Y son precisamente estos lugares muertos los que fuerzan a Markopoulos a consumir sus años bajo el viento cálido, en medio de la suciedad y el hedor, entre las sombras de los bulevares desteñidos que se alejan del centro en busca de aquel pavoroso arrabal donde habitan, amontonados y oscuros como sus cabañas de adobe, los olvidados por la vida.

Esta vez, el aspecto del profesor parecía aún más ruinoso que la noche de nuestra primera visita. Enterrado bajo una montaña de papeles que tratan del asunto de Akenatón y Tell-el-Amarna, esperando desde hace tanto tiempo que alguien se decida a costear nuevas excavaciones en las ruinas de la ciuda maldita, Markopoulos recobra de vez en cuando un gramo de euforia, que dista mucho de ser agradable, y se consagra al opio y al vino en una medida que yo sólo sabría considerar excesiva. Si las arrugas de su frente, abundantes y prematuras, provienen de estas últimas costumbres, o bien de la dificultad para concentrarse en sus investigaciones, es algo que no podría precisar sin arriesgarme a una conclusión demasiado fácil, obvia y poco documentada. Sólo puedo decir que, en esta ciudad donde los fantasmas de la colonización europea se mezclan con la fantasmagoría latente de la ciudad de Atón, el fantasma macilento que es el profesor representaba el único oyente capaz de corresponderse con mi obsesión, también llena de fantasmas que serpentean, agresivos, en alguna parte del cosmos.

De este modo, sentados en la lóbrega habitación que le sirve de estudio; el profesor, al otro lado del escritorio; yo, con la silla apoyada en la ventana abierta a la abigarrada confusión de la noche; deleitándonos los dos con la incomparable suavidad del opio; de este modo, digo, empecé mi narración...

COMO SEÑALABA USTED hace un momento, profesor, salimos de su casa muy borrachos. Especialmente Charlie que, en realidad, no se tenía en pie. Recuerdo una noche muy agradable, por lo fresca, de lo cual se quejó usted alegando que sin duda sería portadora de un frío mucho más intenso. Y Dennis, con aquella tendencia suya, tan genuina y encantadora —en definitiva: tan adolescente—, a reírse sin tregua de su propia e inagotable capacidad de decir tonterías, comentó que, al fin y al cabo, el frío de Egipto sería equivalente a la canícula de Roma durante el mes de agosto. La mezcla de conversaciones intrascendentes y el griterío que organizamos los cuatro por las calles solitarias no anunciaba, siquiera remotamente, el horrible destino que me aguardaba agazapado bajo el bochorno del *khamsin*, ese viento que es viejo como la soledad de una noche a orillas del Nilo y, como ella, amenazador. También sería injusto insinuar que la noche no tenía magia, no confesar que tenía una gran fascinación. Pero ninguna de estas constataciones, que sin duda usted aguarda a modo de elogio por su decisión de confinarse aquí para toda la vida (y no seré yo quien se lo eche en cara, como dice que acostumbran a hacer sus parientes de Éfeso); ningún encomio que pudiera usted dedicar a las noches de diciembre, que yo he maldecido tantas veces en mi prisión; nada, nada conseguiría endulzar el recuerdo de mis sufrimientos futuros, los indescriptibles tormentos que tuve que soportar antes de sucumbir a los dictados del Mundo Macho.

Ese opio es una tentación, profesor. Y la acepto, diantre, la acepto; no dudo un momento en hacerlo. También era tentador aquella noche, y si entonces no dudé en aceptarla, con menos motivo lo haría hoy, que recuerdo cómo todo empezó a partir del opio; y sé que si lo fumo, si voy aspirando con fuerza, si vuelvo a salir de esta casa tambaleándome como Charles aquella noche, si paseo por la Corniche, indefenso como una doncella, tal vez consiga que los dos brutos me sorprendan bajo cualquier porche y me rapten de nuevo; tal vez lo consiga, profesor, tal vez...

Sí: sé perfectamente por qué el Mundo Macho me eligió a mí, que no soy tan hermoso como debiera, ni tan perfecto como es de desear. Y esta razón, esta evidencia, es más cruel que toda la crueldad que el Mundo Macho ha convertido en ley, religión e historia a la vez.

¿Los yanquis? Cierto, cierto: los tres eran muy simpáticos y, cosa rara dado su antecedente nacional, tenían una mentalidad más filosófica que científica, más propia del romántico instruido que del pragmático al uso, inspirado por la trivialización del espíritu y sus formas. Sí, sí: los tres, aunque tal vez Charlie menos que los otros; y, sin embargo, un idealista byroniano cuando encontraba una botella de whisky; imagínele, pues, sobrecargado por aquel opio, que representó para nosotros una especie de necesidad turística vital que no habíamos podido satisfacer en Luxor. Los dioses le bendigan por habérnosla satisfecho. Sí; que Alá, o Atón, o Rediós le bendigan, profesor.

Pero comprendo su impaciencia. Le hablo de una amenaza, incluso insinúo una tragedia, y seguidamente no explico los hechos y me embarullo en simplezas alejadas de cualquier cosa que pueda merecer su interés. Y, sin embargo, después de haber contado tantas veces mi peripecia (tantas, pero jamás creídas), debería tener cierta práctica y no perderme en un rosario de explicaciones inocuas, como si mi salud estuviese realmente afectada y los médicos no se equivocasen cuando intentaban convencer a mi representante de que necesitaba reposo absoluto; que ni pensar en actuaciones públicas, ni plantearme la posibilidad de volver a Egipto, cuna de lo que ellos llaman mi paranoia agresiva. Como si ellos hubiesen tenido razón, sí, con sus órdenes tajantes, la decisión inapelable, el tono severo que se iba perdiendo a lo lejos porque yo echaba a correr, huía de la clínica con la cartera repleta de dinero que Larry dejó sobre la cama (Larry es mi representante; si pudiera me mantendría encerrado a piedra y lodo, y sólo me permitiría salir de la jaula para grabar discos y actuar ante mil histéricas y firmar cheques...).

Pero le robé la cartera, sí, mientras él se entretenía en la habitación vecina, hablando con los médicos. Nada me importaba, sólo pensaba en volver a Minia. Era como una pesadilla, un incesante martillear; incluso en el vuelo Ginebra-Atenas me desperté chillando: «¡Mundo Macho! ¡Mundo Macho!» Y nadie me entendía, y bajo el avión sólo veía muchas nubes, formas macizas, como un vómito muy blanco, que permitían entrever, a través de algunos claros, el azul del mar, salpicado de ondas diminutas.

LOS LABERINTOS DE MINIA aquella noche de diciembre: ¡ah, qué sensación de dulce soledad!, ¡qué manifestación tan estética del vacío, del hundimiento total en algo inalcanzable, difícil de explicar, pero que vas comprendiendo paso a paso, mientras te dejas deslizar en una caída suprema, cuyo final podría ser la indiferencia absoluta hacia todo cuanto pudiese ocurrir, cuanto pudiese implicar el futuro inmediato...!

Con los dos compañeros que me quedaban despiertos —pues a Charlie, dormido de puro borracho, lo arrastrábamos entre los demás—, seguí remontando a pie hasta la Corniche. Hablábamos de aspectos de nuestra vida, pero yo reservaba mi incógnito, quería olvidar esa mi vulnerable situación de pequeño ídolo público de un país que, para ellos, sólo significaba la torre Eiffel, el Louvre y, tal vez, Notre-Dame. Del mismo modo que, para mí, su América de los grandes mitos se reducía a cuatro cosas mal aprendidas en el cine y a un edén de *night clubs* y cadenas de TV, donde me hubiese interesado expansionar mi fama europea a base de actuaciones fabulosamente pagadas. Es decir: intercambio de tópicos para ir alimentando el tópico, tan explotado, de las amistades de quince días que mueren al finalizar el viaje.

No les confesaría nada. En la muerte de Minia, en el núcleo mismo del gran sueño del opio, bajo los artesonados victorianos cubiertos de polvo, entre las modestas mezquitas que íbamos dejando atrás a medida que nos acercábamos a la Corniche, el secreto sobre mi oficio y mi situación en el mundo me otorgaba una deliciosa sensación de inmunidad. Sólo de vez en cuando surgía el recuerdo de Larry, de su vigilancia draconiana: aquel empeño en aprovechar al máximo el atractivo público de mi voz, el impacto de una carrera que, en el fondo, debo por completo a su administración, incluso a su tiranía.

Pero me gustaba olvidarme de mi esclavitud a un micrófono y reír con Dennis y Morgan sobre el azar que nos reunió, siete días antes, en el comedor del Winter Palace, únicos extranjeros en un lugar quc, como Luxor, tiene garantizado un turismo selecto durante la época dorada del invierno, plácida y dulce. Mientras, insisto, las amenazas de ataques judíos no sigan ahuyentando a los clientes.

Así pues, paseábamos sin rumbo fijo, y en un momento del paseo oímos el ruido de unos pasos que iban haciéndose progresivamente más rotundos y parecían caer sobre los nuestros. Dennis se volvió y dijo que dos hombres completamente vestidos de negro, como surgidos de la noche y confundidos en ella, nos seguían con intenciones poco claras. Morgan y yo acogimos el temor de nuestro amigo bromeando a costa de una realidad que ya habíamos comprobado en Luxor: cuando en la soledad de una noche de invierno, a orillas del Nilo, una pareja de hombres se decide a seguirte, sólo cabe esperar una amenaza a tu pobre virginidad.

El opio es pérfido, profesor: lo fue aquella noche, y vuelve a serlo ahora. Por supuesto, puedo dejar de fumarlo, pero el que llevo tomado me empuja hacia el viaje, y el bacilón me devuelve la sensación de navegar sobre una nube, de perder el miedo a aburrirle con esta historia que me llena de horror y a la vez me excita como un pene sometido a flagelación. Mire: es tal el bochorno, que me desnudo ante usted; y lo hago sin pudor, porque la historia que me dispongo a contarle se viste con pocos velos: es una historia de angustia, de crueldad, de macabra placidez y, sobre todo, de gente desnuda. Lo fue desde que Morgan comparó los mantos negros de nuestros seguidores con los tuaregs que, de niños, vimos en alguna película en tecnicolor; lo fue desde que los dos hombres se escondieron bajo algún porche, bajo alguna cenefa bordada de hadas y flores victorianas...

Dejó de inquietarnos lo que minutos antes temíamos: ese posible ataque a nuestra improbable virginidad. Era absurdo lanzarse a reflexiones miedosas a causa de dos pobres transeúntes que tal vez regresaban de jugar a los naipes con los amigos; que acaso buscasen putas, y pare usted de contar. No, amigo mío: nada había en aquella presencia, en aquella persecución, que nos empujara a presuponer la insólita tragedia que nos aguardaba, oculta bajo el misterio de la noche, bajo la impensable profundidad de los absurdos. Nada nos anunciaba el drama, y, sin embargo, el drama estaba a punto.

SOY EL HIJO DEL SOL, profesor; soy Nebjeperura, y mi inmortalidad está asegurada porque mi muerte anual, cuando dejo solo a Epura Epsamón durante el invierno del Mundo Macho, se convierte en suprema resurrección cada primavera, cuando regreso con los rayos de la vida, que he arrebatado a Aquel que Manda en el Tiempo, enemigo mortal de Cobra Macho, la fuerza primigenia del Mal que creó el Universo y engendró a Epsamón en el gran vientre del Sol, del mismo modo que Epsamón me engendró en la fuerza de su padre para que yo fuese el Co-Divino, desde el principio de todas las historias. Yo soy la vida, igual que Epura Epsamón es el poder de la vida: el poder único, que existe más allá de cualquier medida. Todos los dioses del Mundo Macho exigen el culto a la fuerza, a la capacidad de infligir sufrimientos y de padecerlos, como demostraciones excelsas de las cualidades superiores de la raza. Pero yo soy la belleza y la vida, soy el espíritu, la cultura; me representan Citereo o alígero, y los jovencitos de Lur procrean en mi nombre, en las cuevas donde habita la Bestia Llamada Hembra, cuando llega la Fiesta de la Fertilidad. Yo soy divino, profesor, y ni siquiera este opio, ni siquiera las amenazas de Larry y los médicos suizos, conseguirán que lo olvide. Mi jerarquía es categórica y está intacta, porque es ley de Cobra.

Pero en aquella noche de Minia, yo no presentía que estas jerarquías pudiesen existir en ningún lugar del universo; tal vez porque ni siquiera en el sueño más ebrio imaginé la existencia de una realidad como la del Mundo Macho, cuyos enviados —ahora lo sé— se ocultan por todas las esquinas de nuestra civilización, a la espera de un momento de debilidad que les permita alcanzar el poder universal por el camino de la fuerza del guerrero, o, si es más conveniente, con la astucia de la serpiente. Aquella noche de Minia me hallaba fascinado por la dulce, perfecta paz del río, por la magia de las necrópolis que se adivinan en la ribera oriental, más allá de las palmeras que el viento mece con una dulzura excepcional.

Dennis y Morgan forjaban proyectos para algunas noches de juerga exótica, no bien llegásemos a El Cairo. Yo no les escuchaba. La delicuescencia del escenario propiciaba una pereza a pensar, a rechazar, aceptar o, simplemente, discutir cualquier proposición de futuro. Quedaba muy lejos la preocupación de los primeros días, el miedo a la rabieta de Larry, obligado a anular una serie de contratos que le habrían reportado muchos beneficios, y a mí, beneficios aparte, más agotamiento del que ya me dominaba cuando me escapé. El dominio de Larry, su voluntad de hacerme vestir, sonreír, fotografiarme e incluso andar como él quería, eran recuerdos que se iban perdiendo en aquella placidez escogida. Y, finalmente, fue esta placidez la que me venció.

Mi indiferencia estaba dirigida por una urgencia de soledad y un imperioso deseo de conocer por mí mismo aquella nueva realidad; un deseo que rechazaba la compañía y, sobre todo, las conversaciones de los demás. Entre el Nilo y yo, sólo se tendía un paseo con jardincillos maltratados por el tiempo y la suciedad aportada por el choque de muchos vientos; entre aquel tiempo y mi necesidad de aproximarme a él, sólo se alzaba la voz incoherente de mis compañeros de opio, que me explicaban lo fascinante que fue vivir en Jeddah los primeros meses, cuando llegaron allí para enseñar inglés a los soldados árabes. Y, de repente, ya estaban explicando lo aburrido que resultaba ahora, después de haber vivido allí tanto tiempo. Para ellos, aquellas vacaciones en Egipto, y la posibilidad misma de contarme su vida castrense, constituían una especie de liberación.

Su liberación iba aproximándose a la mía: al maravilloso resultado de no tener que encontrarme en el escenario, arrojando sobre mis admiradores unos rayos de divinidad que ellos mismos, influidos por la sabia publicidad de Larry, habían aprendido a otorgarme. En mi carrera, yo era el hijo de un sol creado por los engañosos reflectores que deslumbraban a los hijos del siglo. Y lo sabía. Y aunque no me desagradaba del todo, sí me sentía su víctima y, al mismo tiempo, sabía que me convertía en verdugo.

Cuando, cediendo por fin a mi deseo, Dennis y Morgan se llevaron a Charlie y me dejaron a solas, enfrentado a la oscuridad del Nilo, sentí como si la angustia que me acomete en el escenario, llegado el momento de los saludos, cuando estalla el alud casi metálico de aplausos, volviese a dominarme con una fuerza que la soledad no conseguía vencer. En aquella muerte de los siglos, junto al Padre Nilo, rememoré el implacable huracán de los ruidos que han acompañado mi carrera y también mi vida por todas las ciudades que he visitado, por todas las calles en las que he vivido. El estrépito de un aplauso incesante se mezclaba con las escandalosas bocinas, siempre descompasadas, que obsesionaban mi mente. Era la sinfonía de mi siglo; y si aquella noche no lograba olvidarla, ya era inútil esperar que pudiera conseguirlo nunca.

En el corazón de la noche crujían de nuevo unos pasos que no oí hasta tenerlos muy cerca y a mi alrededor. Me disponía a recriminar a mis amigos por no respetar mi deseo de soledad, pero, al volverme, me encontré con los dos hombres de antes: mantos negros hasta los pies, fez y turbante que les cubrían boca y frente, de forma que, entre tanta negrura, sólo aparecía la llamarada de los ojos, intensa y amenazadora. Vistos tan de cerca, ya no podía confundirlos con una sombra: eran estatuas cinceladas en una extraña piedra negra que, desde luego, no se parecía al mármol.

Reencontrando en esta imagen cualquier momento de peligro de alguna película-ensueño de mi infancia, retrocedí sin saber qué hacer, sin decidirme entre la necesidad de proferir un grito de espanto, o bien de echar a correr. Ellos permanecían inmóviles, y entonces descubrí que tenían una mano oculta bajo el manto: de hecho, empuñaban una cimitarra de puño de oro y con enormes rubíes incrustados. Después apareció una hoja enorme, brillante como un relámpago. Y la luna le añadió destellos de brutalidad.

A partir de esta visión, fija en mis pupilas como una luz hipnótica, sólo recuerdo un golpe muy fuerte en la cabeza, un sueño sin fin, y un turbio remolino, en cuyo desorden latían los consejos de Larry, las bocinas estridentes de mis ciudades, y un ejército de jinetes, vestidos de negro, cubiertos hasta los ojos, cabalgando por un desierto de arena blanquísima, casi nieve, que se perdía hacia una distancia incalculable en tiempo y espacio...

Sólo eso, hasta que desperté.

PERO MI DESPERTAR no se parecía a ningún otro; y la pesadilla, lejos de desaparecer con mi retorno al mundo consciente, ocupó, a partir de entonces, un lugar sustancial y determinante en mi vida. La pesadilla fue mi modo de vida.

Al abrir los ojos, apareció debajo de mi cuerpo una extensión muy blanca, como el desierto del sueño, y unas botas doradas, que caminaban produciendo aquel avance tan especial. Sentía los miembros completamente entumecidos y, cuando quise mover los brazos, me asaltó un dolor intensísimo, como un tormento. Por una razón que al principio no entendí, estaba imposibilitado para realizar cualquier movimiento de brazos o piernas. Y sólo podía levantar el cuello hasta una altura mínima, la única que me permitía la postura en la cual me transportaban.

Me habían dejado completamente desnudo, y, a juzgar por la llaga en que mi cuerpo se había convertido a causa de las quemaduras del sol, hacía horas que duraba aquella marcha, aquel viaje de mi inconsciencia. Me llevaban como un cordero que acaba de ser sacrificado o va camino del sacrificio: colgaba cabeza abajo, tobillos y muñecas amarrados a un tronco que los raptores transportaban sobre sus hombros, ambos en silencio, sin contestar a ninguna de las preguntas que yo formulaba de forma inconexa. Sólo se detenían de vez en cuando para darme agua, pero no me desataban; tampoco se preocupaban de la sangre que goteaba por todo mi cuerpo, resbalando desde las muñecas y los tobillos, insensibilizados ya a cualquier tipo de dolor que pudiesen recibir a partir de entonces. O esto supuse en aquellos primeros momentos de mi espanto, cuando aún no podía imaginar todos los dolores físicos que mi cuerpo habría de soportar cuando me otorgasen los privilegios de Co-Divino sobre la Tierra. Aquello parecía la culminación de todos los males posibles, y, sin embargo, no era más que el principio: mi nacimiento al Mundo Macho.

Los raptores siguieron marchando en silencio durante varias horas, y yo iba perdiendo sangre; el mundo temblaba ante mis ojos y el cuerpo entero ardía con una intensidad progresiva, bajo el azote del sol.

Sólo veía avanzar la arena en pliegues infinitos: pequeñas dunas dentro de cada duna, dibujos que se convirtieron en una serie de líneas alteradas, cruzadas entre sí y sobre las cuales iba proyectándose mi sombra horizontal. Pero, finalmente, ya ni siquiera pude ver aquella blancura, porque mi visión se hizo roja: tanto sol había soportado. Y de nuevo sentí que la conciencia escapaba, y sólo oía, lejano, muy lejano, el jadeo de los hombres que me sostenían. Después, un gran vacío.

UNOS GRITOS ME HICIERON recobrar el conocimiento. Seguía atado, pero ya no avanzábamos sobre el desierto; para mi sorpresa —mayor si cabe que las anteriores—, me balanceaba sobre un paisaje de increíble fertilidad. Entonces hice mío el grito, y fue de pavor, pues el paisaje parecía hundido en el vientre del mundo. Mis raptores me transportaban por encima de un precipicio en cuyo fondo rugían enormes cascadas que se perdían en la humareda de su propia espuma. En este trance, sólo las cuerdas que me mantenían amarrado al tronco evitaron que el propio impacto del despertar me precipitase en las profundidades.

Y al instante me pregunté si sería volador el tronco que me sujetaba.

Pero eran mis dos raptores quienes se encargaban de dirigir el singular trayecto. El que antes caminase delante de mí, se hallaba ahora en la otra parte del abismo, que sin duda habría cruzado a salto de liana, pues el puente de cuerdas estaba roto. Pugnaba por mantenerse en pie sobre un saliente de la montaña, pero éste era tan estrecho que el menor movimiento en falso podía arrojarlo al abismo, arrastrándome consigo.

Si mi terror necesitaba mayores estímulos, bastó comprobar que el hombre tenía los brazos en alto y sostenía con ambas manos la punta del tronco; el otro extremo era recibido cuidadosamente por su compañero, quien permanecía sobre otro risco de la montaña opuesta. Y yo continuaba vagando por el espacio, a una altura tan inaudita que incluso las cascadas, los bosques y los prados del fondo parecían elementos de un diorama diminuto encerrado en una bola de mágico cristal.

Entonces estalló un aullido aterrador, que fue perdiéndose hacia abajo: el cuerpo del primer hombre caía por el riscal, seguido por un alud de piedras enormes con un estrépito semejante al de un seísmo. En un instante, cuerpo y piedras se esfumaron entre los vapores de las cataratas, allá en lo más profundo.

Mi grito enlazó con el eco del desdichado; resonó en las rocas que me rodeaban, expresó todo el espanto que llevaba reprimido en mi interior, todo el dolor de los miembros entumecidos, de la sangre que continuaba manando. Y el tronco, al que ya sólo sostenían las dos manos del otro raptor, fue a dar contra la parte inferior del saliente que le servía de plataforma. Sentí el golpe de las piedras contra mi carne desnuda, y después quedé colgando, en lo que mi delirio juzgó un desamparo absoluto. Me equivocaba. Desde lo alto, las fuertes manos del desconocido sujetaban el tronco e intentaban controlar su vaivén. Con los ojos cerrados, con el grito ininterrumpido, me sentí izado lentamente.

Gracias a la prodigiosa fuerza de mi raptor me hallé sobre la plataforma, apoyado contra el muro de tal modo que, incluso atado al tronco, la postura se me hizo más cómoda o, cuando menos, soportable.

El hombre se quitó la capa y me reveló el más pintoresco aspecto de guerrero que nunca imaginase. Su uniforme era la desnudez total, aliviada sólo por algunos aditamentos no menos pintorescos. Las botas doradas, que yo empezaba a conocer de memoria, le cubrían las piernas hasta la rodilla; guantes también de oro le protegían los brazos, y la parte superior del pecho se defendía con una coraza del mismo metal pero que, de hecho, era poco más que un enorme medallón. Guantes, botas y coraza constituían el único hábito del soldado, además de un cinturón de cuero negro, tachonado, del que colgaban un cuerno de caza y una cimitarra, protegidos por fundas de marfil con esmeraldas incrustadas. Y entre esos atributos, propios del guerrero profesional, destacaba un pubis teñido de púrpura, cuyo vello diríase el marco rococó para un pene descomunal.

Sonrió el joven; y, de haber tenido humor para algo, tal vez hubiese pensado que ya era hora. En correcto francés me comunicó que el peligro había pasado, y que pronto llegaríamos a Lur. Seguidamente empuñó el cuerno de caza y lanzó al aire un sonido clamoroso, violento. Yo empezaba a recuperarme del dolor de las ataduras, pero la impresión de oscilar sobre aquel abismo, de ver cómo se desplomaba en sus simas nuestro acompañante, no era de las que se pueden borrar con facilidad. Incluso hoy, pasado tanto tiempo, me despierto de madrugada y siento que la cama huye de mi cuerpo, y sigo colgando sobre aquel espacio infinito, con las manos del atleta como único, casi imposible, contacto con la tierra firme.

Un trueno fragoroso resonó en lo más profundo de la montaña. Era el ruido de la piedra que se rompe, de la tierra que revienta, del volcán que escupe su ira. Y la montaña se abrió de par en par, y aparecieron unos peldaños que conducían a un gran pasadizo excavado en la piedra viva y festoneado por antorchas enormes cuyas llamas danzaban mecidas por el aire que llegaba del exterior. El hombre que a partir de entonces sería mi carcelero devolvió el cuerno al cinturón y desenvainó la espada. Yo incliné la cabeza sobre su hombro y, exhausto, me dejé conducir.

Y aún pensaba que, después de tantos avatares, ya no habría destino que pudiese importarme. Ni siquiera el más horrible.

Sólo que aquel destino era ya el definitivo; era mi prisión. Porque, cuando el hombre cortó las cuerdas que me habían mantenido atado y me llevó en brazos como si transportara una pluma, entré definitivamente en el Mundo Macho. Y mientras descendíamos los peldaños (de impecable basalto, que contrastaba con la aspereza de la roca), la gran puerta se cerró a nuestras espaldas, emitiendo el curioso silbido que caracteriza a los dragones.

De súbito, un estado de alerta.

Mi carcelero me arrojó al suelo, y a continuación me arrinconó conra la pared. Se oían pasos que provenían del fondo de la escalera. A medida que fueron haciéndose más rotundos, delataron la angustia de alguien que corría hacia la salida.

Astor, que tal era el nombre de mi guardián, apagó las dos antorchas que tenía más a mano, y quedamos en una penumbra que nos protegía de los ojos de los demás, pero dejándonos la visión del entorno. Los pasos iban aproximándose, y Astor levantó la espada en actitud de ataque y defensa a la vez. La puerta se cerraba más lentamente de lo que se había abierto, y los dos cuerpos que subían corriendo aún tuvieron tiempo de ser bañados por un rayo de luz del día.

Eran un muchacho y una mujer de lo más extraños que pueda imaginarse. Él llevaba la cabeza rasurada, lo mismo que el resto del cuerpo, visible porque iba completamente desnudo, como Astor, y, al igual que éste, sólo se cubría las partes correspondientes a las botas, los guantes y el pectoral. Pero todos estos accesorios no eran de oro, como los de Astor, sino de acero, lo cual evidenciaba que el mancebo pertenecía a una jerarquía inferior. La mujer era la imagen exacta de la miseria: un cuerpo lleno de costras, greñas hasta los talones, la desnudez apenas cubierta con una piel de vaca que habría servido de alimento a todos los piojos del país. Los zapatos, ya casi inexistentes, eran también de piel y los sujetaba con cuatro cordeles raídos. El estado decrépito de aquella mujer hacía imposible precisar si era joven o vieja. No tenía edad. Él la arrastraba por el suelo, como si la fatiga pudiese más que la angustia. Jadeaban ambos, pero, cuando estuvieron más cerca, me di cuenta de que los aretes que colgaban de las orejas del mancebo temblaban tanto como el cuerpo de la fugitiva. Y en pleno jadeo corrían con mayor desespero hacia la salida, mientras la puerta se cerraba inexorablemente.

La habrían alcanzado a tiempo de no mediar la intervención de Astor, quien surgió de la oscuridad y, con un formidable salto, separó a la mujer del joven y le desafió, tocándole el pecho con su espada de hoja anchísima. La fugitiva rodó por las escaleras. Profería unos aullidos estremecedores, con la mano levantada hacia la salida en un último, desesperado, intento de alcanzarla.

El grito del mancebo fue como el de una fiera a la que acaban de herir de muerte. Se lanzó sobre Astor desde dos peldaños más arriba; pero el violento choque de los cuerpos no consiguió hacer vacilar al capitán, quien rechazó al fugitivo contra la pared mientras la puerta acababa de cerrarse definitivamente.

De rodillas, el muchacho y la mujer se golpeaban el pecho y aullaban cada vez con más fuerza, con la cabeza agitada como si fuesen dos espantapájaros. Iban a abrazarse, pero Astor se interpuso y chilló la señal inconfundible de una orden lanzada hacia más allá de las tinieblas.

No pasó mucho tiempo y éstas se rompieron con el resplandor de multitud de antorchas esgrimidas por hombres que vestían el mismo uniforme que Astor (pero también con materiales de una jerarquía inferior), y blandían lanzas cuyas puntas se posaron contra el pecho del fugitivo. Después de dar algunas órdenes, y mientras los soldados ataban las manos de los prisioneros, Astor me cogio del brazo y, sonriendo, dijo que yo no debía asustarme en absoluto, porque yo era «especial». Y antes de seguir nuestro descenso miró hacia atrás y sonrió de nuevo: me señalaba la gran puerta de basalto, la puerta que sólo puede abrirse desde dentro del Mundo Macho, y jamás desde fuera. Tal vez la sonrisa de Astor significaba que el único peligro era, precisamente, el intento de salir al mundo exterior. La huida.

¿VERDAD QUE AÚN no le he hablado de la cobra que Astor ostentaba en el pectoral y de las más pequeñas de las botas y los guantes? Era un signo distintivo de mi obsesión; del mismo modo que es parte indivisible de la imaginería religiosa del Mundo Macho. Así, la cueva daba a un bosque de helechos gigantes en cuyo principio se levantaba una muralla de proporciones ciclópeas, con una gran puerta coronada por la estatua, grandiosa y amenazadora, de una cobra real erecta, en actitud de ataque. Al volver la vista, descubrí que esta bestia litúrgica también estaba grabada en el pectoral de los soldados que nos seguían y, en menor tamaño que la de Astor, en cada una de las botas y guantes que completaban los uniformes. Y es precisamente esta Cobra Macho la que puebla mis sueños: la forma sinuosa que, cada noche, me arrastra al grito, me hunde en la caída hacia el abismo, me obliga al delirio.

Seguidamente, reparé con mayor exactitud en las características físicas de Astor, de sus soldados y del fugitivo. Todos eran jóvenes —Astor tendría veinticinco años, y el fugitivo no llegaría a los veinte—, pero sus proporciones eran tremendas, y recordaban a las figuras más exageradas del titanismo agresivo de algunas esculturas clásicas. De estatura descomunal, habían desarrollado sus músculos sin perder ese equilibrio supremo de cada parte del cuerpo que el Mundo Macho exige para lograr que la raza cuente con el poder desmesurado que otorga la fuerza y con la belleza que reside en el perfecto cultivo de la estética. Todos ellos eran de piel bronceada, resplandeciente como ungida por el aceite que suelen utilizar los modelos de ciertas revistas de fisioculturismo. Y en el aspecto sobrenatural y soberano de aquella raza de gigantes, destacaba la exigencia básica de un origen ario: soldados y oficiales tenían el cabello más rubio y los ojos más azules que jamás viera en mi Europa, exceptuando acaso a los hombres del Norte. Comparada con los atletas de Astor, la prisionera parecía negroide.

Llegados a esta parte de mi historia —no a un momento del sueño del opio, como podría usted pensar, o han pensado ya otros antes que usted—, considero justo hacer honor al paisaje, a la mezcolanza de formas insólitas que me acogía y que, aun hallándome bajo el dominio del espanto, no podía dejar de contemplar, estupefacto y fascinado a un tiempo; del mismo modo que no puedo dejar de describírselo ahora, pues, con el trastorno que le habrán provocado mis rodeos, privarle de tan extraordinaria información podría ser cualquier cosa menos justo.

Una vez traspasada la muralla, lejana reminiscencia de un trabajo de cíclopes, Astor me guió por un camino no demasiado ancho sobre el que colgaban, cual abanicos para uso de gigantes, ramas y hojas de árboles sin final visible, retorcidos entre sí hasta formar un ovillo que los convertía en selva impenetrable. De hecho, más allá del camino no podía verse sino una oscuridad nocturna, resultado natural de tanto espesor. Los árboles que bordeaban el sendero tenían los troncos más gruesos que pueda imaginar, y algunos parecían de madera petrificada —lo eran, según me contó Astor—. A medida que el camino descendía hacia otra cueva tan gigantesca como la anterior, el cielo parecía más alejado de mis ojos. Más allá de la oscuridad que reinaba entre los árboles, podía oír el canto de pájaros grotescos, múltiples chillidos, disonantes o roncos, que hubiesen podido ser de ranas del tamaño de los elefantes. Pertenecían a aquel mundo tenebroso de la selva virgen (el Mundo Macho tiene dos: la que termina a la entrada del país, y la que da al desierto de los herejes y a las montañas bermejas donde vive la Bestia Llamada Hembra. Pero es una zona que ni siquiera los más osados ciudadanos de Lur se han atrevido a explorar).

De vez en cuando me volvía para observar a los dos fugitivos, que los soldados escoltaban a cierta distancia, y cuya suerte me preocupaba dada la violencia con que los tratase mi raptor. Pero con sólo levantar la mirada descubría todo el camino que llevábamos recorrido, toda la distancia que nos separaba de la cueva de entrada y, ya, de la primera muralla ciclópea conocida como la Puerta Cobra.

—Es la muralla más antigua del Mundo Macho —me explicó Astor. Después introdujo una serie de topónimos y sonrió ligeramente, como si diera por supuesto que yo los conocía—. El recuerdo de estas piedras va mucho más allá de nuestras leyendas más antiguas, incluso antes de que el Padre Sol transmitiera sus rayos a Epsamón para que éste, a través de ti, los hiciera llegar al pueblo. Desde mucho antes de todas las historias, nuestros más remotos antepasados nos dejaron testimonio de una primera muralla encabezada por la Puerta Cobra: una construcción muy primitiva, que el tiempo destruyó.

Pero cada nuevo descubrimiento se inscribía en el ritmo de mi angustia. Poco a poco, la flora ciclópea, los ruidos clamorosos de pájaros sin nombres civilizados, daban paso a la conciencia de sentirme prisionero y al imperativo de averiguar qué lugar constituía mi prisión. No le extrañe este despertar repentino de la inteligencia después de tantas sorpresas y de tanto horror. Al contrario: reconocerá usted que si, en cualquier viaje sencillo, una cierta dosis de curiosidad es más que natural, en mi caso era pura moderación.

No era menos moderada la actitud de Astor, frío como los guías de oficio y siempre a mi lado, atento y ceremonioso, pero sin piedad ni simpatía. Un cierto respeto de su parte y un cúmulo de cumplidos, a veces exagerados, me sorprendía lo indecible en un bruto que me arrebataba de mi mundo sin demasiadas consideraciones. Al mismo tiempo, su silencio, su interés por dejar bien acabado un trabajo concreto —y en aquella ocasión el trabajo era yo—, me hacían adivinar que el impulsor de sus acciones no era él mismo; que más bien trabajaba para una tercera persona.

—Sé que debes estar hambriento, monseñor —comentó—. Ha sido imperdonable no prestar atención a tus necesidades fisiológicas; pero antes de entrar en Lur intentaremos remediar la falta.

Miré a mi alrededor y no vi más que selva. Selva y aquellas montañas altísimas e irregulares, violadas, si acaso, por el laberinto de peldaños de mármol que íbamos descendiendo. No se veía signo alguno de humanidad. Sólo nosotros dos, los prisioneros y aquellos soldados.

—¿Antes de entrar en Lur? —pregunté.

—Sí, antes, monseñor. Habrá que aguardar la llegada de la noche, para que podamos hacerlo en secreto. No estaría bien que el pueblo viese a Nebjeperura antes de su consagración.

—¿Y quién es Nebjeperura? ¿Ese prisionero, tal vez...?

—Tú eres Nebjeperura, monseñor. El que es Co-Divino sobre la Tierra. El que nace de Epura Epsamón como Él nació de Cobra y del Sol, en el principio de todas las historias.

Imposible saber si se burlaba de mí. Su aspecto podía ser tan inescrutable como cuando llevaba el rostro cubierto, pues le educaron para servir sin hacer preguntas, aunque éste era un detalle que yo desconocía entonces. Le habían formado como un titán para ser jefe de un ejército de titanes, en correspondencia con la fuerza y el colosalismo de las estatuas que ya nos rodeaban. Porque, de pronto, el camino semisalvaje se había convertido en un sendero delicioso, adornado con estatuas de atletas que mostraban inscripciones referidas a los grandes generales que, en el pasado, formaron en la milicia del Mundo Macho. Lo abrupto de la selva y la montaña se trocaba ahora en un orden perfecto, de una belleza geométrica y en modo alguno reseca, pero sin concesiones a un mínimo de feminidad. De hecho, todas las estatuas del paseo eran masculinas, así como las de los grandes monumentos funerarios que, separados entre sí por pinos de copa muy recortada, habían sido construidos en segundo término.

Astor me explicó que nos hallábamos en el inicio de la Vía Herculana, la cual enlaza la capital del Mundo Macho con las montañas de donde llegábamos y que son conocidas con el nombre de Sierra Prohibida. Era una de las múltiples vías de comunicación que Epsamón mandó construir a lo largo de su reinado eterno; vías que comunican Lur con los puntos más importantes de un país que, al parecer, no era tan pequeño como yo había creído. Y de todas estas vías, la Herculana se caracterizaba especialmente por el honor de contener los sepulcros de los grandes patricios, que vienen a morir al templo del Final Viril.

Pero una nueva información de Astor contribuyó a acrecentar mi asombro:

—Sólo los sacerdotes de este templo tienen derecho a ver a Nebjeperura antes de la consagración. Por tanto nos detendremos aquí y tú podrás descansar, tomar un baño y comer con tranquilidad. Después seguiremos la marcha hacia Lur, en un carruaje más adecuado a tu rango.

Entre aquellas estatuas de magnífica musculatura, entre aquellos sepulcros en los que creí ver copias de ciertos templos romanos de planta circular, me sentí más amenazado que nunca. Y, al comprender que estaba definitivamente perdido, me postré ante mi guardián y, besándole la mano, supliqué por mi libertad perdida.

Y sucedió que Astor, antes tan complaciente, me lanzó una mirada despreciativa que contenía toda la violencia de un verdugo. Levantándome de un tirón, me obligó a caminar a su lado con la cabeza erguida. Sólo hizo un comentario:

—Nebjeperura nunca se arrodilla ante nadie. Nebjeperura nunca suplica.

Cuando llegamos al templo del Final Viril, los soldados encerraron a los dos prisioneros en una gran jaula y yo fui recibido por varios sacerdotes que, al igual que el fugitivo, llevaban la cabeza completamente rasurada. Vestían túnicas transparentes de lino blanco que dejaban el sexo al descubierto, pero tenían el pecho cruzado por una piel de tigre. Entre ellos destacaba la figura soberbia del Gran Exarca, cubierto de oro hasta los pies. Él fue quien me rogó que aceptara entrar en el templo bajo palio.

Así, rodeado por los sacerdotes y aturdido por sus cantos, perdí a Astor de vista. Y con la pérdida momentánea de quien había sido mi raptor y después mi carcelero, me sentí más indefenso que antes.

PUSIERON A MI SERVICIO a dos sacerdotes adolescentes, cuyo inexplicable respeto hacia mi inexplicada persona no evitó que, de vez en cuando, me dirigieran algunas miradas de desconfianza, como si no acabasen de creer que yo, sucio de sangre y polvo, pudiera ser el verdadero elegido para Co-Divino. Dadas las circunstancias, no era difícil adivinar que cualquier tentativa de interrogatorio por mi parte sería extremadamente mal recibida; y así las cosas, decidí cenar sin preocuparme de nada y, después de un baño encantador, dormí tranquilamente hasta la hora de reemprender el camino hacia mi prisión definitiva.

Durante el tiempo que transcurrió entre nuestra llegada al templo y el sueño al cual me entregué con tanto placer, no me sentí con fuerzas para reconsiderar mi situación. Podían aguardarme muchos peligros, y cada uno mayor que el anterior; pero ya era evidente que nada podía hacer para evitarlos. El sueño, el desfallecimiento y la delicuescencia que nos invade cuando la profunda certidumbre de la muerte ha logrado robarnos incluso el miedo a morir, me arrastraron a una especie de estado hipnótico, del que hoy sería incapaz de asegurar que no me hubiese sido provocado, tal vez por arte de magia, tal vez mediante alguna droga en el vino. No necesito decirle que me dormí apenas me dejaron caer en un lecho inmenso, elevado sobre cuatro columnas salomónicas y cuyo colchón estaba formado por una gran cantidad de plumas, que, a juzgar por su tamaño, pertenecían a algún pájaro de dimensiones absolutas.

¿Podrá usted imaginar mi sueño de aquella noche? No es difícil. Recogía todas las constantes de mi angustia y me abría a un rosario de obsesiones que empezaban a desarrollarse, nuevas y rampantes, como resultado del mundo insólito al cual acababa de nacer hacía pocas horas. Flotaban por mi sueño la expresión airada de mi representante, que me buscaría desesperadamente por las noches de París; los desproporcionados anuncios que jalonan, con letras de neón, los paisajes de mi mundo habitual; las bocinas estridentes que han acompañado siempre mi vida; y, en fin, los aplausos metálicos que puedo escuchar al final de todas mis actuaciones, cuando me encuentro frente a la masa anónima que se pierde en la gran oscuridad de la sala. Pero también aparecía la reciente pesadilla de la gran Cobra que domina la entrada al Mundo Macho; los matorrales de flores colosales que crecen junto a la ruta de peldaños que nos había conducido al principio de la Vía Herculana; los sepulcros de planta circular, con enormes bóvedas de cañón decoradas con estatuas de mármol, que rodeaban el templo del Final Viril...

En mi pesadilla, yo era consciente de hallarme recluido en algún recinto de aquel templo, y también sabía que los lejanos cánticos que me llegaban desde hacía rato pertenecían a una realidad muy concreta, que no aceptaba concesión alguna al escapismo. Estos cánticos, esta realidad, me hicieron despertar por completo y volví a sentirme solo, y de nuevo tuve miedo.

Una sola pluma de la cama era suficiente para cubrir mi cuerpo, y sólo imaginar el tamaño del animal a que podía pertenecer me hacía víctima de nuevos temores. Asociaba aquellas plumas con las dimensiones de la flora que había visto durante mi itinerario hacia el templo, y, como lógica correspondencia, obtenía la idea de una fauna antediluviana, más allá de cualquier medida que mi siglo pueda considerar normal.

También los objetos de la habitación eran desmesurados, empezando por el lecho y terminando por los incensarios suspendidos a ambos lados del gran baldaquín que me cobijaba. Al igual que las patas de la cama, las columnas del baldaquín eran salomónicas, laminadas de oro, y los incensarios impregnaban la estancia con una atmósfera de perfumes organizados en vapores, de una dulcísima pesadez que aumentaba mi estado letárgico. Algunos rincones estaban ocupados por muebles de madera finísima, mesitas de marfil de una blancura impecable y gigantescos almohadones de piel de tigre esparcidos por el suelo, junto a un estanque artificial que llegaba hasta la terraza y de cuyas aguas brotaban lotos resplandecientes, papiros de tallo delicadamente áulico y tulipanes cuyas corolas parecían cálices de rojo alabastro.

Esta alianza entre la barbarie y el refinamiento iba más allá de la estancia, se prolongaba hacia el otro extremo de la terraza; y al salir pude comprobarlo, pues se abrió ante mis ojos otra visión fabulosa: un paisaje extremadamente dulce que se correspondía, con gran precisión, con las distintas formas arquitectónicas que el tiempo había ido dejando en él.

Desde la terraza del templo del Final Viril, todas las contradicciones que condicionan la fisonomía del Mundo Macho aparecieron ante mí de forma deslumbrante. Acompañado por el eco insistente de los himnos religiosos, mis ojos vagaron sobre aquella visión fantástica sin acertar a detenerse en nada concreto, perdidos en la inmediatez de la fascinación.

Así era el Mundo Macho.

Las montañas que se perdían entre las nubes servían

de cinturón a un valle que dijérase metáfora de la paz: un valle grandioso, surcado por diversos ríos, estanques y cascadas que, en aquella hora de la tarde, recibían un postrer rayo de sol que enrojecía el agua. Los bosques y los parques distribuidos alrededor de la inmensa Lur, capital del Mundo Macho y de todo su Imperio, no tenían el feroz aspecto de la selva que habíamos dejado atrás, antes bien parecían el capricho de algún jardinero inglés, fantasioso en extremo. Por todas partes resplandecían las tonalidades doradas de una bonanza que, en el Mundo Macho, suele durar hasta las primeras violencias del invierno, corto, sin embargo, porque yo, Nebjeperura, no tardo en regresar de mi periplo a las tierras de la Nada, de mi lucha contra Aquel que Ordena el Tiempo y Odia al Hombre. Y la placidez del paisaje se acentúa con la irrupción de una inmensa pirámide que emerge del centro del valle y llega a ser más alta que cuantas rocas la rodean. Es el eje espiritual del país y de su religión..., incluso de su política, porque, en el Mundo Macho, religión y administración política forman una misma entidad inseparable. (Más tarde, Astor me explicaría que fue precisamente en la pirámide donde Epura Epsamón recibió la consagración del Sol.)

El bucolismo del paisaje me había distraído de todas las angustias que yo tenía motivos más que suficientes para ir alimentando, y por ello no me di cuenta de que los cánticos, antes lejanos, se habían ido aproximando: ya estaban junto a mí. Me giré, asustado, al notar que alguien me acariciaba la espalda. Pero encontré ante mí a un Astor sonriente que se había cambiado de ropa y en lugar de su escueto uniforme llevaba aquellas vestimentas que tantas veces he podido ver en los cuadros del renacimiento florentino: mallas a rayas negras y rojas que le llegaban hasta la cintura (pero dejando abierto el triángulo del sexo), chaqueta roja con mangas negras y de anchísimo vuelo y un bonete rojo sobre la cabellera que, lavada y peinada ya, le llegaba hasta la nuca. Detrás de él formaban ordenadamente los miembros del coro sacerdotal, que seguían entonando sus salmos.

El cabello áureo de Astor, su rostro bronceado, recibían un toque de resol que le daba la apariencia de un ser menos amenazador que antes. Diríase un serafín con cuerpo de atleta. Mi carcelero de miel y azúcar. Y, siempre, mi informador...

—Desde las trincheras donde se dedica a aniquilar a los enemigos del Imperio, el triunfante Epsamón nos ordena que abreviemos al máximo el proceso de tu consagración, para que puedas entrar cuanto antes en Lur en calidad de Co-Divino. Será esta noche. Síguenos, pues, monseñor.

La tranquilidad apenas intuida desde la terraza, recuperó la barbarie de horas antes. Al salir de la estancia, bajo palio y rodeado por el cortejo de sacerdotes rasurados, la paz era sustituida por largos pasadizos de rocas sin pulimentar, contra las cuales resonaban todos los salmos que, invocando la fuerza y el sacrificio, sólo conseguían remitirme a un nivel de crueldad que ya adiviné ante los primeros paisajes del Mundo Macho. La lóbrega estrechez de los pasadizos y su iluminación mediante fogariles de hierro muy pesado sostenidos por brazos de un oro delicadamente trabajado, marcaban nuevas contradicciones entre dos sensibilidades, una de civilización, de barbarie la otra. Y Astor no me revelaba ningún enigma.

La mentira de unos cánticos que ponían a los dioses y la eternidad como pretexto de una fiesta de sangre me fue revelada de inmediato, cuando, pasado uno de los recodos del laberinto de rocas, desembocamos en un pasadizo más largo que todos los demás, cubierto por una bóveda ennegrecida a causa del humo y con un gran número de atletas crucificados en cada pared: cuerpos desnudos, en tensión, cuyos miembros estaban clavados en la roca viva con clavos que tenían por cabeza enormes piedras preciosas. Avanzábamos entre las víctimas, y nuestro cortejo de túnicas blancas, encabezado por Astor y el Exarca en actitud de plegaria, suscitó en los moribundos unos gritos de entusiasmo; vítores patrióticos que, según Astor, iban dedicados exclusivamente a mí. Es decir: a pesar de que muchos de aquellos hombres llevaban días crucificados, les quedaban fuerzas para saludar a una pobre criatura que, sin proponérselo, venía a reinar sobre su raza.

Comprenderá usted cuánto me extrañara que los asesinos condenados a un suplicio tan vergonzoso y terrible alentaran, a pesar de todo, unos sentimientos cívicos de tan alto nivel. Aquella actitud invitaba a pensar que, en el Mundo Macho, los perseguidos por la justicia tenían más calidad humana que los que la dictaban y la administraban.

Pero he aquí que Astor me desengañó con una pequeña aclaración admirablemente concisa: los crucificados eran ciudadanos libres, algunos incluso pertenecían a la alta nobleza, y cumplían las leyes básicas del Mundo Macho. Acudían al templo del Final Viril para terminar allí sus días con la dignidad que corresponde a quienes no tienen mácula de que avergonzarse; quienes habían merecido el honor ciudadano de la muerte que decreta el Estado porque habían cumplido con todos sus deberes cívicos y raciales a lo largo de una vida que debía concluir necesariamente a la edad de cincuenta años. Y ni un día más.

La naturalidad con que Astor me proporcionaba tales explicaciones, mientras desfilábamos entre los cuerpos crucificados, pudo enloquecerme casi por completo de no haber tenido ya bastantes razones para compadecerme a mí mismo. Me hablaba de una ley de vida que exigía la muerte al cumplir los cincuenta años; y yo, que tenía veinticinco, avanzaba en aquel momento hacia un destino que podía ser tan cruel como el de aquellos hombres, e incluso más. A ellos se les exigía que sacrificasen su tiempo antes de que la senilidad convirtiera su cuerpo en un harapo de carne agotada que pudiera ser vergüenza de la raza. A cambio, obtendrían tumbas monumentales, edificadas conforme a las proporciones de lujo y titanismo que exigen los cánones arquitectónicos del Mundo Macho. Desde niños, habían sido educados en la idea de una perfección física que no podía decaer con el paso de los años; y ellos lo habían aceptado, acaso antes de nacer, porque así estaba escrito, desde el principio de todas las historias, en los libros que forjaron la grandeza del Mundo Macho.

Pero yo no tenía nada en común ni con esta raza ni con este mundo, y, sin embargo, era conducido a un sacrificio que se me exigía para que ellos mismos pudiesen convertirme en la glorificación máxima de su ideal de perfección. Los mártires me saludaban desde su agonía voluntaria porque yo era la imagen en la cual deberían mirarse, a partir de entonces, las Juventudes del Mundo Macho. Yo, que había sido secuestrado de mi mundo y de mi profunda angustia de miserable mortal, me convertiría en el espejo donde se reflejaría la voluntad de una nueva generación; del mismo modo que en la imagen de Epsamón Divino se reflejaba, desde siempre, la voluntad de todo un pueblo, de toda una Historia.

PERO EN CUANTO DEJAMOS ATRÁS el corredor de los crucificados, Astor hizo que me detuviera ante una gran puerta de hierro y me anunció que la Consagración sería una prueba muy difícil de soportar; pero que sólo la superación del dolor me haría digno de ser tratado como un hombre y, después, como el representante de los dioses sobre la Tierra. Yo no tenía respuesta, pues era evidente que me sentía envuelto en una elección que estaba muy lejos de solicitar. Una vez hube aceptado lo inevitable, con actitud típica de prisionero, sólo me quedaba navegar, indefenso, en la barca que mis raptores quisieran fletar; y decidí que era preferible ser considerado un hombre antes que un perro, o tal vez un esclavo.

Pero yo soy humano, profesor; soy un mísero mortal, sensible tanto a la angustia como al placer, a los latigazos del dolor como a los de la alegría. Hasta entonces nunca me había planteado la posibilidad de pasar seriamente por divino; y esta idea me hacía temblar con igual intensidad que la de pasar por perro o por esclavo. Durante los años que he viajado de escenario en escenario, de sala de grabación a pistas de *night club*, siempre me he resistido a creer lo que la publicidad de Larry intentaba imbuir en la mentalidad de mis admiradores: que yo, miserable pedazo de carne, era el pequeño dios privilegiadísimo en el Olimpo de los mitos chillones que ha creado mi siglo. En más de una ocasión he sido víctima de esta maniobra, profesor, pero, en el fondo de mi angustia de adorado, siempre quise preservar el punto de cordura que me hiciera sentirme uno más entre todos los ángeles caídos en la condición humana: pobre, inhóspita, mortal, y, sin embargo, la única que poseo.

Sin imaginar qué desagradable sorpresa me preparaban (y presentía la peor), comprendí que mi actitud y mi resistencia a partir de aquel momento podrían decidir cuál iba a ser mi grado de hombría según aquellos bárbaros: determinaría, al menos, mi derecho a ser considerado humano como ellos. Para Astor y para todos los que iban a conocerme cuando hiciese mi entrada triunfal en Lur, yo era un objeto del cual se podía disponer; una especie de extraña bestia sin voluntad propia, completamente indigna de lo que el Mundo Macho ha denominado «raza elegida». Y ello sin olvidar que todas las sorpresas que poco a poco me habían hecho prescindir de la costumbre de pensar o actuar, podían hacerme parecer un títere imbécil. Así pues, me urgía convencerles de mis disponibilidades, no tanto de titán (que ya llegaría el momento) como de hombre.

Y debo insistir en que ni siquiera me permitían escoger. Una orden de Astor, unas leyes ancestrales, toda una extraña forma de civilización, me lanzaban a mi destino y me robaban lo que me distinguía como hombre: mi albedrío.

Dije a Astor que intentaría superar con éxito todas las pruebas, y él me anunció que, una vez superadas, necesitaría descansar muchos días y muchas noches. Me miró después con no poca lástima y, de un violento tirón, me despojó de la túnica azul y quedé completamente desnudo. Los sacerdotes iniciaron un nuevo cántico, de ritmo agresivo, que a partir de las primeras notas fue acompañado de un ruido de tambores procedente del otro lado de la puerta de hierro. Y cuando otros sacerdotes la abrieron desde dentro, me encontré en la gran basílica que contiene el altar nacional de Cobra, rodeado por su inmenso lago de fuego.

Astor me acompañó hasta la orilla del estanque, y unas llamas altas como casas me hicieron sentir un calor insoportable que me obligó a retroceder. Se me ocurrió pensar que tal vez la consagración consistiría en el fuego, y tuve que morderme los labios para no gritar. Allá, en lo alto, podía ver la enorme bóveda que coronaba aquella especie de gran panteón, la guarnición dorada que parecía imposible que no se hubiese resquebrajado a lo largo de los siglos, a causa del calor de las llamas. Al mismo tiempo, la colosal estatua de Cobra, en actitud eternamente erecta, surgía del otro lado del fuego, y, a pesar de la elegancia de sus líneas, sintetizaba todas las amenazas de que yo había sido objeto hasta aquel momento.

Y es que, como he insinuado, como afirmaré, profesor, la amenaza y la muerte tienen, en el Mundo Macho, las formas sofisticadísimas del arte más evolucionado.

Como en el caso de los sepulcros de la Vía Herculana, la configuración de aquella gran nave, de su bóveda grandiosa, respondía a un modelo arquitectónico romano; y su colosalismo me recordaba algún monumento conocido. Se trata de una construcción esférica, con una galería de columnas corintias que sostienen un primer piso, formado por multitud de nichos que guardan, desde tiempo inmemorial, los mármoles que representan a las divinidades del Mundo Macho. La bóveda, hemisférica, arranca de este primer piso, y presenta una superficie que se diría carcomida por multitud de artesones que otorgan al conjunto una grandeza imperecedera.

Y puedo asegurarle que, apenas el Sumo Sacerdote de Cobra descendió los peldaños del altar rodeado por los acólitos, reconocí, en su dalmática bordada con filigranas de oro, otro recuerdo de mis estudios de arte. Contrastaba estrepitosamente con las túnicas de lino transparente de los sacerdotes comunes la toga de plata maciza del Exarca de Suer (que se había desplazado secretamente a la comarca capitalina para asistir a *mi* ceremonia) y el taparrabos de malla roja que caracterizaba a los acólitos, adolescentes todos ellos. Asimismo, el bucle sumamente airoso de los efebos no guardaba relación con los adornos que cubrían la testa del Sumo Sacerdote, del mismo modo que la suya no consonaba con la cabeza rasurada de los subalternos más inmediatos: lucía el cabello trenzado y se tocaba con una mitra de oro de la cual pendían tres sartas de perlas, y sus borceguíes eran de seda morada, con otras tantas hileras de rubíes. El vestido, solemne, estaba formado por dos partes superpuestas; la de debajo era una dalmática de terciopelo, del mismo color que los zapatos, y formaba mangas abiertas, cayendo, libres, casi hasta los pies; la parte superior era una toga-tabardo con predominio del oro, material que en el Mundo Macho puede hallarse fácilmente. Y todos aquellos elementos cuya grandeza y lujo empezaba en el atuendo me recordaban ciertas ceremonias primitivas del culto cristiano.

En un esporádico momento de lucidez, mientras el Sumo Sacerdote me rociaba con un incienso de perfume turbador, me di cuenta de que, al igual que el Exarca, tendría más de sesenta años y que, por lo tanto, no se había sometido a la ley de autocrucifixión a la cual se había referido Astor. Esto ponía en crisis mis primeros conocimientos de las leyes del Mundo Macho: ¿qué secreto privilegio respetaba la vida de los sacerdotes —y la de algunos coroneles, como supe después— dentro de un orden de valores que decretaba la muerte de cualquier individuo al llegar a los umbrales de la vejez para mantener históricamente viva la exuberancia y la perfección estética del Machismo?

Pero no tuve tiempo de profundizar en mi pensamiento; mientras el Sumo Sacerdote elevaba los brazos hacia la imagen de Cobra, dos acólitos avanzaron hacia nosotros sosteniendo con gran respeto sendas almohadas de terciopelo carmesí, y sobre una de ellas reposaba un estilete muy largo, cuya punta estaba al rojo vivo.

Para disimular el pánico permanecí completamente inmóvil —lo cual suele producir el efecto de un valor capaz de resistir cualquier atrocidad—; fijé la mirada en el hierro candente, mientras me abandonaba a los brazos de dos sacerdotes que me condujeron hasta un ara larga y estrecha como un banco de mármol, y de cuyos cuatro extremos sobresalían sendas Cobras de bronce, a guisa de agarraderos. Entonces me obligaron a tenderme boca abajo y con grilletes de oro me sujetaron una mano a cada cobra; hicieron lo mismo con los pies, de forma que me encontré con el cuerpo abierto en forma de aspa. Colocaron debajo de mi vientre uno de los almohadones de cachemira, para que quedase en alto el trasero. Huelga decir que la situación no podía estar más clara.

A partir de aquel momento ya era imposible pensar en una remota posibilidad de huida. Mientras los cánticos iniciaban un ritmo más veloz, siguiendo el compás de un frenético timbal, diría que belicoso, yo apreté los dientes con todas las fuerzas que aún me quedaban. Sólo esperaba el contacto de aquel fuego contra mi carne. En un momento de espanto definitivamente histérico, lancé un aullido que se repitió muchas veces, con toda una gama de modulaciones diversas, según iba golpeándose contra los espacios, tan armónicamente distribuidos, de aquella bóveda sensacional.

Mi desazón aumentaba a medida que retrasaban el supremo instante del suplicio. Incapaz de ver cuanto estaba ocurriendo a mis espaldas, comprendí al menos que sólo el primer contacto con el hierro candente me indicaría el instante del dolor. Podía suceder en cualquier momento, en cualquier segundo. Pensaba: «¡Ahora!, ¡ahora!»; pero el hierro se aplazaba y yo apretaba los dedos sobre el cuerpo erecto de las cobras y mordía el mármol del ara y, en un desesperado intento por desatarme, incorporaba la parte inferior del cuerpo, casi saltaba. Pero el tormento no se producía, y los sacerdotes cantaban, y los golpes de timbal ya eran delirantes. Es decir: un segundo se convertía en siglos.

Empezaron a pasar el fuego por mi espalda, siempre cuidando de que el estilete no me cortara, y yo lo sentía milímetro a milímetro, a medida que iba bajando hasta rozar las ancas que yo seguía levantando desesperadamente. Cánticos y tambores formaban un himno de batalla. El estilete se aproximaba a su destino, y de repente, con una precisión horripilante, mi verdugo, sea quien fuere, me introdujo lentamente la punta candente en el ano.

Usted puede imaginar lo que fue sentir el fuego en las profundidades de mi virginidad. Y, se lo juro, profesor, aún no he sabido expresar a nadie cuáles fueron exactamente mis sensaciones en aquel momento alucinante.

¿Necesito decir que me desmayé?

SU REACCIÓN ME PARECE lógica, profesor: la desconfianza, la ironía, el rechazo dictado por cierta mentalidad filosófica..., sí, todo eso es muy natural. Comprendo que cualquier fragmento de mi relato es suficientemente increíble como para justificar que sea escuchado como el sueño de un loco o de un drogado. Sobre todo porque no puedo aspirar a aclarárselo con algo que se parezca lejanamente al rigor o a la razón. De este modo, todas las partes de mi historia pueden parecer una sucesión inconexa de fantasmas y verdugos; una retahíla de violencias gratuitas, de crueldades que no puedo llegar a convertir en advertencia grave y desesperada, porque, puestas a no tener, no tienen siquiera una lógica interna. Y el conjunto resulta ser reflejo obsesivo de la pesadilla que sólo yo he padecido, que sólo yo padezco. Le hablo de la Vida Nueva a la cual me lanzó el destino.

Pero me apresuro a explicarle que yo he tenido dos «vidas nuevas»; es decir, dos principios inesperados de vida después de la que mis padres y su circunstancia me dieron. La primera vez, Larry me sacó de las propiedades de mi padre, allá en Bretaña, para encumbrarme hacia esta dudosa cima de la música del siglo, desde la cual soy soberano de un reino multitudinario a cuyos súbditos ni siquiera conozco. La segunda vez, cuando esta situación se había tornado tan insoportable que necesité huir a Egipto en busca de vacaciones desesperadas, una orden que Epsamón habría dictado desde su palacio, en la cima de un reino que nadie de nuestro mundo conocerá jamás, me arrebató de mis realidades y me depositó en lo más alto de una adoración obligada que me ha aprisionado hasta el tormento. En ambos casos, la Vida Nueva surgía de muchos momentos alimentados en mis sueños de adolescente, cuando las revistas de cine o los tebeos de aventuras me imbuían un sentimiento de envidia hacia los ídolos que el cine, la aventura o la canción habían creado para deslumbrarnos. Mi primera metamorfosis, ídolo de un reino pop, y esta segunda vida nueva, en calidad de Nebjeperura, eran la puesta en escena, de mis fantasías más secretas; y apenas me hallé instalado en ellas, fui descubriendo que muy a menudo la fantasía puede ser amarga, cruel y destructiva. Porque en ambos casos —yo, ídolo popular, o yo, ídolo del Mundo Macho—, en ambos fui utilizado como instrumento amargo, cruel y destructor.

Sí: Larry entra en tratos con una fábrica de gafas de sol, y los fabricantes saben que si yo me fotografío con esas gafas y no con otras, su venta subirá durante el verano; Larry sabe que, si salgo una noche con una muchachita que aspira a hacer cine, ella aparecerá en las revistas de chismes y sabrá pagar de algún modo tal promoción. La moda, las gafas, incluso la filosofía de nuestro siglo, dependen de mí; y los comerciantes del Mundo Macho lo comprendieron desde el primer momento, y lo explotaron a conciencia cara a la juventud del país. Porque, en realidad, estos dos sistemas no son tan diferentes como puede parecer a primera vista. La Vida Nueva a la cual me arrojó Larry, y la Vida Nueva en cuyos secretos me aleccionaba Astor, tienen puntos de contacto tan obvios que mi éxito en Lur ya no puede serme extraño, del mismo modo que no me extraña la portada de cualquier revista que reproduzca mi imagen con el jersey que una determinada fábrica me ha propuesto exhibir a cambio de dinero.

De este modo aprendí por qué motivo, sin conocer yo la existencia de un lugar llamado Mundo Macho, Epsamón Divino pudo levantar un día el bastón de su poder ilimitado y decidir para siempre el destino de un pobre muchacho bretón.

Otra Vida Nueva empezaba para mí en el palacio real de Lur, algunas semanas después de mi iniciación en el templo del Final Viril. E insisto en la cronología para sugerir el tiempo que tardé en recuperarme de las heridas que la penetración del fuego me había producido. Estaba iniciado en el rito sagrado del dolor, que todo lo sublima y a todos endurece, y ya sólo me faltaba iniciarme en el rito de la violencia y del mal, que enseñan a dominarlo todo. Quedaba el Dogma de la Crueldad, que fortalece al hombre, lo hace menos vulnerable y lo acerca a la justicia impasible de los dioses de la Fuerza Macho. La verdad es que mi estancia en la segunda Vida Nueva habría de inducirme a una continua meditación sobre estos temas básicos, siempre rodeado por un universo donde el lujo, la sensibilidad y la barbarie encajaban amistosamente con el primitivismo y el refinamiento cultural.

Así pues, al despertarme completamente curado de mis heridas, me descubrí en un conjunto de habitaciones que parecían el museo donde descansase, perfectamente amalgamada, toda la historia del Arte. Mi perplejidad aumentaba con cada nuevo objeto que descubría y con todos los que iría descubriendo a lo largo de muchos días y muchas noches consumidas paseando por las estancias de palacio, en desesperada pugna por combatir el aburrimiento.

El ala del palacio que me fue destinada contenía las dependencias residenciales de una mansión romana, pero sólo el atrio y las termas seguían ortodoxamente ese estilo, ya que, en el dormitorio, en la biblioteca y en la sala de música, había sido añadida una decoración que contradecía el original: de hecho, la sala de música era una habitación de cúpula trapezoidal, decorada con grandes frescos de imaginería bucólica y cantidad de *trompe-l'oeil* en las paredes, las cuales estaban divididas en entrepaños barrocos que aislaban las pinturas de acuerdo con su temática (los temas tenían un sabor muy decadente a causa de las proporciones rubensianas de las figuras y también del vestuario, capaz de presentar a un Aquiles con casaca del siglo XVIII y a un Patroclo que, en vez de lanza, disparaba un arcabuz). La cama de la alcoba representaba un gran cisne de oro en forma de barca, rodeado por biombos de laca negra con dibujos japoneses y de tamaño superior al de una persona. Detrás de estos biombos se veía el techo, adornado con cenefas estucadas de imaginería floral que a su vez enmarcaban escenas de la vida cotidiana en la Venecia del *Settecento*. Por todas partes colgaban cortinas de terciopelo, seda y damasco, que formaban tendales de muy vistosa apariencia que separaban los diversos espacios y en cuyo dorso se hallaban enormes vidrieras góticas que daban paso a una neblina entre roja y azul cuando les daba el sol.

Los objetos no podían ser más heterogéneos; ánforas griegas, incensarios turcos, armaduras medievales, candelabros hebreos, y unas vitrinas colocadas en los nichos de las paredes que contenían toda suerte de piezas de anticuario: relojes de bolsillo de la fábrica Breguet (realmente impensables en un mundo que sólo utilizaba los relojes de sol y de arena), porcelanas K'ang Hsi, cruces polícromas de la escuela lemosina, terracotas al estilo Della Robbia (a causa de sus vírgenes, esas terracotas se consideraban «paganas»), jarroncitos Capodimonte, guerreros etruscos y, entre otras muchas cosas, unos polichinelas sicilianos que recuerdo especialmente, pues su expresión violenta me aterrorizaba cuando, alguna noche, me despertaba en medio de un sueño demasiado agitado.

Aquella misma noche, Astor envió un esclavo a mi habitación. Solicitaba mi permiso para comprobar que todo estuviese en orden, y quería saber si Nebjeperura, restablecido ya de sus heridas, tenía a bien arreglarse para asistir a la Fiesta de la Purificación de la Raza. Yo estaba aún demasiado asombrado, no sabía qué hacer, qué decir, ni siquiera qué pensar. Así pues, sólo se me ocurrió preguntar a qué fiesta se refería Astor. Muy reverencioso, el esclavo me comunicó que su deber era servirme, pero que ello no le permitía estar enterado de asuntos que no eran de su incumbencia, y cuyo conocimiento incluso podía reportarle severísimos castigos.

La insolencia del efebo, llamado Avitachí, no parecía corresponder a la idea, tópica si se quiere, que solemos tener de la esclavitud; y la nobleza de su porte tal vez me habría parecido justificada de haber sabido, entonces, que los esclavos palatinos son, precisamente, los hijos de los ciudadanos más ilustres de Lur. Bajo Epsamón, la relación padre-hijo está abolida desde el principio, y cuando los muchachitos cumplen los diez años, se les saca de la Casa de la Vida, donde han sido criados desde su nacimiento, y se les adscribe a un destino público ya definitivo, que empiezan a realizar al cumplir los quince años, a partir de una ceremonia que se efectúa después de las Jornadas de la Reproducción, bajo el mecenazgo de Homo Demeter.

Avitachí tendría unos dieciocho años, y había elegido la condición de esclavo palatino, lo cual no sólo no le privaba de elegancia natural; antes bien, se la había acentuado, pues, me apresuro a repetirlo, este cargo público no se parece a la esclavitud tal y como nosotros la consideramos: es un título meramente formal, incluso honorífico, puesto que los esclavos de verdad reciben el nombre de Bestia de Servicio, y la mujer —última categoría de humanidad en la escala de valores ciudadanos del Mundo Macho— recibe la denominación de Bestia Llamada Hembra. Engendrados y educados para ser bellos, los adolescentes del Mundo Macho han sido preparados, además, para encajar a la perfección en una sociedad que proscribió de sus principios básicos cualquier concesión a lo vulgar. Y, de este modo, más que esclavos, los efebos del palacio real, la Iglesia o las principales mansiones del país, son objetos preciosos: cultivados en música y en poesía, conocedores de las más delicadas facetas del arte de la conversación, se diferencian notablemente de la juventud destinada a la milicia, la cual es educada desde la primera infancia para incorporarse a las diversas falanges *junior*, y recibe más un adiestramiento físico que una educación de la sensibilidad. Yo soy, por supuesto, el espejo que refleja ambas facciones de las Juventudes Macho, pues he sido adiestrado para inspirar a los púberes que con sus voces blancas deleitan las noches de los patricios de Lur y, al mismo tiempo, me han hecho fuerte para ser ejemplo de aquellos que, en el campo de batalla o en la vida cotidiana, deben ofrecer un pecho más bravío y poderoso que la más puntiaguda de las lanzas del hereje enemigo.

Pero entonces yo ignoraba estos detalles. El cuerpo de Avitachí, desde la cabeza a los pies igual al del fugitivo de la montaña, con las mismas botas, los mismos guantes e idénticos pendientes circulares como único uniforme de servicio, sólo me permitía asociarlo al otro desdichado con la condición de esclavitud, de la cual —supuse al instante— habría querido huir en unión de su compañera. Esta idea me explicaba, momentáneamente, la furia de que Astor dio muestras al descubrirlos; y, pues todas las sociedades bárbaras acostumbraban a castigar con gran crueldad a los esclavos que intentaban escapar, sospeché que el castigo de la pareja sería terrible. Sin embargo, no podía suponer el espectáculo que el machito protagonizaría aquella misma noche.

Astor había cambiado otra vez de indumentaria. Vestía botas de terciopelo rojo, guantes del mismo tejido y color, y una cota de malla que sólo le llegaba hasta el vientre: continuaba con un cinturón de cuero tachonado y, naturalmente, la desnudez total hasta las rodillas, donde terminaban las botas. El tono del terciopelo era agresivo, y las vacilantes llamas de las velas que llenaban la estancia le arrancaban un suave centelleo.

Astor hizo una reverencia muy cortés, y seguidamente se excusó por haberme tenido abandonado. De todos modos, esperaba mi perdón al aducir que, durante los dos meses de mi letargo, había acudido a velarme tres veces al día; celebraba mi buen aspecto (eso implicaba un elogio para los médicos de Lur), y confiaba en que las vendas de muñecas y tobillos podrían disimularse con brazaletes y ajorcas de alto precio.

Me apresté a decirle que nunca había llevado brazaletes ni ajorcas, y que tampoco necesitaba llevarlos ahora; pero Astor acababa de golpear un enorme gong de oro, y, apenas llegó Avitachí, le ordenó que preparase mi atavío de la forma más conveniente. El muchacho salió, para regresar con cuatro mancebos que me empujaron hasta un espejo de oro pulido y me ataviaron de acuerdo con las indicaciones que les daba Astor, de forma que cuando me levanté de la banqueta ya ostentaba la doble corona del Imperio, un manto como el de Astor, un cinturón de rubíes y diversos brazaletes y ajorcas en forma de cobra, serpenteándome por los brazos y los muslos. Si algo he agradecido en alguna ocasión, fue que no tuvieran la ocurrencia de afeitarme la cabeza; lo cual, basándome en Avitachí y en el fugitivo, creía obligado para todos los efectos de Lur. Atribuí la excepción a que yo había sobrepasado los veinte años y no estaba destinado a ser esclavo selecto pasadas las Fiestas de la Reproducción. Yo estaba adjudicado de antemano.

Astor aplaudió mi aspecto, y yo insinué si podría cubrirme el sexo, pregunta que provocó una gran risotada en mi repulsivo guardián. Pero cuando insistí, ya en tono suplicante, Astor adoptó una actitud severa y, como inmediato pregonero de las leyes establecidas, me explicó que el poder de Lur era un poder macho; que las divinidades eran machos, y los atributos de la virilidad imperial debían exhibirse siempre, a fin de que fuesen ejemplo de la perfecta virilidad colectiva.

Seguidamente me comunicó que Epura Epsamón, Sumo Condottiero de los ejércitos de Lur, me enviaba desde el frente su bienvenida y lamentaba no poder recibirme personalmente. De este modo me dispensaba el tratamiento y el honor que mi dignidad y mi jerarquía pública merecían, y al mismo tiempo me hacía saber que su impaciencia por venir a mi encuentro era enorme, y que, mientras durase su ausencia, Astor procuraría que no tuviese quejas de la hospitalidad del Mundo Macho. Además, me comunicaba que el mismo Astor, gran capitán de la guardia palatina, sacerdote honorífico del culto de Cobra y oficial del Servicio Secreto, sería el encargado de escoltarme hasta la Fiesta de la Purificación de la Raza, donde mi presencia, en tanto que Nebjeperura, era absolutamente necesaria. Y, al igual que hiciera antes, Astor efectuó una airosa reverencia indicándome la salida: una gran puerta de marfil flanqueada por dos de los efebos.

Sin abandonar una conversación que pretendía ser amena (siempre las noticias sobre las victorias más recientes de Epsamón en la Guerra Santa) y cada vez más sonriente si yo me decidía a concederle, de vez en cuando, un amago de sonrisa, Astor me guiaba por pasadizos interminables, construidos con un cristal que cubría paredes, techo y suelo, de forma que podían reflejar hasta el infinito cualquier objeto que se colocara en el centro. Debo decir que ni esta suntuosidad, ni la gentileza, acaso engañosa, que me dedicó Astor a lo largo del camino, lograron borrar de mi mente la noción de cárcel que me asaltaba: una idea obsesiva y pronta a convertirse en estado anímico permanente.

Nunca me había visto desnudo con la insistencia que proponían los espejos pues, al reflejar mi paso sobre cuatro superficies, me dividían en una infinidad de sombras de mí mismo, entre las cuales las más ambiguas podían ser el sueño de ser libre y el sueño de ser joven. Y también reproducida miles de veces la soberbia figura de Astor, la cual, como contraste con mi propio cuerpo, parecía colocada allí para recordarme que mi fuerza física era sólo un espejismo. Uno más, quiero decir. Como mi libertad antes o después de Astor. Como mi juventud, que un día u otro agonizaría.

Pero este mundo que me rodeaba no parecía haber sido nunca joven; ni siquiera Astor, cuya atlética apariencia pregonaba la cuidadosísima práctica de todo un sistema de disciplina gimnástica, que arrancaba del orden fundamental que regía el Mundo Macho. Cada anacronismo, cada desnivel repentino entre una sala de apariencia suntuosa y una lóbrega gruta, separadas por puertas de oro labrado delicadamente en pequeños retablos alegóricos, obedecía a una voluntad de que existiera el desnivel, nunca a una casualidad o a una negligencia y, ni que decir tiene, a una concesión al experimentalismo. Incluso en el arte, el orden del Mundo Macho explota la abrumadora serenidad producto de una madurez impuesta; la rigurosa, exacta, tranquilizadora geometrización de las formas; la disciplina estética más estricta, que excluye el constante sentido del riesgo a caer en el caos de la imaginación y la improvisación que son maravilla innegable de los objetos jóvenes, de sus sentidos abiertos, de sus latidos en alboroto constante.

Los pasadizos de los espejos desembocaban en una vasta sala excavada en la roca viva, sin concesión alguna a lo que entenderíamos como civilizado; pero, incluso aquí, un solitario trozo de alabastro labrado en las más exquisitas lucubraciones del barroco indicaba que podía ser un rincón donde Epsamón gustara de meditar un rato, en el corazón de un primitivismo que ya no podía ser más salvaje. Después, ese contraste de las formas daba a unos densos jardines colgantes, llenos de flores monstruosas en su magia coloreada, de belleza tan colosal como desproporcionada.

A continuación, otra sorpresa: una escalera mecánica que se adentraba en las profundidades de la tierra y llegaba a un vestíbulo de paredes ilustradas con jeroglíficos y con el techo sostenido por cien columnas de capiteles papiriformes; después del vestíbulo había otras escaleras mecánicas, esta vez colosales, que nos llevaban a diversos puntos de la superficie. Entonces descubrí que el palacio real se hallaba situado en la más alta de las cinco colinas que rodean la ciudad, y en la primera de las cuales nació la colectividad que habitó Lur, miles de siglos, miles de historias atrás.

Siempre maquinalmente, coleccionando más y más cosas incomprensibles a cada nueva visión de aquel mundo que me elegía, me detuve en un peldaño de la escalera mecánica (el pasamanos estaba hecho con estucados de motivos que recordaban carteles de la *Belle Époque*), y fui transportado lentamente hasta el parque que da entrada al palacio y cuyas palmeras ya se entreveían allá en lo alto.

De pie, en un peldaño inferior al mío, Astor seguía explicando las victorias de Epsamón en las guerras expansionistas del Imperio Macho. Y, al mirar el cuerpo de mi guardián, recordé que un día, en el metro de Londres, mientras la escalera me llevaba hacia la estación de Charing Cross, yo iba mirando los anuncios de una película de Tarzán, con el cuerpo del atleta y su piel de tigre reproducidos de manera obsesiva, uno junto al otro, uno junto al otro...

Las estatuas y esfinges situadas a ambos lados de la avenida que empieza en el parque del palacio real y termina en el gran templo de Homo Demeter, me ofrecían una nueva visión de colosalismo acentuado por los obeliscos de las Victorias y la severa perspectiva con que el conjunto se me presentó apenas salí de la escalera mecánica. De hecho, la avenida parecía una inmensa prolongación de las paralelas que formaban los pasamanos de la escalera y que, en el exterior, incluía las estatuas, los obeliscos y las esfinges, levantadas sobre pilares macizos y que representaban, invariablemente, rasgos de clamorosa masculinidad, exagerada aún más por el león reglamentario que servía de cuerpo. Todas tenían una altura dos veces superior a la de las casas más altas de la ciudad, e incluso eran más elevadas que las agujas desafiantes de las torres de una sociedad bancaria con evidentes reminiscencias de catedral gótica.

Detrás de las esfinges, en un ambiente iluminado por antorchas de un tamaño anormal pero que ya empezaba a parecerme corriente en todas las iluminaciones del Mundo Macho, brotaba una multitud abrumadora de templetes, que tan pronto evocaban el románico como el griego dórico o el barroco vienés, y numerosos edificios civiles, además de los palacios de los más ricos personajes de la ciudad; y surgían por doquier palmeras y magnolios perfectamente organizados, araucarias, cactos y helechos gigantes, plácidos olmos que rodeaban, en algún espacio verde, enormes fuentes talladas en los muros de algún edificio de formas cúbicas o trapezoidales...

Este impresionante paseo, denominado Vía del Harén de Homo Demeter (cuya grandeza, según pude apreciar después, sólo podía compararse a la Vía Sacra y al Forum Imperial), conducía directamente al gran templo, cuyo ingreso sólo estaba permitido al «pueblo fuerte», que incluye las jerarquías más importantes de Lur, empezando por la Iglesia y terminando por los artesanos. De hecho, el «pueblo débil», las categorías inferiores al artesanado, sólo podía ver la curiosa manifestación de Homo Demeter el día de la Fiesta del Harén, cuando la divinidad monta en su barca dorada y se desplaza hasta ese templo desde su residencia oficial, situada más allá de las murallas.

Mientras avanzábamos por aquella Vía sumamente concurrida (yo iba recostado en el interior de una basterna recamada de damasco rojo y con las cortinas corridas, pues el pueblo sólo puede ver a Nebjeperura una vez al año; Astor, como buen soldado, me escoltaba a caballo), mientras la multitud se arrodillaba a nuestro paso, comprendí que ningún espectáculo, ninguna manifestación de titanismo, superaría, o podría igualar siquiera al espectáculo que constituían los jardines, el gentío, las esfinges y, finalmente, la gran mole del templo tallado en la roca viva y que cerraba la avenida, allá al fondo.

Miedo y sorpresa. O espanto y extrañeza. Añada usted sinónimos. Cuantos quiera. Cualquiera que fuese la adjetivación, allí había una mezcla de sensaciones que me impulsaban a detener todo intento de explicarme la realidad, de reducirla a términos racionales. De repente, el universo, antes increíble, suntuoso y a la vez brutal, sólo representaba una gran incógnita: ¿de dónde había salido, cuáles eran sus orígenes, qué causa podía explicar la enorme amalgama de historias y estilos que contenía?

Pero estaba demasiado ebrio para razonar en términos adecuados. Y lo peor era que ignoraba de qué droga.

Siempre a caballo, Astor iba informándome acerca de la avenida que recorríamos mientras peatones, literas y cuadrigas se apartaban apresuradamente para cedernos el paso. Yo permanecía detrás de las cortinas de muselina azul, que me protegían de la mirada de los demás sin impedirme la visión de palacios, esfinges, templos y árboles raros que íbamos dejando atrás, entre aquella multitud que era siempre del género masculino y en su gran mayoría exhibía, desnuda, la parte inferior del cuerpo.

En un instante determinado se me ocurrió preguntar a Astor dónde estaban las mujeres del país; y él, introduciendo la cabeza por las cortinas, sonrió de una forma tan irónica como insinuante.

—¿Eres un bromista nato, o sólo finges, monseñor? ¡Ah, dioses, dioses! Si lo eres, deberías disimularlo por cortesía hacia tu pobre servidor. En caso contrario, ¿qué ganas con fingir lo que no eres...? ¿Aún no has comprendido, monseñor, que te encuentras en la capital del Mundo Macho?

Por supuesto, lo había comprendido. A partir del momento en que recobré la conciencia de mí mismo, dispuse de todos los momentos, de todas las presencias humanas que necesitaba para constatar sin dudas ni interrupciones que había ido a caer en un lugar donde el macho era el rey. Y, sin embargo, esto solo no bastaba para hacerme suponer que la presencia de la hembra se hallase excluida, incluso proscrita...

¿Cuál era el papel de la mujer en el Mundo Macho? ¿Sería posible que la única que vi hasta entonces, la que encontramos en la cueva huyendo con el joven de la cabeza rasurada, fuese sólo un espejismo, una aparición de mi delirio en un momento y una angustia en que todos los espejismos hubiesen sido posibles? De ser real, ¿dónde estaba la mujer? ¿Dónde, en caso contrario, el espejismo?

Pero el espectáculo que yo debía presidir aquella noche no iba a tolerar preguntas de este tipo, y la corriente de ignorancia que me había arrastrado hasta entonces, seguiría deslizándome no bien Astor me ayudase a bajar de la litera, repitiendo una reverencia que fue imitada por todos los presentes, y me ofreciese el brazo para guiarme entre una gran cantidad de triclinios, profusamente ocupados, hasta llegar a una tribuna adornada con cortinajes de lamé y desde la cual se divisaba una gran parte de los jardines pertenecientes al templo donde debía celebrarse la ceremonia.

El parque era un recinto cerrado; estaba limitado, de una parte, por la montaña abrupta que contenía el templo, y, de la otra, por las rejas que nos separaban de la avenida. Además, era un recinto que nada tenía que envidiar, en frondosidad, a los jardines del palacio real. Aquí, sin embargo, los árboles podían ser salvajes como en las montañas; y las estatuas iluminadas que sobresalían por encima de los matorrales adquirían el dudoso aspecto de una amenaza basada exclusivamente en el poder supremo de la belleza. Manifestaciones, a escala inmensa, de una belleza y un temple que tenían su principio y fin en la figura masculina; titanes de mármol, bronce o alabastro que representaban no sólo invenciones típicas del Mundo Macho —es decir, de la mitología que le es genuina—, sino copias exactas y aumentadas del Laocoonte griego, del David y el Baco florentinos, del Apolo de Belvedere, y una muy cuidada rememoración de aquel apoteósico Celta herido que, según averigüé cuando ya conocía el gran secreto del Mundo Macho, se conserva en un museo de Roma.

Otras estatuas de notoria nombradía se hallaban repartidas por los jardines: discóbolos, aurigas, Marte todopoderoso y, en fin, un Sebastián más concebido a la manera pagana que acorde a los cánones de la ortodoxia católica, pues su desnudez estaba acentuada hasta la exhibición del pene, era descaradamente atlético y se hallaba en una postura de sufrimiento que aportaba un pathos muy particular, parecido al placer.

Entonces, Astor se detuvo con gran respeto y dijo:

—Éste es Epsamón.

Miré y volví a mirar atentamente al coloso bajo cuyo tormento paseaban, bebían o se tendían en triclinios los invitados que aguardaban el comienzo de la ceremonia. El cuerpo del santo, retorcido bajo la lluvia de flechas, se emparentaba con el Marte dominador, y contrastaba con la ligereza, casi femenina, de aquel suave Mercurio, algo burlón, cuyo pie alígero parecía dispuesto a perderse por el espacio de un momento a otro...

Astor se mostró orgulloso al repetir:

—Epsamón Divino. Epura Epsamón. Nuestro Dueño.

—Imposible. ¿Me has tomado por tonto? Es san Sebastián.

Entonces Astor levantó el brazo y, a distancia, trazó el perfil de la estatua en el aire. Desde mi perspectiva, parecía como si Astor acariciase los rasgos del mártir.

—Sólo Nuestro Amo podía salir con vida de un tormento semejante. De todos los titanes de Lur, sólo él podía sobrellevar la venganza de los herejes, sobrevivir a los sufrimientos que le infligieron al hacerle prisionero, y seguir siendo tan arrojado como antes, tan poderoso como siempre... Sólo él, de entre todos nosotros, podía volver a ser el león que nos guía, y sin el cual, monseñor, quién sabe qué sería de Lur.

Y al reparar en mi expresión, añadió:

—Por ello, siguiendo su alto ejemplo, todos los jóvenes de Lur aprenden a sufrir los más terribles tormentos; y aunque al principio les duela, al cabo todos se sienten felices de ser adiestrados en la agonía, porque saben que de este modo se acercan a la madurez...

—¡No es natural! —exclamé, ya en los límites de la desesperación—. ¡Todo eso es demasiado absurdo!

Pero ninguna perspectiva era natural en el Mundo Macho; o, por lo menos, no a mis ojos. La misma dimensión ciclópea de esculturas que, por otra parte, me sabía de memoria, no sería justificada en cualquier otro lugar donde la proporción y la estructura no hubiesen sido consideradas, como aquí, cánones que pueden variar de acuerdo con la necesidad de dotar a la raza de la máxima belleza y la máxima potencia. Y yo mismo, acostumbrado a un mundo que ha perdido, desde hace siglos, el gusto por la grandeza, me empeñaba en considerar las palabras de Astor de acuerdo con la pequeñez que yo conocía, recordaba y representaba, en lugar de ceñirme al hiperbólico titanismo con cuyas constantes me obligarían a familiarizarme a partir de entonces.

—¿Y ese David? —pregunté. Y hubiera dado cualquier cosa por saber qué secreto intercambio cultural pudo cruzarse entre la Galleria dell'Academia y el Mundo Macho. Pero Astor cercenó la posibilidad de cualquier nueva pregunta.

—Son las divinidades del Mundo Macho —dijo en

un tono extremadamente seco—. Los dioses del pathos; los señores de la fuerza, el dominio y la belleza. De todo cuanto es grande, poderoso e invencible. Y Epsamón es su representación viviente sobre la Tierra. Y tú, preguntón excesivo, mejor harías sacrificando a los dioses en agradecimiento por haber sido el elegido entre todos los jóvenes hermosos.

¡Al diablo, profesor!; ¡al diablo él y sus motivos de agradecimiento! Un garrotazo capaz de aturdir a un elefante; dos días colgado cabeza abajo; mi cuerpo quemado por el sol del desierto; una violación que, para colmo de males, se efectuó con un hierro candente y, encima, el rufián osaba insinuarme que ofreciera sacrificios de agradecimiento a dioses desconocidos.

Me disponía a responderle con palabras que posiblemente faltan en las cartillas de su país, cuando sonó un gong descomunal situado en la primera plataforma del templo, y todos los invitados se levantaron de los triclinios y se arrodillaron al paso de un séquito presidido por el Sumo Sacerdote de aquel culto. Descendía el séquito las escalinatas, y al llegar junto a mí unos novicios empezaron a rociarme con incienso y perfume de sándalo, mientras los invitados volvían a arrodillarse entonando una especie de canto gregoriano, pero con palabras pertenecientes a su extraña lengua. De hecho, el único que permanecía de pie era Astor, quien tendió el brazo hacia mí, y, siempre sonriente, exhibió el dorso de la mano, esperando que yo depositara la mía para guiarme entre el pasadizo formado por los triclinios; un pasadizo que terminaba en la tribuna imperial.

No se requerían excesivas luces para comprender que, siendo yo tan respetado, incluso adorado, estaba muy lejos de correr ningún riesgo inmediato; así pues, me dejé conducir por Astor mientras los sacerdotes, altísimos y enjutos, tocados con pelucas de varios pisos y de todos los colores, seguían nuestro itinerario entonando el salmo que, en el Mundo Macho, suele preceder a las Fiestas de la Purificación.

En la tribuna había dos triclinios, y yo ocupé uno de ellos. Apenas me hube tendido (siempre siguiendo las indicaciones de Astor acerca del porte que debía adoptar), mi repulsivo guardián levantó los brazos en señal de invocación y gritó: «¡Nebjeperura!», que, por la unión del prefijo «Nbj» al concepto «nepu-ra», significa «Co-Divinidad sobre la Tierra», puesto que, en la lengua imperial «nepu-ra» significa, precisamente, «única divinidad sobre la Tierra».

Esperaba que Astor se tendería en el otro triclinio; pero no fue así, pues hacerlo equivaldría a un sacrilegio. Era el asiento único, sagrado e intocable de Epsamón, tan rico y maravilloso que, aun siendo riquísimo el triclinio de cada invitado, el de Él sobrepasaba cualquier descripción en lujo y buen gusto. Otro tanto sucedía con la banqueta que Astor ocupó a mi lado, dado su privilegio de capitán de la guardia palatina. Pero antes de sentarse, profirió por tres veces el grito triunfal, y siempre fue coreado por la aclamación de mis súbditos. A continuación, el Sumo Sacerdote, que había llegado al pie de la tribuna, consagró la ceremonia a la gloria del ausente Epsamón y a sus triunfos en la Guerra Santa; y estas dedicaciones coincidieron con una nueva apoteosis, mezcla de cánticos, vítores y fanfarria ejecutada por los soldados que, en doble hilera, acababan de aparecer en la pronaos del templo.

Y toda la avenida de las esfinges, que se perdía a lo lejos, más allá del parque, hacia la colina del palacio real, iluminóse de repente con miles de luces mientras enormes reflectores dibujaban, sobre la oscuridad del cielo, una gran cruz gamada que fue acogida con grandes aplausos al tiempo que brotaba de los pedestales de las estatuas una humareda de diferentes colores, que esparcían los mismos perfumes con que yo era rociado. Y, entonces, Astor se me aproximó más de lo que el protocolo permitía, y, en voz baja y tierna, de forma que sólo yo pudiera oírle, me dirigió la primera palabra en la lengua de Lur. Una palabra que, si usted me lo permite, no voy a traducirle, por pudor.

—*Ashnar.*

Con los efluvios de mil colores, los cánticos iniciáticos, los vítores, las luces, las hogueras, los reflectores proyectados hacia el cielo, se formó una suerte de niebla entre cuyos recovecos aún podía entrever diversos cortejos que descendían solemnemente las escalinatas del templo. Eran hombres, por supuesto, pero sus testas, teñidas de oro, plata y lapislázuli, correspondían a ciervos, toros, águilas, guepardos, e incluso aves del paraíso con plumas de chillona policromía, que se arrastraban por los peldaños y temblaban al viento o se agitaban según el ritmo del descenso.

Detrás de este cortejo venían los grupos buitre, león, leopardo y elefante, cuyas diferencias físicas, al igual que el desarrollo de sus órganos genitales, estaban de acuerdo con la potencia de los animales que representaban. Estos individuos transportaban cinco bandejas colosales, muy bien adornadas con flores y piedras preciosas. Y si bien, desde abajo, mi visibilidad era harto imperfecta, es decir, no me permitía ver los manjares, cabía suponer que eran deliciosos, tanto si estaban refinados como si se servían en estado salvaje.

Debo decir que, al reconocerlos, no entendí por qué razón cada bandeja transportaba a un adolescente semiquemado (si no se interpretase como humor negro, diría que semirrustidos; pero deberé decirlo de cualquier modo, porque lo estaban); y aún entendía menos por qué iban adornados con uvas, ciruelas, ananás, dátiles, patatas, e incluso *ratatoulle*; pero al buscar la mirada de Astor no necesité esperar la respuesta.

La repentina comprensión de las características de la ceremonia me impulsaba a gritar de terror, y tal vez de asco prematuro; pero un grito inesperado del propio Astor me hizo enmudecer. Acudieron dos soldados, que cambiaron unas palabras con mi guardián, y éste, indignado, les gritó algo que sonaba a una orden más que terminante; de manera que los dos partieron a cumplirla lo antes posible, y Astor se encaró con los sacerdotes y los invitados para rogarles un poco de paciencia, que le fue concedida, pero no sin que algún bacante delatara una cierta impaciencia, llegándose hasta los muchachitos para examinarlos, atados como estaban entre los racimos de uvas, las ciruelas y las piedras preciosas, aguardando su turno para la muerte. Y esperaban con los ojos muy abiertos por el espanto, llorando, mordiéndose los labios, temblando incluso, a pesar de que las parrillas les habían dejado dorados.

Si, como respuesta a las preguntas que aquella situación me planteaba no conseguía hallar explicación alguna, menos aún me la proporcionaba el inaudito silencio de las víctimas. ¿Por qué no chillaban, en su dolor atroz? ¿Tan valientes eran, que podían soportarlo en silencio?

Astor intentó explicarme aquella mudez, describiéndome una etapa anterior al ágape, y que consistía en cortar la lengua de los adolescentes para que sus chillidos —los cuales, él mismo lo reconocía, serían «incluso probables»— no echaran a perder la grandeza litúrgica del momento y la placidez digestiva de los bacantes.

Así fue como supe que la Fiesta de la Purificación contaba con diversas etapas esenciales, y que el joven que semanas atrás intentara escapar del Mundo Macho debería sufrirlas todas, una tras otra, en presencia de los invitados. Y ellos aceptarían de muy buen grado la preparación en público de un manjar sumamente agradable. Pues quien más, quien menos, tenía sus nociones culinarias.

Al verme palidecer, Astor comentó que probablemente me sentiría un poco incómodo antes de integrarme por completo a las costumbres del Mundo Macho; pero que, de cualquier modo, no debía darlo a entender en aquel momento y lugar, pues no sería cortés de mi parte sorprender a los invitados con una repulsión que, al mismo tiempo, les provocaría una cierta violencia por el solo hecho de sentirse muy superiores a mí.

—Por otra parte —añadió Astor, en tono despreciativo—, sería el sentimiento propio de cualquier persona civilizada al ver que alguien tiene la debilidad de compadecer a los débiles, los deformes, las hembras, la miseria... Es decir: la escoria del Mundo Macho.

Una mirada más minuciosa me explicó las teorías de Astor y, por extensión, la ley tácita del derecho a existir en el Mundo Macho. Los sacrificados de aquella noche serían, evidentemente, una escoria de aquel esplendor: imposibilitados para existir en una raza que se quiere perfecta, los adolescentes rustidos padecían taras físicas evidentes —y las que yo no podía percibir, por insignificantes, me las indicó Astor—; taras que podían ser un dedo más corto que otro, una mirada torcida, la cabeza desproporcionada, una oreja demasiado grande y, por supuesto, los hombros o el pecho estrechos (sabemos que las leyes estéticas del Mundo Macho son taxativas en lo referente a la anchura mínima de hombros y pecho de sus súbditos). Por otra parte, también era una falta gravísima, condenada desde muy antiguo, cualquier intento de huida. Y es importante remarcar que, en tal caso, ni siquiera la perfección física más indiscutible puede salvar al reo de la muerte.

Porque entre los adolescentes, inmolados en razón de sus mínimos defectos físicos y raciales, sobresalía la figura del joven rebelde de la cueva. Él era la víctima que los sacerdotes se habían olvidado de cocinar, creyendo que el primer sacrificio de la estación del Crecimiento del Río, cuando todo se purifica, sólo se reservaba a los impuros de mañana (es decir, a los adolescentes que es necesario sacrificar hoy mismo para evitar la progresión del defecto). Y era precisamente el fugitivo quien más se resistía, debatiéndose con todas sus fuerzas, pero en vano, ante los soldados que le arrastraban hacia una gran hoguera encendida entre las estatuas de Marte y de Epsamón-Sebastián. Era él, sí, rebelde hasta el último momento, rompiéndose las venas en su forcejeo contra las cadenas que ceñían sus muñecas, aullando hasta que fue definitivamente atado de pies y manos a cuatro cuerdas que, tensadas desde lo alto de ambas estatuas, le dejaron colgado en rígida cruz de aspa mientras mi repulsivo guardián, ignorando el último aullido que pudo lanzar el mancebo antes de que los sacerdotes le cortasen la lengua (esto provocó un abundante río de sangre, que salía de la boca y chorreaba cuerpo abajo), mandaba a los sacerdotes y a los esclavos que empezasen a servir los impuros ya condimentados.

La luminotecnia, de rayos extremadamente espectaculares, y la gran variedad de colores del humo que flotaba ante las estatuas, daban a la escena el aspecto de un sueño de orate más que la apariencia litúrgica que se pretendía. Pero cualquier posibilidad de acogerme a la embriaguez como evasión, de llegar a convencerme de que todo aquello era una pesadilla, queda excluida por completo apenas recuerdo de manera inequívoca mi aceptación de las exigencias del Mundo Macho y de la necesidad de ser, allí, el Nebjeperura.

No, profesor: ni pesadilla, ni locura, ni nada que se le

parezca. Insisto en que abandoné el opio cuando empecé a hablar. Olvidemos, pues, esta suposición. Estoy sereno. Quiero ser objetivo, aunque no lo consiga completamente. Intento describirle un mundo, una realidad externa con todos los detalles posibles; y si de vez en cuando mezclo en la narración el recuerdo de mis sensaciones, deberá usted perdonarme atendiendo a que es profunda exigencia del recuerdo lo imposible de una objetividad total, y que, por otra parte, el recuerdo en sí mismo favorece cualquier desliz hacia el delirio. Porque yo siento, profesor: no soy de piedra. Ni entonces ni ahora. Tenía, y tengo, todos los sentidos en guardia.

Por otra parte, el horror no se olvida fácilmente.

El horror acompaña durante mucho, muchísimo tiempo...

CADA MORDISCO de los comensales, cada contorsión desesperada de los cuerpos que agonizaban en las bandejas, correspondía a un incremento de la iluminación a lo largo del paisaje extendido entre el templo y el palacio real. Y la música, en su insistente percusión, había alcanzado un crescendo capaz de enloquecer.

Los sacerdotes más jóvenes, los de la cabeza de bestia débil, depositaban sobre las mesas bandejas que contenían a los muchachitos impuros, y, mientras tanto, una *chorus line* formada por bailarines núbiles, teñidos de verde y púrpura, empezó a evolucionar alrededor del fugitivo, quien permanecía tenso a causa de las cuerdas que tiraban de su cuerpo; acto seguido, le arrancaron la piel, requisito indispensable para una perfecta higienización de los manjares.

¡Delicioso grado de *civiltà*! Mientras las tenazas de oro se deslizaban por los músculos tensados de aquel cuerpo doliente, algunos invitados empezaron a comer uvas, ciruelas o el bambú que servía de relleno al vientre abierto de los impuros; de hecho, el muslo del más joven —un apuesto púber que, sin embargo, era cojo— presentaba diversos cortes sangrientos, profundos pozos que delataban la ausencia de la carne que ya masticaban con suma gula los ocupantes de los triclinios más cercanos.

Los incensarios despedían vapores rojos, azules, verdes o amarillos; en los primeros peldaños del templo, las trompetas resonaban con estruendo creciente, las estatuas de las divinidades del Mundo Macho palidecían al lado de la muy barroca manifestación de Cobra-Ra, gran monstruo de oro que representa al Sol; la avenida de las esfinges parecía más inmensa que nunca; el pueblo débil confinado más allá de las rejas, celebraba verbenas, acudía a los mercados y paseaba de acuerdo con su forma de celebrar la Fiesta...

Una vez arrancada la piel del fugitivo con rapidez sorprendente, untaron su cuerpo con aceite y lo ataron a un palo que fue colocado sobre dos horquillas levantadas a cada lado de un montón de brasas; así, ya en la broqueta y girando sobre las llamas, el cuerpo empezó a calentarse y, poco a poco, fue tomando un agradable color tostado. Mientras tanto, los invitados cortaban más carne de los cuerpos de los impuros, pero sin afectar a sus órganos vitales, pues formaba parte esencial del pathos exigido en la ceremonia que los sacrificados permanecieran vivos hasta el último momento; conscientes de que eran devorados. Y yo, recordando que el fugitivo no iba solo cuando intentó ganar la salida del Mundo Macho, pregunté a Astor qué habían hecho a la mujer.

—Por el momento, la Bestia es sagrada —dijo él sin apartar la mirada de un niño que aún no había sido tocado—. Es sagrada porque este traidor, antes de decidir la fuga, la dejó preñada. Y hasta que la criatura nazca y podamos saber si es macho o hembra, la Bestia no podrá recibir su castigo.

—¿Y si la criatura nace hembra?

—Vivirá con sus hermanas de deshonor: en las cuevas rojas, cerca del desierto. Y, al llegar a la pubertad, será el miserable coño en cuyas tinieblas el macho engendrará hijos que puedan continuar la gloria del Imperio. Como ha sido desde el principio de todas las historias, monseñor.

¡Enigmas, enigmas, enigmas! ¡Siempre el absurdo de los enigmas!

Decidido a desenigmatizar un poco la situación, pregunté si la fugitiva correría la misma suerte que su compañero (cuyo cuerpo era ya tan sólo una gran herida, muy requemada); pero Astor, sin dejar de vigilar la bandeja que contenía al niño desconocido, soltó una gran carcajada con la cual parecía tildarme de panoli, y exclamó:

—¡Estás completamente loco, monseñor! ¿Desde cuándo una hembra merece la misma suerte que un macho..., aunque sea un macho tarado? ¿Quién, de todos nosotros, sería capaz de ultrajar a los Dioses de la Fuerza imponiéndoles el sacrificio, no me negarás que desagradable, de seres tan débiles?

Reconocerá usted que todo aquello era cada vez más difícil de entender; y el despropósito se complicaba aún más si recordamos que, durante mi tiempo en el Mundo Macho, cualquier referencia a la Bestia Llamada Hembra había despertado, en el reducido auditorio que se me permitía tener, un sentimiento que no era tan sólo de ironía, sino incluso de espanto en algunos casos. La única hembra, y aun sucia y enfermiza, que me había sido dado ver era aquella que, a pesar de merecer una pena tan cruel como la de su acompañante (que se estremecía mientras le hacían girar sobre el fuego), no podía ser castigada porque era demasiado débil; y, al mismo tiempo, no era tan débil como para no merecer un tratamiento sagrado a causa del hijo que había engendrado en ella, precisamente, un súbdito del Mundo Macho.

Entre tantas dudas, quedaba una que no podía dejar de convertir en pregunta:

—Y dime, Astor: ¿cómo hacen el amor los súbditos del Mundo Macho? ¿Entre ellos, tal vez? Espero que me entiendas: hablo de las relaciones carnales... ¿Utilizáis a los esclavos, los soldados, o...?

Astor se escandalizó enormemente de mi suposición:

—Anda con cuidado —me dijo—; anda con mucho cuidado, pues la idea que acabas de insinuar es herética. Hablas de prácticas totalmente reprobables, porque atentan contra los dioses, que quieren la fuerza y no la debilidad. Y nada debilita tanto el cuerpo, nada le resta tanta salud y belleza, como el inútil desgaste del sexo. Por ello, los súbditos del Mundo Macho sólo se desgastan una vez al año, precisamente en las Jornadas de la Reproducción, y aun para cumplir con un deber, que es el de crear vida, no el de entregarse a inútiles goces.

De cuantas sorpresas venía recibiendo, la de conocer la represión colectiva de un mundo que tenía como ley andar con el pene al aire, tuvo el valor de dejarme tranquilizado. Porque era obvio que si el sexo estaba prohibido en el Mundo Macho, no tenía ya razones para temer que me hubiesen llevado al palacio de Epsamón para satisfacer sus devaneos reales.

Ahora bien: si yo no estaba destinado a ser el amante del gran señor, si toda aquella carpintería no correspondía en absoluto a una sociedad de pederastas, ¿cuál sería mi situación en el Mundo Macho, con qué serie de fetichismos extraños sustituían aquellos hombres las necesidades básicas que su religión y su gobierno habían convertido en tabú?

Pero, si tiene usted en cuenta que en la Universidad de Lur había un gran número de estudiantes de Derecho que se esforzaban en memorizar las Leyes, los Códigos y los Usos del Mundo Macho, comprenderá cuán anormal resultaría que yo entendiera tanta sapiencia recién llegado al país. Sin embargo, Astor no pensaba igual, ya que mis preguntas provocaron en él una nueva mirada de compasión y aquella sonrisa —¡siempre la misma!— con la cual los adultos suelen fingir que perdonan generosamente la dorada inconsciencia de los jóvenes.

Mientras tanto, el fugitivo era conducido lejos de las miradas de los invitados, pero cerca de las nuestras, y Astor me obligó a contemplar, no sólo el momento en que su cuerpo, encendido como una brasa, era atado sobre una bandeja, sino, incluso, cuando uno de los sacerdotes lo abría en canal y, después de extraerle los intestinos, rellenaba las entrañas con ciruelas y almendras, lo cosía con una aguja de proporciones nada normales y, como todos los objetos del ritual, de oro. Yo me tambaleaba. Doquiera que mirase encontraba la misma visión de carnes cortadas y sangre goteando por los labios pintarrajeados de los comensales, mientras los músicos de cuerpos teñidos de azul y testa de pez-espada ejecutaban madrigales renacentistas, cantados por efebos teñidos a su vez de púrpura y con la cabeza en forma de paloma.

Ya cosido el fugitivo, lanzados a cualquier rincón de la improvisada barbacoa los intestinos que le habían extraído, Astor ordenó que se le sirviese, convenientemente adobado con especias de las provincias orientales. Seguidamente, hizo callar a los músicos y, con los brazos en alto dirigidos hacia las estatuas, anunció que había llegado la hora de que le sirviesen a su propio hijo, llamado Sató. Y cuando él mismo me lo tradujo al francés, expresé un estupor que, a causa de su habitualidad, ya no escandalizaba a nadie. Pero pedí más explicaciones. Especialmente sobre aquella paternidad que el repulsivo Astor me revelaba de repente.

—Epsamón no quiere errores en el acto de engendrar la vida. Las divinidades del Mundo Macho no suplican la perfección: la exigen. Y castigan cualquier error, cualquier desliz que traspase el supremo orden establecido. Los mismos dioses que velan por nuestra grandeza aceptarían el sacrificio de un hijo propio si fuera menester sacrificarlo. Dime, pues, monseñor: ¿no hemos de aceptar nosotros?

Los jóvenes cabeza-halconados acababan de llegar a la imperial tribuna y, en medio de la expectación general, depositaron otra enorme bandeja a nuestros pies. Allí, rodeado por todo tipo de frutas salvajes que puedan considerarse deliciosas, yacía el niño, sujeto con cordeles de oro, asado como los otros y de una extraordinaria belleza física, sólo alterada por el pecado de ser estrábico. Este defecto físico le obligaba a mirar de soslayo, por lo cual, en su intenso sufrimiento, no se sabía exactamente si estaba mirando fijamente a su padre por lo de la fuerza de la sangre o se limitaba a expresar su desesperada impotencia.

Todos los rostros de la fiesta, bellos y pintados como máscaras de un carnaval irreal y alucinante, quedaron pendientes de los movimientos de Astor, quien cogió un cuchillo y un tenedor mientras los miembros del niño se ponían en tensión y la otra víctima, el fugitivo, había ya dejado de ser el centro de la atención general para convertirse en un patético salpicón de carne presta a mil pulquérrimos mordiscos.

—¡Aguarda! —exclamé—; oh Astor, te lo ruego..., al menos dime..., asegúrame que tengo razón..., que es imposible que sea hijo tuyo...

—¿Por qué?

—Tú eres muy joven.

—Lo tuve a los catorce años —dijo, encogiéndose de hombros—. Yo cumplí mi deber civil y religioso; él, sin embargo, no ha salido como manda el Mundo Macho.

—Pero..., pero ¿no ves cómo te mira?

—¿Cómo quieres que me mire si es bizco?

—¡Entiéndeme de una vez! Te mira de ese modo porque para un hijo ha de ser terrible que le sacrifique su propio padre... ¡Eso, por lo menos, no podrás negarlo!

—Si sufres por ello, alégrate como corresponde a tu juventud, a tu rango y a la sublimidad de esta ceremonia. Él ignora que yo sea su padre... Si mal no recuerdo, ya te expliqué cómo, al nacer, todas las criaturas van a la Casa de la Vida, y pasan a ser del Estado y de la Historia... ¡Ay monseñor, deberías anotar las lecciones en un cuaderno, porque observo que tienes muy poca memoria!

Protesté, chillé y estuve a punto de llorar; pero todo fue en vano. Astor se preparaba a cortar la carne del hijo.

—Yo lo engendré..., y tal vez no puse bastante esmero.

Apoyó el tenedor contra el estómago y con la otra mano utilizó el cuchillo para efectuar un corte profundo y largo. El niño intentaba encogerse, en busca de un alivio relativo; pero las cadenas doradas con que lo habían sujetado le impedían hacerlo; abría la boca, se mordía los labios, pero al carecer de lengua le era imposible proferir un solo grito. Finalmente, cuando el estómago quedó abierto de arriba abajo, salieron dos palomos colocados en lugar de las entrañas; y los pájaros volaron muy alto, mientras los invitados gritaban, bebían y terminaban de comerse a los donceles que precedieron al hijo de Astor.

Mil veces supliqué que cesara la ceremonia; rodé por el suelo, sobre las alfombras de terciopelo rojo y las pieles de tigre y oso. Ocultando la cabeza entre las manos; gritaba «¡Basta! ¡basta! ¡basta!»; y no cesaba de gritar y de golpear el suelo con los puños cerrados, invocando a cualquier deidad que no perteneciera al Olimpo del Mundo Macho...

Pero Astor ya masticaba la carne de su hijo, y tenía los labios enrojecidos por la sangre que le goteaba por la barbilla, y reía como un loco, con la fuerza de sus veinticinco años, con su furia desbocada, con toda su maldita masculinidad.

Entonces me dijo:

—Tú has de dar el ejemplo, Nebjeperura. De hecho, tú debieras haber sido el primero...

Y sus palabras contenían, velada, una carga tan fuerte de amenaza que tuve miedo. Tanto temí que mi contención no correspondiese a lo que ellos esperaban del elegido de Epsamón, que me levanté muy lentamente hasta alcanzar el repugnante bocado que Astor me ofrecía.

Al principio sentí el dulce sabor de la sangre, y al instante, casi simultáneamente, la tibieza del rustido y un asco que no conseguía vencer: era el sabor insólito de un pene. Y cuando en el tiempo venidero llegara a acostumbrarme, incluso a desear aquel sabor, sabría que el de aquel niño había sido suculento. Pero entonces no tenía perspectiva suficiente para apreciarlo.

De este modo entré en la comunión que me iniciaba a un nuevo misterio del Mundo Macho. Y mientras masticaba el pene proscrito, volví a perder el mundo de vista, me desmayé entre los gritos dionisíacos, los cánticos, el olor a incienso, el frenético vuelo de los palomos que habían salido del hijo de Astor, y la música de un arpa, suave y lejana...

LLEGADOS A ESTE PUNTO, y dado que su mirada de estupor no puede deberse solamente a la fuerza del opio, empiezo a entender que no me he explicado demasiado bien. Si no quiero arriesgarme a que vuelvan a tomarme por loco, me conviene colocar inmediatamente algunos puntos sobre más de una i. La continua sorpresa de la Vida Nueva nunca consonaba con explicaciones inmediatas de Astor o de cualquier otro a quien me aproximara con ganas de saber. Yo conservaba el impacto del primer espanto, aquí, en Minia; y este mismo impacto era el que me guiaba sin tregua. La retahíla de paisajes, efectos decorativos, colores y ruidos, vestidos y desnudeces, sangre y vino que se desarrollaba a mi alrededor desde que despertase en el desierto, favorecía muy poco la entrega a una lucidez, por pequeña que fuese. Y, por otra parte, cualquier pregunta o protesta que pudiese dirigir a Astor sólo recibían, como respuesta, aquella sonrisa cortés pero severa, dispuesta a servirme, pero despreciativa y en absoluto propensa a una limosna de comprensión.

Me habían sido impuestos una serie de deberes dictados por una civilización que no era la mía, pero de la cual yo era príncipe. Cierto que, en días futuros, Astor o los preceptores encargados de mi educación me irían aclarando algunos enigmas, acostumbrándome a una apreciación y a una obediencia a las reglas; pero, a pesar de todo, yo estaba convencido de que siempre habría un último secreto del Mundo Macho que no me sería revelado y cuya ignorancia me consumiría día y noche. Pero este secreto, que era la verdad sobre los orígenes del Mundo Macho, sólo lo poseía Epsamón, amo y señor de todas las verdades; y mi destino debería ser, en este punto y para siempre, la ignorancia total, por más que la acumulación de elementos externos como las costumbres, el mobiliario, la arquitectura, los vestidos, el *atrezzo* en general de aquel gran escenario, me hiciesen concebir unas hipótesis que, por otra parte, sólo conseguían sumirme en una creciente confusión.

Pero esa composición de lugar corresponde a lo inexplicable de mi narración; y yo me había propuesto ordenar sólo las cosas que puedan formar para usted una imagen concreta y coherente del Mundo Macho y su amenaza latente, dejando aparte todos los elementos no resueltos o imposibles de resolver; y quiero cumplir mis propósitos, aunque luego no sepamos la forma de situar en el orden de la lógica estos elementos caóticos pero que, entre sí, y dentro del concepto reconocido (la verdad aceptada, de antemano, de que el Mundo Macho existe) tienen una coherencia total.

Así pues, intentando organizar mi progresiva comprensión, alejándola del caos en que me había instalado —y que, evidentemente, me codiciaba—, establezco unos primeros puntos de información y de conocimiento a partir de los cuales, profesor, podrán ser entendidas muchas cosas de aquella nueva realidad. A pesar de que ya empiezo a olvidarme de su presencia, profesor...; es como si le ignorase a usted, y a medida que el opio le va adormeciendo, profesor, siento, una vez más —una de tantas—, que hablo para mí solo.

... Me despertó el efebo Avitachí, y sería temprano, porque el sol lucía pálido sobre los parques del palacio y la luz que se filtraba por las ventanas góticas era muy suave. Después, al encontrar a mi alrededor el lujo refinado y los objetos de suma exquisitez que decoraban la estancia, sentí como si la barbarie de anoche hubiese sido una pesadilla..., otra parte, quiero decir, de aquella pesadilla que soportaba desde hacía tantos días y que, de hecho, podía contener tantas partes. La gigantesca cabeza del cisne a modo de baldaquín de mi cama, los paisajes venecianos del techo, las vidrieras ilustradas de las ventanas (en ellas, la repetición del tema Sebastián ya se hacía sospechosa) y, en fin, los numerosos cirios de todos los tamaños instalados en un sinfín de candelabros altísimos, me aproximaban demasiado a visiones artísticas familiares para que pudiesen aterrarme al primer golpe de vista. Después, la sola visión de Avitachí, que esta vez vestía un jubón medieval hasta el vientre y se tocaba con peluca blanca, de paje ochocentista, me recordó todos los cuerpos de la noche, sus intentos de retorno a la naturaleza mediante el desnudo inferior y la entrega a una libertad original del cuerpo que nuestro siglo, nuestra civilización, suelen asociar especialmente con las tribus salvajes. Y la humillación absoluta y, al mismo tiempo, la hostilidad que me demostraba mi esclavo con sólo formularle yo un par de preguntas, contribuían a darme la inequívoca sensación de que entre la pesadilla de anoche y la pesadilla de la mañana sólo se tendía, como zona diferencial, la pausa del sueño.

Mientras los otros esclavos me preparaban el baño en la piscina interior, charca redonda recamada con azulejos negros y abundante en lotos y nenúfares que flotaban sobre un agua sumamente perfumada, se me anunció que Astor había venido a recogerme con el fin de dar juntos un paseo informativo; es decir, que sirviera para ponerme en contacto con algunos elementos de la vida cotidiana del Mundo Macho. Ordené que le hicieran pasar de inmediato, y él obedeció un poco a disgusto porque, a pesar de todas las confianzas y de todas las investiduras, no está bien considerado que Nebjeperura se deje ver en público mientras se baña.

Debo decir, de paso, que nunca conocí baños tan deliciosos como los que tomaba en el palacio de Epsamón. La espuma era prodigiosamente abundante, prodigiosamente rosada, olía a flores exóticas, y dos esclavos me enjabonaban y me daban masajes. Resultaba sumamente exquisito extender la mano y atrapar, entre la espuma, algún nenúfar. La piscina se hallaba instalada en una rotonda cubierta por una cúpula de cristal esmerilado, y al filtrarse por ella la luz del sol se deshacía en un polvillo azul que coloreaba las paredes, las numerosas ánforas de plata y las delicadas cráteras colocadas sobre pedestales de alabastro, entre las cuales se deslizaba una especie de madreselva que sólo se encuentra en Lur y produce una diminuta rosa negra que purifica los interiores con un perfume limonado. También había bancos de mármol negro, y en uno de ellos fue a sentarse Astor, quien de nuevo vestía su uniforme de guardián en servicio activo. Al servicio exclusivo de mi persona, ya que viene a cuento recordarlo.

Mi imaginación estaba a punto de estallar por la cantidad de preguntas que hubiese deseado formular; al mismo tiempo era consciente de que mi privilegiada posición en el palacio de Epsamón me permitía una actitud de exigencias extremas hacia quien, contradicción extrañísima, no dejaba de ser mi carcelero. De este modo, pensé que en vez de perder el tiempo suplicando información como prisionero, me convenía empezar a tratar a la gente con la actitud adecuada a Nebjeperura. Puesto que me habían investido de tal, sería para cualquier cosa menos para ser humilde. Es decir: me convenía utilizar la severidad, el tono despótico y el desprecio hacia los demás que son la actitud más adecuada al Co-Divino.

—Hace dos días que aguardo tus explicaciones —dije a Astor mientras los esclavos me secaban con toallas de satén. Y procuraba que mis palabras tuviesen un tono despótico.

—¿Qué quieres decir, Nebjeperura?

En labios de Astor, era obvio que el tratamiento oficial empezaba a favorecer mi situación.

—Tus explicaciones y tus excusas por... por... la insolencia con que he sido tratado, naturalmente.

—¿Insolencia, monseñor? Que no llegue a oídos de Epsamón. El simple hecho de pensar que has sido maltratado lo más mínimo, bastaría para mandarme al tormento. Así pues, espero que me ahorres una acusación directa y, en ausencia de Epsamón Divino, te limites a transmitirme cualquier queja que tengas. Hazme cualquier pregunta como la que ahora te hago yo: ¿insolencia, por qué y de qué manera?

Intenté aclarárselo. De hecho, yo había utilizado la palabra «insolencia» como podía utilizar la de «crueldad». Pero no era el momento de echarme atrás. No era el momento de vacilar. Así pues, convertí mi actitud temerosa e indecisa de anoche en otra de severidad porque no había sido contestada ninguna de mis preguntas, y se me había dejado en un ayuno total de «porqués» y «cómos».

—Si ésta es tu única queja, monseñor, todo quedará solucionado dentro de breves momentos. De hecho, he venido a recogerte para llevarte a conocer nuestras formas de vida. Si me hubieses dejado hablar, me habrías ahorrado esta humillación...

Di un paso en falso:

—Yo no quería humillarte, Astor...

—Sin embargo lo has conseguido. Y te lo agradezco.

¿Tanto podían cambiar las cosas en una sola noche?, y ni siquiera en una noche completa, sino a partir del momento, ya avanzado, en que me dejaron desmayado en mi lecho de cisne. Cualquiera fuese la explicación o la situación, Astor se había arrodillado ante mí y —lo crea usted o no— me besaba los pies. Que un joven tan alto y fuerte ofrezca tan increíbles muestras de acatamiento, no es algo que ocurra todos los días; de manera que, impulsado por el mal efecto que me producía, le di un puntapié en la boca. Él, por toda respuesta, apoyó la frente contra el suelo y expresó de nuevo su apasionado agradecimiento.

—¡Levántate! —exclamé—. ¡Levántate de una vez, perro! Y, si quieres serme útil, te ordeno me expliques inmediatamente a qué viene la extravagante alegría que me expresas...

—La alegría, la felicidad de ser humillado por Nebjeperura no tiene precio —dijo Astor levantándose del suelo, pero manteniendo siempre la cabeza baja—; no hay nada que pueda comparársele...; sólo tiene algún parecido con el tormento soportado en nombre de Epsamón Divino. Por ello te digo, monseñor, que, a partir de ahora, tu despotismo podrá disponer de mi vida; tu despotismo me libera, porque tú pasas a disponer de mi voluntad: ya no debo preocuparme por decidir. Porque tú me ordenas y yo no tengo más alternativa que obedecer, ¡oh, Nebjeperura!; y puedes convertir mi cuerpo en un saco de carroña arrojada a los leones de tu zoológico, o puedes vestirlo de oro y llenarlo de dignidades, según te parezca; pero, en cualquier caso, me liberas, porque, de ahora en adelante, ya no necesitaré decidir...

La violencia, la crueldad, el orgullo, e incluso la belleza de que Astor diese pruebas anoche, durante la ceremonia, desaparecieron por completo, convirtiéndolo en un muñeco que oscilaba entre el miedo y el gozo; que temblaba y sonreía a la vez mientras uno de los efebos me ofrecía una bandeja de plata que contenía un látigo de cinco lenguas acabadas en puntas de hierro. Astor gemía:

—Si es tu deseo, soportaré los latigazos hasta el desmayo, y cuando recobre el conocimiento estaré dispuesto a sufrirlo más veces..., todas las que desees, monseñor.

Rechacé el látigo. Todo aquello era demasiado confuso. Y más se confundía a medida que un nuevo elemento entraba en juego.

—Sólo quiero la libertad —dije.

—La libertad eres tú, Nebjeperura. Eres tú, porque asumirás la libertad de todo el pueblo de Lur y nos librarás del peso de soportarla. Incluso serás la libertad de Epsamón.

En aquellos momentos, en medio de tantas tonterías, mis nervios volvieron a padecer la misma tensión de anoche. Y un sudor muy frío, que nada debía a los vapores del baño, iba goteando por mi rostro.

—¡Por favor, Astor! ¡Explicaciones! ¡Te lo ruego! ¡Oh Dios mío, no puedo más...!

Entonces, los fenómenos sufrieron una inversión fatal, y fue como si toda mi sensación de prisionero regresase de repente, reflejada en el repentino cambio de la expresión de Astor. Si ante mis intentos de despotismo él pareció menguar hasta lo ínfimo, ahora volvía a su actitud normal, a toda su altivez, violenta y dominadora, de guardián implacable. Cogió el látigo que me ofreciese y volvió a depositarlo en la bandeja, que el esclavo se llevó no sin dirigirme, también, una mirada de desprecio.

—Así pues, disponte a seguirme. Pero procura darte prisa, que la jornada es corta y hemos de ir lejos. ¡Corre!

Así recobró el tono de dueño de mi esclavitud. Me condujo a lo largo de los pasadizos de los espejos hasta que llegamos a la encrucijada de donde salían las diversas escaleras mecánicas, algunas de las cuales penetraban la tierra hacia los subterráneos en lugar de subir a la superficie. La alternancia de habitaciones suntuosas y civilizadas con pasadizos de roca adusta y salvaje, volvió a producirse; y la severidad de Astor, a pesar de su sonrisa forzadamente amable, amenazó con alcanzar una hostilidad que, lo comprendí muy bien, yo mismo me había ganado como contraprecio de mi condescendencia.

Así fue como decidí metamorfosear mi carácter de una vez por todas, y cogiendo en un arrebato el látigo de oro que mi repulsivo guardián exhibía como símbolo de su autoridad, le golpeé el rostro tres veces consecutivas...

—¡Ah perro! Te he pedido explicaciones, pero veo que tendré que exigírtelas a costa de tu sangre.

—¡Nebjeperura! —exclamó él—. ¡Oh, Nebjeperura, monseñor!

—¡Puñetas! Ahora ya sé que es inútil tener lástima de los perros. Compruebo que la amabilidad de vuestros superiores no sirve para que funcionéis mejor.

—Estás en tu pleno derecho a ejercer el despotismo, monseñor. Tú *has de ser* el despotismo.

Se reanudaba el efecto inmediato de la violencia, y asimismo la extraña complacencia de Astor. Es decir: él regresaba a la única posibilidad de acceder a mis intentos de aproximación. Y, al mismo tiempo, yo volvía a la condena de tener que estar solo en la cima de las cosas. Reencontraba el punto más alto de la soledad, propia de todas las divinidades sobre la Tierra.

Pero a menudo yo había sentido aquella sensación de soledad en medio de la admiración y la reserva de los demás. ¿Acaso mi experiencia de los últimos días no era una vertiente muy original de las infinitas posibilidades que puede ofrecer la soledad, y una faceta, no negaré que impensadísima, de su habitualidad? ¡Ah, pero este problema no le interesa demasiado, profesor, puesto que prefiere usted dormir! Me deja la narración para mí solo, la convierte en autoconfesión, hace que yo sea de nuevo un fardo de soledad, una carga que usted se niega a aligerar, aunque sólo fuese con los cuatro consejos que yo esperaba, aunque sólo fuese con la limosna de su credulidad (y conste que ya no hablo de la razón, porque sé perfectamente que nadie me la dará nunca). Así, permite usted que navegue lentamente hacia el monólogo interior, absurdo en estos momentos y, con todo, avasallador, penetrante, consolador y no sé cuántas cosas más...

La soledad; ¡maldito estigma, profesor! Yo la sentí, tuve que acostumbrarme a ella y aprender a existir solo. Oh, sí: en el escenario de mis recitales, en la pista de mis actuaciones en *night-clubs,* sentí que otros resplandores me dejaban solo y a la vez grande; solo y a la vez grande en una dimensión que yo no puedo explicar a mi público, ni siquiera a Larry, porque a ellos sólo les importa mi voz, mi apariencia, los gestos estereotipados que voy fijando mientras bramo...

El drama se repetía en Lur. Al menos, esto lo reconozco. Insistir en mi esperanza de un poco de amistad por parte de Astor, Epsamón, Larry o cualquier otro ser humano, sólo es repetir el drama. La última derivación del ridículo en que puede caer el problema de la soledad apenas entra en conflicto con la apreciación de los demás. El «numerito de la soledad», como se lo denomina cuando explicas las razones que te hacen sentir así. O, como diría Batsá una noche: «Estás considerado Co-Divino, y te quejas. ¿Te has detenido a pensar qué sentirías si mañana te llevasen a trabajar a la cantera y te obligasen a arrancar piedras con los esclavos y arrastrarlas a través del desierto para construir los grandes anfiteatros de Lur? ¿No te parece que entonces tendrías todos los motivos para sentirte muy solo, muy desgraciado y muy víctima?

No lo sabía. No lo sé. Tal vez fuese igualmente la soledad. Distinta, con otros latidos, pero soledad al fin y al cabo. En esto son siempre idénticas la soledad de los hombres y la de los dioses. Aguarda agazapada el momento de entrar en acción, la primera oportunidad. Yo, muchacho normal, ser anónimo; yo, cantante de fama; yo, Nebjeperura; yo, esclavizado en las obras del anfiteatro, y, finalmente, yo: un cadáver. ¿Qué importa la manifestación de mí mismo? *Ella* siempre permanece. No hay salvación.

—DEBES PERDONARME, Nebjeperura —dijo Astor—. Sabes perfectamente que un deseo tuyo es una orden para mí. O, mejor dicho, monseñor: una orden de tus labios se convierte en mi deseo.

—Así pues, ¿siempre me veré obligado a emplear la fuerza?

—Simplemente tu voluntad, Nebjeperura. Oh, tú, que eres el Co-Divino, no puedes permitirte..., ¿cómo te lo diría?..., ningún tipo de sumisión a la debilidad de tus siervos. Yo, aunque esté situado entre los más altos del país, no por ello dejo de ser uno más entre los siervos de cuya vida, de cuya muerte puedes y debes disponer. Y si algo entra en mi deseo de ahora y en cualquier deseo que pueda alimentar en adelante, es precisamente servirte con toda perfección, convertirme en tu perro, porque eso es lo que Epsamón me ha ordenado que hiciese hasta que él en persona regrese a Lur, y sea tus ojos y tu voluntad del mismo modo que Él y tú mismo como pareja seréis los nuestros.

Y mientras nos acercábamos a la salida (de forma que ya no necesitábamos antorchas para iluminar aquella parte del subterráneo), Astor insistía en justificar que, si había postergado sus explicaciones sobre la realidad del Mundo Macho, sólo se debía a su deseo de hacer posible que cada explicación coincidiera con la correspondiente comprobación puesta a mi alcance; y con este fin, había organizado para aquel día, primero de la semana, una serie de excursiones a los alrededores de Lur; así, cuando Epsamón regresara de la Guerra Santa no me encontraría tan ignorante de *mi* realidad nacional. Tampoco dejaba de pronunciar palabras de excusa cuando me exponía que la otra causa de haber esperado tanto para informarme, era que encontraba muy plausible que, después de ciertas incomodidades del viaje y de ciertos espantos (naturales, dadas las circunstancias), necesitara sin duda un reposo.

—No has pensado mal —concedí, en tono siempre severo—. Sin embargo, pudiste adivinar que las pruebas a las que he tenido que someterme no son nada importante para mí, pues en tanto que Co-Divino, me hallo inmunizado contra estas tonterías. Y espero hacerme entender de una vez por todas: quiero saber qué hago, con quién, dónde, cómo y por qué... Lo digo por tu bien, perro miserable. Si no haces lo que debes, sabré cómo hacértelo pagar.

De este modo quedó muy claro que cualquier posibilidad de relación amistosa entre Astor y yo debería tardar mucho tiempo y mucho esfuerzo; deberían romperse muchas cosas antes de establecer una corriente afectuosa; debería ceder la correspondencia de dominio sobre sumisión que el Mundo Macho exigía incluso en el amor y en la creación de vida.

CONVENCIDO DE QUE era imposible llegar a buen puerto mediante la amabilidad o la gentileza en el trato, utilicé lo mejor de aquel despotismo recién aprendido para preguntar a Astor adónde conducía la salida de la cueva, boca de luz que ya permitía ver algunos soldados de la guardia palatina situados junto a uno de los colosos de granito, cuyas dimensiones quedan explicadas con las proporciones que la figura humana alcanzaba en comparación. Basta con decir que aquellos guardianes apenas les llegaban a la mitad de un solo dedo del pie, cosa verdaderamente notable si se tiene en cuenta que los soldados del Mundo Macho, sobre todo los de la guardia palatina, pueden alardear de una estatura descomunal. Estos soldados de las milicias imperiales son voluntarios, y Astor me aseguró que cualquier joven mínimamente ambicioso de Lur aspiraría a ingresar en ellas, porque es uno de los más altos honores que es dado recibir en el país. El cuartel es de una belleza extraordinaria, y está integrado por tres partes, separadas entre sí por callejones que conducen a la muralla ciclópea; pero estas partes están unidas unas a otras por puentes de delicada arquitectura: sobre el callejón se levantan unos arcos ojivales sostenidos por esculturas de mármol que reproducen motivos de flora y fauna, además de una imaginería humana que recuerda sospechosamente la arquitectura religiosa de nuestra Edad Media europea. El palacete central tiene una lonja muy antigua, cuyo mármol forma un ajedrezado blanco y rosa; delante está la plaza de los Condottieros, de belleza indescriptible cuando nace el día. Esta placeta, toda de mármol y muy bien cuidada a pesar de cierto hedor procedente de los establos que ocupan el tercer cuerpo del edificio, tiene en el centro una fuente de alabastro cuyos caños son a su vez trescientas figuras, la mitad de las cuales reproducen el rostro de Epsamón sobre un cuerpo de león alado y la otra mitad se divide entre grifos míticos y la representación del Tronco Universal —tema básico de la cosmogonía de Lur— donde se enrosca el símbolo motriz de esta Iglesia: Cobra. Los motivos se alternan de manera perfectamente ordenada, siempre creando una sensación de paz que contrasta vivamente con la función bélica de los cuarteles. Es muy usual hallar en esta fuente a algunos miembros de la guardia que descansan conversando, o bien bañándose, mientras esperan que llegue su turno de servicio.

Los otros dos edificios que forman la parte frontal de la plaza (cerrada a cada parte por la roca viva, que soporta el palacio real y dos templos) están destinados a servir de establos, como ya le he dicho, y alojan la Casa de la Prueba, cuyo delicioso aspecto exterior (dos galerías de arcos venecianos, si no me equivoco) no hace suponer, siquiera remotamente, los objetos de tortura que contiene. A ambos lados de la salida de los túneles que conducen a las escalas mecánicas del palacio se yerguen los colosos que he citado, representando también a Epsamón revestido con la Corona de los dos Países y el símbolo Cobra. Tan grandioso tocado queda a la altura de los jardines colgantes de Epsamón, quien utiliza una puerta sita en el ojo de uno de sus colosos para bajar en secreto; y es que por el interior hueco del coloso desciende una escalera de caracol que sólo el Divino y sus más adictos servidores están autorizados a utilizar.

Al ver estos colosos, al examinar su rostro descomunal, me di cuenta de un hecho sorprendente en extremo: los rasgos que reproducían no guardaban relación con las estatuas de los caños, ni éstas con las estatuas de Epsamón que se levantan por todos los rincones del palacio, o con el Sebastián que Astor me enseñó ayer. Espero que lo entienda: de hecho, no había ninguna representación de Epsamón que se pareciera a las otras; así pues, todas podían ser auténticas o podían ser falsas.

—Bueno, Astor, ¿empezamos?

—¿Empezar qué, monseñor?

—Las explicaciones. Todas. Y rápido, Astor, muy rápido. Explícame de una vez dónde me encuentro.

—En Lur, monseñor. La capital del Mundo Macho.

—Eso ya lo sé, bestia. Pero, ¿dónde diablos se halla situado este mundo?

—¿Situado, monseñor? No sé a qué te refieres.

—¿Estamos en Egipto, Astor?

—¿En Egipto, monseñor? Todo lo que ves, hasta mucho más lejos de cuanto puede abarcar tu mirada, corresponde al legado histórico y cultural del Mundo Macho. Y es una herencia legítima, hecha de siglos que son exclusivamente nuestros desde el principio de todas las historias. Así pues, monseñor: ¿qué tiene que ver Egipto con ello?

—No abuses de mi paciencia, hijo de perra, porque la tengo ya más que agotada. Yo fui raptado en Egipto. Fui raptado en Minia, para ser más exactos. ¡No intentarás hacerme creer que me encuentro en otro planeta...!

Es cierto que yo había leído fabulaciones de este tipo en libros o tebeos de ciencia-ficción, pero era demasiado absurdo suponer que pudiesen suceder en la realidad, ni siquiera en el sueño más loco al que hubiese podido arrojarme una noche de LSD, cuando el bacilón te empuja al viaje y, en él, puede crearse cualquier transmundo de auténtica locura. Era absurdo imaginar un trasplante espontáneo a cualquier planeta remoto, como aquellos en cuyos cráteres mis héroes de papel habían hallado civilizaciones de hombres-halcón, de mujeres-topo, de donceles-león y reinas-egipcionadas, falso sueño de una Atlántida colocada al alcance de un consumo ingenuo. Es cierto que en aquellos itinerarios domésticos cualquier fabulación, por abracadabrante que fuese, había sido posible y posibilitada; pero al fin y al cabo sólo fueron concesiones a un tipo de fantasía que mi aburrimiento cotidiano, incluso histórico, había necesitado.

¿Descartaría, sin embargo, la evidencia de un viaje aún más alucinante que los producidos por cualquier droga?

Astor, con su ingenuidad de indígena, me suministró la respuesta:

—Te equivocas de base, monseñor. Ninguno de los mundos que nombras existen entre nosotros. Todo empieza en el Mundo Macho: todo termina. No hay otro planeta, no hay otras tierras, no hay otros reyes. Es una realidad única, Nebjeperura. Y el resto es un sueño que tú has tenido en vano.

Mientras los soldados de la guardia palatina me saludaban besando el suelo y dos capitanes preparaban los caballos, yo intentaba disimular el vértigo que se había apoderado de mí apenas las palabras de Astor me ilustraron acerca de la posibilidad de que aquella vida mía de entonces, los instantes recientemente vividos en el Mundo Macho, fuesen una existencia auténtica, que rechazaba mi personalidad de antes y la convertía en un espejismo. «El resto es un sueño que tú has tenido en vano», me decía Astor, negando de este modo cualquier contacto con el mundo exterior. Y eran palabras que se repetían en mi cerebro con un eco clamoroso, aunque sin ahogar mi deseo de conocimiento, mi derecho a situar todos los elementos en una perspectiva más o menos coherente y dilucidadora.

Dos soldados, que no se atrevían a levantar los ojos, me calzaron unas botas altas hasta las rodillas. Ni siquiera la preparación conseguía distraerme de mis preocupaciones; pero lo consiguieron de forma total unos gritos terribles que salían de la Casa de la Prueba. Toda la exquisitez de la fachada, de tímpanos primorosamente adornados con relieves y grupos plásticos de marfil, quedaba disminuida bajo el espanto que inspiraban aquellos gritos, cada vez más fuertes, cada vez más crueles.

Fustigué los labios de los dos servidores provisionales y, con las botas a medio atar, exigí la atención de Astor.

—¿Qué sucede ahí dentro, Astor?

—Nada que no sea natural, monseñor. La prueba de los voluntarios para el reemplazo de la guardia palatina.

—Quiero verlo.

—Es mejor que subas a tu caballo, monseñor. En caso contrario, se haría tarde para visitar los lugares que quiero enseñarte. Recuerda que hoy empieza tu conocimiento del Mundo Macho. Conviene activarlo para cuando llegue Epsamón.

—Esto forma parte de mi aprendizaje, Astor. Guíame tú, que eres mi siervo.

El tono imperativo ya no era en absoluto equívoco, y Astor debió de comprender que no desaprovecharía la oportunidad de hacérselo sentir. Cualquiera que fuese mi antojo, se había convertido desde muchos siglos antes en la imperiosidad que todo un pueblo sabría obedecer. Y también en la necesidad que tenían de obedecerla.

Me introdujo en la Casa de la Prueba, y los guardias que contemplaban la iniciación de los reclutas se arrodillaron a mi paso, como si obedecieran al poder de muchas órdenes tácitas que nada ni nadie podrían cambiar. Todos estaban situados alrededor de un pozo enorme, en cuyo fondo se celebraba la iniciación de los mozos, que siempre son escogidos entre los más altos, fuertes y rubios de la raza elegida. Pero cumple decir que incluso siendo impresionante en exigencias, su prueba lo era menos que el sacrificio en el templo de Homo Demeter. Aquí no se les pedía que devorasen a unos adolescentes imperfectos: las exigencias se limitaban a una resistencia física que demostraba no sólo machismo en un sentido religioso, sino también capacidad para soportar la vida difícil de la milicia, o la variedad de torturas que podía sufrir el soldado si cayera en manos de los herejes y éstos quisiesen obligarlo a confesar proyectos secretos del ejército macho.

Por ello, la iniciación consiste en una serie de tormentos denominados «básicos» o «elementales», pues no causan la muerte: suplicios que abarcan diversas pruebas —flagelación, hierros candentes, el borceguí que aprisiona el pie entre dos maderos y de este modo va aplastándolo, inmersión del cuerpo en una caldera de aceite hirviendo...—, pruebas todas rematadas por el sacrificio del dedo pulgar del pie, que los reclutas de Lur ofrecen a Epsamón en prenda de fidelidad. De hecho, el Templo de la Prueba cuenta con prestigiosas catacumbas en cuyos muros se exhiben, colgados a modo de exvotos, los dedos de los reclutas de la guardia palatina desde muchas generaciones hasta hoy.

Si los mozos han demostrado su valor en las pruebas elementales, pasan a resistir el frío en el interior de una inmensa nevera; o bien el calor en unos baños de vapor que pueden alcanzar temperaturas demenciales. De hecho, algunos aspirantes han salido enloquecidos de estas termas ardientes, por lo cual fue preciso sacrificarlos durante las fiestas de Purificación de la Raza. Pero si salen bien parados, aún les queda arrastrarse por el fango, entre campos de cactos, o bien sobre mesas con cuchillos dispuestos con la punta hacia arriba, cuchillos que hay que aprender a evitar porque tienen la hoja impregnada de una sustancia venenosa. Todo ello revelará una capacidad para resistir las adversidades atmosféricas que puedan afectarles en tiempos de guerra y, también, para salir de las trampas que pueda tenderles el enemigo. Se trata de una preetapa, seguida de la del adiestramiento militar específico, que es cuando el recluta aprende a preparar trampas más mortales que las de los herejes, a clavar la lanza en los puntos vitales del cuerpo humano y a infligir al enemigo tormentos más feroces que los suyos.

Mientras Astor me exponía esta segunda etapa, yo la asociaba con mi propio período de servicio militar en un campamento cualquiera del Midi, lejano y olvidado. Cierto que a mí, como recluta, no me exigieron el sufrimiento físico a una escala tan titánica, pero es posible que dejase en el cuartel más de un dedo del pie. No me pregunte cuál, ni tampoco en qué medida, porque no estoy seguro de si sabría contestar; pero siempre que, a partir de entonces, me he entregado, devoto, a un mínimo de marihuana, he reencontrado una sucesión de imágenes que comprendían mi juramento a la bandera francesa, las artes de matar que se me habían enseñado tan perfectamente, el dedo que cortaban a los reclutas en la Casa de la Prueba, la vigilancia obsesiva de Larry, la voluntad que dejé en manos de los oficiales del campamento y la locura de mis admiradores cuando corren detrás de mí en una masa chillona que recuerda algún himno bélico, primitivo y acompañado por todos los tambores de una batalla ancestral...

Como aquel himno pomposo, que cantaban los reclutas del Mundo Macho mientras aguardaban su turno para la prueba:

Gloria ai Numi! ognun rammenti
Ch'essi reggono gli eventi,
Che in poter de' Numi solo
Stan le sorti del guerrier.

Su! del fiume al sacro lido;
Sien barriera i nostri petti;
Non echeggi che un sol grido:
Guerra e morte allo stranier!

Guerra!, guerra!, sterminio all'invasor
Guerra!, guerra!, va signor di aquesta
Terra... oh Epsamon!
Va e ritorna vincitor!

¿Podía evadirme a una sorpresa mayúscula? Como ya le he dicho, podría ocurrirme lo más grande y la sorpresa sería vencida por la fuerza que tantos descubrimientos a la vez me habían enseñado a alimentar. Pero ahora me hallaba ante unos mozos entusiasmados con un himno bélico cantado con palabras que podía garantizar como totalmente italianas. ¿Era, tal vez, una canción de moda, llegada al Mundo Macho por un juego de interrelaciones que sería el colmo investigar? ¿O tal vez los italianos, puestos a pensar cosas locas, fundaron un Istituto de Cultura en Lur? Cuando se llega a dudas de este tipo, cualquier concesión a la extravagancia tiene que resultar, forzosamente, un hecho normal.

Mientras salíamos de la Casa de la Prueba, pregunté a Astor:

—¿En qué idioma rebuznaban éstos?

—No rebuznaban, monseñor; *cantaban* el Himno de la Guerra Santa. Y era en tu honor.

—Cuestión de matices, estúpido. No desvíes el tema, como haces demasiado a menudo, y dime en qué lengua cantaban.

—En un dialecto reservado a la milicia de Lur, monseñor. ¿O tal vez esperabas que utilizasen el dialecto del «pueblo débil»?

Me dirigió esta última pregunta con tanta ingenuidad, que descarté inmediatamente la sola idea de que estuviera burlándose de mí. Y, sin embargo, insistí:

—No te rías, perro, o tendré que arrancarte la piel a latigazos.

—Monseñor: tú me pediste información y yo te la doy.

—Entonces, ¿por qué me ocultas que los reclutas conocen el italiano?

—¿El italiano?

—Como tú conoces el francés, perro.

—No te entiendo, monseñor. ¿Qué quiere decir «italiano», y qué quiere decir «francés»?

—«Francés», lo sabes perfectamente, es la lengua de mi país. Es esta lengua que tú dominas a la perfección y gracias a la cual hemos podido entendernos desde el primer momento.

—Pero, ¿qué lengua, monseñor? Yo me limito a utilizar un dialecto reservado a los sacerdotes de Cobra...

—¡Basta! —exclamé mientras le golpeaba el rostro con la fusta—. ¡Quiero la verdad! ¡Te la exijo de una vez!

Él inclinó la cabeza y enjugó la sangre que le brotaba de la nariz. Cuando volvió a mirarme, parecía sumamente agradecido y lamía su propia sangre con rara avidez.

—Lo que te digo es verdad, monseñor —mostró la palma de la mano, abierta en un perfecto saludo romano—. ¡Te lo juro!

—¿Cómo te explicas, pues, que yo pueda entenderte sin haber estado antes aquí? ¿No te parece que este hecho por sí sólo ya demostraría...?

No me dejó terminar.

—... demostraría, monseñor, lo que todos sabemos: tu divinidad te capacita para entenderlo todo, para saberlo todo...; demostraría que las Juventudes del Mundo Macho no se equivocan al considerarte el dios de la sabiduría y de las artes.

Aunque aquella nueva prueba de servilismo era tan alarmante como el culto a la violencia o al canibalismo de anoche, yo había aprendido la lección de no expresar demasiado a menudo mi sorpresa, y obtener de aquel modo la obediencia de Astor; obediencia que en aquellos momentos me era más necesaria que nunca. Y diré, de paso, que si el precio de mi seguridad era su servilismo, no iba yo a retroceder a la hora de aceptar ambas cosas como condición ineludible para mi supervivencia.

Por otra parte, Astor parecía mucho más contento a causa de mi actitud; la suya, enigmática a pesar de la apariencia de certeza que tenían las respuestas, ya empezaba a vacilar entre la adoración al dios que yo era para él y un afán por resultarme mucho más humano.

Y es que, precisamente, repitió la palabra de la noche anterior:

—*Ashnar.*

¡Singular dulzura la de su tono!

Desde aquel día, y por todos los que siguieron, la misteriosa palabra de Astor se prolongó en una frase que él pronunciaba constantemente con todo el agradecimiento, toda la pena de un alma abierta a un sentimiento nuevo y desconocido:

—*Ashnar oua, Nebjeperura, oua-t ashnar-it.*

AGONÍA, PROFESOR; agonía que ni siquiera concede la piedad de otorgar el consuelo supremo de la muerte. Agonía incluso en las religiones, que conllevan desde su origen la semilla de una herejía congénita, que los grandes dioses se empeñarán en destruir aplicándose con tanta crueldad como amor depositaron en la creación. Todo es destrucción, profesor; destrucción y agonía en forma de crueldad que nos infligimos los unos a los otros por medio de las relaciones, por medio del amor, por medio de la gran mentira de los gobiernos o las adoraciones a la divinidad. Desde niño, en mi país lejano, fui educado en la creencia de que Aquel que Ordena el Tiempo y es Todo Bondad creó el mundo en seis días, creó al hombre a su imagen y semejanza; desde entonces, mi religión me ha contado que la Serpiente perdió al hombre, porque ella es la reencarnación de Aquel que se Rebeló y a quien el gran creador convirtió en Ángel Maldito, tiniebla que se opone a la luz, muerte del espíritu que niega la vida eterna. La religión de mis padres me enseñó a creer en el Bien y a temerlo, de forma que no adoré el Mal hasta que no creí en Cobra, Origen Macho de todas las fuerzas del universo, Tronco Universal de una religión en la que la crueldad es virtud y la agonía tiene otro sentido, y aquello que para nosotros es luz se ha convertido en tiniebla, y las tinieblas tienen el sentido redentor que para nosotros tiene la luz. Epsamón cabalga, feroz, contra las regiones del Mundo Macho que son heréticas en dioses, habla y características étnicas, y sobre ellas ejecuta la voluntad de destrucción que los dioses de la fuerza ordenaron al principio de todas las historias. En el Mundo Macho, los ángeles malditos son signo de bondad, y los ángeles buenos son signo de pecado. La serpiente es la vida que no tiene límites: así empezó el mundo, me enseñan ahora, y el hombre fue creado por el Mal, fuerza que sublima la debilidad innata a la raza y le desafía a alcanzar el acto titánico de la destrucción. Y los dioses que crearon el Mundo Macho destruyeron a los que no creen en ellos y que, sin embargo, también fueron originalmente su creación. Yo mismo, que soy Divino, no acabo de entenderlo.

¡Oh, profesor! El hilo de la narración escapa y yo regreso a los orígenes de todas las cosas. Tomo de nuevo los millones y millones de siglos que me han precedido y el mundo se me presenta desnudo y terrible; aún no ha sido creado, es el relámpago que engendra la vida sobre el vacío del Universo a punto de ser parido. Todo es oscuridad: en este espacio virgen no baila un solo astro, ninguna estrella, ninguna chispa que no sea la del fuego que alimenta al Poder Macho. Detrás del micrófono, mientras me desgañito en las canciones que el público quiere oír, veo esta oscuridad inmensa al otro lado de unas luces poderosas que me enfocan desde las baterías; veo la oscuridad impenetrable, el espacio virgen que no envía sonidos hacia mí, sólo insignificantes chispas que se unirán para crear vida. Ahora siento los ruidos, el gran trueno que ensordece, la cascada de rostros que ya son vida, la uniforme mueca de esta sociedad que me crea en cada canción que le dedico, en cada canción que se desliza sobre mi espíritu sin dejar nada de él. Más allá de este caos, más allá de todas las culpas originales que yo pudiese llegar a sentir, Cobra se levanta, hincha la gran cabeza sobre los estucados del palco más próximo al escenario, y me dice:

«Mucho antes de que Epsamón empezara vuestra historia, yo creé el Universo: hice salir el fuego del agua, el agua de las nubes que habían salido del fuego; hice la piedra y los árboles, todas las flores que brotan en las ramas del gran tronco de la vida, creé al hombre contra la voluntad de Aquel que Ordena el Tiempo, y Él dijo al hombre que yo había creado: "Te maldigo, hijo de la Serpiente, porque has sido hecho en contra de mi voluntad; te maldigo porque yo sabía que al lado del Bien existe el Mal y quería protegerte de él, quería evitar el sufrimiento de cualquier criatura que pudiese nacer de esta lucha inacabable, y por ello preferí renunciar a la creación. Pero la Serpiente, uno de mis ángeles malditos, creó las cosas con el poder del Mal, y el último día de la semana te creó a ti, hijo de la agonía, y por ello seas para siempre maldito. Y envío contra ti a todos los ángeles de mi infinita bondad, todas las chispas de mi Tiempo eterno, que te perseguirá por los siglos de los siglos..."»

Oh, profesor: este Tiempo va más allá de todo mi dolor; empieza millones de siglos antes de cualquier alegría que pueda llegar a conocer, del Bien o del Mal que pueda cometer en el breve espacio de mi vida. Se remonta hacia un pecado sin nombre, que no sé cuándo cometí; pide una purificación que desconozco; me mata porque me declara culpable de no sé qué crimen. Ésta es mi agonía, finalmente aceptada: engendra muchas más, mientras el mundo es creado a cada instante y se destruye una milésima de segundo después; mientras Aquel que Ordena el Tiempo, enemigo mortal de Cobra, engendradora del Mundo Macho —como el Sol, violado por la Serpiente, creó a Epsamón Divino—, lucha contra Cobra en las más antiguas raíces del Gran Tronco Universal, en un combate de tal magnitud que escapa a todos los pasos, a toda mi memoria, a todos los recuerdos del mundo...

¿De quién soy hijo, profesor? ¿Nací, como me enseñaron en mi país, de Aquel que Ordena el Tiempo y Odia al Hombre —ese a quien adoran, sin embargo, los herejes del Mundo Macho—, o bien fui creado por Cobra, que se rebeló en la gran lucha por la forja de la creación? «Escucha bien, heredero de la agonía: yo te engendré, hace muchos siglos, en el vientre supremo del universo. Fuiste una fuerza que había de ser eterna, y Aquel que Ordena el Tiempo montó en cólera y contó tus días para siempre. Al Mal, que era tu fuerza primigenia, se opuso el Bien, te dio el dolor para vencerlo, hizo de ti un pedazo de carne débil que vacila entre ambas fuerzas, acortó tus días y tus noches y te arrojó a la fatalidad de la muerte. Pero yo te creé poderoso y malvado, y en mi rebelión prolongada en los siglos te di las fuerzas que te hiciesen volver continuamente a este mundo que yo domino. Yo soy el Mal, y tú eres mi hijo, y por ello resucitarás siempre, mientras la gran contienda no quede resuelta para toda la eternidad. Aquel que Ordena el Tiempo te roba la vida, y yo te arrebato a la oscuridad de la muerte y te resucito a cada ciclo histórico para que tu fuerza no se pierda, para que mi rebelión tenga continuidad, siglo tras siglo, hasta que el tiempo se agote a sí mismo. Y son mis sacerdotes quienes velan por tu retorno a la Tierra; son ellos quienes ostentan el poder de comunicarse con tu espíritu errante y hacerle volver con la manifestación que resulte más adecuada al tiempo nuevo, a las necesidades religiosas y políticas de cada nueva etapa de la lucha de las fuerzas del Mal contra la voluntad aniquiladora de Aquel que Ordena el Tiempo...»

Sí, eran las doctrinas que Cobra me revelaba cada mañana, durante mis plegarias en la capilla privada que se me destinaba en su templo. Eran revelaciones propias de una iniciación que iba cumpliéndose rigurosamente, y que habían de llevarme a penetrar en los grandes misterios. Después, el altísimo lugar a que había sido destinado sería ya indiscutible, nadie podría arrebatármelo porque yo lo habría ganado de acuerdo con las supremas ordenaciones del Mal. Y, al mismo tiempo, jamás podría escapar de él.

Y era porque, además de las agonías de una condición humana diferente de la que me había sido inculcada por los sacerdotes de mi religión, yo aprendía en las revelaciones de Cobra que existí en el Mundo Macho mucho antes de mi reciente llegada, muchas veces antes, tal vez; que volvería a existir allí después de mi muerte, y que, por esta causa, cualquier intento de huida era imposible. Sí, profesor: ésta era la verdadera agonía, jamás sentida antes, imposible de comunicar a alguien que, como yo, no esté iniciado en los Grandes Misterios de

Cobra. Es la agonía de saber que la muerte no existe, que las vicisitudes que arrastro una vez cada dos siglos volverán a presentárseme con cada nueva reencarnación; que mi espíritu permanecerá inexorablemente condenado a volver a la vida, siendo rey o esclavo, inteligente o tonto, sano o enfermo, en posesión de otro rostro y otros músculos, dominador o esclavizado a otros cuerpos, y sea como fuere, siempre miserable. La agonía se repetirá siempre, profesor, porque Cobra quiere que la muerte no exista; y tal vez esta misma conversación la repitamos en siglos venideros, usted o yo, con rostros diferentes, voces que no serán las de ahora, en la Minia distinta que el futuro habrá decretado: no nos reconoceremos en esa nueva reencarnación, como no podemos reconocernos en la de ahora; como no podemos recordar, en este presente, el rostro que tuvimos hace muchos años, tal vez siglos, cuando tuvimos la misma conversación en Babilonia, en el París de Luis XV, quién sabe si en la tan próxima Tell-el-Amarna...

Agonía. Agonía convertida en la obligación de no morir; en el deber de regresar siempre. Agonía que se convierte en religión; doctrina convertida en ley de todo un pueblo creado por las fuerzas del Mal que, curiosamente, eran adoradas como si fuesen fuerzas del Bien. Mundo Macho. Mundo Macho.

Y tú, Cobra, ya que te hallas en todas partes, escúchame: Soy tu hijo, lo sé, y desde que me iniciaste en los grandes misterios, mi enemigo es Aquel que Ordena el Tiempo, derrotado por ti, vencido en sus intentos de lucha para evitar que, en la preñez de la creación, surgiera esta monstruosidad que tú, Cobra Macho, denominaste hombre.

Agonía, profesor. Agonía de saber que la muerte no existe. Agonía de saber que yo, entre todos los hombres, fui elegido para descubrir el gran misterio de Cobra.

Pero mi narración tiene un hilo, o debería tenerlo; y el hilo de esta primera parte, cuando yo era aún un novicio, debe conducirlo Astor necesariamente. Repulsivo y odioso a mis ojos, aquel déspota cabalgaba siempre a mi lado y me instruía acerca de los más insignificantes detalles de la realidad a la cual yo empezaba a pertenecer; pero lo hacía sin aportar la menor claridad acerca de las cosas que desde un principio me habrían servido para llegar al fondo de todo el problema: no simples detalles de una superficie, por otra parte apasionante, sino el núcleo esencial, la verdad última; los orígenes del Mundo Macho, la finalidad de aquella batahola que poco a poco iba perdiendo el aspecto divertido de escenografía teatral, libre de cualquier compromiso, y se convertía en realidad viva, segura, que existía y oprimía a pesar de todos los absurdos imaginables. Sin embargo, ninguna de estas revelaciones era posible: la verdad última del Mundo Macho se ocultaba, siempre, bajo la densidad de la verdad oficial. Una vez aceptada esta evidencia tendría que recurrir a la astucia y aprovecharme de la función de instrumento a que se prestaba Astor, en todo momento y para todas las cosas.

Aquel día se limitaba a enseñarme las tierras de labranza que rodeaban Lur; tierras fértiles, por supuesto, y generosas en aquella flora gigantesca; monstruos creados por el hombre, que yo había observado ya en el parque de palacio y en los bosques de los alrededores. Las dimensiones colosales correspondían igualmente a los terrenos destinados a la agricultura o al pastoreo, y en este aspecto no es raro que la economía agraria del país sea tan próspera desde siempre. Los cultivos se extienden hasta mucho más allá de donde termina la provincia de Lur, y es frecuente ver en ellos a trabajadores desnudos, titanes que se doblan incansablemente bajo el ardor del sol, haciendo uso de aquella fuerza característica de la raza, sometidos a una disciplina que explica la perfección de su trabajo. La bonanza del tiempo, siempre propicio, tanto en la época de siembra como en la de las recolecciones, garantiza la eficiencia de estos hombres que están al servicio de los grandes propietarios de Lur, ya que las tierras, conquistadas tiempo atrás al enemigo (la gran batalla de Lur le dio la supremacía sobre las otras provincias del Imperio), suelen ser de propiedad privada. Ahora bien: al no existir la familia en el Mundo Macho, los terrenos son adjudicados por el Estado; de forma que, cuando llega la autocrucifixión de cada patricio, el Gran Consejo otorga su herencia a quienes se han distinguido por sus acciones de guerra o, simplemente, por una conducta pública ejemplar (la Iglesia queda excluida de esta ley, por ser propietaria de terrenos intransferibles desde el principio de los siglos). Un dato curioso: nunca se ha dado el caso de que algún terreno de Lur fuese adjudicado a uno de los trabajadores que se haya distinguido labrando la tierra; eso origina el hecho, no menos curioso, de que, mientras los propietarios cambian continuamente, los trabajadores siempre son los mismos.

Cuando pregunté a Astor dónde vivían los campesinos, él me guió hacia un poblado de casas de adobe, todas de un solo piso, que en aquel momento recibía los últimos rayos de un sol ya moribundo tras el horizonte. Formaba un conglomerado muy tranquilo, y ofrecía un aspecto totalmente distinto de la confusión de luces, colores y mezclas de estilos arquitectónicos que yo había visto en la capital. La sequedad espectral del lugar, que sería insoportable cuando el sol luce de lleno, le daba un aspecto de bucólica cárcel cerrada en sí misma, casi inexpugnable. Sin que en apariencia le faltara nada, algo se echaba de menos. Tal vez era lo mismo que me faltaba a mí, entre las columnas de mármol, las cortinas de terciopelo, el ajedrez de alabastro y toda la decoración que corresponde al Co-Divino.

Al comentar con Astor aquella sensación, él me contestó un tanto ofendido:

—¿Confundes a los trabajadores de Lur con los esclavos, monseñor? Sólo tu divina inexperiencia te justifica. Debo decirte que estos hombres son libres, y viven aquí como podrían vivir en Lur, en Baskeatá, o en cualquier ciudad importante del Imperio. Tal vez incluso vivan mejor. Porque aquí, en los pueblos, no tienen necesidades superfluas, y en la ciudad se convertirían en víctimas de estas necesidades.

—¿Víctimas, Astor?

—Víctimas, monseñor. Porque querrían más de lo que necesitan para vivir, y, como sin duda sabrás, ésta es la única forma de obtener la satisfacción de sus caprichos innecesarios. ¡Felices, ellos, en su existencia casi ciega! Porque es cosa sabida: la vida urbana crea, además de caprichos, muchas más limitaciones para ganarse la vida que los pueblos.

—Pero, ¿viven aquí por su propia voluntad? Quiero decir... si lo han escogido.

—Lo ha decidido el Estado, monseñor. Cuando el adolescente sale de la Casa de la Vida preparado para iniciar su existencia de ciudadano...

—¡Ah, sí! Ya sé. El Estado decreta cuál es el lugar de cada uno, ¿no?

—Así es, monseñor. Y es ley natural, impuesta desde hace siglos: ley de Epsamón...

—Porque Epsamón es...

—... el Estado, ¡naturalmente!

Pensé que aquellas leyes no estaban tan claras como el repulsivo Astor daba por descontado, pero yo no sabía cómo contradecirle. De hecho, todas mis ideas, todos mis esquemas estaban destinados a hundirse apenas rozaban la lógica del Mundo Macho. Las nociones de civilización que me habían sido inculcadas en Europa se tambaleaban aquí estrepitosamente; como, más adelante, se tambalearían mis ideas religiosas, incluso mi sentido de lo erótico. Me hallaba sometido a un ininterrumpido proceso de integración, y yo sabía que nadie podía ser tan fuerte para resistírsele. O tal vez yo fuese más débil de lo que pensaba.

Ni siquiera Astor era tan fuerte, disciplinado y fanático como su actitud hacía suponer, pues, en un momento dado de sus lecciones, hizo una mueca de aburrimiento y fue fácil comprender que ya estaba cansado de tanta teoría, de tantas explicaciones, oficiales o no. Y al ver que yo acogía de buen grado este gesto, aprovechó para sugerir que cabalgásemos hasta una aldea muy próxima, donde se celebraba la romería de Cobra, que convoca a un gran gentío procedente de todos los lugares de la región. Yo celebré la idea, y él me entregó un yelmo provisto de visera que me cubriría medio rostro: permitiéndome un anonimato más que feliz, pues no convenía que el «pueblo débil» viese el rostro de Nebjeperura antes de la primavera absoluta.

—No habrá nada mejor —comentó Astor—: ver las cosas al natural; participar en ellas te puede reportar mucho más provecho que una explicación mía; aunque fuese perfecta. Por otra parte, podrás ver de cerca la representación viviente y multiplicada de Cobra, de cuyo culto tendrás que ser Sumo Sacerdote antes de que Epsamón te consagre como su segundo sobre la Tierra.

Mientras me aconsejaba la mejor forma de lucir el yelmo, me dijo también que cada mañana debería ir al templo de Cobra, donde después de numerosas meditaciones y plegarias se me aparecería el Dios y me iniciaría en los Grandes Misterios, no sólo de su culto, sino del orden que rige el Mundo Macho y, en general, toda la creación. Pero me importaba muy poco en aquel momento, porque deseaba contemplar la extraña romería, a pesar del temor de verme obligado a participar en ella como precio de mi aprendizaje.

No tardamos en llegar al pueblo de Feverah, que mostraba una arquitectura elemental; pero al hallarse situado al borde de un barranco, ofrecía además la fantástica visión de muchas casas que diríanse a punto de precipitarse en la profunda nada. Cabalgamos rodeados de un intenso hormiguero humano: de cuerpos que entraban y salían del villorrio, a pie y a caballo, y así nos dirigimos a la plaza principal que, como en todas las villas del país, tenía en el centro un pequeño templo, santuario de la divinidad local bajo cuyo aspecto suele representarse Epsamón para las provincias de su gran Imperio. Y es sabido que la urbanización de muchos pueblos del Mundo Macho tuvo su origen en esos templos, a cuyo amparo fueron edificándose casas y palacios, hasta que, con la ordenación de las calles y la creación de ensanches y de futuras zonas de desintoxicación de espacios, se alcanzó la estructura actual.

En la plaza, la animación era muy grande: la multitud, abigarrada y chillona. Veíanse carros adornados con guirnaldas, esquilas de buey y cuernos de caza; saltimbanquis desnudos que llevaban el cuerpo teñido de los más variados colores (su apariencia, sin embargo, es mucho más pobre que la de los mimos, equilibristas y bailarines, teñidos de oro, que suelen alegrar las calles de la capital todas las noches del año); tenderetes repletos de cirios, recordatorios, exvotos, incienso, relicarios y otros objetos de la devoción a Cobra; vendedores de frutas, bebidas refrescantes, objetos de magia; incluso todo un escenario improvisado, donde unos actores de poca monta interpretaban la curiosa historia de un noble de Lur que, malaconsejado por su lugarteniente, desconfía del efebo que el Estado le ha confiado para su educación y lo estrangula con un pañuelo de seda, después de haberle recomendado que rezara a Cobra sus oraciones para que le perdonara en la otra vida y no le hiciese reencarnar en el cuerpo de un esclavo o un hereje. Dado que yo mostraba cierta curiosidad por conocer el final del drama, Astor me invitó a desmontar y me condujo hacia otra dirección, diciéndome:

—Puedo contaros el final, monseñor: la he visto representar muchas veces.

—¿Tan buena es, que aplauden tanto?

—El corazón del pueblo se enardece con estas fábulas, monseñor. Es la escena del pañuelo la que más aplauden, porque anuncia plenamente el triunfo del Mal. El lugarteniente, decidido a perder al efebo, enseña al amo el pañuelo de seda que le delata de un delito que, en realidad, no ha cometido. Es un acto de villanía que sólo tiene un fallo: su falta de categoría. Incluso un hereje podría llegar a estos extremos.

El solo hecho de asociar aquel argumento con algún otro que yo hubiese visto o leído en mi tierra, ya me hacía temblar; porque si llegaba a la conclusión de que toda aquella ceremonia, diálogos incluidos, estaba más que arraigada en mi propio bagaje cultural, la ironía de las interrelaciones propondría de nuevo el enigma de siempre: la búsqueda de los orígenes; y una nueva obsesión de estas características corría el riesgo de ser sumamente peligrosa. Especialmente si consideramos que el acto que para mis compañeros de civilización era moralmente reprobable, para el Mundo Macho constituía la gran virtud que preparaba al hombre para las grandes acciones determinadas por el imperativo del Mal, puesto que, según la lógica del país, el lugarteniente calumniador era el héroe positivo, y el efebo-víctima era negativo, por demasiado débil. Pero entonces no había asimilado aún que este culto a las fuerzas que consideramos negativas era, en el Mundo Macho, la razón de Estado que sostenía todo un edificio ideológico; principio y fin, tanto del sistema como de su voluntad de expansión.

Astor me mezcló con la multitud que saltaba y bailaba por las calles, me hizo pasear entre un grupo que llevaba a cabo una procesión de palmas por las cuales se enroscaba una cobra viva (es la manifestación popular del Gran Tronco Universal) y, finalmente, llegamos a la plaza del Templo, donde una nueva escena no esperada me lanzó hacia un mayor espanto y una repugnancia más intensa.

Coreados por los salmos de sacerdotes jovencísimos, cuyos cuerpos estaban embutidos en ceñidas pieles de serpiente —de hecho, eran una segunda piel—, hombres y adolescentes desnudos adoraban a más de un centenar de cobras, grandes y pequeñas, que danzaban en el propileo y descendían por las escalinatas del templo. Las bestias, provocadas tanto por los salmos como por la cercana desnudez de sus adoradores, se izaban más de un metro por encima del suelo, e hinchando la cabeza hasta hacérseles casi redonda, parecían dispuestas a lanzarse sobre el primer cuerpo que se les aproximara. Sin embargo esto no ocurría, y el culto se cumplía de una forma increíblemente pacífica, como si los atletas y las serpientes hubiesen nacido juntos, hubiesen sido separados después y, ahora, al cabo de los años, se reencontrasen para amarse en su madurez respectiva como cuerpos y como fuerza.

Nadie parecía temer a las cobras; al contrario: juntaban las manos y, arrodillados, besaban la tierra a pocos milímetros de la bestia que, erecta, dilataba y contraía la cabeza redonda, siempre emitiendo unos silbidos pavorosos; otros bacantes se las colgaban del cuello, dejaban que se enroscasen por la cintura o entre los muslos, y, entonces, la cabeza de la cobra se agitaba en busca de los ojos humanos, a los que hipnotizaba mientras el bacante caía en éxtasis, y a veces lamía el cuello erecto de la bestia. Otros llevaban cestas que, al abrirse, dejaban ver unos ojuelos negros, de intensidad y penetración estremecedoras: poco a poco, salía la Cobra particular que cada campesino de Lur tiene en su altar doméstico, y la bestia se mezclaba con sus compañeras, de forma que todo era una superficie viscosa, de anillas grises que se enroscaban entre sí mientras los cuerpos, anchos y duros, se elevaban con el peso de la cabeza hinchada que las hacía oscilar alternativamente hacia adelante y hacia atrás, en un balanceo sumamente armonioso y acaso fascinante. En el altar principal, que había sido trasladado al exterior para que pudiese ser visto por los romeros, se mostraba un ejemplar de Cobra Macho que yo no conocía: de cintura para abajo era una serpiente; de cintura para arriba, un atleta con rostro helenizante, rubio, por supuesto, y de cuya nuca surgía un abanico y de cada una de sus intersecciones brotaba una cobra de oro, de tamaño menor. Al lado de esta manifestación de Cobra, los sacerdotes de piel-de-serpiente entonaban salmos sobre los milagros de la reproducción y la proximidad de la primavera, que llegaría en cuanto Nebjeperura volviese del país de la Nada. Y multitud de adolescentes desnudos, pero con el cuerpo adornado con ristras de cascabeles, bailaban saltando por encima de las cobras más pequeñas o, si se trataba de alguna cobra real, por debajo de su cabeza hinchada.

Entonces, Astor me sonrió y, pasando entre los adoradores y las bestias de las escalinatas, fue a buscar una cobra de cuerpo tan ancho que necesitó agarrarla con las dos manos y, de este modo, rodearla. Su cabeza completamente hinchada, la señal en forma de V como marcada con un estigma de fuego, y la fuerza de los coletazos que buscaban el cuerpo de mi guardián, eran señales suficientes para convencerme de que, en el peligro que implica cualquier cobra, aquélla era una emperatriz de la mortalidad.

Al ver que Astor se dirigía hacia mí cargado con la serpiente enroscada alrededor de los muslos, deseé echar a correr y no detenerme nunca más; pero el onirismo que caracterizaba a la escena, el ritual adormecedor de los salmos, el ritmo monótono de las serpientes que se movían entre los efebos bailarines y, a veces, dentro de sus cuerpos, me dio la fuerza de voluntad necesaria para soportar una visión que colmó los límites de lo increíble: Astor besaba a la Cobra; su lengua robusta y los dos hilillos delgados que constituían la lengua de la bestia se encontraban; cada lengua penetraba en las encías del otro, se deslizaba sobre ellas en un beso que nadie ha podido imaginar, que nadie creerá jamás. Y precisamente a este beso sagrado me invitó Astor, y tuve que aceptarlo.

Tiempo después, en la clínica, junto al lago tópicamente suizo, yo recordaba el beso y me despertaba gritando, sumido en un charco de sudor. Entonces, una enfermera vestida de rosa, que ofrecía una comprensión digna de consultorio radiofónico, me inyectaba algo para que pudiese dormir tranquilo y, contrariamente a sus propósitos, contribuía de este modo a devolverme la pesadilla, la visión de la testa hinchada de Cobra que iba acercándose a mi rostro mientras yo abría la boca para recibir su lengua...

Pero allí, en Feverah, cerré los puños con todas mis fuerzas y no grité: el beso que Cobra me proponía fue recogido como quiere el Mundo Macho: apasionadamente, en busca del éxtasis, como una necesidad religiosa. Sentía sobre mis encías el cosquilleo de aquella lengua vil, pero superé el asco, vencí el mareo que me acometía, evité el desmayo. Me había costado mucho conquistar el respeto de Astor y no quería perderlo aunque hubiese de soportar todos los tormentos, todas las repugnancias de la historia pasada y de cualquier historia que esté por llegar. Mientras el sol remataba su caída y era ya evidente que debíamos regresar a Lur, percibí que Astor empezaba a considerarme uno de los suyos.

PERO PASABAN LOS DÍAS y Epsamón no regresaba de la Guerra Santa; y yo, prisionero entre todos los esplendores del gran palacio, empezaba a experimentar cierta complacencia; no conformismo, entiéndame, sino algo parecido a la acomodación que provenía de la costumbre, del deseo de decidirme a aprovechar las cosas a mi alcance.

Ya que en ausencia de Epsamón me correspondía conservar las más elementales formas del protocolo, decidí creer que mi prisión, aun siendo tan opresiva, no dejaba de ser, por lo menos, dorada; y así esperé que esta resignación me compensara la falta de otras cosas importantes, entre las cuales esa mínima concesión a la locura que los humanos, a menudo y no en vano, asociamos con la libertad. La vigilancia del repulsivo Astor ya no representaba una carga tan enojosa como antes, o, por lo menos, no la representaba en Astor mismo, que había empezado a mostrarse simpático, e incluso tierno; pero sí en el aspecto amo-esclavo que él se empeñaba en dar a nuestra relación. Es cierto que, de vez en cuando, condescendía a ser amigo más que siervo o guardián (entonces nadábamos juntos en la piscina, hacíamos carreras de caballos o jugábamos al ajedrez), pero estas ocasiones aún eran excepcionales, porque el sentido de un orden supremo podía más que su dote de humanidad, tan poderosa como la evidente belleza que lo adornaba. Y, en cualquier caso, no olvido que su tarea incluía un apartado, importantísimo, que podíamos clasificar de didáctico (trabajo que, en él, era permanente). Según las exigencias de aquel didactismo, él era responsable de convertirme en un gran señor, un caballero digno del Mundo Macho; de forma que cuando Epsamón volviera a palacio, vencedor de los herejes, encontrase en mí la divinidad perfecta.

—Y no sólo Él —comentaba Astor—, sino todos tus súbditos y, muy especialmente, las juventudes del Mundo Macho, pues, como te he dicho tantas veces, deben mirarse en ti como en un espejo. Tu presencia es ya política y religiosa, monseñor, y cada uno de tus actos, cada ademán, cada mirada, son enjuiciados en este sentido. Incluso tu aspecto, tu vestido, tus aficiones, el peinado, la forma de pintarte los ojos. En estos momentos, las juventudes del Mundo Macho sabe perfectamente qué gambeto gusta a Nebjeperura para bajar a cenar con los exarcas de las provincias azules; y este gambeto, su color exacto, invariable, se ha convertido en el atuendo apropiado para las grandes ceremonias, para las diversiones de la noche denominada sábado que, como sabes, es la del gran esparcimiento; saben, nuestros jóvenes, de qué color es el manto de terciopelo con el cual te envuelves al salir del baño, con qué estilo de natación has deslumbrado a tus siervos, si las botas te gustan abiertas por delante, lisas o con el gran pliegue bajo la rodilla. Las tiendas de Lur han agotado los birretes con que te tocas cuando cabalgas en la caza del jabalí, la clámide que eliges para leer cómodamente tendido en la biblioteca, en la paz del atardecer; incluso las plumas que, como es presumible, llevarías en lo alto de la armadura si hoy mismo hubieses de incorporarte a la Guerra Santa, secundando a nuestro señor Epsamón. En pocas palabras: tú eres la imagen que presentan las juventudes del Mundo Macho a cada hora del día, según las necesidades de cada situación y de cada lugar en particular. Sólo falta que seas para siempre como un espejo en la moral, en las creencias, en la actitud política e incluso en los gustos culturales.

—Francamente, nunca hubiese esperado que, como modelo, yo diera para tanto... Coge un grano de uva y pélamelo, Astor... Y te diré, de paso, que nunca he escogido un vestuario que tú no me hayas ofrecido.

Astor peló un grano de uva y me lo ofreció.

—Un vestuario exquisito —dijo—: ¿acaso no es de tu agrado?

—Al contrario: me ha parecido divertidísimo disfrazarme de griego para reposar, de pintura prerrafaelista para el almuerzo del mediodía, de Adán para practicar deportes, y de egipcio para ir a adorar a Cobra. Considero que, como Carnaval, no se puede pedir más; pero me gustaría saber qué ocurriría si, por un casual, llego a elegir un vestuario que tú no tengas previsto. Supongo que toda la disciplina de las Juventudes se desbarataría.

—De ningún modo, monseñor. Cualquier extravagancia tuya, por inesperada que sea, llegará a los sastres de Lur una hora después de que tú la hayas adoptado. Y en un plazo máximo de dos semanas, las tiendas del Mundo Macho estarán provistas del atuendo que la juventud necesita para parecerse al primer joven del país. De hecho, todo tu vestuario potencial está ya reproducido en miles de artículos que los jóvenes de Lur agotan diariamente en las tiendas. Quiero decir, con todos mis respetos, que cualquier vestimenta que elijas, sirve. Bota o borceguí; sombrero de ala ancha o birrete; manto o toga; manga de gramalla para cubrir el brazo o brazalete..., cualquier cosa, monseñor.

—¡Fantástico...! Pélame otro granito... Así pues, todos los jóvenes de Lur, excepto los esclavos, llevarán el cabello largo como yo, se pintarán los ojos como tú me has enseñado a pintármelos...

—Tú los llevas como ellos, monseñor. Es moda antigua en Lur. La importó la reina de Saba cuando vino a visitarnos en tiempos del judío Salomón.

—Muy preciso. Y precioso, ¿no? Es decir, que no hay escapatoria. Los jóvenes del Mundo Macho tienen que ser iguales a mí en todo, y yo, siendo como soy Nebjeperura, no podré ser diferente de ellos...

—Una regla válida para todos nosotros, sí. Todos menos los sacerdotes de Cobra y los jefes de la Guerra.

—¿Y por qué ellos no, Astor?

—Ellos tienen otros modelos, monseñor.

—¿Que son?

—Ellos mismos, por supuesto.

Cuando me dio el otro grano de uva, pelado con exquisito esmero, dibujó aquella sonrisa de complacencia típica de las conversaciones que se desarrollan con toda normalidad, aunque, al fin y a la postre, resulten tan poco satisfactorias como la que acabábamos de tener. Paseábamos por uno de los jardines colgantes: el que se abre sobre el patio del cuartel y queda exactamente a la altura del rostro de uno de los colosos de granito. Tener tan cerca la boca de Epsamón, boca lisa y redondeada en no sé cuántos metros de piedra muy trabajada, hizo que me estremeciera. De repente me acometió la pregunta que había mantenido callada durante muchos días.

—¿Cómo es Epsamón? Quiero decir, físicamente. Un día me dijiste que sus representaciones son...

Era el tipo de pregunta que Astor siempre rechazaba, y esta vez no constituyó una excepción. Se volvió para pelarme otro grano de uva, y permaneció en silencio. Me vi obligado a repetir la pregunta, y, cuando se decidió a mirarme, lo hizo fijamente, como si me reservara una sorpresa.

—Lo sabrás cuando llegue el momento —dijo—. Sólo te ruego que tengas paciencia, porque no está en mi poder ni en mis atributos hacerte esta revelación.

—De acuerdo. Y ¿quién me la hará, llegada la hora?

—Estarás iniciado en los grandes misterios de Cobra, y sus más altas jerarquías sacerdotales considerarán si es el momento apropiado para revelarte lo que ni siquiera yo puedo saber.

Al contemplar de nuevo los rasgos monumentales del rostro de Epsamón, al otro lado de las palmeras enanas que limitaban la terraza, tuve un presentimiento que no podía dejar de consultar con Astor, quien, complaciente, me servía una copa de alabastro con inscripciones jeroglíficas; una copa cuya transparencia dejaba ver unas burbujas juguetonas y deliciosas, parecidas a las que produce el champagne.

—Mirando estas estatuas llego a una conclusión, Astor: la representación no es realista, ¿verdad?

—Un día te lo dije, monseñor. Es simbólica.

—Y ¿por qué, tratándose de Epsamón?

—Por eso mismo, monseñor. Y te ruego que no me hagas más preguntas a las cuales sólo puede contestar tu destino, que es...

—Ya lo sé. El destino del país.

—Exactamente. Sé tú un amo piadoso, y sea yo tu siervo más fiel, el que más te adora..., lo cual sólo podré demostrarte si me limito a cumplir el programa didáctico que me ha sido fijado.

Pero en el programa figuraban prácticas tan horribles como las que ya le he contado a usted, profesor; y yo aún no había logrado vencer el miedo y el asco que muchas de estas cosas me inspiraban, mientras mi hermoso guardián ya empezaba a mirar mis repulsiones y mis espantos con aquella sonrisa de simpatía que, como también le he dicho, se iba convirtiendo en afecto sincero. En cualquier caso, la frecuencia de su compañía, los ratos larguísimos que estábamos obligados a compartir, le pusieron en situación de compadecerme el día en que vino a anunciarme uno de los nuevos sufrimientos que tendría que soportar; y, si bien se empeñaba en no aclararme del todo los misterios que me angustiaban —o tal vez tenía razón cuando decía que no podía hacerlo—, estoy muy seguro de que no se hubiese compadecido tanto algunas semanas antes, cuando le gustaba dejarme en la ignorancia por placer; cuando se divertía maltratándome a causa de mi humildad.

Hacía ya una semana que todas las mañanas me llevaba al templo del Gran Tronco Universal, donde elevaba mis plegarias a Cobra en la capilla privada dentro de la cual, si él y los sacerdotes no me mentían, la meditación, el ayuno y otras formas del ascetismo debidamente establecido me darían acceso a la revelación de los Grandes Misterios. Y fue precisamente una de aquellas mañanas cuando, cumplidas ya todas las ceremonias, y mientras me preparaba para volver a palacio utilizando uno de los pasadizos subterráneos que me evitarían ser visto por el pueblo, llegó Astor y, después de arrodillarse como de costumbre, me pidió que despidiera a mi séquito porque necesitaba hablar conmigo en privado. El Sumo Sacerdote de este culto nos introdujo en una sala especial y, apenas nos quedamos a solas, Astor empezó su discurso:

—Tu estancia entre nosotros ha demostrado con creces que la elección de Epsamón Divino no fue desacertada. Has ido aprendiendo nuestra lengua, has asimilado nuestras costumbres, has obedecido las sabias medidas de nuestra religión y has conseguido que el pueblo te deseara, que la juventud de Lur se mirara en ti como en un espejo. Has demostrado que no careces de grandeza, pero aún te falta superar ciertas pruebas. Para conseguirlo, los sabios de la capital intensificarán las lecciones, te someterán diariamente a cursos más intensivos, mediante los cuales, y con tu esfuerzo soberano, llegarás a ser el más sabio de todos nosotros; y comprenderás que esta exigencia es fundamental, pues, como miembro superior de nuestras clases dirigentes, tú debes poseer toda la sabiduría que nosotros nunca poseeremos, y así podrás regir más acertadamente nuestras voluntades, dirigir nuestros pensamientos, e incluso nuestro gusto. Ahora bien: ¿de qué serviría tu capacidad intelectual si no fuese acompañada de la fuerza, en primer lugar, y de la voluntad de aniquilar, en segundo pero no menos importante reto? ¿De qué servirían las letras que leerás en nombre nuestro, si no ofrecieses la estampa de la belleza absoluta (y el poder no es nada si no es bello), la belleza y la fuerza forjadas en la palestra, en los juegos, en la vida al aire libre, en la suprema armonía de la virilidad compartida? Y, al mismo tiempo, ¿qué serían tus leyes (que han de ser implacables hasta la crueldad) si vacilases un momento, bien por piedad, bien por debilidad, a la hora de ejecutarlas? ¿Qué serían, igualmente, todas aquellas virtudes, si llegado el instante del sufrimiento este tu cuerpo, que el pueblo debe adorar, se revelara indefenso, endeble, capaz de desmayarse al primer suplicio?

—¿Y quién dice que yo tendré que sufrir suplicio? —pregunté, ingenuo—. ¿Acaso no soy el Co-Divino?

—Lo eres, y, por serlo, tu vida y tu resistencia deben ser modelos a seguir por todos nosotros, que al ver, en las Fiestas del Vino, el ejemplo de tu poder macho, aprenderemos a no vacilar ante los peligros; igual que cuando nos llegue el momento de presentarnos en el Templo del Final Viril para terminar allí dignamente nuestros días y evitar que la raza se vea ultrajada con las vejaciones de la senectud.

—Me hablas de una nueva ceremonia, y aún no he tenido tiempo de asimilar el significado de las anteriores. ¿Qué es eso de la Fiesta del Vino? Yo diría que en este país hay más fiestas que días tiene el año.

—De las Fiestas que solicitan tu presencia para que el pueblo conozca que has regresado vencedor del país de la Nada, demostrando una vez más el gran poder del Mal, ésta es la segunda, y representa la primavera que tú nos devuelves con los rayos de la vida. Seguidamente, participarás en las Jornadas de la Procreación, donde engendrarás la vida ante todo el pueblo. Estas dos ceremonias certificarán que eres inmortal, porque las presides cada año desde el principio de todas las historias.

De este modo deduje que había existido otro Nebjeperura antes que yo, y que Epsamón me necesitaba para que mi presencia convenciera al pueblo de que los grandes mitos del Mundo Macho nunca morirían, porque estaba escrito que fuesen inmortales, y que siempre fuesen creídos.

Y, sin embargo, ¿dónde estaba aquel Nebjeperura que partió, como cada año, hacia las tierras de la Nada y no regresó, como cada año, para devolver la primavera al Mundo Macho? ¿Qué desastroso fin pudo tener el compañero de Epsamón, cuando ahora tenía que ser yo, un pobre trovador del consumo europeo, quien entregase los rayos de la vida a un mundo que dependía de ellos? Era muy posible que el Nebjeperura del pasado año hubiese cumplido ya la cincuentena y estuviera crucificado en las cavernas del templo del Final Viril; incluso era probable que, joven todavía, muriese en acto de batalla al lado de su señor, y se ocultase su muerte en nombre de una suprema razón de Estado. Eso explicaría, con toda seguridad, que me raptasen para sustituir a un mito necesario; pero, de cualquier modo, no abandonaba la duda que me perseguía desde aquella noche de Minia: ¿por qué, entre todos los hombres, tuve que ser yo el elegido?

Preguntárselo a Astor hubiese sido perder el tiempo, dados los antecedentes. Decidí seguir la comedia. Y, a pesar de todo, la mañana había sido muy provechosa, porque las palabras de Astor me habían aportado alguna luz sobre uno de los enigmas que me obsesionaban. Y reconocerá usted que, dada mi situación, lo que puede parecer poco era realmente muchísimo.

—De acuerdo, Astor. ¿Debo entenderlo exclusivamente como un deseo de Epsamón, o bien como una orden que es obligado obedecer?

—Monseñor: entiéndelo como un ineludible imperativo de nuestras leyes, las cuales son Epsamón, quien, dicho sea de paso, no sería Divino si no fuese, Él mismo, la ley.

Preceptos de este tipo me los inculcaban día tras día, en clases de siete y ocho horas de duración, los sabios que habían sido designados como mis maestros y que, cosa curiosa, habían llegado a la vejez como los sacerdotes sin acatar el rito del Final Viril. Esto fue lo primero que me sorprendió cuando aquellos hombres de aspecto patriarcal me llevaron a la biblioteca privada de Epsamón: la biblioteca donde yo debía seguir las lecciones y que contenía una cantidad de libros como nunca había visto en parte alguna del mundo; libros de todo tipo, en todas las lenguas conocidas, encuadernados en piel humana de prisioneros o esclavos (en el Mundo Macho hay toda una industria que utiliza la piel de los prisioneros muertos para hacer tapas de libros, pantallas, portamonedas, ceñidores, e incluso zapatos; y esto se explica porque los prisioneros, o quienes pertenecen a la esclavitud auténtica, no tienen derecho a la gloriosa muerte de la crucifixión voluntaria).

Los celadores de la cultura me esclavizaron en aquella tarea intensiva que me hizo aprender por la fuerza un sinfín de materias sorprendentes que más adelante le expondré, y que, a causa de las infiltraciones de culturas exteriores, le sorprenderán tanto como a mí. Pero no es de eso de lo que quería hablarle ahora, sino de esa otra preparación, también intensiva, a la cual me sometió Astor, siempre decidido a que yo llegara a ser el ejemplo juvenil necesario para la generación más reciente del Mundo Macho. Y para conseguir esta preparación, de la cual se habría encargado Epsamón personalmente si los asuntos bélicos no le hubiesen retenido tanto tiempo en tierras de herejes, se presentaba cada mañana en mi atrio personal y me azotaba.

La primera vez me sorprendí mucho, porque, incluso siendo una práctica harto difícil de soportar, no era tan terrible como las palabras de Astor me habían hecho presentir. Acostumbrado a la evidencia de que en aquella tierra cualquier crueldad no sólo era posible, sino cotidiana, pasé la noche en vela sospechando que me cortarían un dedo del pie como a los reclutas de la guardia palatina, que me aplicarían la penetración mediante el hierro candente, como ya había sucedido una vez, o algo por el estilo. Cuando confesé mis temores a Astor, él estalló en una carcajada, y adujo que los dedos de mi pie eran demasiado preciosos para ser malgastados («¿Qué dedos más serenos podría besar nuestro pueblo, y en especial *tus servidores más próximos*?»). Y a continuación se sonrojó como un niño atrapado en su primer escarceo amoroso.

En el atrio, cerca de la piscina, había dos pequeñas columnas de mármol negro, en las cuales no era la primera vez que reparaba, pero sin preguntarme nunca si podían tener otra utilidad que no fuera la estrictamente decorativa. Después de una breve ceremonia que tenía algo de iniciación litúrgica, el hermoso Astor golpeó el gong y Avitachí trajo unas cadenas de oro con las que me ataron de manos y pies a las pequeñas columnas, y me dejaron allí abierto, en forma de aspa, postura que en los tormentos del Mundo Macho representaba la figura digna de los privilegiados. Además, como, según Astor, las primeras veces percibiría dolor, aquella postura me dejaba la cabeza en libertad para echarla hacia adelante o hacia atrás, de acuerdo con el impulso que solicitara mi cuerpo en busca de un alivio desesperado. Seguidamente cerré los ojos, puse los miembros en tensión y me mordí los labios mientras oía los pasos de Astor, que se alejaban a fin de tomar más impulso con la distancia.

El primer latigazo hendió el aire, me golpeó la espalda y yo grité de una forma desgarradora; tanto, que Astor se acercó y me dijo:

—Comprendo que de momento te quejes, monseñor; pero convendría que aprendieras a reprimirte de ejercicio en ejercicio, porque no es precisamente una vergonzosa declaración de dolor lo que el pueblo espera de ti.

A duras penas pude gemir:

—Ten paciencia... Todo llegará...

—Lo sé, monseñor, lo sé... Y si tú pudieras verte con mis ojos, atado de este modo, con la espalda sangrando... ¡Ah, serás digno del Mundo Macho, y cada latigazo te hará desear uno más! Lo pedirás como si fuese una dádiva preciosa, monseñor, porque tu vida, tu sentido de la existencia, ya no podrá prescindir de esta maravillosa sensación, de ese aprender que tu cuerpo, tu voluntad, vencen con grandeza la incomodidad que los más débiles consideran fatal.

Retrocedió y volvió a azotarme; al principio, haciendo una pequeña pausa entre uno y otro azote; después, muy seguidos, hasta que la espalda llegó a ser una gran llaga que mi apuesto guardián acudió a lavarme con hiel y vinagre mientras yo le insultaba con la autoridad que me confería mi sagrado despotismo. Pero en esta ocasión se dolió de mis insultos, porque, al parecer, no era justo que yo, magnánimo señor, dejara sin agradecer el esfuerzo que él, como amigo, debía realizar al administrarme el sufrimiento.

La cotidiana aplicación de aquella disciplina alcanzó pronto una complicidad entre víctima y verdugo que convertía el tormento en un simple ejercicio de estudiante, como los trabajos de caligrafía que los sabios me ordenaban cada noche para que se los llevara realizados a la mañana siguiente. Es cierto que el adiestramiento del machismo implicaba dolor; pero yo me daba cuenta de que Astor tuvo razón cuando alegaba que el sufrimiento soportado con regularidad me capacitaría para aceptarlo cada vez con mayor complacencia. Al mismo tiempo —y eso iba a saberlo con el paso de los días— me otorgaba una extraña dependencia del martirio, como si el daño inicial se convirtiera, a partir de un momento determinado, en algo sin lo cual ya no podría vivir. Y era obvio que, en ese aspecto, el dolor bien soportado, el sufrimiento que se aprende a desear, puede ser una forma de cultura como otra cualquiera.

Debo decir que la superación del dolor, o, mejor dicho, la superación del espanto frente al dolor, vino asociada a una sublimación del asco de matar, virtud en la cual nunca esperé sobresalir. Astor sabía perfectamente que me quedaban muchos prejuicios en este sentido; por lo tanto, no era de extrañar que me mirase con gran pena el día en que vino a buscarme para ir al Jardín del Fauno, donde me aguardaba el pelotón encargado de ejecutar a Avitachí..., y que yo debía presidir en un primer aprendizaje de las lecciones de violencia bien administrada; porque es bien notorio, y nada erróneo, que las violencias más pequeñas capacitan al hombre para avanzar hacia las leyes absolutas de la destrucción general. Y, de este modo, la crueldad, administrada al principio en dosis mínimas, va en aumento a medida que progresa el aprendizaje, hasta que alcanza aquellas apoteosis culminantes que hacen o deshacen la Historia; y es muy cierto que los tormentos que aprendemos a infligir en la tierna carne de un esclavo adolescente engendran, después de mucha práctica, la Guerra Santa, en la cual Epsamón es ahora diestro porque ya lo fue, de joven, en azotar a placer a todos sus siervos. De este modo era evidente que si yo triunfaba en aquel adiestramiento, ya no vacilaría cuando, en un futuro, tuviese que ordenar la ejecución de los traidores, la muerte en masa de los enemigos herejes, la destrucción de sus ciudades, de su libertad. Y es que todo aquello constituye un requisito indispensable para una perfecta educación de príncipe.

Ignoro si sabré expresarle con toda exactitud el horror de aquella primera ejecución, el vértigo inaudito que inspira a un alma no educada el hecho de robar, lentamente y a sangre fría, este latido de vida que los grandes dioses depositaron en cada fuerza de la creación. Sin embargo, existe ese horror, y no hay nada que pueda comparársele, aunque uno llegase a asumir por completo las leyes del Mundo Macho, según las cuales una existencia individual no tiene la menor importancia, porque su único valor consiste en hallarse sometida al absoluto del Gran Tronco Universal, o bien al Estado, que es su forma más organizada puesta al alcance de los hombres. Como muchos otros tormentos que hube de contemplar mientras no acepté que cada ejecución puede suponer un vastísimo placer, el suplicio del mancebo que hasta hacía poco fuese el encargado de despertarme cada mañana constituyó uno de los golpes más duros que me correspondió soportar y superar durante la primera época de la Vida Nueva.

PERO COMPRENDO que el orden de la narración incurre en faltas imperdonables, y que tantas reflexiones me alejan de algunas escenas básicas para la comprensión de la historia. Ahora mismo, animado por el interés que despierta en mí la organización y las costumbres del Mundo Macho, efectúo un inmenso salto y le hablo a usted de un suplicio sin explicar cuáles fueron las causas. Y es menester que se las exponga, pues ni siquiera en un país tan absurdo como el Mundo Macho se organizan ejecuciones y tormentos sin que la víctima los haya merecido. No sería justo; y la justicia, aunque sea en un aspecto extravagante, existe en Lur y se hace respetar: Avitachí, debo decirlo, sufrió tormento y muerte porque era de justicia que lo sufriera. Era reo y criminal. Explicarle a usted la razón de esta culpa será el principal objeto de este fragmento. Y si deja de fumar opio (sobre todo porque, al ver cómo se aficiona, siento la tentación de volver a él), si me escucha usted con atención, no quedará decepcionado.

Todo empezó días antes, una tarde, en el atrio; cuando yo me hallaba haciendo los deberes impuestos por mis maestros (analizar unas doctrinas sobre la belleza, que recordaban a Platón como el azul recuerda al azul), Avitachí tañía la lira, instrumento en cuyo manejo era particularmente diestro. Recuerdo que la puesta del sol doraba las columnas con un resplandor mortecino, que favorecía cualquier tendencia a la melancolía. La música, de antiguas resonancias, milagrosamente ineducada, aumentaba aquella sensación con una dulzura que la hacía muy lejana, como si no proviniese de la superficie, sino de los más profundos abismos de mi interior. A medida que se perdía la luz, mientras el viento me traía todos los perfumes del parque, mi memoria volaba hacia otro tipo de delicuescencia que ya no toleraba el ejercicio de la razón, ni siquiera el estudio de textos tan sublimes como los que se me ordenaba aprender.

Ya he dicho que la altivez de Avitachí fue muy agresiva desde que nos conocimos, pero aún debo añadir que aquella primera actitud no varió en lo más mínimo durante todo el tiempo que estuvo a mi servicio. Su historia me era desconocida, y, si bien tiempo atrás me habría interesado conocerla, ahora ya no me importaba en absoluto, porque los intentos infructuosos de ganar su confianza habían acabado por cansarme. Me resultaba tan desconocido como la melodía que tocaba; de hecho, él sólo existía para crearla.

Pero aquel día, cosa curiosa, aprovechó la ausencia de Astor, quien había ido a una fiesta de gala, y se abrió completamente a la simpatía y a una actitud cercana al intento de comprenderme, como si quisiera ayudarme. Huelga decir que nunca había dejado de ser ceremonioso, servicial a más no poder; pero, insisto, siempre de una forma distante, inalcanzable. Sin embargo, aquella noche prescindió de muchos protocolos obligados y, desde el primer momento, quiso dejar muy claro que era humano.

Yo me había levantado para dar un paseo por el claustro contiguo, construido en un encantador estilo románico; y hacía ya rato que estaba sentado en el borde cubierto de musgo de la fontana. Inconscientemente, acariciaba los peces; no pensaba sino en los tilos mecidos por el viento, cuando percibí que la música había cesado. Y al ver que la imagen de Avitachí coincidía, en el agua del estanque, con el reflejo de las galerías de arco de medio punto que tenía sobre mi cabeza, levanté la mirada y le descubrí a mi lado.

—¿Monseñor añora alguna cosa o algún lugar?

La pregunta me extrañó profundamente. O, tal vez, más que la pregunta, fue el hecho de que pudiese interesarle mi respuesta.

—Tal vez sí —contesté—, pero no sé qué.

—¿O quién, monseñor?

—No sé. Supongamos que sea *quién*...

Se sentó a mi lado, sin ni siquiera pedir permiso. Tanto atrevimiento me hizo notar que ni por un momento perdía su altivez.

—¿Acaso monseñor añora una... mujer?

—¡Una... mujer!

¡Ay, dioses! En aquel preciso lugar, junto a un surtidor formado por leones y palmeras de piedra, aparecía una extraña criatura que me devolvía un nombre casi olvidado. Venía a hablarme de la mujer sin utilizar ningún adjetivo despreciativo, sin incluirla en una especie zoológica inferior, refiriéndose a ella con la naturalidad que yo utilizaba en Europa, mucho tiempo antes, cuando aún no había olvidado que necesitaba hacer el amor de vez en cuando sin que me importase la perfecta conservación del cuerpo.

—Una mujer, sí —dijo él—. He velado muchas noches junto a ti, y sé que la necesitas. Hablas a menudo de ella en tus sueños.

—Supongamos que sea así..., supongamos que la Vida Nueva no ha podido desterrar la inquietud que me provoca este recuerdo. Pero ¿por qué razón me hablas de este tema tú..., tú precisamente, uno de este país?

—Porque yo, monseñor, no soy de este país.

—Perdona, pero...

—Yo no nací en el Mundo Macho, monseñor. Y en mi tierra, cerca del mar, hay dos mujeres que me aguardan: mi madre y Hathor, que es joven y bella, y deseable.

Entonces recordé que bajo el birrete de lamé dorado, había una cabeza rasurada, exactamente como la del joven que intentó escapar del Mundo Macho...

—¿Eres un esclavo de orden inferior? —le pregunté, intranquilo por cada palabra que pudiese pronunciar—. Es eso, ¿no? Te hicieron prisionero durante la Guerra Santa y...

—En mi tierra, soy hijo del rey. Pero mi padre no se las da de divinidad. Ha sido elegido por su pueblo, monseñor, y ahora dirige nuestros ejércitos contra el exterminio brutal de vuestro Epsamón. Mi padre está junto a sus súbditos, y camina entre ellos y los escucha. Y nadie imita su forma de vestir, del mismo modo que nadie se peinaba como yo.

Muy bien: hijo de rey hereje contra dios absoluto. Su altivez contra el orgullo y el despotismo que yo intentaba fingir. El combate se establecía sobre la base de una absoluta igualdad, excepto en una cosa: él sabía que, con la simple mención de la palabra *mujer*, todo mi cuerpo se había estremecido. Esto me colocaba en sus manos, porque ambos sabíamos que cualquier cosa que él pudiera pedir a cambio de devolverme aquel sueño medio olvidado iba a concedérsela sin dudarlo.

—De tus palabras deduzco que quieres hacerme un chantaje. Querrás la libertad, por supuesto. ¿Qué me darás tú, a cambio?

—La mujer, monseñor. No la Bestia Llamada Hembra; no la máquina reproductora del Mundo Macho, sino la Mujer, simplemente: bella e inmensa, madre y amante como lo es allá, en tu tierra; capaz de hacerte volver a ti mismo. Porque yo sé, monseñor, cuántas veces has pedido a Astor que te llevara junto a ella; y Astor te lo ha negado porque él sólo ha conocido el sexo una vez al año, en las Jornadas de la Reproducción. Él es una criatura del Mundo Macho, monseñor, y cree en la pureza del cuerpo, que da al país una raza de titanes bellos e invencibles; pero tú no crees ni creerás nunca tal cosa. Tú no ansías tener un cuerpo perfecto, el temple sin vida de un dios de mármol; sino que lo darías todo: poder, divinidad, riquezas y cultura, a cambio de aquella única fuerza que conociste lejos del Mundo Macho, cuando ni siquiera soñabas en el horror de tener que reservar para las Jornadas de la Reproducción toda tu fuerza de humano..., la fuerza que, después de las fiestas, deberás enterrar bajo un año de ejercicios en la palestra, adiestramientos en el dolor y otras mentiras por el estilo...

—¿Y tú me ofreces...?

—Que tu manantial de vida no se agote en una ceremonia de estatuas; que vuelvas a saber qué es, hacia qué paraísos te empuja, cómo te da la medida de tu libertad, también olvidada...

En aquel instante se apoderó de mí el temor de que

todo fuese una maniobra que el gobierno del Mundo Macho hubiese preparado para ponerme a prueba. Recordaba a los dos fugitivos del primer día, el destino incierto de la mujer y, sobre todo, el final del muchacho, devorado por sus hermanos en el templo de Homo Demeter. Pero, a pesar del miedo, la sonrisa de Avitachí me animaba, y tal vez quería decirme que mi caso era muy distinto, porque yo era la divinidad sobre la Tierra y podía disponer de todas las leyes del Mundo Macho. Por lo tanto, decidí que haría mi santa voluntad (y en este caso, profesor, ya sabemos que «santa» no es un simple adjetivo enfático).

Lo más sorprendente era que, incluso antes de conocer mi respuesta, Avitachí ya se había preocupado de pedir los caballos al cuartel; había encargado otros dos de refresco, y los soldados no le opusieron dificultad alguna, porque él puntualizó que obedecía órdenes de Nebjeperura. Mientras bajábamos por las escaleras metálicas y, después, por el pasadizo excavado bajo el palacio, él iba contándome su historia: Avitachí, que, en la lengua de Lur, significa «Melodía de los barrios del Muelle», no era su nombre, sino el que le impusieron cuando Epsamón se lo llevó en calidad de rehén precioso, pues tenerlo en palacio constituía una garantía de que el rey de Auer rendiría la plaza sin condiciones. En realidad se llamaba Glauco, que, en la lengua de los herejes —considerada dialecto inferior por los sabios de Lur—, sirve para denominar un color verde más pálido que los otros y, al mismo tiempo, a un molusco muy difícil de pescar porque su azul luminoso lo confunde a menudo con el agua del mar y la caricia de la luna llena. Le llamaremos Glauco a partir de ahora, y, de paso, me ahorraré las explicaciones que me dio sobre el destino que esperaba a su pueblo si el rey Plauto se rendía a Epsamón para salvarle a él la vida. Eran sucesos terribles: las ciudades de Auer serían destruidas, como todas las que Epsamón había conquistado a los herejes; cortaría la lengua a todos los hombres y, después de afeitarles la cabeza, serían llevados como esclavos a Lur, donde se les emplearía en obras de construcción hasta que muriesen; las mujeres jóvenes serían encerradas para siempre en las cavernas de la reproducción, y las que no sirviesen para dar hijos al Mundo Macho —entre las cuales figuraba la propia madre de Glauco—, serían pasadas a cuchillo, como se ha hecho siempre cuando es Epsamón quien vence. Y Epsamón vence siempre.

Los oficiales de la guardia palatina no parecían extrañados por mi antojo de cabalgar de noche: además, les parecía muy normal que me hiciese acompañar por un servidor, como correspondía a mi rango y como exigía mi seguridad personal. Pero me di cuenta de que un soldado muy joven me miraba fijamente, tal vez espiándome, como si sospechara algo. Pero no era la sospecha lo que me intrigaba en él, sino el hecho inequívoco de haberle conocido, de haberle tratado no durante mi estancia en el Mundo Macho, sino en una vida anterior. La pintura de los ojos, azul como exige el Machismo, la escasa vestimenta propia de los soldados y el cuerpo desarrollado de una forma apoteósica, le prestaban un nuevo aspecto; pero no tanto que fuese imposible reconocerle.

Pensé en él durante mucho rato, mientras cabalgábamos a toda velocidad por los campos de Lur y los dejábamos atrás para adentrarnos con la mayor rapidez posible en las sombras protectoras de la selva.

—Tengo la sensación de que nos estaban vigilando —dijo Glauco, mirando continuamente hacia atrás—. Nos urge ganar tiempo, pues podrían sospechar nuestra huida y nos perseguirían.

Los rugidos de las fieras, invisibles entre la maleza, me hicieron olvidar rápidamente la impresión que me produjo el soldado que viera antes; del mismo modo que la impaciencia por volver a encontrar a una mujer hacía que me olvidara del miedo inmediato producido por aquellos rugidos. En esta historia, profesor, todo es una cuestión de sensaciones que se imponen, que van triunfando unas sobre otras y se anulan entre sí de acuerdo con los terrores del momento, de acuerdo con sus urgencias. La duda, el miedo y la necesidad de la esperanza pueden presentarse seguidos, e incluso mezclados, y el resultado es siempre un augurio, ya placentero ya terrible. Son momentos de gran tensión los que preceden al dolor o la alegría; y tanto la presencia del soldado a quien creí reconocer, como los ruidos de la selva, implicaban una premonición que el mismo Glauco había captado. A medida que avanzábamos entre aquellos árboles que apenas dejaban filtrar los rayos de luna que nos servían de guía, los cánticos de los pájaros parecían gruñidos, y eran como aullidos de desesperación, tal vez un coloquio entre los muertos enterrados en los panteones ilustres que se hallan al otro lado de la selva, antes de abandonar la Vía Herculana. Y Glauco me comunicó que apenas saliéramos de aquellas arboledas espeluznantes llegaríamos al territorio prohibido.

Y así fue. Dejamos atrás los últimos árboles de la selva y apareció ante mis ojos una enorme llanura, en forma de pendiente muy pronunciada, que llegaba hasta el desierto. Allí concluían los dominios de Epsamón y empezaban las tierras de los herejes. Más allá de las primeras dunas, la arena estaba cubierta de huesos, restos de los muertos en una guerra de expansión tan antigua como el Mundo Macho: una guerra que, en realidad, era el precio permanente que pagaba por su grandeza; una guerra que es la historia de todas las conquistas que esta colectividad ha realizado desde que, al abandonar el valle donde empieza Lur, envió sus legiones a crear un imperio que no tenía parangón en toda la historia que la mente de los hombres podría recordar.

Obedeciendo a una indicación de Glauco, me volví y, en el otro extremo de la selva, pude distinguir una montaña muy irregular, coronada por una pirámide natural. Era de piedra roja, resplandeciente a la luz de la luna y con algo de fantasmal. Y yo había leído en los libros de geografía que detrás de aquellas montañas, en medio de las mismas, se formaba el valle estéril donde habita, salvaje y peligrosa, la Bestia Llamada Hembra.

Me disponía a lanzar mi caballo al galope, pero Avitachí sacó la espada y en un segundo la sentí sobre mi cuello. Mi cómplice ya no sonreía, y su altivez de príncipe se había convertido en furia de guerrero: hizo alarde de una brutalidad inesperada, y yo dejé caer las riendas y, más ingenuo que nunca, pregunté por qué rompía el pacto...

—No hay tal pacto —contestó—: yo no soy un rehén, sino un espía con la misión de convertirte a ti en rehén de Auer. Aquí no tienes a nadie que defienda tu dignidad. Aquí, «monseñor», estás en poder de los hombres de Auer.

—¿De quién dices? ¿Qué estúpida película intentas colarme?

—Estás en poder de los soldados que mi rey ha mandado al recibir mi mensaje. Se hallan ocultos entre los árboles, y te cargarán de cadenas y te llevarán a presencia de nuestro rey. No de mi padre, porque te he mentido, sino del gran señor que gobierna con justicia y bondad a mis padres..., no desde el principio de todas las historias, porque no existe tal origen, sino desde que la madurez le hizo apto para gobernar según el veredicto del pueblo y hasta que el final destinado a toda vida humana lo lleve al reino de Aquel que Ordena el Tiempo...

No supe qué decir. Tanto me acostumbraron a ser obedecido, que el hecho de obedecer ahora me parecía una regresión extravagante.

—Pero... pero... tú...

—Yo sólo soy uno más de los jóvenes que luchan contra el invasor. Como muchos de mis compañeros, me infiltré entre las Juventudes de Lur; y, como ellos, arriesgo en mi empresa la suerte y la vida. Sólo esperaba el momento de poder sacarte de palacio y, sobre todo, que no tuvieras a Astor a tu lado. Te informaré, «monseñor», de que la fiesta que esta noche le ha tenido alejado de ti será considerada como una importante coyuntura en la inmediata victoria de mi rey sobre el tuyo... Y, ahora, ¡apéate de una vez! Y no intentes defenderte. Nuestros hombres no vacilarían en matarte, porque sabemos que eres la pieza clave para conseguir que todo el poder, todo el esplendor del Mundo Macho, se hundan en un solo día.

Hasta mucho tiempo después no fui capaz de comprender el significado de estas últimas palabras, pero empezaron a intrigarme desde el primer momento. Y mientras Avitachí, empujándome con la espada, me obligaba a bajar del caballo, miré a mi alrededor, buscando a los hombres misteriosos que estarían dispuestos a encadenarme. De repente, Glauco emitió un silbido, levantó los brazos y gritó a sus compañeros. Pero la respuesta fue terrible. Y no para mí, como sin duda esperaba mi raptor...

Oí un grito que, desde los árboles, quería prevenir a Glauco de un gran peligro; pero ya era demasiado tarde, porque al anunciar aquel aullido el fracaso de los planes previstos, la mano de Glauco, que esgrimía la espada hacia el cielo, fue cortada de tajo por un hacha que voló desde los matorrales. Glauco rodó por los suelos, gritando y frotándose el muñón sangriento, y al punto salieron de entre la maleza los soldados del Mundo Macho, blandiendo sus cimitarras. Al frente de la tropa, Astor empuñaba otra hacha, y entonces comprendí que fue él quien había arrojado la primera. Vestía de gala, con clámide de lino blanco y sandalias doradas, pero sus manos y brazos estaban cubiertos de sangre. Al verle, Glauco intentó incorporarse mientras con la única mano que le quedaba apretaba su muñeca cercenada. Mas sus intentos fueron inútiles, porque Astor dio un salto colosal y, antes de que el traidor tuviera tiempo de escabullirse hacia el desierto, se arrojó sobre él profiriendo un prolongado grito de guerra y le cortó la otra mano de un nuevo hachazo.

Los gritos de Glauco no sólo eran producidos por aquella tremenda violencia, sino también por la visión de los cuerpos de sus partidarios, que los soldados del Mundo Macho sacaban de entre los matorrales. Retrocedí un paso. El espanto quedaba relegado a un segundo plano; mejor dicho, ya no había lugar para él. La visión de aquellos cuerpos superaba cualquier impresión, cualquier otro sentimiento.

—¡Me alegro de no haber llegado tarde! —exclamó Astor, mientras me rodeaba el hombro. Y yo me apoyé en él y estallé en un llanto histérico. Pero Astor no me despreciaba, como las otras veces en que me había visto en el mismo estado. Tal vez empezaba a comprender. Tal vez se hacía cargo.

—Conocíamos los planes de ese traidor y montamos una guardia especial que le seguía en todo momento. La fiesta sólo fue un pretexto: era necesario dejarte a solas con él, provocar la huida. Hemos tomado el atajo de las montañas, que él desconoce, y así llegamos antes que vosotros: justo a tiempo de aniquilar a sus cómplices. Míralos bien, monseñor, pues éste será el castigo de todo aquel que se atreva a atentar contra tu persona.

Los cuerpos yacían ensartados en las lanzas de los soldados del Mundo Macho, pero antes habían sido ejecutados a golpes de hacha. Ahora, las lanzas levantadas exhibían los cadáveres mutilados a modo de trofeos de guerra. Aquellas carnes estaban abiertas con tajos enormes, y la sangre caía sobre los soldados. El hombre que gritase entre los matorrales aún respiraba, y antes de morir miró a Glauco y exclamó «Viva la Libertad» o algo por el estilo. Los otros cuerpos tenían cinco o seis hachas clavadas; y cuando los soldados movían las lanzas, las heridas iban ensanchándose. Pero ni siquiera eso podía hacer padecer a las víctimas más de lo que ya habían padecido.

—Gracias —murmuré, siempre apoyado en el pecho de Astor—. Para la próxima vez aprenderé a no ser tan ingenuo.

Glauco mostraba ahora los dos muñones ensangrentados, y mientras un soldado le ataba los pies a la silla de mi caballo, para que yo pudiese arrastrar su cuerpo en señal de victoria, él gritó:

—¡Serás ingenuo mientras seas un vulgar lacayo del Mundo Macho..., mientras seas un esclavo y no descubras que en tu ignorancia reside su fuerza!

—¡Hacedle callar! —exclamó Astor—. ¡Hacedle callar ahora mismo!

Aunque los soldados lo mantenían aferrado por el cuello, Glauco continuaba gritando:

—¡Escucha! ¡Escucha! Para ellos, tú eres mucho más importante que Epsamón... ¡Tú eres el Mundo Macho! En el *Palazzo* del Lago sabrás...

Astor, siempre ágil, cayó como un relámpago sobre el prisionero y le golpeó la cabeza con ambas manos. Glauco perdió el conocimiento, y los soldados acabaron de atarlo a mi caballo: huelga decir que lo arrastré hasta el palacio, como si la victoria hubiese sido mía. Los soldados iban a recibir una buena recompensa a cambio de no contar lo sucedido, y, de aquel modo, mi fama no sufriría un golpe perjudicial. Todo perfecto: nada había sido dejado a la improvisación. Pero, al observar la feroz expresión de Astor, sus rizos desordenados, empapados de sudor, sobre una frente de verdugo en contraste con la túnica de lino blanco, pensé una vez más que la civilización más refinada, la belleza más lograda y la extrema perfección cultural no consiguen triunfar sobre la crueldad. Y que el despotismo sigue siendo amo y señor del universo, aunque se oculte bajo aquellos tres disfraces y reciba, a lo largo de la Historia, multitud de nombres diferentes, que pretenden ser disimuladores.

—Las leyes son muy severas en estos casos —me decía Astor mientras cabalgábamos hacia los Jardines del Fauno al despuntar el alba—. El traidor no debe morir en seguida; al contrario: que sienta el impacto de cada flecha, una a una. Después, cuando se halle agotado, encenderemos la hoguera que lo consumirá completamente. Pero es imprescindible que esté vivo; y, para ello, los arqueros, honrados con tu presidencia, tienen la orden de no dirigir los tiros hacia los puntos vitales del cuerpo. Si son expertos, el reo puede soportar incluso cien flechas vivo. Y algunos hubo que, antes de ser consumidos por las llamas, soportaron hasta ciento cincuenta.

Llegamos al Jardín del Fauno, paraje de aspecto idílico donde el día ya se manifestaba en mil tonalidades de dulzura acentuada por la profunda serenidad de los contornos. ¿Quién podía pensar en la muerte, y menos aún en el sufrimiento, inmersos en aquel bucolismo perfecto? Imagine una llanura donde la primavera pareciera haberse anticipado, como en un suspiro inexplicable, y que, sin embargo, fuera imposible no explicar. La llanura aparecía surcada por estanques fugaces, a cuyas orillas, y a veces en su interior, se levantaban ninfeos de formas pálidas, templos de cúpula dorada, pequeños arcos de triunfo de pasadas centurias por los cuales se deslizaban, traviesas, multitud de madreselvas apenas sugeridas en la impresión total del paisaje. La luz se descomponía; los colores de las flores y del agua manchaban la suntuosidad de un espacio completamente verde, de césped exquisitamente cultivado que recubría a modo de tapiz las colinas de los alrededores. La brisa soplaba tenue, y daba a las hojas de los almendros floridos, a las ramas del espléndido mirto, a los verdes abanicos que penden de los chopos, la placidez de un orden que tuviera, como única finalidad, la victoria de la vida sobre la muerte. Y sólo la presencia de los arqueros interrumpía la imposible belleza de un cromo que pronto estaría teñido de sangre y quemado por las llamas, como la carne del joven Glauco.

Estaba atado al tronco de un roble y le habían cortado los pies, de manera que brazos y piernas no quedaban sujetos por las muñecas y los tobillos, sino por los cuatro muñones. Además, su pecho delataba las señales de las tenazas al rojo vivo que le habían aplicado para obligarle a confesar los nombres de los otros espías de Auer infiltrados en la corte de Lur o bien en la capital. Reconocí que la alusión de Astor sobre la poca costumbre de Glauco a soportar el sufrimiento era cierta. El muchacho estaba aterrorizado y gritaba que no quería morir; de forma que, sólo con oírle y ver cómo su cuerpo se debatía inútilmente intentando soltarse, se me hacía un nudo en la garganta. Aún me parecía admirable que, con los brazos y las piernas cercenados, aquel harapo de carne humana anhelara seguir con vida, pero resulta que la fuerza del instinto vital, incluso en casos en que parece inútil seguir adelante, puede llegar a extremos de verdadera tozudez, ya personal, ya colectiva (su empeño no conseguía contestar a una de las preguntas básicas de las lecciones de Lur: ¿no es preferible terminar de una vez con un cuerpo mutilado o con una nación enferma? ¿Por qué los cuerpos enfermos, por qué las comunidades víctimas de debilidad histórica, no pueden ser piadosamente asesinados con un certero y elegante golpe que acelera de una vez el curso de la historia sin darle tiempo a transmitir su debilidad a otros cuerpos, a otras comunidades sanas?). Teorías aparte, yo me sentía dominado por el terror; y cuando Astor me ofreció el arco dorado que yo debía tensar, se me cayó de las manos junto con la flecha. Pero lejos de despreciarme, como hubiese hecho de suceder en los primeros días de la Vida Nueva, los bellos ojos de mi guardián me animaron, como diciéndome: «No te preocupes, lo superarás. Siempre te has portado magníficamente, has aprendido muchas lecciones, y nada permite suponer que la de hoy vaya a ser una excepción.» Y, en tono sumamente amable, me preguntó si aún me dolían los latigazos de la mañana.

Me situé en cabeza del pelotón, y los arqueros me miraban con gran respeto gracias a la verdad oficial de mi «gesta» gloriosa, al atrapar al prisionero sin ayuda de nadie. Atendiendo a mi rango, se me concedió el privilegio, tan solicitado siempre, de lanzar la primera flecha. Muy tenso el arco, apunté a la rodilla de Glauco, y si bien la flecha fue a dar en el muslo, escuché los entusiastas aplausos de Astor quien, lejos de criticar mi error, fue comprensivo y elogió que, a pesar del nerviosismo propio de mi iniciación, hubiese colocado la flecha en un punto tan doloroso para la víctima. Seguidamente, entre los «No quiero morir» y los «Asesinos» que iba gritando el adolescente, cada arquero disparó su flecha, y unas fueron a dar en el pecho, otras en el vientre, muchas en los muslos, y algunas en el cuello. Al llegarme el turno para iniciar la segunda vuelta, noté que Astor me miraba con sorna y curiosidad a la vez, y yo, sin dejar de temblar, decidí demostrarle que era perfectamente capaz de aprender cualquier género de lecciones, incluso sin ayuda de los libros. Entonces apunté a la boca de Glauco, y la poca destreza que antes demostré de modo tan penoso, me valió esta vez un éxito sorprendente, porque la flecha entró por el ojo derecho de la víctima y, brotando de la herida un líquido amarillo-sanguinolento, el condenado profirió un grito más estridente que todos los anteriores y se desmayó.

Como quiera que Astor decidió aguardar a que el prisionero se restableciera para rematar el suplicio en sus mínimos detalles, decidí darme un paseo por el parque mientras los soldados se emborrachaban y entonaban himnos de guerra. Pero al mirarlos un poco distraídamente, volví a descubrir el rostro que no me era desconocido, el soldado que ya no me resultó extraño la noche en que Glauco intentase raptarme. Un soldado que, a pesar de la semidesnudez que imponía el uniforme, el casco que le cubría media frente y el pectoral con el símbolo de Cobra, me remitía a mi última noche pasada aquí, en Minia, y a los tres últimos rostros que vi antes de despertarme en el desierto sin retorno.

—¡Dennis! —exclamé al recordar de repente quién era el soldado. Y gritaba más asombrado que nunca; como si la realidad volviese a girar vertiginosamente sobre sí misma, como si las cosas que había empezado a comprender no fuesen nada comparadas con las que no llegaría a comprender jamás.

—¡Dennis Branden!

MÁS QUE UN MOMENTO de respiro para la prisa que va dominando mi narración, cada una de mis interrupciones busca el recuerdo, la evocación siquiera breve, apenas sugerida, del horror que seguía a cada sorpresa que el Mundo Macho, sus costumbres, sus seres, me iban deparando. En el recuerdo, tal vez incluso más allá, permanece, además, la emoción de lo que en un momento dado intentaba descubrir, de la incógnita que seguía a cada nuevo descubrimiento (en el caso de esta interrupción en mi relato, el descubrimiento de Dennis), y la certeza de que, a partir del conocimiento, quedaban todavía muchos más enigmas; que era forzoso adentrarse en un nuevo gran misterio, turbador, en busca de una nueva verdad que podía ser la explicación de todo un conjunto o, simplemente, la entrada a otro laberinto en cuyos recovecos cada nueva proposición acaso se explicaría menos que las anteriores. En el recuerdo, esta alternativa tiene el poder de dejar la historia abierta, imposible de ser completada, al menos por el momento. La narración vuelve a interrumpirse al filo de la duda, lo cual hace que su continuidad se extravíe. Son lagunas que me llevan hacia el instante evocado, que me lanzan a revivirlo con más fuerza; pero es sólo el instante, y no la narración en sí misma lo que cuenta. Cortando bruscamente mi narración, mientras aprovecho para comprobar que su sueño significa aburrimiento, que sus ojos drogados ya no contemplan con interés mi, digamos, odisea, intento explicarme una vez más las cosas, y, nuevamente, las cosas permanecen inexplicables.

¿Cómo podría expresar de otro modo el intenso temblor que me acomete aún hoy, en este mismo instante, apenas aparece en la narración el rostro, la peripecia, el temple extrañamente transformado de un Dennis convertido en soldado del Mundo Macho, formando parte del pelotón de ejecución con el grado de sargento, desnudo y cruel como los otros, y, como ellos, irreconocible, comulgando de buen grado con el sacrificio del joven espía, gozándolo plenamente, con risotadas estruendosas, y quién sabe si excitándose con los chorros de sangre que originaban el impacto de las flechas en el cuerpo agonizante? Hoy, como entonces, siento el vértigo inaudito de comprobar el gran poder de asimilación del Mundo Macho, poder que Astor siempre elogiaba, pero que, en el fondo, yo no podía imaginar tan fuerte. Asimilación e integración: he aquí los preceptos que encontraría personificados en el comportamiento de Dennis, el muchachito yanqui que un día fue capaz de reírse de su propia capacidad de decir tonterías, con encanto adolescente, y que ahora, al encontrarnos de nuevo, quedaba incapacitado para ser otra cosa que un titánico verdugo adiestrado, además, en las vergonzantes reglas del vasallaje.

Que su propia sumisión le enseñaba a colocarme a mí, Nebjeperura, en el sitial más elevado de unas jerarquías presididas por las grandes figuras de piedra que le ordenaron adorar, me lo demostró asaz elocuentemente cuando, al aproximarse a él, se arrodilló y, besándome los pies, murmuró una plegaria en perfecto italiano, lo cual me avergonzó un poco, porque yo, diosecillo viviente, no sabía pronunciar con un mínimo de corrección el dialecto de las milicias que yo mismo mandaba. No era, sin embargo, la única sorpresa de carácter lingüístico que Dennis me reservaba, porque cuando se atrevió a hablarme dando respuesta a mis preguntas, no lo hizo en el inglés que habíamos utilizado en Minia, sino con la rara perfección que, en la lengua vulgar del Mundo Macho, sólo podían alcanzar, presumiblemente, quienes la han aprendido de niños y desde niños la hablaron. Y Astor, siempre protector, acudió a mi lado. Sonreía con gran satisfacción; sin duda por comprobar que el alcance del poder integrador del Mundo Macho seguía siendo invencible, infinito, no dejaba un solo cabo suelto. Y al mirarme, tierno y didáctico a la vez, quizás aspiró a recordarme que yo mismo caminaba hacia una idéntica asimilación de aquellos preceptos, ya históricos.

La expresión de Dennis no dio a entender que antes de aquella mañana, mucho antes de aquella dimensión del Mundo Macho en la cual coincidíamos, hubiese existido otro mundo, otra historia de ambos, en la cual pudimos coincidir. En el clarísimo contexto de nuestra cárcel —insisto: dorada—, las relaciones se establecían de una forma inequívoca; y la nuestra sería para siempre una relación de jerarquías. Nebjeperura se acercaba a un simple sargento, le distinguía con su atención, incluso le premiaba con una mirada: ¿qué podía haber de extraño en el hecho de que él se sintiera recompensado y, arrodillándose, se considerase deudor de mis divinas deferencias?

Astor parecía comprenderlo tan claramente, conocía con tanta perfección el juego jerárquico implícito en cualquier relación que yo pudiera establecer con mis súbditos del Mundo Macho, que ni siquiera se le ocurrió formularme la pregunta más lógica para aquella ocasión; es decir: ¿conocía yo de antes a aquel soldado a quien favorecía con una deferencia que nunca dediqué a los demás? Lo mismo, en definitiva, que extrañaría a mi representante si, entre la multitud de jovenzuelos y doncellitas que me esperaban a la salida de un recital, bajo el aguacero de invierno, distinguiese yo a alguno concediéndole el honor de ocupar un lugar en mi coche mientras los otros se mojaban en la espera de un apresurado autógrafo sobre un bloc insignificante.

Sin embargo, al inclinarme para formular algunas preguntas a Dennis Branden (lo cual criticó Astor inmediatamente, pues, a pesar de tantos progresos, yo aún no había aprendido que es indigno de Nebjeperura inclinarse ante nadie que no sea Epsamón Divino), y al dirigirme a él en inglés, mi guardián me miró extrañado y fue obvio que empezaba a intuir algún misterio. Al poco, dio algunas palmadas, preguntó si nuestra víctima se había restablecido del primer desmayo y ordenó a los soldados que se reorganizasen para proseguir la ejecución. El sol ya empezaba a brillar sobre la pineda que podía vislumbrarse al otro lado del ninfeo de Serapis; era una luz mucho más potente, que iluminaba amapolas, margaritas, jacintos y enormes rosales que brotaban por todas partes, pero no individualmente, sino en forma de gigantescos matorrales, pues ya dije que, en el Mundo Macho, tiene la flora un tamaño monstruoso. Otro día, intrigado por esta fecundidad a escala titánica, pregunté a Astor acerca de sus orígenes, y él me explicó: «¿Acaso lo habías atribuido a una simple voluntad de la Naturaleza, monseñor? Si pensaste así, te equivocabas. Sería otorgar a la Naturaleza unas posibilidades que sólo puede tener de un modo accidental, nunca voluntario, puesto que es la intervención del hombre, dueña y señora en tal dominio, la única capaz de lograr la creación de fenómenos como los que acabas de ver. Los sabios del Mundo Macho han violado con su sabiduría la matriz misma de la

Naturaleza y, domándola, han conseguido hacerla más titánica, ponerla al nivel de la voluntad macho que rige el Universo, y de cuya mixtificación más sublime formaría parte el hombre. Porque la Naturaleza es elemento hembra, monseñor, y está escrito que la hembra sólo existe en tanto que complemento del Machismo, verdad última de todo poder que se estime válido y perdurable. ¿No te lo han explicado los doctos sacerdotes de Cobra? Desde el principio de todas las historias, desde que el Mal derrotó al Bien y dio lugar a la forja de la Creación, el poder macho busca a su contrario para engendrar el gran desorden del mundo, que le es necesario para afirmarse como fuerza básica; y en esta lucha no resuelta reposa, eternamente, el supremo equilibrio del Universo. El poder, siempre macho, engendrará en la Naturaleza, hembra, sólo para dominarla, para adueñarse de ella, pues ¿qué sería el Poder si no dispusiera de elementos para poder ejercerse, de fuerzas inferiores a las que dominar como prueba irrefutable de su propia grandeza, de su propia invulnerabilidad? Los principios de la Creación emanan de esta lucha constante, de la cual es hijo el hombre, titán porque tiene como padre al Poder original; débil también, porque nació de un coito entre el Poder y la Naturaleza. Y, heredero de padres tan malavenidos, siempre deberá tener un brazo al servicio de uno, y el otro brazo dominando a la Fuerza hembra; y es precisamente al acatar el precepto del dominio cuando el hombre se hace digno de una paternidad tan titánica. Así, estas flores que ahora ves, enormes como no existen en las leyendas más disparatadas de los antiguos, esas flores son el símbolo de la legitimidad del hombre, que les ha dado, con sabiduría, todo el poder del padre a partir de una creación de la madre, la cual, dicho sea de paso, las creó el día en que el miembro macho entró en sus profundidades vulnerables y las transformó en fuente de vida. De este modo, obedecemos el precepto que dice: "El Poder será rey de la fuerza madre y siempre ha de dominarla, porque está escrito que la rebelión de las fuerzas hembras acabaría con la grandeza del Mundo Macho." Así, desde que la historia es historia, y desde que Epsamón es único, los sabios se aprestan a castigar la rebelión de las fuerzas hembras, que se levantan, salvajes, contra el gran Poder universal y campan a su antojo en la creación de formas débiles, que hemos sabido metamorfosear a la altura de los dioses titánicos que nos guían, del Poder que las engendrara en las cosmogonías que tú conoces y en las cuales ningún elemento es hembra. Así, la flor que crece tranquila en el prado, el árbol que vive inofensivo en el bosque, la cascada que se precipita por las montañas y el río que baña, en su crecida, las tierras donde germinan las cosechas anuales de dos provincias, fueron separados de su origen, el vientre de la Naturaleza, para poder recibir, con la inyección del poder macho, aquel miembro que les da belleza, los hace útiles, con fuerzas más poderosas que la vida. Del mismo modo, los hombres del Mundo Macho realizan cada año su peregrinaje a las cuevas de ganado donde habitan las máquinas de concebir, y atacan con los atributos del Machismo la innoble debilidad de aquellas que, sin su pene, no tendrían ningún sentido en el mundo, como no lo tendría la Naturaleza si el Poder no la poseyese a cada nuevo paso de la Historia. Porque, del mismo modo que el hombre es hijo del Poder, la hembra es bastarda de la Naturaleza, hija a quien el Gran Padre Universal no quiso reconocer y a quien urge dominar, como el Poder, siglos atrás, dominó para siempre a las fuerzas débiles, en la victoria que le da razón de ser como se la da, al hombre, la histórica derrota sobre la Bestia Llamada Hembra.»

Pero, si bien es cierto que la intervención del macho y de su religión habían logrado convertir la espontaneidad de árboles, flores y estanques en una monstruosidad fabulosa, no por ello la mañana dejaba de presentar un agradable aspecto, incluso delicuescente; aspecto y delicuescencia que convertían en sacrilegio la ejecución de Glauco. Entre la serena paz de la niebla matutina, rota paulatinamente por los rayos de la vida, bajo el rocío que ya había empapado aquel cuerpo a punto de morir, Glauco sólo me parecía, horas antes, la imagen onírica de una crueldad que continuamente me era propuesta y que, por repetida, empezaba a perder sus efectos. Fue una visión tal vez imaginada, atribuible a una pesadilla que no podemos dejar atrás al despertar. Ahora, con el trino de los pájaros, con los pavos reales extendiendo sus abanicos de variado colorido junto al árbol en cuyo tronco se convulsionaba el mártir en los últimos espasmos del dolor; con el resol que hacía a la sangre resaltar aún más sobre el rosado brillo de la piel, toda la ceremonia parecía más que cruel: era excesiva, y, lo que es peor, aburrida. Al mismo tiempo, el enigma de Dennis originaba en mí una insoportable curiosidad, y apartaba mi interés del suplicio que yo presidía y de cuyo pathos debía aprender tantas cosas esenciales para un Co-Divino. Y si Dennis se volvía de vez en cuando para mirarme, lo hacía sin una sola mirada de complicidad que delatara su recuerdo del encuentro anterior. Entonces se me ocurrió una última posibilidad desesperada: «Tal vez Dennis desea comunicarse conmigo, pero sabe que estamos vigilados; sabe que, en estas circunstancias, y dados mis privilegios, sólo una orden dictada por mi persona podrá favorecer una entrevista que le permita confesarse por entero, incluso proponerme algún plan para escapar del Mundo Macho...»

Trastornado en busca de tantas posibilidades para un encuentro con quien podía revelarme muchas cosas de un destino tan parecido al mío, pero que, a la vez, tenía que haber sido distinto en tantos aspectos; excitado por la posibilidad de aproximarme a mi situación desde una óptica opuesta, tal vez tanto o más apasionante que la que hasta entonces fuese la mía, olvidé que la vida de Glauco ya se estaba agotando, y que todo su cuerpo aparecía cubierto de flechas, tantas, que un soldado iba rompiéndolas para que pudieran caber otras.

La idea de ver mi orden cumplida, y la posibilidad de zambullirme, acto seguido, en algún estanque de los más placenteros del parque, me ofrecía un consuelo inmediato, y la impaciencia me indicaba que ya no podía demorar por más tiempo la culminación del acto de justicia. Y cuando comuniqué a Astor mi voluntad, me dijo que apenas estuviese preparada la leña para quemar el cuerpo del asaetado, yo mismo, con mi sagrada mano, aplicaría el fuego purificador. Ni siquiera me inmuté, porque, puestos a ser crueles, unas llamas no tenían ya la menor importancia; y también porque estaba demasiado preocupado intentando hallar las palabras que convirtieran mi deseo de entrevistarme con Dennis en una orden rotunda que Astor no estuviese en grado de discutir. Mientras, Dennis iba acumulando leña alrededor del árbol del suplicio: era uno más entre los soldados que, indiferentes, cumplían un rito que, en el Mundo Macho, podía ser cualquier cosa menos insólito.

Astor me observó fijamente y sonrió:

—¿Me anticipo a tu deseo, monseñor, si sugiero un baño y un poco de natación para después del suplicio?

—Te anticipas a medias —dije, señalando a Dennis—; quiero nadar, sí; pero, antes, exijo una entrevista con aquel sargento.

La sonrisa desapareció de su rostro. Esbozó una expresión de sorpresa.

—¿Es... un deseo, monseñor?

—¡No! ¡Es una orden, perro!

Bajó la cabeza, humillado, y ordenó a uno de sus hombres que le diese una antorcha encendida. El soldado se la entregó y él la puso en mis manos, como si mi aceptación de rematar el ritual sangriento fuese el intercambio justo para la entrevista que yo había solicitado y que tan vital era para mí. Como era vital para el orden del Mundo Macho que yo, aquella mañana, aprendiera de una vez por todas la gran responsabilidad de otorgar la muerte, primero a escala individual, y después, a medida que avanzara en mi aprendizaje, a escala colectiva. Así, con un intercambio de miradas, breves y de asentimiento, tanto por su parte como por la mía, Astor ordenó al mismo soldado que avisase a Dennis, con el fin de que se purificase para celebrar una entrevista conmigo no bien cumpliese yo mi acto de afirmación.

El pelotón formó con marcialidad, descansaron los arcos y observaron mi avance hacia el árbol, a cuyo tronco atado Avitachí lloraba dulcemente, sin fuerzas ya para gritar. Tenía la cabeza caída sobre el hombro y apenas se le veía el pecho: tantas flechas albergaba ya; todo el cuerpo era un charco de sangre, formado por riachuelos que se cruzaban sobre una superficie de carne completamente agujereada, en la cual ya empezaban a chupar algunas moscas, enormes como sólo pueden serlo las del Mundo Macho, gracias a la intervención de sus científicos, y que, como es norma en los vocablos zoológicos de este país, son designadas con el género masculino (es decir: *tabor*). Al llegar junto a la víctima, le oí murmurar algunas palabras y me miró tan fijamente que era imposible no entender que quería decirme algo muy importante. Entonces, por primera vez, recordé todo lo que quería comunicarme el día en que Astor le cortó las manos, y, fingiendo que tiraba de sus cabellos para infligirle un mayor sufrimiento, aproximé su cabeza a la mía.

—Epsamón —murmuró él a mi oído—. Escucha, Epsamón Divino...

Pensé que estaba delirando. Que su confusión era propia de la muerte ya cercana.

—No lo soy —dije—. Te equivocas.

—Tú. Epsamón Divino... —dijo él—. Tú, Epsamón..., cerdo...

A medida que yo tiraba de sus cabellos, fue volviendo la cabeza, y parecía como si, entre tantos dolores como había soportado, aquél fuese el mayor de todos. Repitió sus extravagantes palabras, y escuché a mis espaldas las recomendaciones de Astor, que parecía algo impaciente y me instigaba a encender la leña, apilada hasta las rodillas de Glauco.

—El *Palazzo* del Lago del Tiempo —murmuró el agonizante—, el secreto... Tú...

Pero yo sabía que estaba a punto de morir, que era cosa de pocos segundos, y que el Mundo Macho no me perdonaría que le dejase expirar sin aplicarle el último sufrimiento, el definitivo, aquel que prolonga la consciencia del dolor hasta el punto exacto en que se corta la vida. Además, sabía que todo cuanto se me exigía disculpaba cualquier antojo de crueldad, incluso el más excesivo, que pudiera acometerme al aplicar el tormento. Así pues, miré directamente a Astor, quien me animó con una sonrisita desafiante. Entonces, mientras Glauco seguía murmurando sus absurdas palabras, sus referencias a Epsamón y al *Palazzo* del Lago (pero, ¿qué *palazzo*?; ¿qué lago?), me reí del secreto que me anunciaba y, movido por una ira contra no sabía qué, tiré de nuevo de sus cabellos hasta conseguir que quedara mirando al cielo, y acto seguido hundí la antorcha en su rostro. Los rasgos de Glauco quedaron ocultos bajo las llamas.

Profirió unos gritos espantosos, que sirvieron para animar aún más mi urgente necesidad de dominar su vida, dirigiéndola hacia la muerte con lentitud a través de un dolor que estaba en mi mano administrar y dosificar. Él aullaba, yo chillaba, Astor y los soldados, Dennis incluido (o él más que los otros), aplaudían como locos, me trataban de divino con vítores que me ensordecían mientras, sosteniendo la antorcha, iba sacando la cabeza de Avitachí del fuego sólo para permitirle respirar unos segundos y, después, volver a sumergirlo entre las llamas, de forma que pronto estuvo completamente quemado: la carne se desprendía de sus mejillas, los ojos se deshacían, los labios se resquebrajaban como el fango en un horno antiguo y, al partirse, la flecha que tenía clavada en el ojo aumentó el tamaño de la herida, y por el orificio que íbase ensanchando podía verse el cerebro, con el fuego que empezaba a penetrar en él. Yo me reía como nunca me había reído hasta entonces (días después, Astor me diría que la voz y la risa se me habían hecho más poderosas) y, en plena risotada, animado por los aplausos de mis súbditos, arrojé la antorcha entre la leña, y el cuerpo de Glauco no tardó en estar rodeado por las llamas mientras la cabeza, a consecuencia del dolor y la derrota, efectuaba movimientos desesperados, frenéticos, como un espantapájaros sacudido por un furioso vendaval. Finalmente, todo su cuerpo desapareció bajo las llamas y los soldados se arrodillaron ante mí y me adoraron.

El tiempo que siguió a este suplicio sirvió para llevarme hasta un estanque, donde Astor había hecho levantar una gran tienda que diera intimidad a mi reposo y pudiera protegerme de cualquier mirada indiscreta. Pero no recuerdo nada de este itinerario porque estuvo dominado en su totalidad por una impaciencia que se aproximaba a la histeria. En el final de aquella cabalgada bajo la frondosidad habitual en los parques palatinos, surgía intermitentemente la sonrisa de Astor, siempre a mi lado, admirativo en escala progresiva; y, desde otro fondo, aún más remoto, surgían las palabras que Glauco me había dirigido como un aviso, como la pista idónea para descubrir un misterio necesario, seguramente vital..., tanto que era capaz de llevar a un pobre adolescente a la muerte más horrible que pueda administrar una divinidad sobre la Tierra.

—Astor...

—Permíteme que te elogie, monseñor. No tengo palabras, no...

—¡Ni las necesito, perro! Contéstame sólo a una pregunta: ¿existe un lago muy especial, con un *palazzo* muy especial?

Él palideció. Detuvo el caballo, desmontó y aferró las bridas del mío con tanta violencia que me hizo vacilar sobre la silla.

—Te lo ruego, monseñor: olvida las palabras de los locos. Nunca te he pedido nada; nunca te pediré nada a partir de ahora..., pero escucha hoy mi consejo: olvida las palabras de los locos.

—Esto quiere decir que el *palazzo* existe. Y, al parecer, debo deducir, por tus palabras, que yo no seré bien recibido en él. Me pides que lo olvide por alguna razón muy concreta, ¿verdad?

—Por la única cosa que tiene interés para mí, monseñor..., tu vida.

Nos miramos fijamente a los ojos y permanecimos así un buen rato, hasta que yo desmonté y me puse a su lado. Nos hallábamos en la entrada de la tienda, y el lago ya resplandecía con tonalidades más vivas, porque la primavera empezaba a ser una realidad. Me cogí del brazo de Astor y, quizá por vez primera, nuestra conversación se amplió hasta los límites de una confianza extrema. Él temblaba.

—Escúchame, Astor: la esclavitud que me ofreces, las lecciones de los sabios, la aplicación que he demostrado sufriendo el dolor y aprendiendo a infligirlo, no conseguirán hacerme olvidar la única cosa positiva que me ha enseñado el Mundo Macho: mi necesidad de comprender.

—Monseñor: la necesidad de comprender puede desembocar, muchas veces, en alternativas fatales.

—Y las aceptaré, amigo mío, porque la madurez que acabo de adquirir en el seno de la crueldad y en esa suerte de jerarquía que os empeñáis en otorgarme, también incluye mi madurez de hombre; y te prometo que, a partir de ahora, no temeré nada que antes no haya visto y probado; no amaré ni odiaré cosa alguna si antes no la he comprendido. Y mi primera comprensión será este mundo: será el saber, de una vez por todas, de dónde proviene, quién lo creó, dónde está situado. Seré lo que queráis que sea, pero no sin antes saberlo todo..., aunque el precio de mi sabiduría consista en convertirme en un miserable. Y, para empezar a enterarme, hablaré ahora mismo con este soldado, a quien un día conocí fuera del Mundo Macho, y te exigiré que me digas ahora mismo por qué me ocultas cuál es el lago, cuál el *palazzo*, y, en resumen, qué hay en él, qué representa...

Astor me cogió de la mano, que permanecía apoyada sobre su brazo, y dijo que haría pasar al soldado al interior de la tienda, donde, por otra parte, yo podría comer fruta muy escogida, refrescarme con vino helado y prepararme para un delicioso baño. Pero, en el fondo, él sabía que aquellas evasivas no conseguirían apartarme de mi pregunta; y volví a repetírsela dos veces más. Obligado a contestarme, murmuró simplemente:

—En el *Palazzo* del Lago del Tiempo, dueño mío, se encuentra tu destino.

La idea de aquel lago especial del que Glauco me había hablado con una vehemencia tan desesperada, y que Astor temía como una terrible amenaza contra mi pobre destino, empezaba a obsesionarme con la misma intensidad que todas las obsesiones que ya cobijaba en mí, o incluso en mayor grado; y, a pesar de la paz aparente, tanto del agua como de los bosques que la rodeaban, el estanque elegido para mi baño me servía de asociación con el misterioso lago, y era, por esta razón, una presencia perturbadora.

Pero durante el tiempo transcurrido entre la primera sorpresa y esta última, yo había adquirido un estilo, había aprendido ciertos modos y maneras que evidenciaron su utilidad cada vez que tenía que enfrentarme con las personas y la realidad del Mundo Macho; así que sabía plantearme las cosas con cierta astucia, y ya las organizaba racionalmente, de cara al provecho o al daño que podían aportarme; y no creo necesario decir que todo ello formaba parte del sentido utilitario que el concepto «racional» pueda tener en el Mundo Macho. Ya le he dicho que la actitud que más beneficios me había reportado se basaba en el despotismo, cuyas ventajas tuve ocasión de comprobar en el cambio radical que últimamente había experimentado otra actitud que tenía siempre junto a mí y que era contraria de la mía. Es decir: Astor y el respeto que decidía otorgarme me daban la razón.

Todo aquello implicaba una disciplina muy difícil, porque uno no se endurece así como así; incluso el reconocimiento de la propia crueldad tiene un precio que hay que pagar, a menudo con pena. Sin embargo, yo me había habituado a medir mis sentimientos, a disimularlos cuando se hacía necesario. Aquella mañana, ya sabía que es necesario disimular la impaciencia; que a la amabilidad le conviene ocultarse bajo el manto de la dureza; que la curiosidad no debe hacerse tan evidente como para demostrar a los demás hasta qué punto los necesitamos: a ellos, a sus explicaciones, a la sabiduría que puedan comunicarnos. Me habían vendido una máscara, y si yo quería que Dennis me revelara su enigma —puesto que sería parte integrante del gran enigma del Mundo Macho—, necesitaba ocultar el rostro tras la máscara, aunque el precio del encubrimiento consistiese en no recordar que Dennis y yo tuvimos en otro lugar una amistad, breve pero sincera, y que, al fin y a la postre, éramos víctimas de un mismo drama... o de un mismo sainete.

Por otra parte, era evidente que unos momentos antes, en los Jardines del Fauno, él no me había reconocido, o no había querido reconocerme. Las conjeturas que podían formularse a partir de este hecho eran, como siempre, muy variadas: tal vez Dennis me había reconocido, pero prefería disimularlo por razones de estrategia; tal vez le intimidaba mi nuevo aspecto de Co-Divino, que, en aquel país, me situaba muy por encima de él; tal vez le habían drogado y no era dueño de sus actos, o, puestos a suponer, acaso creyera que el drogado era yo, y que, si me saludaba y yo no le reconocía, era un paso en falso que pudiera costarle la vida.

Astor, cosa extraña en él, no quiso estar presente en mi entrevista con Dennis: de repente me devolvía unos derechos de los cuales yo había aprendido a prescindir desde que él se convirtió en mi guardián. Sin embargo, no abandonaba la voluntad de servirme. Antes de salir de la tienda, se ocupó personalmente de que los siervos dejasen una pequeña ánfora con vino helado y tres bandejas que contenían carne rustida, pescado dorado, fruta de la selva, quesos varios y pan de miel. Se ocupó de que los almohadones de damasco esparcidos por todas partes constituyesen para mí una adecuada garantía de comodidad; me preguntó si deseaba algo más y, antes de salir, me recordó que, cuando me apeteciera tomar el baño, no tenía más que avisarle golpeando el gong que se hallaba junto a los triclinios, con el símbolo de Cobra pintado en rojo. Salió de la tienda y reapareció al poco, anunciando a Dennis. Después se quedó fuera, presidiendo personalmente la guardia, para asegurarse de que yo no sería molestado.

En aquella estancia perfumada en exceso, donde sólo la suavidad de la seda y la abundancia de objetos de oro macizo lograban romper la soberanía del rojo, Dennis no me recordó en absoluto a aquel muchachito yanqui, de apariencia universitaria, que fuese durante los días de nuestro trato en Minia. Muy al contrario: su pectoral de acero con la gran imagen de Cobra, sus botas altas hasta la rodilla y el cinturón de piel de leopardo por toda indumentaria, no lo diferenciaban en absoluto de cualquier sargento del Mundo Macho. Tenía la piel tan bronceada como el resto de mis súbditos; su mirada era igualmente inexpresiva, sus manos se habían tornado fuertes y duras; me atrevería a decir que incluso había aumentado de estatura, en una medida muy notable y esperanzadora para los bajitos de todo el mundo. Y cuando, en días sucesivos, le viera calzado con sandalias, y no con la bota cerrada del uniforme, me daría cuenta de que también le faltaba el dedo pulgar del pie.

Era evidente que tenía que vérmelas con alguien que había sido adiestrado con el mismo esmero que me adiestraron a mí. Tal vez incluso mejor. Aclarar las partes de este «tal vez», comprobar el alcance y el éxito de este adiestramiento, serían las directrices de mi investigación, el eje de las preguntas a que pensaba someterle antes de revelar mi juego.

—Batsá a tu servicio, monseñor —exclamó él con solemnidad, al tiempo que me hacía una reverencia marcial—. Dispón de mi vida y de mi muerte, tú que eres divino.

—¿De verdad no me conoces, Dennis?

Fue un paso en falso, lo reconozco. Pero lo di conscientemente.

Él no abandonaba su aire marcial y ceremonioso: antes bien lo acentuó.

—Todos conocen a Nebjeperura, y todos le adoran: pero somos pocos los que tenemos el privilegio de verlo personalmente. Hablar con él, como lo estoy haciendo yo, constituye la más alta recompensa a que pueda aspirarse sobre la Tierra.

—Y, sin embargo, Batsá, tú me habías visto antes de ahora. Intenta recordar.

—Es cierto, monseñor. La noche que estuviste a punto de ser raptado por el espía de los herejes. Yo me hallaba en la puerta del cuartel, vigilando de forma disimulada, como me había ordenado Astor.

—No, Batsá, no. Yo hablo de mucho antes.

—Antes, monseñor, sólo te había visto a través de tus representaciones múltiples. Y en los libros que hablan de ti, desde el comienzo de todas las historias.

A partir de aquel momento, sin abandonar mi actitud oficial, sentí pena por el compañero a quien, ya no me cabía la menor duda, habían administrado una droga muy poderosa, que le robaba el conocimiento y la conciencia de sí mismo. Debían administrársela a todos los muchachos que raptaban del mundo exterior. Y el hecho de que no hubiesen obrado igual conmigo confirmaba, una vez más, que no debía preocuparme por mi persona: incluso en una treta tan básica como hacer perder la voluntad de aquellos a quienes se quiere integrar, ellos me consideraban divino e intocable. Al fin y al cabo, tuve suerte.

Después de examinar nuevamente a Dennis, me dejé caer en el triclinio y él se apresuró a escanciar vino en un gran cáliz de bronce, enriquecido con unas curiosas incrustaciones de oro. Eran figuras humanas, de formas hieráticas: doce barbudos vestidos según la moda bizantina, las testas coronadas por diademas de plata. En el centro, algo mayor que las figuras, sobresalía un cordero que llevaba el mismo atributo circular en la cabeza.

—Te has referido al comienzo de la Historia —dije, fingiendo no conceder la menor importancia a una pregunta que, de hecho, tanto me importaba—. ¿Por qué utilizáis tan a menudo esta frase, los habitantes del Mundo Macho?

Él se mostró algo extrañado. Y yo aún más, cuando me contestó:

—Esto, monseñor, deberías saberlo tú, que regresas de la Nada.

—¡Ah, claro! Por supuesto... ¡yo regreso de la Nada!

—Todos saben que, al contrario de Epura Epsamón, Nebjeperura no es inmortal. Desde los primeros años de escuela, cuando recibimos las primeras lecciones sobre las palabras y las cosas, todos sabemos que, al acabar cada otoño, Nebjeperura muere, y entonces cabalga en su caballo de alas blancas hacia las tierras de la Nada, y allí lucha contra Aquel que Domina el Tiempo y Odia al Hombre. Todos saben que éste es el origen del invierno, que mata la vida: al acabar el otoño, el gran enemigo de Cobra roba el sol, y Nebjeperura, que vive del sol, muere por falta de éste y cabalga para recobrarlo y devolverlo al Mundo Macho. Mientras tanto, Epura Epsamón permanece triste en su palacio, esperando que Nebjeperura regrese, vencedor sobre la Nada, y devuelva consigo la alegría que favorece la reproducción de todas las cosas.

Pero el Divino no permanece triste demasiado tiempo, porque Cobra vela por él y ayuda a Nebjeperura en su lucha contra Aquel que Domina el Tiempo. Y el joven Co-Divino regresa con los rayos de la vida, y por eso es primavera, y por eso crecen las flores, y por eso los hombres del Mundo Macho van en peregrinación hasta las grutas donde vive la Bestia Llamada Hembra y siembran en ella la simiente que es eterna como el poder de Epsamón y como la victoria siempre renovada de Nebjeperura...

—Claro, claro..., no recordaba que he ido a buscar los rayos de la vida.

—Todos lo sabemos, monseñor. Todos sabemos que te ausentarás durante tres meses, y que tu muerte será el motivo por el cual, con tu resurrección, la vida se renueve como siempre ha sucedido. Por ello decimos: «desde el principio de todas las historias», porque tu lucha y la soledad que domina a Epsamón, a tu muerte, son la primera historia del Mundo Macho, inmediatamente después de que Cobra se rebelara en contra del Bien e hiciese la creación, en la cual...

—Lo sé, lo sé: esa lucha es el origen de las historias; y mi resurrección anual es la Historia, que no puede cambiar.

—Exactamente, monseñor.

El prodigio de una doctrina como aquella contenía demasiadas bifurcaciones para explicarla en una conversación que debe ser necesariamente esquemática, a pesar de que el silencio de las calles y el alba que empieza a pronunciarse y el sueño de usted, profesor, me hagan pensar que hasta ahora no he dado demasiadas pruebas de mi capacidad de síntesis. Sólo puedo decirle que no hay religión más complicada que la del Mundo Macho, ni divinidad tan rica en significaciones y complejidad como este su humilde servidor. Y al desconcierto que me producía tanta confusión, podemos añadir otro todavía mayor: que un país que parecía recoger lo más exquisito del arte universal, toda la sabiduría de veinte siglos de pensamiento humano, aún pudiese alimentarse con mitos tan fabulosamente ingenuos.

Pero he aquí que las dudas siguientes sirvieron, al menos, para dejar muy clara una cosa: que la grandeza del Mundo Macho y todo su poder de expansión residían en la profunda complejidad de una religión en la que cada elemento tenía que ser más inexplicable que el anterior; cada dogma debía tener una doble y compleja traducción política, e incluso ideológica. En aquella confusión de dioses de ida y vuelta, soles místicos, combates jamás resueltos, reptiles paternales y engendradores de humanos o titanes a quienes se exigía la educación de la violencia como iniciación a la capacidad adulta del exterminio, pero también la aceptación de la mudez en la vida cotidiana; en aquel dédalo no había nada improvisado, ninguna ley que se remontase a una tradición popular, a una voluntad mantenida a lo largo de los siglos: todo era una manifestación del Poder, y el poder se crea a sí mismo, se autoconsagra mediante un racionalismo espantoso, que no admite improvisaciones ni riesgos de error debidos al azar. Y era seguro que la persona o institución a quien se debiesen los orígenes del Mundo Macho fue tan racional al crear aquella religión como Voltaire cuando atacaba a la de su tiempo.

Y, sin embargo: ¿quién fue el creador?

La pregunta, aunque urgente, no era de las que podía formular a Dennis, pues él parecía dar por sentado que si alguien, en el Mundo Macho, conocía el origen y la finalidad de todo aquel asunto, ese alguien sólo podía ser yo. Así pues, decidí aprovechar la ocasión para enterarme de otros enigmas más cercanos. Y lo haría utilizando un nuevo truco.

—Tú, Batsá, viste cómo intentaban raptarme los herejes. Supongo que no comulgas con sus ideas...

—¡Claro que no, monseñor! ¿Cómo puedes siquiera insinuarlo?

La indignación de Dennis favorecía una inmediata declaración de sus principios. Y pensé que, en el fondo, los titanes pueden ser muy ingenuos.

—¿Y por qué no estás de acuerdo con ellos, Batsá? Te lo pregunto porque, siendo como soy Nebjeperura, me gusta comprobar personalmente si los jóvenes de mi reino han aprendido bien sus lecciones.

—Si me ordenaras arrancarme los ojos con un hierro candente, me los arrancaría sin dejar de cantar tu himno, puesto que he sido educado para ello. Si desde niño me has ordenado que te adore y desprecie a los herejes, para mí será un honor tan grande como el otro demostrarte, ahora, que he aprendido bien la lección. ¿Cómo quieres que no los desprecie, que no los odie con toda mi alma, que no desee fervorosamente ir a la guerra para cortarles la cabeza lentamente, pues así padecerán más?

Todos sabemos que ellos se oponen al dogma de Cobra: creen que el mundo fue creado por Aquel que Ordena el Tiempo, y que Cobra es enemigo del hombre y quiere arrastrarlo a la perdición. Cantan esta herejía en una lengua distinta de la nuestra, y se empeñan en considerarse aparte del gran Imperio que Epsamón edificó para bien de los hombres, en la armoniosa eternidad de la paz. Rechazan todos nuestros dogmas, empezando por tu divinidad; y sólo esto bastaría para incidir sobre mi voluntad y llevarme hacia una cruzada permanente contra ellos. En resumen, monseñor: ¿cómo podría extrañarte que yo rechace su creencia de que el mundo es espíritu y no fuerza, que la fuerza no reside en el brazo, sino en la voluntad, la cual, como todos sabemos, sólo tú y Epsamón tenéis derecho a administrar? ¿Qué hombre dotado de un mínimo de cordura podría creer que no es el Mal la fuerza que da el poder y la paz de los mil años, mientras que el Bien (que ellos adoran) es la despreciable cualidad hembra que sólo se le opone para que Él pueda vencerla continuamente y erigirse en el necesario Poder que debe velar por todos nosotros? Yo estaría loco si creyera un sólo precepto de los que ellos predican; y las doctrinas que tú co-creaste, monseñor, me prepararon para no ser un loco, sino un ser lúcido. Y por ello te digo: muerte para los herejes; muerte para mí si algún día, abandonado por la gracia de los dioses machos, cayera en el repugnante pecado de la herejía.

De repente, la pantalla distancia la visión total de nuestros cuerpos y representa enormes primeros planos con el rostro ampliado a gran escala de Batsá; de este modo, cada músculo será íntegramente apreciado por la mirada que lo observa; cada rasgo revelará los menores movimientos que ha de efectuar acto seguido para expresar o disimular, para ofrecer u ocultar. Los rojos terciopelos que rodean este rostro no tienen más consistencia que la de una remota profundidad de campo: sólo son una transparencia muy difusa, que se insinúa detrás del personaje mientras éste habla moviendo apenas la boca porque todos los actores saben que los labios apenas deben moverse, pues, en caso contrario, el riesgo de exageración es enorme, y la insistencia del primer plano, preciso, grande, objetivo, se convierte en una atroz monstruosidad.

—Has aprendido la lección. Te la sabes. Pero, supongamos que antes, en otro lugar, alguien te hubiera enseñado que el Bien creó el mundo y sólo el Mal se rebeló contra la Bondad de la creación...

Pero quedo al margen de la mirada de Batsá mientras su rostro sigue creciendo y mira hacia adelante, su cabeza cortada a nivel de la frente por el lado superior del recuadro rectangular, su clavícula reposando en la base. Quedo fuera, empequeñecido, mirando el espectáculo desde fuera, admirándome de su pericia dramática cuando él abre la boca más de la cuenta y grita:

—¡Nunca he aprendido eso, monseñor!

—¿Estás seguro, Dennis? —Y, desde mi butaca, yo también grito a la pantalla—: ¡Antes de que te explicasen que el Mal creó el mundo y el Bien se rebeló contra él para ayudar a los heréticos...! ¡Recuérdalo, Dennis!

—¡Monseñor! Tú, que vienes de la Nada, tal vez conocieras allí a ese Dennis de quien me hablas. Dicen que son tierras negras como la noche de invierno..., igual que el invierno cuando tú no ayudas a Epsamón a repartir los rayos de la vida sobre el Mundo Macho...

—¿Y Dennis se perdió en él? ¡Contéstame, perro!

Ha desaparecido aquella enormidad de rostro; él ha retrocedido, todas las formas de la tienda se marcan con extraordinaria precisión, me integro rápidamente en esta imagen, violo los límites de la pantalla, salto al interior de la escena y, apenas me encuentro en ella, cojo a Batsá por la muñeca, se la retuerzo; él se estremece, empieza a arrodillarse lentamente, se muerde los labios, se agarra a mi bota con la mano que le queda libre; llora, y yo noto que vuelvo a tener los pies asentados firmemente sobre el argumento de la película.

—¡Humíllame, monseñor! ¡Humíllame si es tu deseo!

—¡Perro! Tu sangre o una respuesta: ¿dónde se perdió Dennis?

—Tú puedes escapar de la Nada porque tu caballo tiene alas, monseñor, y rompe las tinieblas con su vuelo. Tú irrumpes en el Valle de la Vida, porque desde el comienzo de todas las historias está escrito que así sea. Pero, ¿cómo podría hacerlo Dennis? ¿Quién es Dennis?; ¿quién era, pobre criatura, vil humano sin un ápice de grandeza, mortal sin un aliento de esperanza? ¿Quién era para no perderse en las tierras de las que no se retorna, errabundo para siempre como merecía su insignificancia que los dioses del Mundo Macho supieron maldecir...?

Todas las imágenes son una, profesor, y los dedos de Dennis se agarran a mi bota con mayor violencia, y yo siento que ha aumentado mi estatura, que los tobillos son más anchos y poderosos, que cuando levanto el pie para golpear los labios del perro mi golpe resulta feroz, con una fuerza recién adquirida, y que empieza a ser titánica: por primera vez me doy cuenta de que mis músculos, antes inexistentes (como exigía la moda masculina de los años sesenta, la androginia, casi feminidad, que tanto agradaba a mis admiradores), que esos músculos son ahora masas de acero distribuidas a lo largo y a lo ancho de un cuerpo que nunca volverá a ser simple carne desarrollada por medio del ejercicio, sino hierro templado en el orden contundente que lo convierte en una fortaleza inexpugnable, un bastión que no traicionará, con su debilidad de antes, los deseos que mi voluntad recién nacida empieza a plantearse.

—¡Astor! —grité. Lo hice tres veces más, aumentando progresivamente la intensidad de mi voz, porque tardaba en acudir.

Astor no se sorprendió al descubrir a Batsá tendido en el suelo, enjugándose la sangre de los labios, mirándome asustado. Se arrodilló él también; pero al mismo tiempo yo me agaché y hundí mis uñas en su espalda.

—¡Astor! Una pregunta. Y quiero la respuesta ahora mismo, sin vacilaciones de ningún tipo. ¿Quién es este muchacho?

—Batsá, monseñor. Te lo he dicho antes.

—Me has dicho que era un buen oficial... Ah, sí, lo recuerdo todo perfectamente. ¿Cómo se las ha arreglado para aprender a ser tan bueno en tan poco tiempo? ¿Qué le habéis dado, Astor?

—¿En tan poco tiempo, monseñor? Entró en el cuartel hace cinco años..., el tiempo suficiente para un buen aprendizaje si el recluta es aplicado, como Batsá.

Clavé las uñas con más fuerza, al mismo tiempo que estallaba en una carcajada que intimidó a Astor.

—¡Lo sabía! Pregunta inútil, ¿verdad? Otra cosa, Astor: ¿quién creó el mundo?

—Cobra, monseñor.

—Y Cobra es el Mal. ¡También lo sabía, por supuesto! Y dices que este muchacho no tuvo otra vida en la cual pudiese haber aprendido que el mundo fue creado por el Bien. ¡Claro que lo sé, hijo de perra! Él nació del Mal. Y nunca ha salido del Mundo Macho... Sí, sí: no hace falta que me lo digas. Sé que no hay otro mundo más allá de éste. Y tú..., tampoco tú me raptaste de otra vida, ¿verdad? ¡Contéstame! ¿No me sacaste de mi mundo para traerme a éste?

—Lo sabes perfectamente, monseñor: desde el comienzo de todas las historias, el primer capitán de Epura Epsamón se adentra en el país de la Nada y va en busca de Nebjeperura, que ha ido a rescatar los rayos de la vida para regresar en primavera al Mundo Macho. Cuando el capitán ve que se acerca el caballo alígero de su señor, coge sus riendas de oro y lo guía por el camino que conduce al palacio real.

Le interrumpí con un puñetazo espectacular, que incluso le hizo tambalearse; pero, lejos de dolerse, se aferró a mi bota y posó los labios sobre la abertura frontal. Yo golpeé el gong por tres veces, mientras gritaba:

—¡Era muy extraño aquel caballo alígero! ¡Nada cómodo, perro! ¡Dejé mi sangre en él, atado cabeza abajo, mientras tú empuñabas con firmeza las riendas doradas!

Batsá, muy asustado, me miró, y ni él ni Astor se levantaron cuando entró, corriendo, una parte del pelotón que formaba mi guardia personal. Dije:

—¡Soldados! Vosotros, que me servís, podríais contestarme a una pregunta... —Y mirando con picardía a Astor, añadí—: Que ya nada tiene que ver con las que te hacía a ti. Contestad, soldados: ¿no merece un castigo muy severo quien se atreve a engañar a Nebjeperura?

Sus vacilantes expresiones iban de Batsá a Astor y de Astor a Batsá, como si estuviesen preguntándose cuál de los dos era culpable de tan grave afrenta. Y como quiera que Astor se hallaba más cerca de mí, y de nuevo se agarraba a mi pierna, debieron adivinar que él era el culpable, de forma que su apuro fue mayor que si hubiesen sospechado del otro, porque la culpa de Astor les pondría en situación de castigar a un superior, lo cual ignoro si estaría previsto en las leyes del Mundo Macho. Pero, nada dispuesto a perder el tiempo en dudas, me anticipé a cualquier respuesta con una orden tajante, que imponía mi sacrosanta voluntad por encima de sus probables escrúpulos.

—No necesito respuesta —exclamé—; vuestra obediencia es suficiente, y entiendo que cuento con ella; pues, de no ser así, ninguno de vosotros llegaría a ver la noche. Con ello insinúo, es decir, ordeno, que Astor sea sometido a tormento, ya que él ha sido el ofensor. Ha sido él quien se ha atrevido a mentir a aquel que es divino en Lur mientras dure la ausencia de Epsamón.

El murmullo de admiración de los soldados sólo fue

comparable a la mirada que Astor me dirigía, cada vez más fija a medida que se atrevía a levantar la cabeza hasta que se encontró con mis ojos. Era evidente que se compadecía de sí mismo; pero al mismo tiempo demostraba un singular agradecimiento hacia mí porque sus enseñanzas no habían resultado baldías. Sin embargo, sabía que mi aprendizaje no era completo y que, por lo tanto, todavía necesitaba de su ayuda. Y, paradójicamente, su ayuda consistía en asegurarse a sí mismo un sufrimiento más digno cuanto más terrible.

—Nebjeperura... —gimió.

—¡Calla! Llegó la hora de que sea yo mismo quien decida mis métodos. Y que halle placer al aplicarlos. Tú me has mentido, Astor, y ahora he de contemplar cómo tu cuerpo se retuerce de dolor por mi voluntad: cómo mi albedrío de gran déspota dispone de tu carne, bien sea para destruir en ella la belleza, bien para dirigirla hacia aquellas cimas de titanismo que tan a menudo me has exigido. Pero siempre mediante el dolor..., un dolor más violento, más lacerante que todos los que pudiste padecer hasta ahora.

Para acentuar mi dureza, rechacé incluso la proximidad de Astor, de forma que de un nuevo puñetazo lo arrojé contra la enorme pipa de opio que se hallaba cerca de la salida. Fue recogido por los soldados, que lo recibieron de una forma demasiado respetuosa, por lo cual los miró con gran severidad y, juntando las muñecas, les ordenó: «Atadme, puesto que he ofendido a Nebjeperura y soy reo de sacrilegio.» Con la mirada les indicó que no le demostrasen la menor piedad, y los soldados, indecisos, miraron a Dennis, que seguía tirado en el suelo; después me miraron a mí, sin duda en espera de la orden suprema. Entonces Astor se volvió hacia mí y, con ojos llorosos como nunca hubiese podido sospechar en un macho de su envergadura, suplicó:

—Monseñor: sólo quisiera saber en qué he podido ofenderte. ¡En qué, Nebjeperura, si sólo te he dicho la verdad!

En otra ocasión, tal vez me hubiese parado a considerar que Astor podía ser realmente sincero; que las mentiras que me endosaba sólo eran la verdad oficial que le enseñaron a repetir desde niño y que arrancaba de muchos siglos antes de que él iniciara su propia biografía. Hubiese podido considerar que la mentira puede convertirse en verdad cuando así lo quiere el poder que sobrepasa en fuerza a todos los Astores del mundo; pero en aquel momento yo ya había aceptado lo fácil que puede ser desprenderse de la carga de pensar. La repulsión que Astor me había inspirado meses atrás, y toda la simpatía que sentía por él en los últimos tiempos, se mezclaban inspirando una necesidad insólita de verle sufrir por mi voluntad; de causarle con mis propias manos un dolor tan intenso que no pudiese olvidarlo nunca. Al mismo tiempo, el temor de no estar capacitado para infligir aquel dolor me sumergía en una inseguridad que no sabría precisar, que sólo tenía comparación con el nerviosismo que me asaltaba en otros momentos de mi vida cuando, en espera de salir al escenario, me sentía completamente solo entre bastidores y, al otro lado de las candilejas, adivinaba a la masa oscura y silenciosa que aplaudía mi nombre, anunciado momentos antes por un presentador vestido de smoking negro. ¡Se parecían tanto ambos momentos! El frío temblor que me recorrió el cuerpo de pies a cabeza, la urgente necesidad de orinar, y el imperativo de echar a correr, o saltar y llorar profiriendo aullidos salvajes, sólo podrían ser interrumpidos por la premura de serenarme ante el micrófono o, aquel día del Mundo Macho, cuando la primera serpiente venenosa se enroscara alrededor del espléndido cuerpo de Astor. No había explicación posible. No la había en ambos casos.

Entonces, un soldado señaló a Batsá:

—¿Y qué hacemos con el sargento, monseñor?

Puesto que la mentira de Astor no difería mucho de la mentira de Batsá, antes bien parecía confirmarla, la primera idea lógica fue lo agradable que resultaría contemplar un suplicio compartido por ambos embusteros. Sin embargo, en medio de aquella nueva e imperiosa necesidad de ser dueño del dolor de los demás, surgía una reflexión de tipo práctico que me mantenía unido a mi ansia de conocer la verdadera realidad del Mundo Macho: si dejaba a Astor fuera de combate (lo cual equivalía a pasarme algunos días sin tenerlo a mi lado en todo momento), Batsá podía servirme de guía en una serie de excursiones por Lur, lo cual siempre me había negado Astor so pretexto de que yo debía ser el Oculto (de cuya condición provenía uno de mis nombres religiosos: Nofretakinav; es decir: la Belleza Oculta a los Ojos Profanos). Y para mejor conseguir mis propósitos, nada más apropiado que tener a Astor enfermo, recuperándose de graves heridas, y a

Dennis en calidad de servidor, obligado a aportarme los conocimientos que el otro me había negado.

Pero apenas tomé tal decisión, volvió a apoderarse de mí la necesidad del dolor de Astor; y los razonamientos sobre la estrategia a adoptar fueron abandonados, quedaron sumergidos bajo el impulso de aquella deliciosa impaciencia. Una vez perdonado Dennis, puesto que podía prestarme tan útiles servicios, ya sólo podía pensar en el sufrimiento de mi guardián.

Pero estaba escrito que, desde mucho antes de mi llegada al Mundo Macho, desde mucho antes de que empezasen sus historias, Astor debía padecer por mí: y él lo sabía, y jamás podría aceptar un sufrimiento que no estuviese de acuerdo con su condición de titán, y con la mía de Co-Divino. Así pues, se dirigió a los soldados y sugirió él mismo la clase de suplicio que le correspondía por rango:

—Que uno de vosotros vaya hacia el gran Apis de acero y empiece a encender el fuego en su interior. Seguidamente seré despojado de mis vestiduras y atado a un caballo y el mejor jinete me arrastrará por el sendero de las espinas; cuando mi cuerpo se halle cubierto de sangre, me ataréis boca abajo sobre el lomo del buey sagrado y me dejaréis allí hasta que el dolor me haga perder el sentido. Sé que me desmayaré, porque el dolor será demasiado fuerte incluso para mí, que estoy preparado para soportarlo; pero deberéis despertarme y reavivar el fuego, y lo haréis así hasta que pierda el conocimiento por dos veces más. No me despertéis del tercer desmayo, porque está ordenado que permanezca dos días colgado por los pies en el calabozo de palacio, hasta que mis heridas cicatricen.

Y, de repente, como si se avergonzase de haberse adelantado a mi orden, Astor me miró y dijo:

—Considera, monseñor, que el lugarteniente de Epsamón, sacerdote, por añadidura, del gran culto de Cobra, no podría contentarse con un sufrimiento que no fuese digno de su categoría. Sería el deshonor más infamante que pudieras infligirle.

Aceptando gustoso la golosina que Astor acababa de proponerme, ordené a los soldados que dispusieran los preparativos de la ceremonia, lo cual hicieron inmediatamente, atando las manos de Astor a una cuerda que arrastraba uno de los soldados a caballo. Entonces ayudé a Dennis a levantarse, y le ordené que no se apartara de mi lado en ningún momento, pues se convertiría en sustituto provisional de Astor durante los días que éste necesitara para reponerse de las heridas que las próximas ceremonias iban a producirle.

De este modo se puso en marcha un pintoresco cortejo formado por cuatro soldados de la primera escolta, Dennis, que llevaba la espada de Astor, y yo, montando sobre mi caballo blanco, que no era el alígero, por supuesto. Astor, completamente desnudo, corría detrás del caballo al cual le habían atado; pero llegó un momento en que el jinete espoleó tanto al animal, que mi guardián cayó al suelo, y la cuerda se tensó completamente y le arrastró a trompicones, porque el camino era rocoso e irregular. También él mantenía el cuerpo completamente estirado, y se empeñaba en mantener la cabeza erguida, sin duda por orgullo. Un tirón de cuerda hizo que fuera a dar contra unas peñas muy abruptas que le desgarraron la carne, y un segundo tirón lo lanzó en medio de un terreno que estaba poblado de cactos; de hecho, eran matorrales gigantescos de estas plantas, que, como todas las del Mundo Macho, habían sido transformadas en verdaderos monstruos de la especie. Sus espinas eran grandes como cuchillos, y era fácil suponer que podían producir intensos dolores, sobre todo en un cuerpo que pasaba sobre ellas a tanta velocidad.

Los músculos de Astor desaparecieron entre el ingente bosque de espinas; sólo en algún momento, cuando el caballo que le arrastraba se veía obligado a trotar un poco más deprisa de lo normal, su cuerpo saltaba y surgía momentáneamente mostrando una masa de carne agujereada y un rostro cubierto de sangre. Pero pronto se perdió de vista, porque el verdugo corría más que nosotros, y, a partir de entonces, lo único que quedó de manifiesto en relación con el sufrimiento de Astor fueron precisamente las espinas de los cactos, pues a medida que yo y mi cortejo seguíamos nuestro camino veíamos cómo chorreaban sangre, inequívoca prueba de que habían recibido su tributo de carne.

Cuando víctima y verdugo se hubieron alejado dejando tras de sí una nube de polvo, me dirigí a Batsá, que llevaba las riendas plateadas de mi caballo:

—Después tomaremos un baño juntos. Y a partir de esta noche montarás guardia a la puerta de mis estancias.

—Soy tu siervo, monseñor.

—Sé que no es necesario que te pregunte nada más,

porque es obvio que te han drogado o hipnotizado o ambas cosas a la vez. Pero, de cualquier modo, podrás servir a mis propósitos. Así pues, dispondrás de todo lo necesario para que mañana por la noche podamos salir en secreto de palacio e ir a Lur bajo incógnito. Y así, perro de mierda, me ayudarás a mezclarme con mi pueblo, pues no quiero pasar un día más sin conocerlo.

El tormento elegido por Astor tenía fama de estar reservado a los más privilegiados de Lur, y cumple decir que la magnificencia, tanto del lugar como de la edificación que contiene el instrumento de suplicio, explicaba de sobras aquella estimación. Se trata de un ninfeo de formas sumamente exquisitas, con columnas que bordean la orilla del lago y capiteles de orden corintio, sobre los cuales se organiza un juego de arcos redondos que sirven para alojar a las estatuas, helenizantes, de diversas divinidades del Mundo Macho. De noche, este lugar es particularmente encantador, porque las columnas, de una blancura inmaculada, se reproducen sobre el agua gracias a una iluminación de colores muy suaves y variados; y la imagen, reflejada invertida, que las luces depositan en la superficie del lago, permanece inerte, sin que pueda desfigurarla ni siquiera el rielar de la luna; de hecho, es como si la imagen se fijara en ese espejo, buscando no se sabe qué infinito. Los corpulentos pinos de la colina que empieza precisamente junto al ninfeo, se añaden al reflejo y completan una imagen de augusta serenidad.

En una plataforma de basalto rojo que se adentra en el lago como una pequeña península del sufrimiento se adentraría en el mar inmenso de las delicias, aparecía un templete sostenido por cuatro cariátides que representaban diversas manifestaciones de Nebjeperura-Apolón. Dentro, también encarado al lago, para que las víctimas más ilustres puedan contemplar su propio suplicio reproducido en la superficie del agua, hay una gran escultura de Apis: un buey ennegrecido porque en la barriga, hueca, se enciende el fuego destinado a la víctima. Ya habrá comprendido usted que el refinamiento de este sistema requiere pocos comentarios: la obviedad del cuerpo consumiéndose entre las llamas de una hoguera corriente ha sido cambiada aquí por un sistema de calor interno que va torturando a la víctima con gran lentitud, sibarítica donde las haya. Y no me cansaré de insistir en que no todo el mundo puede aspirar a este suplicio: es preciso haber acumulado muchos méritos en el Mundo Macho para ganarse el derecho a sufrir unas horas sobre el lomo de Apis.

Cuando la víctima se halla colocada boca abajo, con el pecho apoyado sobre el lomo de hierro, atadas las manos a cada uno de los cuernos y los pies a la cola, empieza la auténtica grandeza del suplicio. Así pues, queda crucificado, pero con la ventaja de que, apenas el contacto con el hierro al rojo se le hace insoportable, puede presionar con los músculos de los brazos y de los pies, de forma que el cuerpo, al tensarse, se levanta algunos centímetros, y permanece así, estirado en el aire. A pesar de todo, el calor que desprende el horno interior traspasa el hierro y llega al cuerpo, que debe defenderse de la quemazón y, al mismo tiempo, de la postura agotadora que ha adoptado para evitar el contacto candente. Esta alternancia es lo que da al Fuego de Apis (como se le denomina) una variedad que difícilmente hallamos en otros suplicios del Mundo Macho.

Todas estas etapas fueron aplicadas a Astor, quien, a pesar de las heridas recibidas durante el trayecto, rechazó la ayuda que le ofrecían algunos soldados y se dirigió hacia el buey por su propio pie, aunque tambaleándose. Se dejó atar las manos a los cuernos, los pies a la cola, y seguidamente, tartamudeando, ordenó que alimentasen el fuego, pues el ardor del lomo contra su pecho era, al parecer, insuficiente. Yo veía aquel cuerpo rezumando sangre, con los músculos traspasados por tantas espinas descomunales, y sentía, ya plenamente asumida, la incomparable satisfacción del castigo administrado en acto de servicio a la justicia. Nada hay que pueda igualársele. Y Astor, siempre solícito, no quiso echar a perder la altísima categoría heroica de la situación con un grito de dolor más digno de los herejes que de un oficial del Mundo Macho. Así pues, se limitó a morderse los labios, que también estaban plagados de espinas.

Poco a poco, el ardor pasó del hierro al pecho; un intenso olor a carne quemada invadió el templete, razón por la cual Dennis insinuó la conveniencia de perfumar el ambiente con esencia de sándalo. Me negué a ello, porque tanto aquel olor a carne como la humareda de cada quemadura constituían mi ingreso definitivo en otro mundo: era mi pasaporte para aquel titanismo que mis músculos ya empezaban a adquirir. Al mismo tiempo, la heroica estampa de Astor me inspiraba una necesidad de ser como él; pero no deseaba menos que se restableciera pronto de sus heridas y pudiese volver cada mañana a mis habitaciones para ayudarme en las clases de flagelación.

Entre tantas contradicciones, me acometía otro prurito todavía más violento: necesitaba ser yo, personalmente, quien le atormentara con el dolor más intenso, el que debía marcarle para siempre, al tiempo que convertiría mi castigo en inviolable, en irrepetible. Y él mismo, levantando ahora la cabeza y mirándome fijamente, parecía solicitarlo.

Ordené que introdujeran una espada en el horno y que no la sacaran hasta que estuviese al rojo vivo. Vigilé la operación, y noté que el fuego me atraía como una irresistible tentación, como si fuese realmente mi único trono. La hoja ya tenía un color brillante, entre rojo y azul, y cuando el verdugo la puso en mis manos, yo sentí cómo un calor insoportable iba avanzando desde la punta hacia la empuñadura incrustada de rubíes. Al verme avanzar, y adivinando mi acción, Astor cerró los ojos y murmuró: «Gracias, monseñor, gracias»; y se mordió los labios con más fuerza que antes, de forma que las espinas de los cactos se le clavaron en las encías, única parte del cuerpo de la que aún no brotaba sangre.

Yo empuñaba la espada; me aferraba a los rubíes de aquella arma que siempre había colgado del cinturón de Astor: el primer objeto del Mundo Macho que vi en mi vida, aquella noche en Minia, cuando él la sacó de entre los pliegues de su manto negro.

También recordé con todo detalle cómo el Sumo Sacerdote del templo del Final Viril levantó el estilete el día de mi iniciación; y, dirigido acaso por ese recuerdo, apoyé la hoja de la espada sobre la nuca de Astor, con suavidad, como si fuera una lengua de fuego que acariciara su espalda poco a poco, en sutil descenso. Él tensó los músculos, y todo su cuerpo se incorporó en la medida que le permitían las ataduras; pero, al parecer, el dolor que sentiría mientras yo iba deslizando la hoja por la espalda fue tan intenso que, para huir de él, era preferible soportar el horrible contacto del pecho contra el lomo candente de Apis. Emparedado entre dos fuegos, mi guardián sólo levantó un poco la cintura, de forma que cuando la espada llegó hasta allí y siguió avanzando hacia las nalgas, el ano se le ofreció con una voluntad muy digna del mártir más abnegado. Y con esta violación de fuego, Astor conoció lo que yo sentí aquella noche del Final Viril, mientras a la luz de las llamas del templo bailaba la forma sinuosa de Cobra Macho.

El agua del lago, cubierta de nenúfares, reflejó la ceremonia: fue espejo que reproducía el buey, la cabeza vacilante de Astor y, en segundo término, una espada que se iba introduciendo en las cavernas de mi guardián, hasta que el insensato se desmayó.

Y yo pensé que aquella noche me divertiría mucho por las calles de Lur, mezclado entre mi pueblo.

ESCUCHA, Larry:

Ignoro si debería empezar contando cómo llegué a él, o bien cómo conseguí escaparme. Era el Mundo Macho. Y esta inquietud pavorosa que el viento del desierto se lleva consigo sólo logra hacerme volver; no hace sino lanzarme a la idea, rotunda, inconfundible, de que aún permanezco prisionero. De hecho, a lo largo de los tres meses que permanecí en la clínica, con el sopor de los paseos por los estanques y el parque como única evasión de la insoportable paz nirvánica a que los médicos han querido condenarme, he tenido tiempo suficiente para descubrir que lo importante de este asunto, de esta obsesión, no reside tanto en la forma en que me atraparon o me ayudaron a huir, como en la etapa intermedia, incluso alucinante, durante la cual aquel universo fue real, vivencia de no sé qué pesadilla.

Pero, a pesar de la opinión de los médicos, a pesar de *tus* amenazas y de las exigencias de la casa discográfica (arréglatelas como puedas, yo no puedo pensar en *long plays* ahora; te juro que no puedo), he regresado a Egipto y, al adentrarme en el país, bordeando siempre el Padre Nilo, he vuelto a sentir con toda intensidad, no que la obsesión volvía, sino que nunca desapareció. Al igual que la pesadilla, de la que es recuerdo y presencia permanentes, la obsesión no llega a curarse ni siquiera con la quietud de todos los bosques de Suiza (pero no te lo reprocho: te interesa que yo vuelva a cantar. No encontrarías otra mina como yo. Nadie se dejaría dominar así. ¿Por qué no ibas a buscar el mejor reposo para tu gallina de los huevos de oro?). Los bosques, sí que rodean todas las clínicas, hermosas como un juguete de niño rico, situadas a orillas de los lagos más apropiados. Hoy, al regresar a Egipto (vendrás a buscarme en cuanto me localices, me mandarás a un detective, los periodistas, yo qué sé, pero habré huido de ti, y el Mundo Macho me abrirá sus simas para que yo sea su rey), mientras busco por todas las esquinas a los dos misteriosos personajes que podrían raptarme y restituirme mi trono, la obsesión se materializa en el hundimiento total de mis nervios (ya debería tener mucha práctica en perderme en una sucesión de explicaciones inútiles, como si mi salud estuviese realmente afectada y los médicos no se hubieran equivocado al intentar convencerte de que necesitaba reposo, de que debería permanecer un mínimo de seis meses sin actuar, a duras penas acabar la grabación del *long play* y el doblaje de la película y huelga decirlo ni pensar en volver a Egipto, sino que desde Suiza a casita y reposo absoluto, como si ellos hubiesen tenido razón con sus palabras terminantes la decisión inapelable el tono severo que iba perdiéndose a lo lejos mientras yo escapaba corriendo, huía de la clínica con aquella cartera llena de dinero que tú habías dejado sobre mi cama eres irlandés de lo más tozudo si pudieras me tendrías encerrado con siete llaves y sólo me dejarías salir para grabar y actuar y firmar cheques acuérdate de que la otra vez para conseguir hacer un poco de turismo en Egipto tuve que escaparme y es que estaba ya agotado no podía más necesitaba urgentemente unas vacaciones y mientras tú estabas en la habitación de al lado hablando con los médicos cogí la cartera y eché a correr no había nada que me importara ni siquiera tú sólo pensaba en regresar a Minia era como una pesadilla un martilleo incesante en mi cerebro incluso en el avión Ginebra-Atenas desperté de repente y grité Mundo Macho Mundo Macho y nadie me entendía y bajo el avión sólo veía nubes de formas macizas como un vómito blanquísimo que permitían entrever el azul del mar muy plano). Los bosques de Suiza, sí, los bosques que rodean todas las clínicas, los bosques de Suiza, bellos como un juguete de niño rico, los bosques de Suiza, situados a orillas de los lagos más apropiados, Larry...

¡Sabes ser tan cruel, Larry!

... la obsesión se materializa en el hundimiento total de mis nervios y en un alejamiento de cualquier forma de realidad. El poder de la pesadilla parece romper mi resistencia de antes, y los callejones llenos de lodo a causa del polvo del desierto y el agua de las acequias, se llenan de sombras que vuelven a ser reales, que deberán hacerse palpables de un momento a otro mientras la pobre realidad de esta villa de provincia irá convirtiéndose en las selvas intrincadas del Mundo Macho, en la compacta cadena de rocas que se pierden entre las nubes, y de la cual, si Batsá no me engañaba, yo he sido el único que consiguió salir. Del mismo modo que soy el único que puede contarlo, ahora, mientras busco una entrada de aquella tierra que probablemente no volveré a hallar; el único en contarlo, en haberlo visto, en saber, no sin espanto, que el Mundo Macho existe y, finalmente, el único a quien nunca creerás.

Este pobre loco: yo.

Dime, Mundo Macho: ¿en qué me convirtió Lur? Responde, Larry, mi macho: ¿qué hiciste conmigo mucho tiempo antes de que llegase a Lur?

Hoy, el viento del desierto sopla furiosamente contra las cordilleras del otro lado del Nilo; brama con idéntica fuerza que aquella Navidad del año pasado, o del otro (ni siquiera esto puedo precisarle). Después de que Charlie Walsh, Dennis Branden y Morgan Willard me dejaron solo en la Corniche, enfrentado al misterio del río bajo la noche y a tantos muertos antiguos entrevistos en las profundidades de las necrópolis faraónicas, más o menos próximas. Hoy, el viento del desierto lleva la misma arena; las ratas corren entre la rocalla a orillas del río; la luna hace palidecer las montañas en la otra ribera. Hoy no he dormido, no dormiré, porque el momento está cercano, porque, aunque el profesor duerma el sueño de su opio, asqueado de escucharme, tal vez odiando mi drama y la muerte que no me llega, yo te tengo junto a mí como un fantasma que sólo accede a desvanecerse de vez en cuando para ceder su lugar a otros, pero regresando hoy, mañana, siempre y para siempre.

¡Oh, Larry, Larry!

He perdido los gestos, las sonrisas, las miradas y la forma de peinarme; primero los tuyos, después los del Mundo Macho. He perdido el pensamiento, la ira, la paz, el amor y el odio que me inculcaste; y, luego, he perdido los que me inculcó el Mundo Macho. No reencuentro nada de antes que llegases tú, ni de antes que llegase el Mundo Macho: soy el espectro que, al perder el ayer inmediato, pierde la voluntad que le fuese insuflada, primero por ti, después por Lur. Eso es cierto, Larry; tan cierto como el agua del Nilo cuando la noche se hace muerte: tú me hiciste, y el Mundo Macho me destruía para reconstruirme de nuevo, y ahora no os tengo, y no seré nada hasta que vuelva a teneros. ¡Mundo Macho, Larry macho!

En la cima de la adoración que he despertado, yo he sido la sombra que el siglo quería que fuese; he sido las mil representaciones de la divinidad que el Mundo Macho exigía, y ahora intento reencontrar el punto en el cual todo yo, íntegro y vil a la vez, recomience en la única dimensión que realmente puedo tener.

Por ello te digo, Larry: en esta ciudad, donde los fantasmas de la colonización europea se mezclan con la fantasmagoría latente de la ciudad de Atón, tu dominio alejado en el espacio representa al único lector capaz de corresponderse con mi obsesión, llena de fantasmas que permanecen, vivos y agresivos, en alguna parte del cosmos.

De este modo, sentado en este café con grandes espejos de esquinas biseladas, mientras los viejos fuman una extraña pipa de tubos larguísimos, que no tiene opio (los adolescentes casi campesinos que me miran con expresión equívoca, ofreciéndose desde dentro, o bien desde fuera del café, ¿cómo reaccionarían, por quién me tomarían si me animase a advertirles de que este universo de mitos de plástico que tú diriges puede estar acechándoles en este mismo momento? ¿Me creerían si les pronosticara que mañana, o la semana próxima, tal vez esta misma noche, pueden desaparecer para siempre, catapultados hacia las cimas de la fama, engullidos entre el oro de tus contratos, sepultos bajo la inmensa cantidad de portadas de revista, aislados más allá de las fronteras electrónicas que separan al ídolo de esa selva formada por una multitud angustiada, perdidos en el dorado desierto del disco y de la pantalla?); de este modo, digo, mientras me llega la abigarrada confusión de la última noche que pasaré en Minia, reemprendo esta narración solitaria que tú nunca has querido creer...

LLEGÓ LA NOCHE de la visita a Lur, y Dennis lo preparó todo tal como yo había dispuesto: me disfrazó de soldado raso y procuró que el caballo no fuese blanco, como correspondía a los grandes del Mundo Macho, sino marrón oscuro, que no delata a un jinete de rango elevado. De este modo salimos de las habitaciones co-divinas y, utilizando la escalera interior del coloso de Epsamón más próximo a los jardines colgantes, llegamos fácilmente a la parte posterior de palacio; es decir, al patio de los cuarteles, en cuyo centro las dos fontanas de alabastro esparcían destellos color hueso al ser acariciadas por la luna. Puesto que era la hora de la cena, en la plaza sólo se encontraban los soldados encargados de montar la guardia; éstos ya se habían puesto de acuerdo con Dennis y nos dejaron salir, sin hacer preguntas y evitando las reverencias de costumbre a fin de no traicionar mi personalidad ante cualquier mirada inoportuna que pudiese llegar inesperadamente de los comedores del cuartel. Mientras Dennis preparaba los caballos, yo aproveché para descansar y, una vez más, la visión de la plaza, con las murallas ciclópeas y el espacio cuadrilátero que cortaba la montaña sobre la cual se elevaba la masa barroca del palacio, me produjo la impresión de una barbarie alucinante, como si las primeras construcciones del hombre en una prehistoria muy lejana se hallasen conservadas aquí, convertidas en necesidad de cada día, recuerdo de un tiempo en que no existía otra opción que la de matar o morir: lucha que aún no habría previsto los artesonados marfileños del palacio, las filigranas lombardas de la fontana y la pagoda de plata y lapislázuli que se halla en los estanques de la Fertilidad.

Salimos de los parques de palacio y, siguiendo la Vía Herculana, rodeamos la ciudad con la intención de entrar en ella por la puerta principal (es decir, al contrario de la noche en que Astor me acompañó para asistir a la ceremonia de la Purificación); y apenas nos fuimos aproximando a esta entrada volví a reparar en que la alternativa entre barbarie y refinamiento se reproducía incluso en las murallas de la capital. Aquí, lo mismo que en palacio, era como si cinco mil años de historia hubiesen depositado toda una herencia de formas, colores y sonidos, que convertían la vida urbana en un vastísimo museo de mundos. Pero no existía aquí la herencia de muerte que se halla implícita en toda ruina; al contrario, no había ruina alguna: todo estaba en constante uso, todo formaba parte de una cotidianidad que, o bien había logrado evitar que los siglos hiciesen estragos en los edificios, o bien los había construido de muy reciente. De cualquier modo, esta última suposición no era nada verosímil, puesto que una de las peculiaridades de edificios, puentes, e incluso estatuas, era la pátina que siglos y siglos habían ido acumulando de una forma más embellecedora que destructora; más dignificante de su señorío que dispendiosa y abocada al destino olvidadizo de la ruina absoluta.

Esta parte de Vía Herculana contiene un barrio extramuros que sirve de residencia a los ricos y es sello de dignidad y elegancia, testimonio de un alto grado de nobleza y de ese buen gusto que, en cualquier lugar del mundo, otorga la posibilidad de alejar la propia privacidad del caos urbano. No es que yo entienda demasiado de estos asuntos, pero diría que los espíritus selectos del Mundo Macho acreditan su rango rechazando, precisamente, el estallido ciudadano que ellos mismos han contribuido a crear. Y es que, como en tantas ciudades de nuestro mundo occidental, la vida urbana ha alcanzado en el Mundo Macho unos límites de saturación, una superabundancia demográfica que la han hecho insoportable para cualquier persona que alardee de un mínimo de sensibilidad. Las Cien puertas de Lur (muchas de las cuales pertenecen a diferentes estilos, extremadamente barrocas unas; bárbaras, con enormes leones alados las otras), son ya insuficientes para controlar las entradas y salidas de la multitud que, diariamente, abarrota los mercados de la capital, las escuelas y cuarteles, los templos, las tiendas, los lugares de diversión y, dado que el sistema del Imperio Macho es completamente centralista, los abundantes órganos administrativos que rigen los destinos de muchos pueblos asimilados. Este abigarramiento constituye un espectáculo realmente apasionante, que Dennis se dedicó a mostrarme, no negaré que un poco a disgusto. Es un inmenso hormiguero humano que se diría una reproducción litográfica de lo que para los antiguos debieron ser Nínive, Babilonia o Tebas, con la adición de lo que para nosotros puedan ser Londres, París o Nueva York. Entre las altas murallas, de almenas que dejan entrever la parte superior del *claf*, típico en el tocado de las grandes esfinges faraónicas situadas detrás de la muralla, se adivinan los grandes palacios de columnas papiriformes, separados entre sí por jardines y parques que pueden contener, además, rotondas de formas sinuosas, empinadas como las mayores osadías del *Art Nouveau*, templetes de planta circular dedicados a la divinidad particular de cada mansión, incluso diminutos baptisterios, deliciosos cuando su mármol rosado recibe el sol más tibio del otoño y los lagos adyacentes reproducen su planta octogonal. Detrás de tanta profusión de construcciones lujosas se aglomeraban multitud de barrios comprimidos, con callejones sumamente estrechos, que suben y bajan o se escalonan de acuerdo con las exigencias de las colinas sobre las cuales se hallan edificados desde tiempo inmemorial; aquí, las *insulae*, que pueden tener un máximo de cuatro pisos, se amontonan en una disposición caótica, que sólo puede compararse con la de las callejas del muelle donde, además del caos propio de este tipo de urbanismo, encontraremos las costanillas ascendentes de los artesanos y las pendientes de los menestrales, decoradas con arcos en forma de puentes que recuerdan un tiempo pretérito del Mundo Macho caracterizado por una modesta prosperidad económica, típica del auge de los oficios manuales y el comercio gremial, superada hoy por la industrialización y la constructividad de los grandes banqueros, que hicieron y hacen la fortuna del país con la fabricación de armas para la guerra inacabable de Epsamón Divino.

Cabalgábamos ya por la parte de la Vía Herculana que corresponde a los dominios de los jueces, y Dennis seguía sin pronunciar palabra, como si la gentileza de explicarme el mundo que nos albergaba fuese la cosa más difícil de inculcarle, en aquel momento, mañana, cualquier día del futuro. Yo le miraba de vez en cuando y descubría en su expresión un hieratismo orgulloso que lo hacía cada vez más remoto a mis ojos, como si fuese cierto que nunca nos conocimos antes de entonces. Miraba hacia adelante invariablemente, y sus labios sobresalían con un rictus de una cierta violencia a priori, como si estuviesen preparados para cualquier contingencia que pudiese surgir. Tenía una mano crispada sobre las riendas y la otra sobre la espada, pronta a desenvainarla a la primera emergencia. Era la representación total del genio bélico. Y, si accedía a sonreír, su sonrisa era un simple acto de obediencia al orden que yo representaba, y que le exigía corresponder incluso a mis bromas. Pero no había en él ni un asomo de simpatía.

De las múltiples carreteras que arrancan de Lur y se prolongan hacia todos los rincones del Imperio, la Vía Herculana es no sólo la más importante, sino la más placentera. La barbarie ciclópea de las murallas que se anuncian desde lejos no se delata aquí, siquiera remotamente, gracias al absoluto refinamiento del paisaje y los edificios: las tumbas de la otra parte de la Vía, la que conduce al templo del Final Viril, han sido cambiadas por una sucesión perfectamente organizada de pinos y cipreses, detrás de los cuales empiezan las villas de los ricos, poco visibles a causa de los prodigiosos trabajos de jardinería que colocan una muralla de follaje, flores y troncos entre la vía pública y la entrada de los edificios. Pero, atendiendo a una pregunta mía, Dennis me explicó, ceremonioso y con aspereza, que las formas de cada villa responden a las exigencias del gusto más sofisticado. Curiosamente, alguna era lo bastante alta para lograr superar los árboles y mostrar ante mi embeleso una fachada de formas neoclásicas (con el templete que coronaba la nave del centro y las bóvedas redondas que parecen sostenerlo desde las naves laterales), o bien la equilibrada estructura que aloja tres órdenes de ventanas renacentistas, de serena majestad, separadas por un sistema de acolchado perfectamente distribuido. En cualquier caso, la procedencia extranjera de cada ejemplo, entre los pocos que se dejaban ver, era tan clara que constantemente me remitía a las preguntas que tantas veces me había formulado sobre el secreto profesional de interrelaciones existente entre un lugar como el Mundo Macho y la cultura que alimentó en su día mi historia occidental.

Pero cuando me surgió la necesidad de acorralar a Dennis con una nueva sarta de preguntas, me acordé de los desplantes que recibí cada vez que, en el Mundo Macho, se me había ocurrido preguntar algo. Sin embargo, opté por plantearle el problema sin tapujos:

—Supongo que todas las preguntas que pueda hacerte tendrán, como respuesta, la que dicte la verdad oficial...

—¿Qué te hace pensar así, monseñor?

—Tú mismo, Dennis..., o como quiera que te llames ahora. Basta con mirarte para comprenderlo. Y, también, tu empeño en tratarme de «monseñor».

—¿De qué otro modo podría tratarte? Tú estás muy por encima de todos nosotros.

—¿Estoy, incluso, por encima de la verdad oficial? Responde a esto, y, si quieres, terminamos.

—Tú eres la verdad oficial, monseñor.

Era un círculo vicioso: lo había sido con Astor, empezaba a serlo con Dennis, lo sería con cualquier persona a quien me dirigiese con afán de información.

Yo podía hacer mil intentos por conocer la verdad de aquel mundo; pero todos estaban destinados al fracaso porque, para aquella gente, yo personificaba todas las verdades posibles, y, además, su mundo. Yo: el único condenado a no conocer nunca ni una sola de aquellas verdades, ni siquiera una mínima parte de aquel mundo. ¿O tal vez era otra cosa? Tal vez lo único cierto era que los habitantes del Mundo Macho nunca conocerían otra verdad que aquella mediante la cual eran gobernados: la que me convertía a mí en la verdad y, al mismo tiempo, en el mundo. Esta idea, que al principio había sido imprevista y absurda, empezó a tomar cuerpo y hacerse factible: su ignorancia total desterraba la sospecha de mala fe en todas las evasivas ante cada una de mis preguntas. Ésta podría ser la clave: que lo único que ellos podían revelarme de sí mismos era un aspecto físico, sin duda espléndido, pero parcial, porque una verdad que no conocerían nunca, que nadie les haría comprender, les robó el alma muchos siglos atrás.

—Escúchame, Dennis: esta verdad oficial, ¿también afecta a la arquitectura? Entiéndeme: ¿influye en esta insólita confusión... ese encontrar en mi pesadilla tantas referencias a las formas de nuestra cultura de origen? Dímelo, porque todo el absurdo del Mundo Macho podría aclararse de saber, al menos, por qué extraña razón sus dioses son reproducciones de estatuas que solían aparecer en nuestros libros de bachillerato... Miguel Ángel, Bernini, malas copias de Fidias, mucho mártir cristiano, y, para colmo, esos pilares de templo egipcio...

—Es el templo de la Sabiduría —dijo Dennis sin apartar la mirada de la carretera—; podrás encontrarlo en cualquier enciclopedia del Mundo Macho...

—¡De acuerdo! Incluso puede ser el templo de la Mierda, si te empeñas; lo cual no impide que el templo de Homo Demeter sea griego, y las murallas de la capital una mala imitación de cualquier burgo medieval europeo, con agujas góticas y gárgolas monstruosas por todas partes. Intento explicarte que, en este país, no hay una sola invención original. Todo es prestado. Incluso nosotros dos.

Al parecer, esta última frase impresionó a Dennis de una manera muy especial. Tanto, que tiró violentamente de las riendas y el caballo se detuvo. Con un gesto muy brusco, que sin duda él consideraría el colmo de la insolencia, detuvo también el que yo montaba. Entonces me tomó del brazo.

—Gérard... —murmuró.

Comprenderá usted que, en aquel momento, resultaba muy difícil no morir de asombro.

—Así pues, te acuerdas de mi nombre. Sabes que no soy Nebjeperura.

—Claro que lo sé. Incluso conozco que no es un apelativo genuino de este país, porque, si mis recuerdos de Luxor no me traicionan, el guía lo pronunció como nombre de coronación de algún faraón muy joven, enterrado en el Valle de los Reyes. Sí, amigo mío: me acuerdo perfectamente de todo, pero a partir de ahora no volveré a recordarlo nunca más. Tú has muerto, en tanto que Gérard; yo he muerto, en tanto que Dennis. Y te aconsejo que lo aceptes de una vez, porque fue una buena muerte. La mejor.

Al mirarme directamente a los ojos, recobró por un instante la vivacidad de otro tiempo y pareció animarme a seguirle hacia una lógica que él ya había aprendido a asumir. Como sensación, sólo recuerdo el perfume de los pinos y el viento que, al anunciar el campo abierto, agitaba las plumas de mi yelmo.

—En pocas palabras, amigo francés: ellos me han convencido. Y me alegro.

—¡Te alegras!

—Me alegro, sí, porque todo este misterio, toda esta ley que tú no puedes comprender, correspondía a algo que yo llevaba dentro: la doctrina que necesitaba para ser feliz. La que necesitan los otros...

—¿Los otros?

—Charlie y Morgan. Están aquí. Sin embargo, no son soldados. Han escogido oficios distintos, pero son tan felices como yo en la milicia. Charlie es el protegido del banquero Exfó... Será un banquero importante el día de mañana; y Morgan, en su búsqueda del poder aliado con la mística, estudia en el seminario de la serpiente. En oficios tan distintos, ambos ocupan lugares de privilegio: nuestra asimilación se ha visto bien recompensada, y durante estos años hemos puesto en práctica lo mejor de nosotros mismos, siempre aprendiendo a servir a un orden superior, una raza que no tiene parangón. Y tú no harás nada que pueda decepcionarnos, porque has sido depositario de nuestra voluntad como antes lo fuera Epsamón. ¿Queda todo explicado, MONSEÑOR?

Había algo en aquella declaración de principios que me horrorizó. Existía toda una serie de claudicaciones que confirmaban de qué modo la historia del Mundo Macho no se limitaba al hecho de raptar, sino que se asentaba sobre el de incorporar. Al mismo tiempo se me planteaba el alucinante problema de que aquella costumbre empezase a extenderse más allá de las fronteras de Lur.

—Está claro. Incluso algo que has olvidado, Dennis: lo que a ti te ha servido para realizarte es una doctrina que en nuestro mundo ha recibido y recibe un nombre muy feo. Y tú conoces ese nombre. Lo conoces tan bien, que una noche, en Luxor, mientras cenábamos en vuestro bungalow, te declaraste apasionadamente en contra. ¿Cómo has podido cambiar tanto en seis meses?

Entonces él me miró boquiabierto, como si no pudiese comprender que yo equivocara las fechas de una forma tan patente y manifiesta.

—¿Seis meses, monseñor? ¡Pero si han pasado diez años!

El impacto de esta revelación fue tan grande que mis dedos se clavaron en los músculos de Dennis, y éste, al notarlo, sonrió; pero no sin reprimir un gesto de dolor que expresó mordiéndose los labios. Mi pensamiento volvía a ser una orgía donde ningún objeto de los que me rodeaban podía permanecer quieto; donde los segundos, los minutos, los días habían dejado de tener un significado real y sólo se ordenaban con el curso de una sensación, con el estallido de un impulso que, si bien corto, podía parecer eterno en la memoria. El descubrimiento de esta dimensión de un tiempo remitido a los límites más profundos del absurdo, me confirmaba en la posibilidad de que yo, Nebjeperura, fuese infinito, fuese mortal de ida y vuelta, fuese el gran señor de una condena terrible que dejaba a la vida sin final.

Sin duda, Dennis entendió que ya no tenía deseos de formular más preguntas, pues picó espuelas y me aconsejó que yo hiciese lo mismo, o, de lo contrario, se haría tarde para entrar en la ciudad. Pero yo estaba tan ensimismado que él mismo tuvo que dirigir a mi caballo tomando las riendas. Así proseguimos nuestro camino bajo los pinos y cipreses de la Vía Herculana, y cuando, en un recodo del camino, apareció la impresionante Puerta Imperial, Dennis sonrió de nuevo.

—Supongo, monseñor, que lo que más puede interesarte de tu capital serán los barrios populares...

Asentí maquinalmente, obsesionado por cuanto acababa de escuchar y, al mismo tiempo, fascinado por la impresionante aureola que flotaba sobre Lur, que teñía el cielo con un resplandor rojizo, dueño del horizonte, y destacaba el perfil de las siete colinas por encima de las murallas: majestuosa imagen de un prodigio antinatural que hubiese convertido la noche en día, e incluso eclipsado la fuerza de la luna. Aquel resplandor sobre la ciudad anunciaba el estallido de una noche de diversión perfectamente organizada desde siempre, una fiesta que entendía la alegría como necesidad política y la imperiosidad de divertirse como una nueva e intransferible variante de la gran verdad oficial. En el futuro, yo sabría que la gigantesca aureola que, procedente de Lur, se difuminaba sobre el telón del paisaje, sólo era el precio que toda una sociedad debía pagar para conseguir esa extrañísima forma de paz individual que la indiferencia organizada suele producir.

La riqueza de Lur era el precio, que entonces —y por pocos días a partir de entonces— consideraba yo demasiado caro. Durante el aprendizaje que se me había impuesto, encontré en la biblioteca de palacio todos los libros occidentales que hablaban de historia antigua; obras de un pasado muy remoto que el Mundo Macho quiso asimilar a su presente sin considerar perspectiva alguna. Obligado a estudiar, fui descubriendo cosas estupendas que concernían al itinerario total del mundo, a todas las luchas que el hombre quiso emprender para ir afianzándose en aquella evolución que mi espíritu occidental conoce ahora con el nombre de «civilización». Las lecciones que los sabios me hacían repetir diariamente para asegurarse de que las había asimilado, me acostumbraron a convertir el pensamiento en una disciplina que tú, Larry, me habías robado: una sucesión de eslabones en cadena que, siempre en progresión, introducían una nueva curiosidad después de cada descubrimiento, o convertían a la curiosidad en obsesión por cada cosa nueva que, a partir de aquel momento, pudiese descubrir. Casi sin darme cuenta, fui encontrando a cada paso las bases para una comprensión de las formas que convertían la estética aparente del Mundo Macho en el almacén de una historia, o de muchas, que no tenían ninguna relación aparente con la realidad del país. Había aprendido a distinguir la gran mentira que continuamente se ofrecía a mis ojos, la enorme trampa que, lejos de aportar nuevas claridades con cada nueva identificación, la oscurecían más y más. Y dado que la disciplina del pensamiento aboca a la actitud filosófica, lo que entonces empezaba a sentir como un drama vital era, precisamente, la imposibilidad de utilizar la inteligencia para llegar a la verdad última del mundo que me estaba enseñando a ser inteligente. Situación más demencial todavía porque, si bien la ignorancia acepta pasar por alto muchas evidencias de las que la realidad utiliza para golpearnos a cada momento —dando como cierta la proposición vulgar de que el ignorante no sufre—, la mentalidad filosófica se aterra cuando, empeñada en explorar hasta el fondo del pozo de la verdad, hay alguien que le impide hacerlo.

Mientras el tráfico de la entrada de Lur empezaba a rodearnos con profusión de manifestaciones ruidosas, yo reconsideraba que el estado de felicidad absoluta que parecía desprenderse de todos los rostros que conocí en el Mundo Macho residía, precisamente, en aquella ignorancia; y me preguntaba, acaso por última vez, qué secretos vericuetos habrían seguido todos sus habitantes para alcanzarla. Para ellos, la tranquilidad de espíritu consistía en no saber que el templete redondo dedicado a los Cuarenta Babuinos protectores de la guerra, y que es admiración de todos los *dilettanti* del país, era sólo una reproducción de Bramante, y que, según podría demostrar cualquier libro de mitología de los prohibidos en Lur, los cuarenta babuinos protectores pertenecían a la obsesión religiosa de los faraones del Nilo. Sí, desde luego, era esto. Las cosas que Astor no podía explicarme, las secretas asociaciones que era incapaz de clarificar, no podían existir para él en tanto que enigma, pues, nacido en el Mundo Macho, creció acostumbrado a considerar como formas nacionales y genuinas multitud de obras de exquisito refinamiento occidental colocadas junto al colosalismo más bárbaro y agresivo. Pero yo, al evocar mi único viaje a Lur, el día ya lejano del sacrificio de los niños impuros, recordaba que, tanto la crueldad de la ceremonia como la mezcla de estilos que dominaba toda la avenida del templo, correspondían a una misma necesidad de ocultación dictada por no sé qué extrañas fuerzas. Epsamón Divino, mi amo desconocido, sería el punto altísimo adonde iban a confluir todos los puntos del problema. Él tenía que ser (¿o quién, si no?) la causa y el origen del gran enigma que planteaban la confusión del Mundo Macho y la indiferencia de sus habitantes.

Así pues, conocer a Epsamón Divino se imponía como

la necesidad a partir de la cual tal vez se me concedería la posibilidad de empezar a comprender.

Pues, aunque tú nunca has querido creerlo (¿qué has creído, qué creerás de toda esa historia que mi huida ha dejado abierta para siempre?), aunque tú me mirases tan burlonamente cuando yo, desesperado, te lo aseguraba, seguía sin conocer a Epsamón; ni siquiera sabía cómo era su rostro. Esa ignorancia, esa imposibilidad de conocimiento, se me confirmaba nuevamente mientras avanzábamos hacia la entrada de Lur y contemplaba todas las estatuas que, a modo de propaganda intensiva, iban inculcando en el alma del pueblo la majestad suprema de Epsamón. Como Astor me dijese en cierta ocasión, Él no estaba representado de forma realista, sino reencarnado en cada divinidad que las estatuas personificaban. Epsamón podía tomar la representación del Ra solar, o bien de Marte, el griego, e incluso de una curiosa Astarté que, en vez de pechos múltiples, ostentaba una gran cantidad de penes brotando sobre el arco poderoso que formaban sus piernas. Sí, era evidente que sólo Epsamón podía representar a los grandes dioses sobre la Tierra; que sólo él podía transmitir a su pueblo los rayos solares que yo rescato cada año del País de la Nada; que sólo sus penes múltiples pueden significar la fuerza de la reproducción y, al mismo tiempo, la victoria del poder macho sobre las potencias femeninas de la creación; que sólo él podía estrangular a la hidra, matar al león trífido, destrozar una pared con su puño desnudo... Todo estaba muy claro, tal vez demasiado, porque sólo Epsamón podía atesorar, llevadas hasta la máxima sublimidad, todas las virtudes de la raza, dictar otras nuevas y anular las innecesarias. Y nadie debería conocer su rostro, porque todos sabían que Epsa quiere decir Poder Macho, y el sufijo Amón significa «el Oculto». El que basa toda su fuerza, todo su poder, en el ardid de no mostrarse jamás al pueblo. Y de este modo es respetado y venerado, y se convierte en Estado e Iglesia a la vez.

—He aquí tu templo, monseñor —dijo Batsá señalando un edificio rosáceo que surgía entre jardines, a un lado de la Vía Herculana.

—¿Mi templo, Batsá?

—El santuario de Nebjeperura, monseñor.

Una avenida que conducía de la Vía Herculana al ingreso del templo se hallaba bordeada por estatuas de un gusto exquisito, en cuyas peanas aparecía escrito mi nombre; pero no el que tú conoces, Larry, sino el que me dan en el Mundo Macho desde el principio de todas las historias. La facilidad de la comprensión convertía el asunto en algo obsoleto; mi representación siempre era alguna variante del mito de Apolo y, a veces, de Antinoo y Ganimedes: estatuas lisas, tiernas, de una belleza casi femenina, y en las cuales aparecía con el sexo cubierto de púrpura. ¡Qué extraño complemento de Epsamón me exigía el Mundo Macho! Cada una de aquellas estatuas sostenía, con un brazo deliciosamente cincelado, los atributos de la cultura, de la juventud, de las artes, de la sensibilidad —que no excluye la fuerza—, de todas las virtudes adolescentes que yo estaba destinado a encarnar. Ninguna estatua tenía mi rostro, por supuesto, pero en todas se adivinaba que yo no podría soportar nunca los mismos tormentos de Epsamón, ni luchar como él: que mi destino sería tañer la lira mientras Epsamón descansaba del agotamiento de muchas batallas. Porque está escrito que Epsamón fue creado para la guerra, y Nebjeperura para ser el reposo del guerrero.

Y siempre así:

Las estelas del Mundo Macho reproducen al sol desparramando sus rayos sobre el Imperio, y estos rayos terminan en manos que acarician la cabeza de Epsamón Divino, quien, extendiendo sus prodigiosos brazos, lanza a la colectividad los dones solares. Su figura ocupa todo el dibujo, casi sobrepasa al propio sol; y yo, a su lado, parezco muy pequeño, si bien mucho mayor que el pueblo, reproducido debajo de ambos. A nuestro lado, sobre la balaustrada de los jardines colgantes, se yergue Cobra, velando por nosotros y al mismo tiempo por el pueblo. Yo miro hacia la izquierda y Epsamón hacia la derecha, de forma que a cada lado se encuentra la parte del pueblo a la cual impartimos nuestra bendición. Conmigo está la juventud del Mundo Macho, que viste según mi porte porque yo soy la moda de los jóvenes. Con Epsamón están los ricos, los soldados, la clerecía y los ciudadanos del *pueblo opulento* (artesanos, tenderos, administrativos), denominados de este modo para diferenciarlos del pueblo representado por los obreros del Mundo Macho, que ocupan la penúltima capa del dibujo. Y, debajo, aún encontramos a los esclavos, que llegan diariamente a Lur y tanto sirven para los sacrificios colectivos como para la construcción de obras colosales. Al fondo, proyectado como un *trompe l'oeil*, se halla el mapa del Imperio, los lugares que los soldados de Epsamón han conquistado; las tierras que, después de la Gran Conquista, fueron evangelizadas por los sacerdotes de Cobra.

—Tu templo es el de las Juventudes Macho, monseñor. Y tiene que ser tu orgullo, pues aquí se forjan los hombres del futuro. Mira su resplandor: las luces darán siempre un color rosado, nunca agresivo; es el color que indica la condición de quienes en este santuario se hacen dignos de ti.

Entonces estallé en una tremenda carcajada, que extrañó profundamente a mi compañero.

—¿Tan femenino me ve el Mundo Macho? ¿Tanto como esa estatua?

—Es Nebjeperura Citereo, monseñor. Eres tú, representando a la divinidad de la música. Como con todas las artes que provienen de la sensibilidad. La sensibilidad y la fuerza son...

—¡Lo sé, lo sé! Son virtudes que se complementan, ¿no? Todo se complementa en este país: empiezo a comprenderlo. Pero ahora me río, Dennis. Ahora pienso en un tiempo muy remoto, de hace diez años; un tiempo que esa estatua me ha hecho recordar. ¿Lo ves? En ella aparezco con una lira en la mano, y parece que de un momento a otro produciré unos sonidos deliciosos, inclinaré la cabeza hacia atrás, dejaré caer mis rizos sobre los hombros y echaré a volar. Es divertido, sí. Pero al mismo tiempo no entiendo por qué me asalta una suerte de tristeza infinita, como si el pasado se abatiese sobre mí y yo fuese incapaz de explicármelo. Yo cantaba, sí... Hace diez años, yo salía al escenario con una guitarra y recibía la luz de multitud de reflectores: las luces cambiaban según el efecto que debieran producir sobre un público que me adoraba. Oh, sé que te costará recordarlo, pero entonces yo era muy adorado, y al adoptar esta actitud de la estatua..., la expresión lánguida, los ojos cerrados, los dedos tañendo la lira, con el cuerpo ambiguo que mi década exigía, yo era un Citereo vivo, cada una de mis palabras era acogida con chillidos histéricos, con una salva de aplausos que me envolvían... Sí, amigo mío, Dennis o Batsá, o como quiera que te llames..., los jóvenes de aquella sociedad se vestían con las camisas que yo llevaba, se dejaban los cabellos tan largos como yo, compraban el modelo de moto con el cual yo me había hecho fotografiar en muchas revistas juveniles..., y, en un momento dado, hubiesen aceptado cualquier ideología que yo pudiese sugerirles desde cualquier entrevista en las revistas de música pop. Sí, amigo mío: en aquella sociedad tan lejana yo era el Citereo necesario a unos intereses que me sobrepasaban; era el mediador entre aquellos intereses y unos adoradores que sólo esperaban un gesto mío para aprenderlo de memoria e imitarlo. Tal vez era lo mismo que aquí; exactamente lo mismo, pero mi santuario de entonces era una oficina de publicidad que regía mi representante, y las estatuas que me reproducían no ocultaban mi rostro, antes bien lo explotaban en todas sus expresiones..., es decir, todas excepto la que era auténticamente mía: la que correspondía a mi dolor de hombre, a mi verdad.

—Tal vez aquella sociedad no estuviese hecha de verdades, monseñor.

—Tal vez. Tal vez sólo estuviese hecha de apariencias. Un poco como ésta, ¿sabes? En el fondo, no resultan tan distintas.

La multitud que atravesábamos ahora, con un galope seguro e incierto a la vez, ¿era una simple apariencia? Rostros que hablaban a gritos felices, que bailaban, saltaban, corrían, hacían música, paseaban a pie, a caballo, en cuadriga o litera, pero siempre con la concisión de las cosas que se han convertido en vida, señalando lo irremediable de algún drama oculto. Corrían a toda velocidad cuadrigas de plata, cuyos ocupantes lanzaban mantos vaporosos al viento frenético que producía su propia carrera; mientras literas, sillas de mano o basternas transportadas por esclavos negros, con las mejillas teñidas de oro, se abrían paso entre grupos de mercaderes de provincias, llegados al gran mercado de la capital para establecer tratos provechosos con vendedores y artesanos; había jovencitos que lucían gambetos multicolores, togas de oro pesado o clámides transparentes, medias negras que contrastaban con jubones verdes y enormes sombreros acolchados de los cuales surgía, provocativo, más de un plumero deslumbrante; de vez en cuando, potentados que vestían la toga del ocio se detenían ante alguna villa y alternaban con aquellos jovenzuelos *à la page*; otros paseantes, tan pronto exhibían la túnica del gran patrimonio romano como aquellas capas cortas que, ribeteadas con piel de armiño, dejan las piernas al descubierto y, como es costumbre, el sexo; junto a ellos, una sucesión de mantos larguísimos, con bordados y recamados de oro, mangas que se arrastraban por el suelo mientras sonaba, alegre, el tintinear de los cascabeles que remataban los birretes de los adolescentes recién salidos de la Casa de la Vida; falda corta, de seda plisada, reminiscencia de alguna remota dinastía egipcia, con el gran collar de lapislázuli que, rodeando el cuello, llega hasta los poderosos pezones sin llegar nunca a cubrirlos; y, junto a las complicadas cabelleras renacentistas, otros cabellos también largos, pero que, siguiendo los usos de aquel Imperio, quedan cortados en seco, de forma recta, junto a la nuca, de manera que, libre y esbelto, la potencia del cuello se desarrolla en la palestra como un músculo de gran importancia para la consecución de la belleza general. En resumen: el conglomerado de estilos y épocas que caracteriza las formas externas del Mundo Macho empezaba a imponerse a partir de la figura humana y su vestuario.

—¿Alguna fiesta? —pregunté.

—Ninguna que no sea la cotidiana —dijo Dennis—: la alegría de cada noche en la paz del Mundo Macho.

En la entrada principal de Lur, aquella confusión de gente se multiplicó (y hoy me parece extraño que pueda decir «gente» al hablar de una colectividad que pertenecía toda al mismo sexo). Dos torres enormes, de planta redonda, formaban aquella entrada, abierta en la gran muralla, de cuyas almenas colgaban todo tipo de banderas y estandartes, y multitud de pasquines que animaban al pueblo a creer en la victoria, tan habitual sobre los enemigos herejes. (Y entonces, en medio de aquella confusión, recordé que casi había olvidado la existencia de un enemigo que debía ser exterminado y, por extensión, una guerra apoteósica.) Frente a las torres, en una aglomeración aún más abigarrada, se esparcían infinidad de tenderetes bajo cuyos toldos los comerciantes de las provincias más próximas ofrecían mercancías de todo tipo: telas, lámparas, arneses, perfumes exóticos, terneras, cabezas de toro, collares, muebles de artesanía, esculturas, cuadros, libros viejos, e incluso comidas de inmediata preparación y bebidas que los compradores consumían mientras regateaban el precio de una alfombra tejida a mano o el de incensarios de cualquier tamaño, imprescindibles para las ceremonias, ya próximas, de las Jornadas de la Reproducción (y parece ser que en todas las casas del Mundo Macho hay un altar dedicado al culto de Homo Demeter, del mismo modo que en todos los jardines y los parques de los ricos tienen un templete consagrado a la estatua fálica de Príapo-Ra: el sexo macho bañado por la fuerza del Sol).

Dennis me preguntó si deseaba comprar cualquier fruslería, pero tenía cuanto deseaba y más de lo que podía desear, y mis únicos antojos posibles se relacionaban con cosas que nunca podré encontrar en Lur: tal vez un disco, tal vez un programa de televisión, quién sabe si la crítica de alguna película en mi revista preferida.

¡Oh Larry! ¡Oh profesor! Aún tengo presente, cual una realidad viva que salta de la gran pantalla y me envuelve, aquella entrada en Lur, aquella cabalgata de objetos, voces, rostros, colores y humaredas que surgían a mi alrededor, obedeciendo el trote de mi corcel; siguen presentes cuantas imágenes se me proponían como espectáculo incomparable, a veces sin el menor refinamiento y a veces con una gran exquisitez de los elementos aislados, que contenían tantas cosas que los civilizados hemos dejado ya abandonadas en nuestro uso cotidiano: gobelines cuyos bordados representaban batallas e invasiones sin la menor noción de la perspectiva; iconos de plata que sustituían al Cristo y a la Virgen por los dioses de la fuerza macho en sus versiones más antiguas e imperfectas; sillas de camello recamadas con bordados geométricos o incrustaciones de marfil; enormes tiendas que recordaban, por su forma y los materiales utilizados, las tiendas de los beduinos; imágenes de Cobra en todas sus manifestaciones: desde la solar de Cobra-Ra, hasta la muy sanguinaria Visnú-Cobra, que reclama la vida partiendo de la sangre derramada; macetas con girasoles de enormes corolas y tallo tremendamente musculoso; y, en fin, plantas carnívoras para decoración de interiores, que eran probadas ante el cliente dejando cerca de la planta a un perro atado. (Era un hallazgo de prodigiosa exactitud: el vegetal, que hasta entonces parecía inerte, empezaba a mover las antenas, sacudía sus hojas de tremendas dimensiones y, de repente, la corola empezaba a abrirse, el tronco se curvaba sobre el perro, la boca de la corola se abría aún más, cada labio procuraba alcanzar todo el cuerpo del can y, con la exquisita lentitud que el Mundo Macho exige para la administración de la muerte, el cuerpo del animal iba desapareciendo progresivamente, hasta que fuera de la planta sólo quedaba la cola, que se agitaba sin cesar como demostrando la desesperación que dominaría a la víctima, ya engullida e incapaz de respirar. Finalmente, la planta acababa por tragarse la cola;

y los compradores sonreían, mientras pagaban el importe del artículo que, como acababan de comprobar, estaba en óptimas condiciones.)

Miembros de las Juventudes Canoras recorrían el mercado entonando deliciosos madrigales que originaban sonrisas de complacencia. Eran mancebos barbilampiños, de porte delicado, vestidos con clámides de color añil bordadas con pequeñas perlas del Mar del Sur, las cuales festoneaban la abertura frontal que empieza junto al cuello y termina en el pubis que estos muchachitos llevan depilado por decreto. Con sus rizos larguísimos, por lo común rubios, coronados de jacintos y azucenas, parecían ángeles escapados de algún ideal neoplatónico. Caminaban tocando el banjo o la mandolina, y el más pequeño del grupo, que muy a menudo quedaba rezagado porque las deslumbrantes sorpresas del mercado le distraían, tañía una lira dorada y llevaba un lirio en el pecho. Otros grupos de jóvenes, sólo cubiertos por un tirante de terciopelo negro que empieza en el hombro derecho, pasa entre las piernas y de nuevo se encuentra en el mismo hombro con un cierre de bisutería que reproduce mi rostro, se dirigían hacia otras calles, tocando timbales fabricados con piel de esclavo y cuyo victorioso sonido precede el paso de los sacerdotes de Cobra, quienes, ataviados únicamente con un escueto cinturón de piel de leopardo, pasean la estatua del dios mientras perfuman las calles de Lur con incienso, mirra y esencias de cedro.

El fondo musical se mezclaba con el estruendo de las conversaciones, el galope siempre acompasado de los caballos y el trepidar tumultuoso de las cuadrigas que, en su desconsiderada velocidad, provocaban las protestas de los transeúntes más pacíficos. La pantalla, amigo mío, se llenaba con todas las proposiciones que llevan directamente al olvido de la realidad mediante la fuerza de una fascinación que nos vence sin remedio; las perspectivas de un equilibrio que rechaza cualquier concesión a la fantasía, se abocaban, feroces, sobre las masas humanas mientras los ruidos surgían del respaldo de mi butaca, cual altavoces de una estereofonía donde todo se expresara apoteósicamente, negando tregua a los sentidos. No había ningún color aislado, ninguna forma serena, nada que no se expresara con estallidos horrísonos. Y, entre tanto bullicio, yo empezaba a sentirme muy orgulloso de que aquella multitud, machos poderosos, bárbaros y exquisitos a la vez, me hubiesen elegido para ser depositario de su voluntad colectiva.

CADA VEZ que saludo al público, tú me observas entre bastidores; sé que vigilas la intensidad de mi sonrisa, la forma exacta de apartarme los cabellos con la mano cuando caen sobre mi frente mientras, humilde, inclino la cabeza. Si me vuelvo, te veo allá, al fondo, siempre en segundo término, envuelto en la penumbra donde no llegan las luces de la sala; veo que aplaudes entusiasmado, como la muchedumbre que, al encenderse los focos, me revela sus rostros, me da los rasgos físicos de los gritos, de los «bravos», de los vítores de guerra que tú, amigo mío, pareces coleccionar. Y repito la reverencia cada vez que tú me lo indicas: inclino la cabeza y, al levantarla de nuevo, retiro la greña como tú me has aconsejado, signo ya inseparable de mi personalidad. ¿Acaso no soy el rey? ¿Es que hay otra voz como la mía? ¿No soy el único? Desde un palco, Cobra me lanza sus silbidos y me enseña la lengua bífida que atraviesa los vapores de la tierra; y yo me inclino hacia los bastidores, atrapado entre la fuerza primigenia del Mundo Macho y tu tutela, Larry. Soy el hijo de la agonía y, a la vez, tu hijo. ¿Debo la vida a Cobra o te la debo a ti? Despedirás a los periodistas de las publicaciones menos importantes y me aconsejarás que sea amable con los corresponsales extranjeros; al volver del escenario, empapado de sudor, me cubrirás con un kimono de seda mientras me hablas de dinero; me aconsejarás esta camisa sí, esta otra no, «ahora estaría bien que salieras a la calle con una chaqueta de cuero para dar una apariencia de rebelde», o bien «con el maxi-abrigo ceñido en el pecho para parecer un dandy». Hay que pensar en la gente que aguarda a la puerta del teatro; hay que pensar en los fotógrafos, pero tú, Larry, sólo dejarás que me retraten los que tenemos contratados, pues conocen cuál de mis ángulos fotografía mejor; permitirás que diez admiradores entren en mi camerino para demostrar que soy amable con ellos, pero los otros trescientos se quedarán en la calle, bajo la lluvia, porque estoy muy cansado, ya no puedo más, ya estoy más que harto, Larry. Y Cobra me dice: «Avanzarás a tientas por los oscuros senderos del País de la Nada, hijo de la agonía, y buscarás por todos los rincones los rayos de la vida que roba cada año de los siglos Aquel que Ordena el Tiempo y Odia al Hombre. Cuando tu mano, firme y poderosa, se cierre sobre los rayos, nacerá de nuevo la primavera, y los hombres del Mundo Macho recrearán como todos los años el milagro supremo de la vida.» Una vez en el camerino, me prepararás el calmante adecuado; sabrás lo que no debo comentar con los periodistas; tal vez incluso sientas lástima de mí cuando contemple mi palidez en el espejo que me refleja sin reflejarme. Comprenderé que tus consejos se han convertido en mis gestos, y Cobra guiará mi conducta mientras corro por los pasillos de palacio y me cambias la guitarra por otra más cara, y llego a las cavernas que conducen a la Casa de la Prueba, y el maestro ataca la partitura, y me prepara para la primera nota —primera, pero repetida miles de veces antes y después de ahora—, y tú estás leyendo el periódico en el sofá, y de vez en cuando miras si me sostengo la cabeza entre las manos, no fuera que me desmayase entre las paredes de la cueva, no vaya a ser que el techo se viniera abajo y yo quedara aplastado antes de tiempo, antes de que el inevitable invierno me traiga la muerte y Cobra me entregue el caballo alígero que me permita ir en pos de la resurrección que es mía y al mismo tiempo de la vida. No vaya a ser que me quedara muerto y no pudiese resucitar, y, ¡adiós comisiones!, querido Larry, las pasarías canutas; no podrías pagar más chulos, no podrías comprarte aquel escabel Tudor que vimos en el anticuario de la Ille. De noche, sabré que sólo tú tienes derecho a vivir, y yo permaneceré solo en la cama, con la idea fija de la función de mañana, que es *matinée*, y por eso mejor pagada, pero Cobra rompe las tinieblas del sueño y me grita que vuelva al Mundo Macho, al trono dorado de Nebjeperura que espera, impaciente, el regreso de Epura Epsamón. Y la guerra continúa, y enriquece la Banca del Mundo Macho; y la guerra aún no cesa, continúa, y crucifica a miles de heréticos; y la guerra continúa, pero yo nunca he estado en ella...

Pero debo agradecerte algunas cosas. Cuando Cobra me revela sus misterios, tú brotas de entre la densa humareda y me secas el sudor de la frente, mientras me recuerdas que no debo fatigarme. Cobra me dice: «En tus manos de hijo sagrado están todas las libertades del mundo, y tú eres libre de disponer de ellas. Tu poder es macho, y dominas el Mundo Macho, donde la fuerza es pensamiento y el pensamiento sería debilidad. En medio de la ignominia de la Creación, tú, hijo de la agonía, eres la voluntad de todo un pueblo.»

Pero yo sé que miente. Dispongo de la libertad de los demás, y ni siquiera he necesitado tomarla, puesto que ellos me la otorgaron muchos siglos antes de que yo pensara en pedirla. Dispongo de la voluntad del Mundo Macho, pero ¿dónde está mi voluntad, dónde mi derecho a ser libre? Ni siquiera tengo la opción de correr hacia el *Palazzo* del Lago del Tiempo y saber de una vez cuál es mi destino...

¡El *Palazzo* del Lago del Tiempo! ¿Dónde está? ¿Por qué me lo han prohibido? ¿Qué fábula oculta, qué derecho a la herejía podría darme?

Surges de entre las llamas de Cobra y hablas de dinero, Larry. Tanto velas por mí, que no hay forma humana de perder un solo franco. Mientras, el pianista me adiestra bajo tu vigilancia, y en tu mirada complaciente me doy cuenta de que la voz se me va haciendo más rica. Cada mañana, en la sala de los misterios, cuando canto los salmos de Cobra (generalmente el Tercero, llamado de la Guerra Florida), más de un sacerdote joven se detiene al otro lado de la puerta y escucha. Tú le pedirías dinero por escucharme, lo sé: es una actuación privada que vale tantos miles. Pero Cobra no te lo permitiría, porque ahora yo soy de Cobra, pertenezco plenamente a los misterios que me revelará para que Epura Epsamón me encuentre digno de sentarme a su lado si algún día termina esta batalla contra los herejes, esos bellacos que siempre encuentran fuerza para resurgir desde las profundidades más abismales de una derrota repetida año tras año. Y Astor me explica que los sacerdotes más jóvenes se detienen a escucharme cuando canto, y está tan complacido como tú, orgulloso y feliz porque ha ayudado a crear un discípulo excepcional...

¡Astor, hijo de Cobra, ven como cada mañana a flagelarme, porque ahora ya no me duele! Dame a comer la carne de los adolescentes lisiados, porque ahora ya no me repugna. Llévame la serpiente sagrada, que yo abriré mis labios para recibir entre las encías su lengua cosquilleante. Padre y Madre Cobra: ¡empiezo a ser, finalmente, el sol y la luna del Mundo Macho!

LA LUNA, LLENA como un abanico que sólo se interrumpiese en el último instante de su abertura, hace que el negro cielo —una negrura dominante— se azulee gracias a la enorme aureola que esparce su luz. Las mansiones más modernas de Minia se enjalbegan con el brillo de esta luna, que las hace aparecer cual sepulcros pálidos que no guardasen muertos famosos. Las calles parecen más lisas, tal vez porque la arena del desierto y el agua de los riegos han tenido tiempo para secarse; han creado ya esta capa nueva, un manto más, que mis pasos allanan, una superficie que va imponiéndose a las de ayer, como las de ayer se impusieron a todos los siglos que han ido depositando sobre estas calles la arena del desierto, lejano y, sin embargo, omnipresente.

YO YA ERA NEBJEPERURA; pero el reconocerlo en esta ocasión me inspiró un último destello de pavor que la razón no podía paliar. Yo sabía muchas cosas del Mundo Macho, había entendido su sistema, podía descifrarlo, incluso explicarlo, pero no era esto lo que me asustaba. Al contrario: el terror procedía de advertir que mi despotismo era ilustrado, que mi tiranía sería intelectual. ¿Cuánto tiempo había transcurrido desde que dije a Astor: «La esclavitud que tú me ofreces, las lecciones de los sabios, la aplicación que he demostrado sufriendo el dolor y aprendiendo a infligirlo, no lograrán hacerme olvidar lo único positivo que me ha enseñado el Mundo Macho: mi necesidad de comprender»? Pudieron deslizarse muchos años, muchos siglos, o simplemente unas horas, porque, desde la noche de mi captura en Minia, el tiempo dejó de existir. Pero en años, siglos u horas, había aprendido bastantes cosas como para saber que mis sensaciones ya no temían el atenuante de la ignorancia, y que cualquier crueldad que yo infligiese a partir de aquel momento tendría un valor duplicado: ya sería histórica.

Entonces, presa del pánico, aprisionado en el miedo de mis actos, me acordé de Astor y sus lecciones. Evoqué en un solo instante lo obsesivo de su tutela, sus desprecios, las flagelaciones con que, cada mañana, me acostumbraba a soportar el sufrimiento como decretan las leyes del país. Y se apoderó de mí una loca obsesión por hacerle saber mis progresos, y decirle que mientras yacía en un calabozo por orden mía, yo echaba en falta sus latigazos, y que ahora los necesitaba de una forma más violenta que nunca. Porque ahora yo era Nebjeperura, el hijo de la agonía.

Prescindiendo de Batsá, me lancé a una feroz carrera contra el tiempo y contra el espacio. Pasaban a mi alrededor todas las imágenes desordenadas de la noche; templos dóricos, de forma japonesa; agujas góticas de no sabía qué Ministerio; rostros teñidos de púrpura, verde esmeralda, o añil; cuerpos desnudos, envueltos en seda transparente o forrados de piel de serpiente; sonaban laúdes, timbales, todas las voces de un pueblo que ya era definitivamente el mío. Y más allá de esta carrera, más allá del cuartel y de los sótanos, estaba el calabozo de Astor.

Cuando la guardia me condujo hasta él, mi raptor seguía colgado cabeza abajo. Al oír el ruido de la puerta, abrió los ojos y aulló mi nombre, como si fuese la invocación de una imagen que no le llegaba de la realidad, sino desde la quimera. Por el suelo corrían ratas grandes como conejos, pero yo ya no las temía. Me quité la capa y, acercándome a Astor, exclamé:

—¿Qué has hecho, perro? Hoy he estado esperando tu lección.

Él sonrió, y yo cogí un látigo que colgaba del muro y lo pasé por el fuego. De repente, él empezó a gritar, como temiendo que el castigo fuese para él; pero al momento me di cuenta de que temía por mí:

—No lo hagas —exclamó—. ¡Deténte, monseñor!

¿A qué jugábamos? Él me había adiestrado en una disciplina que tendía a ser cívica y mística a la vez; me había hecho participar de la alegría de hacerme hombre, y ahora, por una ignorada suerte de piedad, pretendía arrebatarme mi derecho a la hombría. Entregué el látigo al soldado que me había abierto la puerta y le ordené que no vacilase en castigarme hasta que perdiese el conocimiento. Lo cual tardó en suceder, porque las lecciones de Astor me habían acostumbrado a resistir durante mucho tiempo y a no gritar hasta después de cien latigazos. Arrodillado en el suelo, apretándome el pecho con las manos, clavando en él las uñas hasta sangrar, empecé a sentir el impacto de cada golpe, y lo celebraba lanzando la cabeza hacia atrás, gritando frenéticamente los salmos que me habían enseñado en el santuario de Cobra.

Colgado por los pies, Astor lloraba.

La anormalidad que implicaba no tener a Astor junto a mí terminó algunos días después, cuando él vino completamente curado dispuesto a guiarme de nuevo entre todas las realidades de Lur. Yo ya sólo podía pensar en ellas, y no bien las asumí, mi cargo imperial adquirió un nuevo significado, e incluso llegó a hacérseme atractivo. Sólo me quedaba esperar que Epsamón ganase definitivamente la Guerra Santa y regresase para investirme con la consagración oficial. Sólo faltaba que el Divino aceptase a Nebjeperura y, a partir de entonces, el verano más esplendoroso reinaría de nuevo sobre el Mundo Macho. Algo que yo deseaba de todo corazón, porque puedo decirte, sin temor a parecer exagerado, que ya amaba a mi pueblo. Mi educación de príncipe acababa de acceder a esta forma de amor, la más generosa a que puede aspirar el hombre.

De cualquier modo, y a pesar de no estar consagrado por Epsamón ni haber completado aún mi iniciación en los Misterios de Cobra, volvía a requerirse mi presencia en una ceremonia de la que el mito formaba parte esencial: la ceremonia de la Reproducción, en cuyo curso Nebjeperura debe dar ejemplo ante todos los jóvenes de Lur y engendrar, en el vientre de una mujer, al hijo que forma parte de las obligaciones políticas de todo macho libre.

Cierta mañana, mientras mis esclavos me mostraban los últimos modelos que, para mí, habían diseñado los modistas de Betarah, llegó Astor y me explicó rápidamente que aquella misma tarde debíamos ir a efectuar una prueba de gran importancia. Según decía, a los sacerdotes del templo de la Reproducción les preocupaba mi capacidad erótica. Temían que si, llegada la fiesta de Homo Demeter, yo subía al altar del dios y no era capaz de efectuar mi función reproductora con la hembra que me habían destinado, los miles de espectadores que contemplaban mi gesta, dispuestos a imitarla, recibirían una impresión tan pésima del poder imperial que las consecuencias podrían ser de una gravedad incalculable. En vano aseguré a Astor que el funcionamiento de mis capacidades era perfecto, y digo en vano porque, para él, yo era un dios virgen, a quien fue a buscar personalmente al País de la Nada, y que, durante los años pasados bajo su vigilancia, no había tenido el menor contacto sexual que probase su eficacia. Era evidente que los sacerdotes tenían razón en sus temores y que la urgencia del asunto determinaba la visita al templo aquel mismo día, y no otro.

Así fue como de nuevo recorrí la selva impenetrable a la cual Avitachí me llevó una noche, para su perdición; y, al igual que aquella vez, la espesura aniquiladora que la creación de Cobra había organizado partiendo de su propio desorden, se alivió al alcanzar la gran llanura de rocas donde empieza, por una parte, el desierto, y, por la otra, la gran pirámide natural que se levanta sobre los habitáculos trogloditas de la Bestia Llamada Hembra.

Vista con la claridad del día, la montaña despedía tonalidades encendidas que contrastaban violentamente con el cielo, colmado a su vez de cierto azul purísimo que sólo la proximidad del desierto confiere. Más allá de la pirámide, sobre el recodo que es cuna de toda la Creación de Cobra, sólo aparecía la pureza de aquel azul tan intenso; debajo, las rocas se apilaban en el caos, como si algún ser más alto que el cielo y la tierra unidos se hubiese entretenido en arrancarlas una por una para dejarlas caer seguidamente. Adquirían formas monstruosas que ningún dedo humano pudo labrar, y a medida que nos íbamos introduciendo entre ellas, percibía que incluso las partes más minúsculas del terreno estaban como recortadas a golpes brutales, de forma que nos veíamos obligados a realizar numerosos descensos por senderos que tan pronto giraban en espirales alucinantes, como bajaban estrepitosamente en recta desnuda, lo cual obligaba a los caballos a acelerar el trote hasta alcanzar un ritmo mortal. En cualquiera de estos casos, nos rodeaban y limitaban aquellas paredes de enormes protuberancias, superficies de arenisca que se resquebrajaron en una época demasiado remota para que aun las leyendas más antiguas pudiesen dar razón de ello. Era como si cada bloque de aquellas montañas multiplicadas entre sí hubiese sufrido, en su propio interior, una multitud de espantosos cataclismos particulares.

La ciudad se componía de agujeros abiertos en las rocas, y era vertical porque los habitáculos aprovechaban la progresión ascendente de la pirámide. Entre covachas, que empezaban junto al valle y terminaban un poco antes de llegar a la cima, serpenteaba un sinfín de peldaños que los habitantes habían construido sirviéndose de los medios más rudimentarios: los que les proporcionaba el gobierno del Mundo Macho eran herramientas casi prehistóricas, porque está escrito que la Bestia Llamada Hembra no debe aprender a utilizar herramientas de inteligencia, pues podría adquirir conocimientos y habilidades que la harían sumamente peligrosa. Y, en eso, las mujeres del Mundo Macho son completamente distintas de las de los herejes, que no sólo gozan con el hombre, sino que, además, han aprendido aritmética, astronomía, historia y bellas artes.

Mientras descendíamos por un sendero menos conflictivo que los anteriores, pero sin dejar de correr el riesgo de que los caballos se despeñaran, pregunté a Astor a qué se debía que en aquella ciudad no hubiese templos, y él contestó que el templo de la Bestia Llamada Hembra es ella misma, pero que sólo tendrá un sentido litúrgico cuando el macho penetre en su interior para crear el milagro supremo de la vida, que coincide con mi retorno al país de la Nada transportando los Rayos del Sol. Acto seguido, añadió:

—Detrás de esas cimas se halla el templo de la Reproducción, al cual nos dirigimos para que puedas cumplir tu prueba. Pero no se trata del templo de la mujer, sino de un santuario donde viven los sacerdotes de Homo Demeter, que cuidan de recibir a los iniciados y destinarles la hembra en la cual deberán engendrar la vida. Es la única jornada del año en que la Bestia Llamada Hembra tiene permiso para salir de su ciudad de cuevas. Llegado este día, los sacerdotes bajan al valle (escoltados por soldados armados, pues la Bestia puede ser peligrosa: se ha dado más de un caso de sacerdotes que han sido devorados) y eligen a las que deberán ser adoradas por el pueblo macho. Entonces, monseñor, unos esclavos debidamente armados las lavan cuidadosamente, las perfuman y las trasladan a las dependencias del templo, donde cada ciudadano de Lur cumple con su deber civil.

—¿Y por qué hay que limpiarlas y perfumarlas tanto?

—¡Oh monseñor! Yo esperaba que te lo habrían explicado tus maestros. Como todas las bestias que viven en estado salvaje, la mujer es sucia por naturaleza, y las enfermedades que se desarrollan entre sus piernas son tan peligrosas que podrían echar a perder la vida de cualquier hombre. En cierta ocasión sucedió algo espantoso: en el cuartel, uno de los soldados más jóvenes se despertó un día aullando desesperadamente, y, cuando sus compañeros acudieron a ayudarle, vieron que se rascaba el vientre hasta sangrar: parecía como si un ejército de serpientes estuviese devorándolo. Todos retrocedieron horrorizados, pues alguien acababa de descubrir que el desdichado tenía el vientre lleno de cangrejos enormes, como las monedas de cinco epsamones, y nadie podía quitárselos porque se agarraban a la piel con sus patas peludas y repugnantes y chupaban la sangre del enfermo. Este drama, ejemplar en cierto aspecto, sucedió porque la mujer que se le destinó durante las jornadas de la Reproducción no había sido desinfectada. En nada exagero, monseñor: la bestia llamada caballo es más limpia que la Bestia Llamada Hembra.

—Y no habéis pensado que, tal vez domesticándolas como domesticamos a los perros...

Astor me miró con ojos de asombro. Su alazán estuvo a punto de tropezar y despeñarse; por suerte tuvo tiempo de sujetar sus riendas.

—¡Monseñor! Lo que acabas de decir es *casi* un pensamiento herético.

—Supón que lo fuese. Ello no impide la posibilidad,

por otra parte demostrada, de que muchas bestias pueden ser domesticadas, e incluso de que pueden llegar a prestar magníficos servicios al hombre.

—¡Ah monseñor! Compruebo que tu humor es prodigiosamente delicioso. ¿Imaginas por un solo momento adónde iríamos a parar si no mantuviésemos a raya a las bestias? ¿Qué crees que sucedió en las tierras de los herejes? Ellos empezaron por adiestrar a la mujer, y una vez convertida en persona, ella se aprovechó reclamando un lugar cada vez más importante en la vida pública. Y no termina aquí. La Bestia Llamada Hembra crió ella misma los hijos que sólo el Estado macho tiene derecho a criar; así como es lógico, afeminó a nuestros súbditos hasta el punto de que organizaron leyes nuevas y débiles: liberaron a los esclavos, compartieron la riqueza estatal y eclesiástica con los siervos y decidieron elegir nuevos gobernantes cada diez años, y de este modo olvidaron el precepto básico de la fuerza, que ordena que sólo un escogido, un titán superior a todos los demás, guíe el imperial destino de la comunidad. En resumen: aquel primer error obligó a Epsamón a intervenir; y desde entonces ya no hay paz en el mundo.

Mientras Astor seguía hablando, yo descubría que en el fondo del valle rocoso se arrastraba una multitud de seres extremadamente pintorescos: eran como bestias muy peludas (más tarde me di cuenta de que cubrían su cuerpo con pieles de oso) y transportaban unos cuerpos muertos, completamente desnudos, casi deshechos, pero que pertenecían a la misma especie. Comprendí que la Bestia Llamada Hembra acababa de hacerse visible, y la magnitud de la sorpresa que aquella aparición me producía me impulsó a pedirle a Astor que nos detuviéramos a observar, sin ser vistos, aquel cortejo que tenía todo el aspecto de un ritual desconocido y, por lo mismo, apasionante.

Astor correspondió a mi deseo con una mueca de condescendencia —como el padre que acepta conceder una golosina al hijo inexperto—. Después, siempre gentil, y con gran dulzura, exclamó:

—Ay, monseñor, cómo te gusta perder el tiempo..., y, sobre todo ahora, cuando nos esperan para algo importante. El espectáculo que tanto deseas contemplar no es más que un desayuno cotidiano.

Estalló el son brutal de un instrumento desconocido —¿tal vez una trompa civil?— que retronó con violencia contra las paredes irregulares que cerraban el valle. Aún no se había apagado el eco, cuando surgieron de las grutas de la pirámide multitud de mujeres enloquecidas que saltaron escaleras abajo, en turbulento estrépito, hasta alcanzar la gran plaza en cuyo centro había unas veinte camas de piedra sobre las cuales yacían los cadáveres desnudos de otras mujeres que un nuevo grupo transportaba desde una especie de cráter; sin duda un fosa común, según dejaban adivinar las pilas de huesos y carne informe, en descomposición, que se amontonaba bajo el sol.

Sonaron más trompetas, siempre con sonidos estridentes, y el valle se convirtió en un amontonamiento de cuerpos; mejor dicho, en una turbamulta de pieles apolilladas, cuyo pelo se confundía con las greñas, largas hasta los talones, y que, a veces, llegaban a arrastrarse por el suelo. Entonces me di cuenta de que los exegetas del machismo tenían razón: no era posible imaginar nada más sucio, visión más repugnante y asquerosa, que la que ofrecían aquellas bestias infames, enloquecidas con sus danzas paganas alrededor de las difuntas, ya putrefactas. Aquellos monstruos me recordaban a la mujer que intentó huir del Mundo Macho; y tal vez la única diferencia residiera en que ellas carecían del espíritu rebelde que, aquel primer día de mi reclusión, parecía guiar la huida de la otra.

Todas transportaban fragmentos de una sucia vajilla de fango, y con una disciplina que, dado el ambiente, resultaba sorprendente y rara, empezaron a formar cola ante las distintas mesas de las muertas. Veinte mujeres cortaban los cadáveres en pedazos bastante considerables y llenaban los recipientes de sus compañeras, quienes se alejaban hacia algún rincón del valle, prontas a devorar el alimento que les había correspondido. Y ante el lastimoso espectáculo que presenciábamos, Astor me acarició la espalda y comentó:

—Observa, monseñor, hasta qué punto llega la incivilidad de las bestias. El espectáculo resulta vomitivo.

—Tal vez. Pero tampoco puedo olvidar que tú mismo, en Lur, me has obligado a comer carne humana. Y no te has detenido hasta lograr no sólo que no me repugne, sino que incluso me guste.

—Te ruego salves distancias. Para el Mundo Macho, comer carne humana es un acto de justicia. Forma parte de una ceremonia excelsa que permite al hombre demostrar la fuerza suprema de su albedrío. En el Mundo

Macho, eso no constituye una necesidad, sino un ritual. Pero aquí, monseñor, las bestias devoran a las bestias de su propia raza porque no tienen nada más para comer. Es típico de la prehistoria que representan, porque sus leyes están dictadas por la urgencia primaria y salvaje de la supervivencia. En lo cual no interviene la filosofía. Ni siquiera la razón.

Es de justicia decir que, aparte las razones de Astor, había unos factores de gusto que obligan a considerar aquel almuerzo en términos de acto abominable. La carne que las bestias engullían era, ciertamente, más asquerosa que todas las que me habían propuesto saborear en las ceremonias de Lur. Allí, por lo menos, la antropofagia de los rituales se nutre de cuerpos jóvenes, a menudo bellos; y nunca se sirven muertos para evitar tanto lo que el hecho tendría en sí mismo de deplorable como la calidad ya pasada de los cadáveres y un posible hedor. Aquí era exactamente al revés: las mujeres engullían una carne amarillenta, ya putrefacta desde el exterior y, por supuesto, también en el interior. Devoraban costillas, tripas, corazón y pulmones semideshechos, y lo hacían con una avidez cotidiana que excluía descaradamente la menor concesión a las exquisiteces y a los refinamientos de la gastronomía, siquiera en un sentido elemental. En Lur, los cuerpos de los adolescentes imperfectos son condimentados con salsas y jugos de invención suprema; se los adoba con todo tipo de especias exóticas, manipulación que ya demuestra toda una tradición de civismo en el gusto; les abrimos el vientre y extraemos sus vísceras malolientes a fin de enriquecer la bondad de la carne con un relleno de ciruelas, ananás, mermelada o chocolate, según corresponda a la salsa circundante; por el contrario, en el valle de la Bestia Llamada Hembra la carne era un habitáculo de gusanos que las devoradoras masticaban con ansia, como si se tratara de una parte más de la carne y de su adobo. De hecho, cada vez que alguna de aquellas mujeres sacaba la lengua, aparecía un enjambre de gusanos que se deslizaban por encima de la misma, untada de una sangre ya seca de aquel color marrón que sin duda corresponde a la sangre de todos los cadáveres putrefactos.

—Tengo más que suficiente, Astor. Sigamos, por favor.

Astor marchaba delante, abriéndome el camino pero volviéndose de vez en cuando para agradecer mis deferencias con miradas de cordero. Era sorprendente que, desde que salió del calabozo, se comportara de modo tan tierno, haciendo inutil que yo siguiera empleando el tono despótico que él mismo me obligó a adoptar, tiempo atrás, con su propia actitud de desprecio. Descendiendo por senderos diabólicos, yo iba pensando que la relación amo-esclavo es una de las más extrañas del mundo; y, dado que así me correspondía tratar a mi pueblo, reconocí en mi relación con Astor una buena piedra de toque para un perfecto comienzo del trato. Si con una sola persona sucedía así, ¿por qué no con mis súbditos, este pueblo que sólo era una prolongación multiplicada del alma de Astor? Cuando yo solía mostrarme gentil con Astor, éste me despreció; cuando fui duro, cruel, e incluso injusto, me temió y obedeció; si desde mi dureza, yo me rebajaba a ser un poco dulce, él me adoraba. Ampliada a escala colectiva, la alternativa no podía ser más reconfortante. La dureza será la columna capital de todo gobernante que quiera verse respetado; y, dentro de esa dureza, un amor extremo hacia el pueblo le capacitará para conceder, de vez en cuando, el mínimo de amabilidad que el pueblo, al no tenerla por costumbre, agradecerá todavía más, aumentando así el amor por aquel gobernante que los dioses tuvieron a bien concederle.

Las teorías que cada mañana recibía de mis maestros se apartaban un tanto de aquella situación, pero, ciertamente, no en sus rasgos esenciales —de hecho, estos rasgos son indiscutibles—, sino, sobre todo, en un aspecto de viabilidad práctica. Así fue como supe que Epsamón, a pesar de ser único e indivisible, no lleva sobre sus hombros todo el peso del gobierno, sino que lo ayudan los sacerdotes del culto a Cobra y, por otra parte, los altos mandatarios de los ejércitos de Lur, puesto que todos ellos constituyen el segundo estadio de una gran torre que, con Epsamón como pináculo irrebatible, se subdivide en diversos estadios, cada uno de los cuales es menos importante de acuerdo con la fortuna privada de las clases que lo componen, y no según sus méritos civiles o religiosos. Esta situación crea, en esta sociedad, una extraña acción recíproca que, según me explican los maestros, sirve tanto para reforzar el gobierno del Mundo Macho como para enriquecer a las clases denominadas «opulentas», sin el apoyo de las cuales no podría existir el gobierno, del mismo modo que sin éste tampoco existirían ellas. Y dado que el recuento es enojoso, paso por alto pequeños detalles, muy secundarios: sólo fueron interesantes algún tiempo, mientras me servían de lección. O por lo menos para estar informado del provecho que puede obtenerse de una situación así establecida desde el principio de todas las historias.

Huelga decir que, a pesar de todo, yo no había conseguido anular por completo la curiosidad que me empujaba a preguntarme constantemente qué principio era aquél y cuáles las famosas historias. Si los Misterios no mentían —y ahora sé muy bien que no—, Cobra creó el mundo y después otorgó a la Raza el poder supremo del Mal para que pudiese defenderse de la ira de Aquel que Ordena el Tiempo, enemigo de la vida. Pero, ¿qué sucedió después, y siempre a partir de después? ¿Cuántas generaciones tuvieron que morir y volver a nacer para morir más veces antes de que naciera Epsamón y recibiese la iluminación de Cobra, en el beso que engendró, con una existencia de miles de años repetidos mil veces, un sistema que es largo, poderoso, insustituible como la vida de Epsamón Divino?

Aquella mañana del valle, las preguntas excluían necesariamente a la Bestia Llamada Hembra, que en la gran plaza de rocalla roja seguía devorando a sus compañeras muertas en un ritual incivil y bochornoso como el acto de parir. Incluso la excluía de los Misterios de Cobra, que nunca revelan dónde engendró el primer macho la línea de descendientes, que, como es sabido, sólo puede germinar en el vientre de la bestia proscrita. Y si Cobra también creó a la hembra, como es lógico suponer —pues no es factible que llegase de la Nada—, ¿qué sucedió, en realidad, antes del comienzo de todas las historias?, ¿qué suceso crucial, o qué lucha frenética, determinó que la hembra fuese bestia y no un ser humano?, ¿que fuese carnaza para la reproducción de una dinastía de titanes, pero nunca aceptada en la grandeza que la raza pretende conquistar? En definitiva: ¿cuáles fueron los propósitos de Epsamón al iniciar esta lucha, al ganarla y crear, partiendo de la Nada, toda una confusión ideológica cuyas piezas, que al parecer encajaban de un modo tan perfecto, no aclaraban, en realidad, ni un solo punto básico, ni una verdad última, la única capaz de explicar el mundo de forma satisfactoria?

¿Por qué yo, raptado para ser de Epsamón, aún no lo conocía ni siquiera en efigie?

Pero apenas dejamos atrás el triste espectáculo de las bestias retenidas en el gueto que sin duda merecían desde siempre, Astor señaló el templo, que ya se vislumbraba en lo alto de una montaña increíblemente azul, y sonrió con ternura:

—Ya vamos llegando, monseñor. Pero antes de entrar, antes de que los sacerdotes den a Nebjeperura la bienvenida que su divinidad exige, quisiera anunciarte una gran sorpresa que te reservaba para hoy: es la recompensa de todos tus progresos, y de los que seguramente demostrarás cuando, en el sagrado altar de Homo Demeter, humilles el cuerpo servil de la Bestia Llamada Hembra bajo tus músculos, ya poderosos.

—Poderosos gracias a ti —dije, en un imperial deseo de ser cortés—. No lo olvido.

—Y, una vez más, tu amabilidad alimentará mi deseo

de ser el objeto de la misma. Pero avancemos hacia la sorpresa. Y es, monseñor, que el día siguiente a la primera jornada de la Reproducción, serás escoltado hasta el desierto de los herejes; desde allí, una nueva escolta de honor como nunca se ha visto en este país te llevará hasta Epsamón para que participes con él en los sacrificios rituales, y contribuyas así a que lluevan sobre la Guerra Santa todas las bendiciones de los dioses del Mundo Macho. Ésta es nuestra costumbre.

—¿La costumbre?

—Lo sabes perfectamente. Es la época en que, devueltos los rayos de la vida al invierno del Mundo Macho, Nebjeperura cumple el sacrificio anual en el templo del campamento. Y en tu honor serán inmolados los prisioneros más jóvenes de las últimas batallas.

«¡Y conoceré a Epsamón!», pensé desde el primer momento, puesto que era lo único que podía interesarme de forma positiva. La sorpresa era, en verdad, bien venida —yo incluso diría que formidable—, y así se lo hice saber al hermoso Astor; y se lo agradecí, y me lo agradeció él.

Y mi agradecimiento no excluía la posibilidad de que, partiendo del conocimiento físico de Epsamón, pudiese llegar al *Palazzo* del Lago del Tiempo, donde, según Astor, se ocultaba mi destino.

PERO, IGNORANDO AÚN la ubicación del lago que ya se me había hecho legendario, tuve que contentarme con la visión deslumbrante del templo de Homo Demeter, que más bien diríase una ciudad porque incluye los recintos privados del monasterio y multitud de palacetes rodeados de parques donde el pueblo de Lur celebra el rito civil de la reproducción. Todo el conjunto surgía como una acumulación de formas sinuosas, de manera que, de no ser por la extraordinaria blancura que unificaba los edificios, hubiese sido muy difícil hablar de una pieza única. Por doquier surgían pagodas de diversas terrazas que contenían muchas bóvedas y sostenían otras nuevas; la maciza acumulación de esculturas contenidas en cada elemento arquitectónico (las esculturas, siempre blancas, cubrían bóvedas, arquitrabes, columnas y capiteles) daba al conjunto el aspecto de una complicada colmena en cuyas celdas las abejas hubiesen permanecido inmóviles y cada vez más aferradas a la piedra. El equilibrio, supremo, encajaba la blancura con la tonalidad extremadamente azul de la montaña, e incluso con el intenso azul del cielo. A ambos lados del camino aparecían hileras de cruces que exhibían, secas desde hacía siglos, las momias desnudas de las mujeres que intentaron rebelarse contra el poder de Lur. Al pasar entre ellas yo no sentía terror alguno, sino un asco de orden inconfundiblemente estético, porque en el Mundo Macho había aprendido a clasificar la belleza de acuerdo con unas reglas muy exactas que, ciertas o equivocadas, no correspondían en absoluto a aquellos cuerpos acartonados, tachonados con clavos que el tiempo y la lluvia habían oxidado de forma que las manchas del orín se extendían por manos y pies, confiriéndoles un color más desagradable todavía. Entonces pensé que si la mujer que me habían reservado se parecía a las bestias que comían en el valle, o a los pellejos colgados a ambos lados del camino, sería muy fácil que los temores del clero de Homo Demeter se confirmasen y que yo no pudiese funcionar en una actividad en la cual, años atrás, había dado pruebas de cualquier cosa excepto impotencia.

Pero diré que los caminos de la verdad son infinitos y, a menudo, difíciles de desentrañar, y que incluso las doctrinas más contagiosas tienen algún fallo que pone vacilaciones en nuestra alma, y le da la posibilidad de redención, el punto de luz que rompe las tinieblas y nos facilita una salida en la cual ya ni siquiera pensábamos. Así me hallaba yo, vencido por las leyes del Mundo Macho y a la vez destinado a un rayo de luz casual que me devolvería la razón, que me retornaría a mí mismo tal y como era antes de llegar a Lur. Y el rayo de luz, el fallo del sistema, iba a ser aquella criatura maravillosa que, surgiendo de los profundos abismos de la esclavitud, restituiría mi adoración hacia el sexo encantador que ya había olvidado.

La noche de Minia me abruma, Larry, y ahora, cuando todo duerme; ahora, cuando ni siquiera me queda el refugio de cualquier cafetucho, soporto la clausura de un hotel que pretende ser de primera (pero es en vano su intento), mientras, a lo lejos, se oye el silbido del Tren del Desierto, lujoso como un relámpago de civilización ya remota que rompe las tinieblas por las cuales tal vez tú, Larry, llegarás a mí. Bajo la bombilla que el viento agita, yo evoco, en trazos simples y torpes, tus rasgos esenciales; temo que el tren se detenga y el viento del desierto, al igual que ayer, al igual que mañana, al igual que siempre, te devuelva a mi lado, y que tú, amigo, representante, hacedor mío, me arrastres de nuevo hacia el escenario, me vigiles apostado entre bastidores, me dictes las cosas que debo negar, sonrías al comprobar cómo afirmo lo que me has enseñado a afirmar. De este modo te escribo, temeroso y angustiado a la vez, convencido de que he logrado liberarme físicamente de ti, pero también sabiendo que en el fondo sigo siendo tu creación, al igual que muchos jóvenes de esta sociedad que tanto dinero te proporciona son, también, una creación mía. Y el viento del desierto golpea los cristales con la misma intensidad de anoche, tal vez con idéntica furia que mañana, pero con la diferencia de que mañana acaso ya no me encuentre aquí. Que mañana, atado cabeza abajo, abra los ojos y vea cómo la arena del desierto va discurriendo bajo mi cuerpo y, al frente, las poderosas botas de un nuevo Astor avanzan seguras, firmes, cumpliendo su misión sagrada, la misma que me hace regresar a mi país para que vuelvan a resplandecer los rayos de la vida y caiga una nueva primavera sobre todo lo que Cobra creó. Sobre todo cuanto fue creado mucho antes de que naciesen los siglos, todo cuanto perdurará por mucho tiempo después de que los siglos hayan alcanzado su fin.

¡Corre, alternativa que arrastro desde siempre! ¡Haz que pueda permanecer en la asunción final de mi destino! No permitas pausas en mi aceptación definitiva: conviérteme en ese hijo de la agonía a quien fueron revelados los misterios de Cobra. Y tú, Larry, si te desesperas al leer en las revistas que mi desaparición puede ser el anuncio de una crisis definitiva, porque mis adoradores de la platea olvidan pronto, sustituyen pronto, adoran pronto a otros ídolos, crea, pues, otro mito a mi altura, otro diosecillo alígero que esté a mi nivel; y llena con su rostro anodino todas las portadas del mundo, todos los carteles que cubran las habitaciones de esta gente que, poco a poco, tal vez sin darse cuenta, ya no podrá resignarse a vivir sin él. ¡Gran dios Cobra, en la habitación de este hotelucho de paredes resquebrajadas como mi siglo, Nebjeperura espera a tus enviados, Nebjeperura desea regresar a su reino, quiere dar la felicidad a su pueblo, iluminarle con los rayos de la vida que ha robado al Gran Señor de los herejes!

¡Oh Larry! ¡Ayúdame, ayúdame! ¡La lengua de Lur me acomete con loca obsesión!; ¡sé que nunca seré capaz de hablar otra! ¡La obsesión me asalta de repente, como la necesidad de cantar para mí solo! Al principio es un desasosiego físico; mi espalda reclama el látigo de Astor; la mano solicita el bastón para golpear el rostro de Batsá; los dedos desean los anillos que arrojan sus destellos hacia todos los rincones del gran salón del trono... *Epura uptusir iu-n'k bnajul...* Epura Epsamón llega cada mañana, rompe la noche y se aferra a los rayos que yo he devuelto al Mundo Macho, los lanza de nuevo mucho más lejos de las terrazas colgantes, los hunde en la inmensa matriz de Cobra, y el día ya es creado... *bauit Atón n'k iu, bauit...!* ¿Es que no te das cuenta, Larry? Habéis obrado como ellos: el peligro se apoderó de mí y todos me dejasteis caer en él..., pero los adolescentes de Minia nunca me creerán; estas muchachas que solicitan mi foto en las revistas no lo creerían; vosotros no queréis comprender, no habéis entendido nada: lo primero es esa necesidad urgente de que salga el sol, Epura Epsamón, y a continuación las Juventudes de Lur acuden al patio del cuartel, se arrodillan ante mi estancia privada y cantan los himnos que acabaréis cantando todos vosotros:

Ussum Abrone
capsea tale
unj inatona
ce siour fayu
u-u-usab Ra!
Nebjeperura
sal maijuda!
Ussum Atona
coberi usne
is vlac antume
Sao -u-u-u ribo
marsoe acaunti
Epsamón Ussum
Ra dor Demeta
homo mau
Ditjma Nau!

Sí, Larry, finalmente remoto: Ditjma Nau quiere decir Mundo Macho. Porque Ditjma quiere decir Macho y Cobra a la vez, del mismo modo que Nau significa Mundo y también Cobra. Las palabras básicas de todo el vocabulario.

¡Qué poco duran las rendijas, y qué mínima luz permiten filtrar! Las palabras y los signos de Lur me salen sin que me dé cuenta. En Ginebra insistías en la urgencia de dejar grabado el nuevo *long-play*, pero apenas empecé a escribir las letras, me salían los himnos que entona la juventud uniformada del Mundo Macho cuando se ejercita en los campamentos colectivos de verano; cuando, al cumplir los años que la raza ya no puede tolerar, avanzan con la cabeza alta hacia el sacrificio supremo del templo del Final Viril; cuando levantan las espadas de hoja triple para hundirlas en el vientre de cualquier miembro de la raza de Auer...

Y entre eslabones perdidos o resquicios que se abren y a continuación se cierran, yo saldré a la Corniche, como todas las noches que he pasado en Minia desde que huí de ti. Ya sé que el sol empieza a levantarse más temprano, y que sus rayos rompen el alba con el vigor de una estación que se renueva. Y todo ello puede significar que un nuevo Astor emprenderá el peregrinaje hacia las sombras de la Nada que ahora me acogen, y guiará mi caballo alígero hacia el mismo centro del Universo...

¡Socorro!

NI LA TURBIA LUZ DE esta habitación, ni el viento del desierto que intenta en vano imponerme su voluntad de locura, tienen suficiente fuerza para iluminar y musicar la imagen que vuelve a mí, resplandeciente, en medio de los delirios del templo, al margen de los sacerdotes, y que no describiré porque se parece demasiado a todas las recepciones que ya me habían dispensado y a las que habrán de dispensarme para siempre jamás. Poco importa la decoración, las salas de marfil que, excavadas en la montaña, conseguían, por obra y gracia de la historia del Mundo Macho, convertir la piedra en bordado, la tenebrosa rocalla en imaginería rococó donde destacaban las figuritas más delicadas que puedas imaginar, multiplicadas hasta el infinito en diversas actitudes de un erotismo refinadísimo —entiende religioso—; figuras que, por vez primera desde que llegué a mi reino, proponían las reproducciones más variadas e imaginativas del acto de amor heterosexual. Nada de esto importa: sólo aquel anchísimo rayo del sol, el más bello entre los que yo pudiese recordar; aquel manantial de sublimidad natural (porque la naturaleza puede ser sublime a ciertas horas del día); la luz que descendía por una gran abertura en cuyo centro, blanca y esbelta como las veinte mil figuritas de amor que la rodeaban, se erguía la virgen, pureza puesta a punto para mi cuerpo.

No, nada había en la virgen de la fealdad, la suciedad y el salvajismo que yo vi en el valle donde habita la Bestia Llamada Hembra. Hubiérase dicho que mi presa era luz celeste, disimulada entre todo el sol que inundaba el centro de la cueva; como un mármol resplandeciente, recién descubierto en la más prodigiosa cantera de un monte donde sólo existieran maravillas; como la tenue preñez del viento después de haber fornicado con la calma, de la noche con el día, del sol con la luna y así cuantos choques de opuestos unieron los lazos del amor fatídico para crear la belleza que no puede ser explicada. ¡Tantas cosas...! Y, en la abundancia, yo sólo supe balbucear una pregunta:

—¿Quién es ella, Astor?

Astor me quitó el pectoral y el cinturón, de forma que quedé completamente desnudo. A continuación, se arrodilló:

—Es toda para ti, monseñor. La prueba que debes superar para que, a partir de ahora, todos podamos adorar tu virilidad.

En el alud de sensaciones que me invadían, con el tumultuoso empuje de un temple que yo recuperaba, la prueba dejó de tener importancia, no significaba nada, porque cualquier prueba necesita método, y mi fuego repentino era desordenado, intrépido y cobarde a la vez, salvaje como el deseo y ardiente como el amor. Hasta mucho tiempo después no percibí que detrás de la virgen se agrupaba una orquestina de arpistas jóvenes y, como ella, bellas y lujosamente ataviadas. No pensé que mi pasión era impuesta, controlada continuamente por los sacerdotes, quienes, arrodillados con Astor, observarían mi actuación a fin de certificar después, ante el pueblo, el alcance real de mis posibilidades. Ni siquiera la densidad de perfumes adormecedores que brotaban del suelo, como nubes que me separaban de aquel prodigioso ser, podían recordar otra cosa que la humareda entre o sobre la cual creemos avanzar cuando nos hallamos sumergidos en la matriz de la ambigüedad de un sueño. Nada contaba; o, por lo menos, nada que no fuese el frío que se imponía al fuego, el temblor de mi piel que, de repente, dejaba de ser aquel trozo de cuero poderoso en que la habían convertido los adiestramientos del Mundo Macho. Y los pasos, tan lentos como temerosos, fueron lo único consciente que supe realizar en aquel instante encantado.

Ella llegó a mí cubierta de sedas que permitían intuir una piel blanca como yo nunca había visto otra; la seda ondeaba al ritmo exacto de la cabellera, negra como la noche, mórbida como el terciopelo y, como éste, inquietante y estremecedora. Los ojos, profundamente negros, me miraron sin intensidad, o tal vez sin expresión ni deseos de poseerme; no había en ellos miedo ni alegría, desprecio o aceptación: eran ojos que se limitaban a existir con la misma laxitud de los brazos, abandonados a ambos lados del cuerpo esbelto y liso, desde el cual surgía, dura y adolescente, la turgencia de unos senos intactos. Y los labios eran carnosos, anchos y lisos como los labios de los colosos que reproducen a Epsamón.

Al llegar al cuerpo, acaricié suavemente los hombros y, sin abandonar mi actitud de dulzura, sin dejar de recordar que los labios de Epsamón eran amenaza de lo incógnito y los de la virgen promesa de cuanto es inmaculado, desabroché una hebilla de rubíes y los velos se deslizaron emitiendo el gemido del famoso hijo de la Aurora. En el éxtasis de aquella proposición, yo no podía pensar que mi amada fuese diestra en el ritual, porque todo su cuerpo me hablaba de pureza. Pero, sin ser maestra en obsesiones, había sido educada en las reglas que Astor me contó después, reglas que dan a la Bestia Llamada Hembra un sentido de utilidad que las clases privilegiadas del Mundo Macho saben aprovechar para sus intereses. Por otra parte, también supe que aquella destreza en la cual había sido educada se consideraba como un hecho de suma liturgia. Pero debo decir que si ella se hubiese revelado como un modelo de torpeza (por cuyo motivo sería castigada con la muerte, pues me estaba reservada desde que nació, y yo soy sagrado y es preciso que se me satisfaga), todo hubiese sido exactamente igual. Y es que, a partir del momento en que la vi, al ser ella luz entre la luz, mi cuerpo ardía en la necesidad de aleccionarla conduciéndola hacia aquel paraíso reencontrado, en cuyo centro ella sería siempre la invicta y yo el vencido.

No hubo acto de amor como aquel en toda la historia del mundo, y Astor me confirmó que, por lo menos, recordaba muy pocos que se le parecieran en toda la historia del Mundo Macho. Me olvidé de cuanto fuese recuerdo o implicase futuro, y ella fue mi reina ocho veces, y al final de cada coito sonó un gong de plata; y entonces Astor vino a buscarme, con extrañas lágrimas en los ojos, y dijo que la doncella era mía mientras se prolongase nuestra estancia en el templo. Tomé a la muchacha en brazos, y ella quedó a mi merced de tal forma que su mejilla aún ardía sobre mi hombro; los sacerdotes aplaudieron mi actuación y, después de muchos elogios y de felicitarse por haber hallado en mí un ejemplo tan magnífico para el pueblo, nos acompañaron a una habitación especial, la más insólita que nunca hubiera visto yo en el Mundo Macho, puesto que, de hecho, era un enorme cubo de cristal, sin más muebles que un gran lecho, también de cristal, y un biombo que sólo era un espejo cuya misión consistía en recibir y transmitir las imágenes que se reflejaban en todas las paredes, techo y suelo. También diré que todo el cristal era opaco, excepto un gran círculo transparente que permitía ver, más allá de un paisaje idílico, la agreste pirámide natural del valle donde habita la Bestia Llamada Hembra. Más tarde, al mirar a través del enorme ventanal único, me di cuenta de que nos hallábamos en lo alto de una montaña de formas alucinantes, y con vapores multicolores, producto de la lava que, siglo tras siglo, había ido acumulando la acción de no sé qué volcán subterráneo.

Llegaba hasta mí, con una sinfonía siempre bárbara e incivil, el sonido de los cuernos de las mujeres del valle.

Dejé a la doncella en la cama (de forma que su cuerpo se proyectase triplemente en el espejo de abajo, en el del baldaquín y en el de una pared), y antes de que Astor se dispusiera a salir por la única puerta, le pregunté:

—¿Cómo se llama, Astor?

Él la miró. Y estaba tan triste como antes.

—«Hembra», monseñor.

—Eso ya lo sé, perro. Pero tendrá un nombre... como tú, como yo, como Batsá.

—Las fuerzas hembras de la creación no tienen un nombre particular, monseñor. «Hembra» sirve para todas las bestias del rebaño.

—Perdona, Astor, pero si no me equivoco, las palmeras tienen nombre femenino.

—En el Mundo Macho, monseñor, no hay palmeras.

—¿Debo soportar que me mientas de nuevo? En los jardines de palacio crecen infinidad de palmeras. A menudo me he tendido a su amparo para leer en paz. Y he visto muchas higueras en los huertos de la provincia. Y, además: ¿qué me dices de las rosas del ninfeo de Serapis?

—Es como si no existieran, monseñor. No tienen nombre.

—El hecho de que no tengan nombre no quiere decir que no existan.

—Todo lo que no tiene nombre es tolerado, monseñor, pero no existe. Dar nombre a una cosa es crearla, prolongar su vida para siempre, como sucede con los ciudadanos honestos, que al morir tienen su nombre inscrito en la tumba para que sean recordados, y esto no sucede nunca con los esclavos, que no alcanzarán jamás la vida eterna (del mismo modo que, de hecho, nunca tuvieron vida pública) porque ningún nombre ilustrará su tumba; y, pues nadie podrá leer su nombre, nada podrá garantizarles la inmortalidad.

Furioso, me lancé sobre Astor, y ambos rodamos por tierra mientras le golpeaba en los labios, como siempre que me consideraba engañado por él (es decir, desde que asumí —o él me hizo asumir— mi derecho a ser autoritario). Mientras le golpeaba implacablemente, le preguntaba a gritos cómo se llamaban las palmeras, las higueras, las encinas; y él siempre contestaba: «Se llaman árboles, monseñor.» Y no había manera de sacarlo de aquí.

Pero no tardé en comprender que, en el sistema del Mundo Macho, en la suprema perfección de su orden, había algo que no funcionaba tan perfectamente como se pretendía, y que la gramática no sólo evidenciaba las clamorosas contradicciones del orden impuesto, sino incluso sus fallos de funcionamiento. No existía la palabra casa, y sí la palabra caserío; una palmera era «árbol» como lo era una magnolia; Cobra era una fuerza padre, y se declinaba con el artículo masculino (de hecho, muchos jóvenes de Lur se llaman Cobrara o Cobraremó), y la luz se convierte en *el* Mal (una vez más, es el concepto Cobra, de forma que en los textos poéticos del Mundo Macho podemos leer *sha-un omnia Cobraener manjeper*, es decir: «Completamente radiante, se hizo la luz del día», que es el principio de uno de los poemas épicos más famosos de aquella cultura y de lectura obligada en la escuela, como es sabido); y, en resumen, la tiniebla se convierte en masculino porque es la transfiguración del Bien.

Decidido a obtener más explicaciones continué golpeando a Astor, sin que él opusiese la menor resistencia; por el contrario, respondía a mis golpes con una inexplicable sonrisa de bondad, mantenía los brazos abiertos en cruz, los puños cerrados, la mirada buscando las alturas, al modo de un mártir cristiano. Y cuanto más le golpeaba y mayor era el torrente de sangre que manaba de sus labios, más inmóvil permanecía, hasta el punto de que quedé yo más fatigado que doliente él. Así, exhausto por mi propia furia, me dejé caer sobre su cuerpo, mis músculos fláccidos reposando en abandono total contra los suyos, pétreos. Él mantenía la cabeza echada hacia atrás, como presa de un éxtasis místico y respirando con inesperada suavidad contra el ritmo descompasado de mi respiración. Así permanecimos, los cuerpos unidos, ensimismado yo en las consideraciones de orden gramatical y sin percibir que los latidos de Astor empezaban a plantear una situación completamente nueva.

Fue un latido dulce y profundo que acaso sin pretenderlo —tan puro era— me comunicó al principio ternura y luego, progresivamente, ardor. Brotaba de su pecho, invadía lentamente el mío, se adueñaba de nuestros cuerpos, ponía una dureza inesperada en los penes que, ya de manera perceptible, íbanse hinchando al unísono.

Pero en un momento dado Astor se incorporó con el terror reflejado en el rostro y me alejó de sí con un empujón que me hizo rodar por el suelo. Acto seguido, se aferró la cabeza con ambas manos y empezó a llorar.

—¿Qué siento? —gritó—. ¿Qué se está apoderando de mí?

Corría, saltaba, aullaba entre, sobre y bajo los enormes espejos, como buscando desesperadamente la salida no sólo del cubo, sino de su propio laberinto. Y lamento no disponer de la simultaneidad que ofrece el cinemascope para unificar todas las acciones y abarcar no sólo mi sorpresa sino los saltos de Astor y, ya, los de la doncella, presa con todo esto de una agresividad tan inesperada como la desesperación de mi guardián. ¡Cuán lejos de mi dulce reina esa fiera corrupta que, arrodillada sobre la cama, empezaba a arrojar sobre Astor los objetos más contundentes que encontraba a su alrededor! Y al mismo tiempo, emitía gruñidos atroces que no supe tomar por insultos hasta que comprendí que ella misma estaba empeñada en una lucha feroz contra el crimen que Astor acababa de descubrir en sí mismo; lucha en la que el odio hacia Astor tenía que estar provocado por algún género de repulsión biológica. Y mientras yo, desde el suelo, contemplaba cómo el cuerpo del titán corría y se multiplicaba entre los espejos (¡mágica, irreprochable armonía de músculos volando por un espacio que no estuviera limitado por horizonte alguno!) ella siguió gritando, convulsionándose; y, comprendiendo mejor que yo los motivos que impulsaban la desesperación del macho, remató sus insultos con frenéticas carcajadas que se prolongaron incluso cuando él consiguió salir de la estancia.

La virgen innominada presentaba ahora el aspecto de un tremendo lince, que no aumentaba mi fuego por sus gracias físicas, sino por la aureola de peligro que todo su aspecto expresaba, y que otorgaba a sus ojos desorbitados por el odio un color liliáceo, tan hipnotizador como la mirada de aquellas cobras que, en la fiesta de un pueblecito ya olvidado, retozaban entre los muslos de los bacantes.

¿Qué podía ser yo para ella? En su mirada, que no era serena y resignada como antes de ser mi reita, ni placentera como en el acto de serlo, había ahora, únicamente, ferocidad y el fervor de una batalla sin tregua, en la cual el enemigo genérico era yo, desde siempre, y en la que, además y a partir de aquel momento, pasaba a ser Astor un enemigo importante y odiado, bien que de otra especie. Porque en la batalla que prometía a mi reina con tanto ardor, yo representaba el macho que le enseñaron a odiar desde niña, pero Astor, con la herejía que acababa de descubrir en sí mismo, se convertía en un rival repentino, cuya existencia era imposible imaginar meses antes.

La batalla entre mi reina y mi raptor sería de resonancias ancestrales. Y el premio para el vencedor era, precisamente yo.

¿Pero de dónde llegaba aquella corriente que, en plena lucha, la hacía ceder bajo la primera caricia que yo me dignase ofrecerle? Su vasallaje no era en modo alguno un mito, como no lo fue el vasallaje de Astor, tan dulce que sería un suplicio para él. Era como una continua alternancia de contradicciones, una sucesión sin freno de sentimientos y emociones; de reacciones a las que, después de haberse producido, se oponían otras totalmente contrarias. El simple contacto de la piel era ya suficiente, y la angustia que despertaban los roces empezaba a convulsionarnos a modo de explosiones en cadena, enigma tras enigma dentro del gran misterio común del Mundo Macho. Adentrado hasta entonces en los grandes embrollos generales, que podríamos considerar de orden externo, yo había olvidado que ningún misterio, ningún embrollo de la realidad que me rodeaba, era capaz de superar lo que hay de sumamente inextricable en el mundo de los sentimientos. De este modo, después de tanto tiempo acostumbrado a explorar únicamente la realidad objetiva del Mundo Macho, era forzoso que ahora me hiciera con otro bastón, otras cuerdas, botas nuevas de suela claveteada, y descendiese, con mi ignorancia a cuestas, hacia las simas más inexploradas del abismo humano.

Pero todas las cosas tenían su relación, como en un proceso que tan pronto podía ser obvio como subterráneo (incluso en el modo de irse desarrollando), y las reacciones que durante todo aquel tiempo experimenté ante las actitudes de Astor se parecían en cierto modo a la actitud de los gramáticos del Mundo Macho, quienes, al negarse a bautizar con nombres nuevos a las formas hembras de la creación, sólo obedecían a un miedo tácito y terrible, que también tendría su origen en el principio de todas las historias. No sé cuándo ni en qué liceo, alguien me contó que, en ciertas civilizaciones primitivas, la invocación del nombre implicaba un modo de desear la forma nombrada o, en otros casos, un modo de exorcizarla. Por supuesto, el reconocimiento de mis sentimientos, incluso de la profunda necesidad de ahuyentarlos, me atemorizó al principio como sucede con las cosas innombradas del Mundo Macho. De esta manera, todas las contradicciones se amalgamaban en un miedo clamoroso, en un espanto que no tenía comparación con ningún otro, como tampoco lo tenía mi temor a conocer el secreto manantial que nutría, con ímpetu calmo, cada actitud de antes o después. Pero el miedo de Astor sobrepasaba con mucho el mío propio en un punto que ya era alucinante: su gente aceptaba la existencia de unas formas hembras, como sucede con aquellas flores convertidas en monstruos de la Naturaleza gracias a la ciencia de los jardineros oficiales; su gente lograba anular al valor hembra mediante el poder macho, siempre vencedor; pero no tenían bastante valor —ni el poder macho era lo suficientemente triunfal—, no ya para reconocer los nombres femeninos, sino incluso para cambiarlos por otros masculinos, lo cual implicaría el reconocimiento de la existencia de lo que ahora negaban.

Entonces, ¿cómo era posible que un sistema tan poderoso, implacable y siempre vencedor como era el de Epsamón Divino guardase, en su correlación de eslabones perdidos, aquel miedo básico infiltrado en las más profundas raíces de unos orígenes que se hubiesen deseado edificados con tal firmeza como para llegar a ser eternos en su fundamento?

Por otra parte, ¿de dónde provenía el rechazo de unos objetos innominados, si, cuando las formas se mantenían vírgenes a cualquier tipo de reconocimiento, no era posible precisar si eran masculinos, femeninos o neutros? Es decir: la decisión inapelable de no dar nombre a las palmeras implicaba la idea de que, en *algún lugar,* aquellos árboles recibían un apelativo femenino. Era imposible que en el inmenso espacio increado que señalaba el dudoso comienzo de todas las historias, las fuerzas o los objetos que aún debían nacer tuviesen ya un nombre que justificara su rechazo. Una vez más, y por comparación, las relaciones del Mundo Macho con un incógnito mundo exterior creaban la duda que me remitía directamente a Epsamón.

¿Quién podría ser Epsamón? ¿Qué universo aún desconocido me revelaría apenas descubriera sus ojos, su autoridad llena de tiempo?

Pensaba en todo esto mientras, con la mirada y la mente ausentes, iba acariciando a mi reina. De pronto, ella recobraba el aspecto puro de antes y, sin una transición que resultara mínimamente explicable, se aferraba a mi cuerpo con toda la violencia del fuego que habíamos encendido los dos bajo la atenta mirada de los sacerdotes de Homo Demeter. Confundidos mis pensamientos, me limité a arrodillarme y empecé a besarle las manos, sin excesivo interés. Pero mi ternura obtenía otros resultados como respuesta: obediente a las leyes de vasallaje que le habían inculcado, ella trascendió la suavidad de los besos y, con gran violencia, me hizo rodar por el suelo, que nos reflejó al mismo tiempo que las paredes y el techo. Una furia tan imprevista me provocó una carcajada angustiosa, con lo cual intentaba darle a entender que no me era posible continuar. Pero ella sacudía la cabeza al modo de los imbéciles, se encogía de hombros y decía cosas en un dialecto que me era desconocido por completo (más que palabras, reconocí un repertorio de gruñidos y gemidos). Sin embargo, ella era la vencedora más obvia de la lucha, porque yo había pasado mucho tiempo aguardándola, y ahora la tenía toda para mí multiplicada en las paredes como un cuerpo que ya formaba parte de mi cuerpo, ligados el uno al otro por una furia que no admitía el cansancio, una furia que, al reflejarse en los espejos, se mezclaba con el cuerpo atlético de Astor que huía, corriendo, contrastados sus músculos de roca con la piel de nieve de la muchacha.

Día tras día, el cubo de espejos reprodujo los mismos contrastes de seda y de roca, la horrorizada huida de mi hermoso guardián, la vida y la muerte de los instintos que se enfrentaron en abierta batalla, hasta que en el aire delicioso de una mañana de primavera sonaron las trompetas de la Floración.

«PASÓ UN PRIMER SIGLO, y después otros millones de siglos, y desde que tus días empezaron en el Mundo Macho, desde que las fuerzas del Mal te dieron ese poder de la agonía, tú reclamaste en vano tu crónica, pediste la explicación de cuantas cosas te han acontecido, predestinado tanto al mundo como a ti mismo, desde el principio de todas las historias. Has ido más allá de todas las averiguaciones posibles, y sólo has encontrado el vacío que nada aclara; sólo el manantial que brota, siempre inexplicable, de los abismos más profundos del tiempo y de la vida. Durante años y años, las historias te han ocultado el punto donde empezaron, y los rostros de tus dioses, moldeados en las colosales dimensiones que el poder exige, nunca te han dado el menor acceso a su espíritu y, así, detrás de sus rasgos de fuerza y belleza soberana, sólo has encontrado la Nada. Como si más allá, más adentro, más acá de cualquier doctrina, el principio de todas las historias fuese lo único realmente falso de mi falacia inmensa, pues la gran revelación que podrías esperar de mí es, precisamente, que nunca hubo un comienzo de las cosas; que en la gran diáspora de la vida que no tiene fin, ningún orden posibilita un solo principio. Y ni siquiera la Nada tendrá nunca un comienzo al cual puedas aferrarte para explicarte a ti mismo qué es el mundo y quién eres tú.

»Pero yo soy Cobra, la fuerza primigenia que engendró el Mundo Macho, y ahora te revelo que ni siquiera tengo la forma que mis hijos han querido darme. Hace muchos siglos —y cada uno de estos siglos suele comprender millones de años—, la superficie del espacio que no tiene fin era la vida, y más allá de esta vida no existía la Nada. No existía el tiempo; no existía el espacio; no había punto que limitase el hecho inmenso e inalcanzable que sólo podrás entender cuando mueras definitivamente y el gran espacio seas tú mismo, como antes, como ayer, como siempre. Hijo de la agonía: yo soy la fuerza que arrastra la luz hacia las tinieblas, y nunca he tenido forma ni la tendré, nunca me he enroscado en el tronco del Universo, inexistente, pues la representación de este universo sobre el cual el Mundo Macho ha querido edificar toda su cosmogonía es imposible de realizar, como lo es la representación de tu espíritu; como lo será, cuando mueras, este mito de que te han hecho objeto, según el cual te adoran, y que requiere mil estatuas, cada una diferente de las otras, para conseguir que seas respetado. Así, el espacio inmenso que soy, que serás tú cuando mueras, que es y ha de ser siempre inalcanzable para quienes pretendan dar forma tangible a las grandes fuerzas de la Creación y que, al representarlas, tal vez sin saberlo, caen en el gran pecado del sacrilegio...»

Cierto, Larry; continúo avanzando a través de los densos efluvios multicolores en cuyo fondo se yergue Ella, o Él, o Ello: fuerza, o poder, o impulso que rompe la claridad y, al mismo tiempo, las tinieblas del universo; cierto, Larry, necesaria e inexorablemente cierto; mi avance se torna tambaleante; tropiezo con las nubes de este humo coloreado que deviene más denso y caluroso, que llega a ser ardiente y forma una espuma turbia que quema mi desnudez y me envuelve como un manto destinado a proteger esta excursión hacia el origen de la vida. Y yo estoy flotando, señor y hacedor mío; floto, esclavo de otro dominio que ya no es tuyo, que ya no es el escenario limitadísimo de vuestros mitos al cual fui transportado, sino otro escenario, mucho más vasto, eterno en tiempo y espacio, ilimitado como los salmos que oigo desde mi muerte, más allá de la madera del ataúd, en la brasa y el tormento de un imposible sueño de comprensión.

YO NUNCA HABRÍA IMAGINADO que pudiese nevar en tierras que ya eran del desierto; y, sin embargo, nevó durante varios días, de forma que te parecerá una nevada increíblemente copiosa si, además de aquella proximidad, tienes en cuenta que ya terminaba el invierno y los árboles florecían con la inequívoca intensidad, con la coloreada exultación que suelen otorgarles los rayos que yo restituyo al Mundo Macho.

«¡Una nevada, tan cercana la primavera!», decía yo. Y la muchacha me miraba, quién sabe si empezando a comprender mi sorpresa.

Ella parecía encantada con mi asombro, y solía enmudecer, juguetona, mientras con palabras que nunca podría entender yo comentaba que su provincia era la más mágica de todo el Mundo Macho, donde, como te he dicho y hace dos días se lo decía al profesor, todas las realidades parecían surgir de un cofre que contuviese los sentidos más genuinos de lo prodigioso. Evidentemente, para ella la nieve constituía algo normal, la costumbre que al filo de la primavera, e incluso cuando ya el calor empieza a ser poderoso, se desencadenaba sobre el Mundo Macho como símbolo de la deformación de un poder sobrehumano que el hombre, con la fuerza que le otorgaba haber nacido de Cobra, era capaz de vencer. Y aquí, magia y máquinas se conjuraban para crear, sobre la Creación primera, año tras año, siglo tras siglo, la gran falacia que el poder reclama, y que a partir de este momento, cuando Astor tome de nuevo, aquí en Minia, las riendas plateadas de mi caballo alígero, será mi propia mentira: la que me estará permitido hacer y deshacer, grande como soy, divino como nadie me discutirá el derecho a ser.

Pero yo, Nebjeperura, me arriesgo a ser tomado por loco en vuestro país de la Nada, y a pesar de mi divinidad reconocida, así en el cielo como en la tierra, nunca lograré comunicaros mi poder y, a la vez, mi espanto. Yo, Nebjeperura, desbocado hacia la vida que existe más allá del sol, cabalgando en mi caballo metálico, ofendido mi sacro oído por el ruido del motor que antes me entusiasmaba, y, sin embargo, rechazando mi mito de trovador del consumo, desciendo hacia los abusos de mi divinidad y te impongo, Larry mío, multitud de nuevos enigmas, multitud de enigmas inmortales.

Yo, el divino. ¿Lo era tanto como para tener todos los secretos revelados desde antiguo?; ¿para ver todos los mitos despojados de los velos, espléndidos y lujosos si quieres, que el Mundo Macho despliega ante los ojos de sus súbditos?; ¿para tener derecho, en resumen, a ser el gran príncipe de leyes que no entendía ni entenderé jamás? ¿Tan divino como para iluminar tierras que obedeciesen a mis doctrinas nunca vistas, a los mitos que yo no había creado, en vez de ser yo quien, desde el escenario, crease, como he hecho hasta ahora, la mitología adecuada a la medida del tiempo, el dominio sobre la atmósfera y, en resumen, la nueva crueldad que, al ser del Mundo Macho, fuese sin embargo mía y de nadie más? Y si todo esto resultaba improbable, ¿qué representaba mi divinidad estratificada en un trono de oro y diamantes (un trono que, justo es decirlo, me parecía ocupar en calidad de realquilado)?

Día tras día, con la mejilla apoyada en el recuadro de cristal transparente (como ojos abiertos en el rostro gigantesco que era la roca viva), y al borde de un abismo que parecía adentrarse hasta el corazón de la tierra, yo pensaba en la nieve, en la primavera y en los rayos que un día llevé desde la Nada (¿dónde estaban hoy?); y, muy a menudo, perdía la noción de las horas, la noción del espacio y el lugar que en él ocupan cosas de cuya existencia tampoco me apercibía, mientras mi reina, desnuda como yo, se encogía a mis pies, como un animalito, acariciándome, murmurando una extraña melodía, tediosa por uniforme, en absoluto creativa y, a pesar de todo, bellísima. En el exterior nevaba copiosamente, y la densa espuma que formaban los copos, coronados por una impenetrable cortina de nubes, adquiría tonos rojizos a causa de la humareda que ascendía de los cráteres activos desde que el mundo es mundo. Y los colores se difuminaban al formar masas más extrañas, en cuyos recovecos la nieve, al moverse lentamente, creaba formas que se deshacían a su vez y volvían a nacer, cual una dinámica obsesiva que, en la mezcla de fuego y vapores de agua helada, llegaba a favorecer distintos juegos de dimensiones, nuevas como otra noción del espacio, formado de repente en corredores, vueltas, abismos y empinadas cuestas por las cuales ya era posible avanzar.

¡Y, de hecho, avanzábamos! Sé que en la sucesión de cosas que llevo explicadas, increíbles, tanto para ti como para el profesor, ésta es la menos verosímil. ¡Pero te juro que avanzábamos! En todos los sueños que he tenido desde entonces, primero en el hospital de El Cairo, después en el de Ginebra, y ahora mismo, mientras paseo absorto por la reencontrada madrugada de Minia; en todos los sueños la soberana matriz de Cobra se ensancha, el manantial brota y, siempre inexplicable, va a mezclarse con la humareda que asciende desde los cráteres, se adentra en ella, avanza, como si la habitación de los espejos que me contenía fuese una nave que acometiese su último viaje, el definitivo.

En el recuerdo, la imagen es completamente objetiva, como lo fue mi percepción de las cosas no bien el cubo de cristal se puso en marcha. Yo mantenía los ojos fijos en el cristal transparente, y sólo veía la mágica descomposición de formas gaseosas que combatían entre sí, mientras el cubo, vertiginoso, se desprendía de la montaña en busca de las profundidades más hondas de la tierra. En el hospital de El Cairo, en la clínica de Ginebra, en cada noche de Minia, he seguido viendo la espesa cortina de vapores, contra la cual parece que estamos a punto de chocar (y entonces el horror adquiere magnas dimensiones) pero se aparta en un último momento, cuando ya me parece que rompo estrepitosamente contra el torbellino de formas amarillas, valles, e incluso cordilleras entre las cuales avanzábamos, implacablemente, en nuestro descenso. Aplasto el rostro contra el cristal mientras en el espacio que tengo ante mí alterna un torrente de líquido hirviente con un mar repentino de hielo amarillo, y los colores infinitos e inexplicables del aire solidificado van deshaciéndose, goteando sobre este único cristal transparente que, en su avance vertiginoso, rompe todos los colores que se le ponen delante, y lo rodean o lo engullen. Empiezo a correr entre y sobre los espejos, alucinando como Astor cuando gritaba: «¡Qué siento, qué siento!»; pero la puerta se convierte en otro espejo hermético, una superficie cerrada de dureza pétrea, pero lisa como las imágenes que se reflejarán en ella: nuevo espejo que, cuando lo golpeo con los puños cerrados, sólo reproduce mi forma, el rostro angustiado, el cuerpo cubierto por un sudor dorado, de manera que mis puños se golpean a sí mismos, mi vientre roza contra mi vientre; y de este modo sigo golpeando contra las otras paredes, siempre inútilmente, puesto que sólo me veo a mí mismo allí, reflejado miles de veces, sobre los espacios reproducidos infinitesimalmente dentro de ellos mismos, contra ellos mismos, como si luchasen entre sí; y el único muro abierto al exterior es este cristal contra el que golpean, obsesivos, los vapores rojos, azules, verduscos, incluso negros, nieve, fuego y lava en el torrente que ya engulle la habitación sin que la muchacha se dé cuenta, inexpresiva siempre, arrodillada aún, rezongando su conato de canción, incapaz de ayudar con un consejo, como en otro tiempo hiciese Astor.

De este modo, otra vez la pesadilla se introduce en una angustia que ya no anuncia la menor esperanza de claridad. Todo cuanto aprendí en el Mundo Macho, todo cuanto fue susceptible de ser clasificado mediante la razón, queda aplastado bajo la gran verdad que deberé aprender de una vez y que encierra definitivamente mi lucha en un fatal callejón sin salida: nunca sabré nada, porque en el fondo de todas las respuestas permanecerá siempre el misterio que no tiene explicación y que sustenta, invencible, la esencia de cada cosa. En eso consistió la revelación de Cobra, cuando el rayo de su oscuridad profunda apareció, deslumbrante, entre todas las tinieblas de colores y sobre las cimas de la gran cordillera encendida que continuaba engendrando pasadizos y gargantas de lava, nieve y rocas vegetales a la salida del cubo de los espejos...

ASÍ FUE COMO LLEGUÉ a las profundidades de la matriz de la vida.

Continuaba golpeando contra el espejo del suelo, siempre duro e inviolable, y la muchacha seguía apoyada en el muro de cristal transparente, cuando una puerta que no era la misma por la que había salido Astor se abrió con lentitud y él regresó a mí vestido con no sé qué especie de mono de metal plateado, tocado con una gran escafandra de vidrio, como si necesitara evitar un aire venenoso o quisiera nutrirse de un aire distinto, muy particular, apropiado a su condición de humano devuelto al reino de las tinieblas. Por primera vez lo veía vestido, pues, como le dije, todos los atavíos del Mundo Macho —desde los militares hasta los de gran gala— exigen como punto de partida una desnudez de la parte inferior del cuerpo, sea mediante un corte en la ropa, sea por la mera acumulación de detalles mínimos —cinturones, hombreras y botas de metal, guantes o gramalla corta— sobre aquella desnudez que tanto complace a los dioses. Tal vez por el hecho de ver al atlético Astor oculto bajo aquel atuendo protector y la escafandra que apenas permitía adivinar el rostro, me excité en la misma medida en que, para otros, resulta entusiasmante ver desnuda a una doncella a la que siempre hubiesen visto vestida. Y debo repetir que, al entrar Astor, mi reina, inmóvil hasta el momento, saltó, furibunda, y empezó a gruñir, babeando y escupiendo a la vez, de tal modo y con tal grosería que tuve que echarme sobre ella y golpearla brutalmente —odiándola por aquel desprecio que, al ir dirigido a Astor, era como si lo infligiese a mi condición de macho—, y habría llegado a matarla si Astor no me sujeta por la espalda dejándome incapacitado para actuar, obligado a contentarme maldiciendo aquella insolencia, mientras la amenazaba con el más severo de los castigos. Pero, lejos de amedrentarse al oír mis amenazas, Astor me arrojó contra la pared, se arrodilló junto a la muchacha y la ayudó a levantarse con insólita gentileza. Seguidamente dijo:

—Ella es sagrada.

—¡Yo soy el sagrado! —exclamé—. ¡Y te juro que, después de esto, haré que Epsamón te corte la lengua, hijo de perra!

—Epsamón —murmuró él con sorna—. ¡Epsamón Divino!

Su rostro adquirió una expresión completamente nueva, un aspecto como no le conocí a lo largo de todo el tiempo —días, meses o años— en que me había limitado a juzgar su nobleza guerrera: bárbara como la de los antiguos y, por lo perfecto de su belleza, incapaz de un mínimo de humanidad. Pero esta vez Astor llegaba como la más genuina representación de la serenidad y, al recoger a la muchacha junto a su pecho poderoso, cubierto de plata, me miró sin respeto alguno, como si lo que yo representaba, mi jerarquía intocable, se hubiese convertido en la materia más execrable de la Creación. Y mi reina, ya de pie, de nuevo inmóvil, parecía una estatua ante la cual se arrodilló Astor, con ternura y devoción, para besarle el vientre. Y después besó el suelo, al modo de un pío adorador. La humareda del exterior ya penetraba en la gran sala de los espejos, y la impregnaba con una dulzura de aromas que invitaba suavemente a la letargia; y yo, indefenso ante aquella fascinación, no habría tardado en perder el sentido si Astor no me hubiese puesto una escafandra como la suya y, después, no me hubiese ayudado a vestirme con las mismas ropas, de forma que pronto parecí la viva estampa de un submarinista ennoblecido por la riqueza de los materiales.

Con la muchacha vestida de la misma guisa, salimos de la estancia y, en vez de encontrarme en el pasadizo de roca, bajamos por una escalera metálica hacia un valle muy profundo, formado de rocas vegetales que rodeaban un gran lago de lava en plena ebullición; como un mar rojo que producía burbujas gigantescas cuyo continuo estallido arrojaba enormes y espumeantes oleadas de fuego sobre otras rocas de azufre, donde agonizaban, clavados de pies y manos, multitud de hombres desnudos, algunos de ellos vivos todavía y otros ya carbonizados, o bien petrificados. Y las alucinadas contorsiones de los vivos, sus aullidos, desmentían las más elevadas idealizaciones del Mundo Macho, otorgando al dolor su dimensión más justa, la que lo hace odioso, la que lo hace castigo y nunca gracia; condenación y jamás privilegio.

Columnas oscurecidas, que aparecían también entre el hervor de la lava, mostraban más hombres atados, cuyos vientres abiertos dejaban caer en el fuego sus entrañas sangrientas que la corriente se llevaba hacia la pequeña cascada de cuya espuma nace el riachuelo que lleva el agua hacia otra cascada enorme, que se adentra en los abismos más profundos de la tierra y cuyo fondo nunca vieron siquiera los mismísimos dioses que todo lo ven. Así comprendí que lo que alimenta el interior de la tierra es, precisamente, la sangre y las entrañas de los millones de hombres que sufren el tormento eterno, atados a las innumerables rocas y a las columnas del Lago del Tiempo.

Y cuando supe que aquél era el lago, volvió a mí, entre gritos de dolor, una voz que me repetía desde siempre: En el Lago del Tiempo, monseñor, se encuentra tu destino...

REGRESA LA OBSESIÓN DEL DESIERTO, el viento suave que me colma la visión de arena, pantalla incómoda que se interpone, con insistencia, entre mis ojos y estas calles donde el agua de los riegos se seca demasiado rápidamente para aliviar, de día, la asfixia del bochorno prematuro. Me han aconsejado que alquile un jeep y visite las ruinas de Antinoé, ciudad muerta que un día fue lujoso regalo de Adriano a su favorito, ahogado, según dicen, cerca de aquí; también me han aconsejado —los habitantes de Minia no cesan de aconsejar cosas— que alquile un taxi con otros turistas y visite la tumba helenizante de Potosiris, en Tunah-el-Gebel. Pero son consejos que me resbalan porque ya soy impermeable a cualquier motivo externo, cualquier paisaje, cualquier provocación que no provenga de mis ansias por contemplar de nuevo las selvas tupidas del Mundo Macho.

Al mismo tiempo, me oculto en la habitación miserable que el profesor tuvo la amabilidad de alquilarme cuando me escapé del hotel, y rezo a Cobra para que Larry y sus secretarias, lanzadas como furias en una búsqueda frenética por los callejones de Minia, no consigan encontrarme nunca. Que el nuevo Astor llegue antes que ellos; que el nuevo Astor tome las riendas de mi caballo alígero y me diga: «Monseñor, ya no habrá vida sobre el Mundo Macho si tú no regresas del País de la Nada, vencedor como siempre.»

En ningún lugar del mundo puede existir hedor más ofensivo que el que me llega desde la calle a esta habitación donde, además, parece que hieden los cadáveres de un millón de serpientes en plena putrefacción. Quienquiera que me lea, ignorando sin duda el hedor de las serpientes muertas, creerá que exagero o que no poseo datos objetivos para efectuar tal constatación. Y, sin embargo, los tengo. Porque este hedor repulsivo acude a mí diariamente como un espanto; vuelve una y otra vez y me transporta al pozo del Lago del Tiempo donde Cobra Macho, el gran símbolo de la Creación única, devoraba a sus compañeras de raza, revelándome así que, en el combate nunca concluido del cosmos contra el cosmos, los dioses deben devorarse entre sí para dar lugar a la vida que triunfa perentoriamente. Esto es lo que he intentado explicar al profesor, entre el sueño inquieto de la droga que me ofrecía y que, nuevamente, he cambiado por un «Cleopatra», garantía cuando menos de un mínimo de lucidez.

No se extrañó al verme regresar, pues ha sabido que un extranjero poderoso acaba de llegar a Minia acompañado por dos secretarias rubias que le ayudan a buscar a un muchacho joven, francés por más señas, que está completamente paranoico y se dedica a perseguir a los adolescentes mejor dotados de la ciudad. No fue necesario que yo acusase a Larry de calumniador infame, porque Spiros Markopoulos sabe perfectamente que, cuando me acerco desesperado a los muchachitos de Minia, mi única intención es prevenirles de la gran amenaza del Mundo Macho, cuyos tentáculos siempre andarán al acecho de las víctimas potenciales de esta ciudad, de todas las ciudades cuyas jóvenes generaciones puedan latir con promesas de futuro para una raza sumamente bella y poderosa. Pero esta limosna se debe a que el profesor es el único capaz de creer a este pobre loco que nunca será creído por nadie, porque Larry estará siempre en guardia, engañando a los demás con el dinero que esté dispuesto a pagar. Incluso es muy posible que, de no ser por la protección de Spiros Markopoulos, a estas horas yo me encontrara ya en el tren, atado de pies y manos por los contratos que Larry ha firmado, ensayando la sonrisa que deberé ejecutar dentro de dos días en el aeropuerto de Fiumicino, mientras los esclavos de la prensa disparan sus flashes y mi mundo respira aliviado, porque, finalmente, me recobra.

Pero yo he gritado: «¡Socorro, socorro!»; y ni Larry ni el profesor, ni sus dioses ni los del Mundo Macho, pueden ya ayudarme. Y, arrodillado ante aquella maltrecha reminiscencia de hombre exquisitamente civilizado —Spiros ya es menos que una ruina—, le he rogado que, como mínimo, aceptara escuchar la continuación de mi historia.

Y cada minuto, cada segundo, tienen un deslizarse que resume lo esencial de todas las urgencias...

PENSARÁ USTED, PROFESOR, que sólo pretendo su ayuda. Y si tal pensara, se equivocaría por completo. Si me equivoco yo, es lícito suponer que, en mi narración, quiero hallar un intento de hacerle depositario de mi aventura, como si, gracias a usted, hubiese de alcanzar la inmortalidad. Si lo piensa, también se equivoca, porque no deseo que sea usted mi testigo; porque sé que mi historia, con usted o sin usted como oyente, pronto será archivada en el caos de recuerdos que le provocará el sueño del opio, o el sueño de vivir. Usted, para entendernos, sólo es el objeto al que puedo poseer ligándolo a una intención que no admite pausas. Y en esta conversación, que ya es sólo un monólogo, yo ejerzo mi gran poder de señor único, y mi trono es oral, y mi látigo cada palabra que le impongo; retahíla de palabras que, lanzadas en cadena, van generando el interés con el cual le tengo encadenado. Usted es mi esclavo, y por ello le ordeno que adore en mí la divinidad del Narrador que, con todas las cartas en la mano, tiene el poder de hacerle ver sólo lo que quiere, de revelarle las cosas que le apetezca revelar y dejarle *in albis* en todo lo que nunca estará usted en disposición de saber, si saberlo se opone a mis deseos.

Porque, en el Mundo Macho, yo he aprendido todas las leyes de la crueldad, y ahora sé cómo aplicarlas, una por una, en variantes tan excelsas que no necesitan ser obvias.

Mi importancia histórica ha sido profética y es incalculable, porque he sabido aportar a la crueldad del Mundo Macho la impensada variante del espíritu. Impensada, digo, pero añado que también ilimitada, porque el espíritu sufre hasta mucho más allá de donde el cuerpo puede aguantar, y ofrece muchas más resistencias a la muerte. El tormento infligido al cuerpo tiene una duración que los héroes pueden prolongar; pero si insistimos, incluso esta prolongación queda sujeta a nuevas reglas, a un código que resulta inevitable cuando el dolor afecta de manera absoluta a un órgano cuya destrucción lleva directamente a la muerte. Y esto no sucede con el espíritu. En su caso, la humillación del tormento puede encontrar todas las resistencias, pero una crueldad sabiamente administrada también sabe abrir los caminos más privados del dolor. Y lo que acaba por triunfar no es la muerte, como sucede con el cuerpo agotado, sino una dosis cada vez más odiada de vida que se renueva, de sentimientos que, heridos y atormentados, no es posible matar como se quiera, sino que viven con más fuerza, acuchillando hasta el final. El tormento que un espíritu puede infligir a otro tiene la ventaja suprema de convertir el dolor en vida insoportable, y la muerte en consuelo imposible.

¿Reconocerá algún día el Mundo Macho que yo instauré este tipo de crueldad, donde una historia de muchos siglos sólo se había preocupado por cultivar las excelencias del dolor que, como un reto, eleva el cuerpo hasta cimas de titanismo y apenas más? Sólo cuando recobre mi trono en el palacio de Lur sabré si el registro de todas las historias recuerda este hito del cual, ahora, en esta habitación maloliente, no sé si sentirme orgulloso o, por el contrario, declararme el hombre más vil de vuestro País de la Nada.

Sin embargo, diré que para una perfecta aplicación de aquella ciencia que yo acababa de inventarme era necesario que alguien descubriese, más allá de su cuerpo perfecto, un espíritu vulnerable, capaz del sentimiento. Durante el tiempo que permanecí en el Mundo Macho, nada me hizo presuponer que la noción de sentimiento existiese y, si alguna vez ha existido, era evidente que alguien, alguna persona, alguna ley, la apartó para siempre en nombre de una raza que pretende basar su poder ilimitado partiendo de la apariencia más recia. Y no supe ver que Astor había cambiado; que había ido desarrollando sacrílegamente el espíritu, al modo de los herejes, asesinando lo que en otro tiempo yo había considerado como mi propio espíritu. En aquella devoción, la de Astor y la mía propia, nacía, para ser inscrita en los libros de acero que registran todas las historias, la verdadera semilla de una herejía que todos los habitantes de Lur llevan en su interior, imborrable reminiscencia de otro eslabón perdido: éste cayó de la mano de Aquel que Ordena el Tiempo mientras luchaba contra Cobra, y es el pecado original que la raza maldita debe purificar con un bautismo de fuego en la Casa de la Vida.

¿LE HE CONTADO YA, PROFESOR, que al entrar Astor en la estancia me reveló la más aproximada imagen de la serenidad que yo pueda recordar? Pues el precio de aquel estado, que conducía directamente a la paz, tal vez había sido el reconocimiento de su gran crimen, perpetrado contra las leyes bajo cuyo imperio nació y vivió pero que ahora rechazaba, consciente de que su camino hacia las tierras de la Nada pasaba por la muerte del cuerpo que había sido baluarte del poder de Epsamón, y que, en sí mismo, como sinónimo de perfección física, tan útil propaganda me hiciese de las excelencias del Mundo Macho. Y al llegar a unos peldaños que comunicaban con un gran puente de rocas, tendido entre la ribera del lago y una gran montaña que sobresalía en el centro y contra la cual iban a estrellarse las oleadas de lava, Astor me dijo:

—¿No tenías tanto empeño en conocer tu destino? Epsamón era quien debía revelártelo, pero yo era el encargado de llevarte ante él; y yo, monseñor, ya no podré hacerlo nunca. Te dejaré aquí, enfrentado a tu verdad. Y veré cómo ella te destruye definitivamente, de forma que puedas ser la bestia más repugnante de Lur..., como aprendí que debía ser aquel que hubiera de regir nuestros destinos, el depositario de nuestra voluntad.

Increíblemente, Astor me reprochaba que yo fuese, ahora, todo lo que él me había enseñado. Cuantas mentiras yo había asimilado se volvían contra mí; y las lecciones que antes no quería aprender, quedaban ya grabadas en mi interior con una fuerza avasalladora, superior a mí mismo e incluso a Astor. El juego de contrarios se acercaba a una culminación estremecedora, y ahora mismo, como mañana, me arrastra a una navegación sin rumbo por un mar de dudas y confusiones donde ya no existe un solo lugar para la razón; un océano en cuyo oleaje se enfrentan entre sí la lógica de lo que el Mundo Macho me ha enseñado a ser y la lógica, completamente distinta, incluso opuesta, que siendo niño aprendí en vuestro País de la Nada. Y en este dualismo, Astor llegaba a mí completamente cambiado, para pronunciar la palabra *Ashnar* una vez más, dispuesto a morir por atreverse a pronunciarla. Pero al momento cambió la ya habitual dulzura de su declaración por una mueca de desprecio.

—Cuando te encuentres ante Epsamón, serás por fin el monstruo que yo he contribuido a crear.

¿Estaba a punto de descubrir, finalmente, el rostro verdadero de Aquel cuya orden me había arrebatado de mi mundo para convertirme en su compañero de reinado, por todas las historias que pudiesen venir a partir de ambos? Entonces se me ocurrió que, en este juego de intereses de alta política, de altísima historia, el sentimiento de Astor, recién descubierto, tenía una importancia capital. Pero ahora sé muy bien que apenas me encuentre en el trono del Mundo Macho, los descubridores como él serán los primeros a quienes perseguiré. Y agonizarán por toda la eternidad en las columnas y las rocas vegetales del Lago del Tiempo.

Astor llevaba en brazos a la muchacha y se mostraba indiferente a mi suerte, como si el solo hecho de mirarme ya hiriese en él aquel sentimiento, aquella ética, que le habían transfigurado por completo. Y en medio de aquel universo de fuego y cuerpos destruidos, abrumados bajo el cielo que era de piedras y de color rojo, infinito como parecía ser todo el conjunto entre y sobre el cual caminábamos, reasumí todas las enseñanzas de Astor y pensé que tal vez la amabilidad con que lo había tratado últimamente era la causa de su desviacionismo. Empujado por la necesidad de hacer sentir sobre él mi autoridad, le asesté un puñetazo, pero con tal violencia

—y, también, con tan poca pericia— que la sorpresa o el impacto le hizo tambalearse y la muchacha se le cayó de los brazos.

La altura del puente era ya importante en aquel trecho del camino pero, además, se erguían desde el fondo las rocas y las columnas más puntiagudas de todo el lago, y la muchacha quedó clavada en ellas. Se hallaban demasiado cerca, rocas y columnas, y las hojas de alguna roca llegaban a enroscarse alrededor de alguna columna: incluso iban a introducirse en las heridas de los hombres atados, cuyos cuerpos, aún vivos, formaban, de este modo, una especie de árbol humano, empapado en sangre coagulada, de la cual se alimentaba su savia. Astor se había arrodillado y miraba hacia abajo, donde el cuerpo de la muchacha quedó clavado: un trozo en una columna, otro en una roca; la cabeza, cercenada del tronco con el golpe de la caída, rodaba ya hacia el río. Curiosamente, una de las columnas le había atravesado el vientre, y no sólo brotaba de él la sangre y parte de las entrañas que son comunes a todos los humanos, sino también una especie de bolsa de placenta en cuyo interior se insinuaba una forma humana y, como cosa más fácil de reconocer, unos ojillos. Arrodillado, Astor se golpeaba el pecho con una de aquellas piedras calientes y me trataba de fiera inmunda, recordándome, de paso, que acababa de matar a un ser sagrado.

—¡Muy bien! —exclamé, ya molesto por tantos misterios—. ¿Quieres decirme de una vez qué tenía de sagrado?

—La vida que tú engendraste —gimió él—; eso era lo sagrado.

Pero los días felices que viví junto a mi reina, creando vida en su maravilloso cuerpo, cedían ahora bajo la urgencia de expresar mi autoridad, de demostrar a Astor que yo era el compañero de Epsamón y, por serlo, no podía volverme atrás aunque lo deseara. Recordaba mi primera ceremonia de la Purificación; recordaba también que él me obligó a devorar a su propio hijo, y se me hacía apasionante demostrarle que había asimilado sus lecciones a la perfección; al mismo tiempo, y no era menos apasionante, podía atormentar su espíritu, recién descubierto, con la idea de que todo cuanto hiciese lo había aprendido de él, y sólo a él debía aquella nueva sabiduría.

Al descubrir que la bolsa de placenta era el producto de mis días, de mis meses o años en el cubo de los espejos, elegí las piedras más afiladas y las fui arrojando contra el vientre abierto de mi reina; y Astor seguía a mi lado, contemplándome inmóvil con expresión de terror a través del cristal de la escafandra, por cuya superficie se deslizaba el vapor que casi imposibilitaba la visibilidad. Las piedras, arrojadas con la admirable puntería que adquirí en el cuartel de Lur, rompían el tejido blanquecino y penetraban en los ojos, en las manos aún informes —eran parecidas a las de las ranitas, con membranas finísimas que unían los dedos—, en las piernas aún no separadas: la bolsa nauseabunda, que era, de hecho, mi única contribución a la vida. Y aquel feto multicolor fue deslizándose a pedazos sobre los rostros de los hombres atados a las rocas vegetales, goteó sobre sus mejillas mientras ellos agitaban la cabeza desesperadamente, abrían la boca de par en par, pugnando por apoderarse del único alimento a su alcance que les permitiría seguir viviendo algo más y, con la contribución de las pocas vísceras que les quedaban, alimentar el curso de los grandes ríos subterráneos.

Pero una reacción insospechada de Astor me dejó atónito. Porque, de repente, se despojó de su atuendo metálico, y pronunciando, en un grito pavoroso, la frase de otros dulces momentos, *¡Ashnar, Nebjeperura, Ashnar!*, se arrojó al Lago del Tiempo. Pero no lo hizo avergonzado, como en aquella otra ocasión en que me insinuó su amor, sino con la nobleza de quien acaba de alcanzar una mayoría de edad que, en millones de casos, no llega nunca en la vida. Completamente desnudo, sin protección alguna, cayó hacia la muerte en un salto digno de ser premiado con la medalla de oro en las Olimpíadas de Lur. Y, como correspondía a su condición y a su valor, el suplicio que recibió en los abismos fue tan impresionante como su destreza olímpica.

—¡Yo he creado al monstruo! —gritaba en su caída—. ¡Yo he creado a Epsamón!

Pero no llegó a las llamas. La fortuna hizo que quedase atrapado por los dientes de los condenados, dientes que se hincaron en su cuerpo con gran avidez y lo mantuvieron suspendido en el aire durante unos momentos. Escuché los aullidos de Astor cuando uno de los condenados le arrancaba la carne del cuello, otro le desgarraba el brazo, otro más los dos muslos, y un cuarto la parte superior de la cabeza. El poderoso atleta que fuese mi guardián y, más tarde, el más directo testigo de mi evolución, intentaba utilizar la mano que le quedaba libre para arrancar de la boca al primer hombre atado los pedazos dispersos de mi hijo, y apenas lo consiguió se restregó por el vientre aquella masa blanquecina, gritando mi nombre y el de Aquel que Ordena el Tiempo y Odia al Hombre. Pero todo no duró ni siquiera un minuto, porque los dientes que le mantenían en tensión arrancaron las partes que apresaban, y él cayó sobre una de las rocas vegetales, mutilado ya en diversas partes del cuerpo, y con el cerebro saliéndosele del cráneo. Entonces tuvo un magnífico gesto heroico, pues utilizó la fuerza que le quedaba para arrancarse él mismo un trozo del brazo que colgaba del hueso y, en un último impulso, me lo arrojó al rostro.

¿Esperaba mi humildad? ¡Ah, tal vez mi arrepentimiento! Pero yo sabía que, en la relación amo-esclavo que mantuvimos desde el principio, él no podía tener la última palabra. Dispuesto a demostrarle mis poderes, me desprendí de la escafandra y en un santiamén devoré una parte del brazo que él me había ofrecido. De cualquier modo, no pude terminarlo: tan abundante era en músculos.

Entonces, la roca vegetal desprendió otras formas de vida tan inesperadas como estremecedoras. De entre las hojas petrificadas surgían arañas rojas y amarillas, no peludas sino espinosas, que cayeron sobre las vísceras de Astor y, después de agujerearlas, se ocultaron en el interior formando túneles, y el cuerpo fue hinchándose de forma desproporcionada, hasta que sólo quedó una especie de bola enorme en la cual sobresalían, devoradoras, las alimañas. Pero Astor ya había muerto, y el Mundo Macho me ha enseñado que la visión de cualquier suplicio sólo puede interesar a un espíritu selecto mientras la víctima conserva un soplo de vida que le empuja a resistir y buscar desesperadamente una posibilidad de supervivencia.

DURANTE MUCHO RATO seguí el camino que me señalaba el puente, y si volvía la vista veía que sólo dejaba a mis espaldas una oscuridad impenetrable, que ni siquiera permitía ver la superficie encendida del lago. Al principio, este telón de tinieblas me dio un poco de miedo, pero apenas alcancé el final del puente y me di cuenta de que la oscuridad iba siendo sustituida por un gran resplandor blanco, sentí el mínimo de tranquilidad que nos asegura la certeza de llegar a alguna parte.

Y llegué a una inmensa plataforma, de mármol tan blanco como el resplandor que se proyectaba hacia las rocas ígneas del cielo; aun siendo la cima de la montaña que se erige, única, en medio del Lago del Tiempo, parecía que no tuviese principio ni final, y sólo había en ella una doble hilera de sepulcros..., como un pasadizo de pequeñas pirámides blancas que diríanse erigidas sobre la Nada. Y al final de aquel interminable pasadizo surgía una nueva colina, siempre de mármol, sobre la cual se levantaba un templo que recordaba en todo al Partenón de los áticos. Pero no había flores, ni hierbas, ni el consuelo de una estrella en lo más alto.

Yo me dirigía al templo, denominado *Palazzo* en los

textos del Mundo Macho, y, al pasar por delante de cada sepulcro, aparecía un sacerdote que empuñaba una cobra y se arrodillaba a mi paso, de forma que pronto hubo muchos sacerdotes, cuyos cuerpos estaban cubiertos por piel de serpiente, cuyas cabelleras eran doradas y los labios y los ojos pintados de púrpura. No sonaba música alguna, sólo el rumor de este viento que el Nilo nos envía desde más allá del desierto; no se percibía más perfume que el hedor de esta droga con que llena usted la habitación y que tanto sueño me provoca. Y cada pirámide era un espejo sobre cuya superficie, por primera vez después de tanto tiempo y de tantos sufrimientos, vi el rostro que Epsamón Divino ha podido tener desde el comienzo de todas las historias.

Entonces adoré a los dioses de lo incomprensible, y su pene me poseyó definitivamente. Se borraron para siempre todas las manifestaciones simbólicas de Epsamón y las mías propias, las que yo había visto a lo largo de mis periplos por el Mundo Macho. Todas las manifestaciones que nos ocultan a los ojos del pueblo, todas las mezclas de dioses que nos prestan sus atributos, toda aquella extraña mezcla de formas externas, desaparecía bajo la evidencia del único rostro que Epsamón había tenido. Es decir: el único rostro que Yo podré tener a partir de este momento.

Epsamón era único, pero no había existido *sólo* un Epsamón. En el mármol de cada pirámide que me reflejaba, con verdad implacable, comprendí de repente toda la historia del Mundo Macho; y le juro a usted, profesor, que no he intentado explicárselo a nadie, tal vez porque sé que nadie (y usted mismo se reiría de la historia, si estuviese despierto) querrá creer jamás que Epura Epsamón y Nebjeperura, el Co-Divino, son una misma persona renovada continuamente a lo largo de los siglos.

Y que desde el primer siglo de la Creación hasta el último, cuando el Tiempo se haya agotado a sí mismo, esta persona soy, precisamente, Yo.

Y COBRA ME DICE:

«Tiembla, hijo de la Agonía, porque contemplarás tu destino, y, como en el mío, verás en él algo que te encadenará para siempre a la anulación total, como me encadenó a mí. Ningún dios ha podido escapar a esta fatalidad, ningún dios ha podido contemplar toda la historia que le ha precedido y seguir siendo como antes. Como yo, que soy el dios en forma de Cobra; como tú, que serás Cobra con la pesada apariencia de una condenación humana que siempre has maldecido, y a la cual, sin embargo, desearás volver a partir de este momento. Tiembla, hijo de la Agonía, porque no bien te sean revelados los misterios sabrás que yo soy su prisionero fatal, como tú mismo lo serás a partir de ahora. Y encadenado al culto que los hombres quisieron erigirme, yo te digo: Me das lástima, hijo de la Agonía, pues también tú entrarás en la divinidad, y ni siquiera de este modo serás el poder, sino sólo lo que el poder quiera que seas.

»Mírame, de este modo encadenado, y sé el nuevo Epsamón que el Mundo Macho necesita...»

Entonces, envuelto por los vapores que iluminan el gran altar de Cobra, pregunté:

—Pero, ¿quién del Mundo Macho? ¿Qué es el Mundo Macho? ¿Dónde y cómo empezó el reinado de Epsamón sobre la Tierra?

Preguntas que siempre aportarían una nueva duda como respuesta. Preguntas que me hacían descender a las profundidades más incógnitas de la sospecha sólo para hacer resurgir, triunfante como siempre, la certeza de que otro punto básico seguiría siendo inexplicable. Y con el derecho a la crueldad que me otorga mi papel de narrador, le ocultaría de nuevo la verdad si no fuese porque el sueño de usted me demuestra que todo esto no le importa en absoluto y que, por lo mismo, la crueldad que quería administrarle en dosis narrativas se vuelve en contra mía, y yo soy quien padece por su culpa, ya que rechaza mi engaño.

Con todo, si esta historia termina no es culpa mía, ni siquiera de la historia en sí misma, que podría prolongarse hasta el infinito como sucede, por otra parte, con cualquier historia del mundo. Cada elemento del Mundo Macho, cada pequeño detalle de una decoración, de un vestido, de una hazaña inscrita con letras de sangre en sus Crónicas, favorecería análisis tal vez interminables, porque cada motivación llevaría a otras nuevas, porque todas se engendrarían, multiplicándose hasta llegar, siempre, a una última verdad que sólo es la inexplicabilidad de los misterios de Cobra, en los cuales quiero ver —o bien, quería— la esencia de la vida. Falso, profesor; todo falso, como el interés de usted, como esta droga que ahora empezaré a consumir puesto que necesito toda la fuerza de la inconsciencia —divina o humana, lo mismo da— para volver a la Corniche, moderar mi paso al oír otros pasos más poderosos, volverme y descubrir entre la oscuridad los ojos inconfundibles del nuevo Astor, que me devolverá a mi trono de Lur donde permaneceré encadenado como Cobra, como Epsamón, como todos los dioses que, un día, decidieron ponerse al servicio del poder del Mundo Macho.

«Mírame encadenado de este modo —dijo Cobra aquel día—; mírame y, a partir de ahora, sé el nuevo Epsamón que el Mundo Macho necesita...»

—Pero, ¿quién del Mundo Macho? —pregunté—. ¿Qué es el Mundo Macho? ¿Dónde y cómo empieza el reinado de Epsamón sobre la Tierra?

Cobra abrió para mí el abanico de todas las historias, y en la abigarrada tempestad del Tiempo que parece deslizarse, y, sin embargo, nunca se ha deslizado, apareció, incorporado a un solo instante, todo el historial de Epsamón, todas las manifestaciones de mi rostro. De la matriz totalmente abierta de los siglos, de los obscenos pezones de la vida, brotó la placenta espesa que flotaba sobre el *Palazzo* del Lago del Tiempo, y la Historia se reprodujo en un momento tal y como yo la había aprendido en la pizarra de mi colegio bretón, tal como puede usted saberla, pero como nunca la sabrá el pueblo del Mundo Macho. Los pezones se hincharon, la matriz se rompió, y en el líquido flotaron todas las ciudades que, a través de la Historia, inspiraron cada edificio de Lur; flotó cada hombre que ideó una catedral, que concibió un palacio renacentista; que, en medio del desierto, erigió la aniquiladora majestad de las pirámides. Resurgió todo el mundo que usted y yo conocemos, toda la lucha del hombre contra la Nada inicial de la vida, y la otra Nada que le espera al morir. Y de cada ciudad en el momento preciso de hacerse, en todos los momentos en que se iba desarrollando a partir de un primer estado de vejez, surgían las calles de Lur tal como yo las había visto, las murallas bárbaras, los campanarios dorados que sobresalían entre las terrazas colgantes de los barrios residenciales, las columnas dóricas de los edificios administrativos, el colosalismo de las estatuas que representaban a Epsamón Divino, nunca igual, nunca reconocible.

¡Epsamón Divino! Mi rostro es el suyo. Soy él.

Surge de la niebla, mandando a sus ejércitos con el bastón dorado de la autoridad suprema, y tiene mi rostro. Transcurren miles de años, y en otra acometida del poder de Lur se coloca la corona de los dos países, y tiene mi rostro. Pasan los siglos, las historias avanzan, Epsamón Divino levanta su espada para descuartizar al rey de los herejes, y nunca deja de tener mi rostro.

—¡Cobra! —grito, ya—; ¿dónde y cuándo empieza el reinado de Epsamón sobre la Tierra?

Ahora aprendo que la cárcel de Cobra es la más cruel de las condenas; el dios supremo es una serpiente monstruosa, un cuerpo que, cuando se levanta, cuando hincha su cabezota descomunal, alcanza la altura de los palacios más altos de Lur. Pero al gruñir, esta bestia siente lástima de sí misma, como todas las víctimas del Mundo Macho, llora por su propio destino y, cuando quiere escapar se lo impiden las cadenas que la mantienen atada, y entonces escupe su veneno sobre un enorme pozo en cuyo fondo de tinieblas millones de pequeñas cobras se devoran unas a otras, agonizan bajo la corriente venenosa que les arroja, desde su altura suprema, ese grotesco señor de todo lo creado. La fuerza que engendró la vida, la explicación que ha patrocinado el gran caos y a la vez el gran orden del universo, gime en su cárcel, y yo quiero saber quién la aprisionó.

Cobra introduce su cabeza gigantesca en el pozo de las serpientes, y yo veo cómo abre sus fauces para engullirlas a todas. La gran fuerza que creó el mundo está hambrienta de vidas como la suya; engulle a las bestias más pequeñas, esas que los hombres del Mundo Macho adoran como representación de una divinidad que sólo verán después de la muerte. Los dioses se alimentan de otros dioses. La gran lucha, el canibalismo supremo de las altas esferas, no debe producirse necesariamente entre contrarios.

Pero yo, profesor, fui raptado en Minia para ser compañero de Epsamón, para transmitir los rayos de la vida al pueblo, siempre a su lado; y ahora, en el *Palazzo* del Lago del Tiempo, descubría que yo, en tanto que pareja, no tenía importancia; que tampoco la tenía Epsamón en tanto que autoridad suprema, que ni siquiera Cobra Macho era una fuerza de la cual no fuese posible prescindir. Los mitos se desmoronaban, profesor; la cosmogonía se hundía estrepitosamente con sólo entrar en el *Palazzo* de Cobra y conocer que éste es, ha sido, será siempre, el gran prisionero. Y, sin embargo, ¿de quién?

De repente, Epsamón Divino. Mi rostro, profesor, estos rasgos que han tenido todos los Epsamones que reinaron en el Mundo Macho y todos los que reinarán después de mí. Miles de Epsamones a lo largo de los siglos aseguraban la persistencia de mis rasgos, y también de mi tristeza. Aseguraban que, desde el principio de todas las historias, Epsamón lucha en la guerra con el rostro cubierto, mientras los invitados de los Sumos Sacerdotes recorren el país de la Nada en busca de aquellos mismos rasgos, de aquel espíritu que se preste a ser domesticado por Ellos, a ser anulado como un día fue domesticado y anulado nuestro Epsamón Divino. Y el día en que Epsamón se rebele, habrá un Nebjeperura a punto para sustituirlo. Y también tendrá mi rostro.

Cuando Epsamón avanza hacia mí, es como si yo me mirara en un espejo. Mis rasgos, colocados en este cuerpo poderoso, se han tornado completamente inexpresivos, obedecen a las palabras que pronuncian los sacerdotes de Cobra, siguen el atajo que señalan las espadas de sus milicias; y, por fin, me revelan la única verdad posible de esta historia que aún no he entendido:

Mitos de Nebjeperura, ceremonias áulicas, salmos y leyendas, son espejismos que comprenden incluso la personalidad de Epsamón. Cesan las voces de la liturgia, enmudece el estruendo de las victorias contra el hereje, se apagan las grandes luces que convierten a Lur en una hoguera de placer ininterrumpido, y en la gran pantalla de algún cinerama destartalado ya sólo aparece la gran verdad del poder. Batsá, Astor, Glauco, la virgen que fue mi reina, miles y miles de extras completamente desnudos, decorados ciclópeos de cartón-piedra, todo, son letras escritas con sangre sobre el enorme cartel que encontraréis a la salida del local y nos presenta a todos desfigurados, contrahechos por la voluntad de un único hacedor que invirtió el dinero en la producción y decretó que nos moviésemos a su antojo de gran dominador.

Epsamón avanzaba hacia mí y yo retrocedía. Cada uno de sus pasos correspondía con otro mío, pasos de una sola persona, rostros que chocaban en el espejo, ojos iguales a los míos, mi propia boca, duplicidad obsesiva de un mito que ponía en los labios de Epsamón mi propio aullido.

—¡Hazme libre! —exclamó Él.

Todo fue demasiado rápido para pedir a la narración un mínimo de coherencia. Cobra continuaba devorando las serpientes, intentando desprenderse de las cadenas, escupiendo gargajos de veneno a las hermanas que quedaban en el pozo y que iban reproduciéndose como yo me he reproducido a lo largo de los siglos; Epsamón, el poderoso, seguía pidiéndome la libertad, y yo retrocedía más aprisa; y así, incapaz de pensar, pero con la angustia latiendo en cada rincón de mi cuerpo, eché a correr sin mirar atrás, impulsado no por la necesidad de saber, sino por una urgencia de protección. Me deslizaba sobre el mármol de la gran llanura de las tumbas que llevan mi retrato; saltaba sobre las cadenas del puente, intentaba no caer en el fuego del Lago del Tiempo, donde los hombres atados abrían desesperadamente la boca y dirigían los dientes hacia arriba, sin duda esperando mi cuerpo; llegué a volar sobre las arañas que aún devoraban los miserables despojos de Astor; vomité sobre el jugo del feto que yo mismo había engendrado y, profiriendo los gritos más espantosos que aquel infierno oyese nunca, me encontré ante el cubo de los espejos y entré.

No quise detenerme, ni podía. Detrás de mí temblaban todos los espectros de un mundo de sombras inexplicables, pero también todas las certezas de una Historia en la que cada forma del poder había constituido una seguridad de aprisionamiento para la vida verdadera del hombre. Aquella persecución no era sólo mía: millones de hombres la padecieron antes que yo, desde dentro o desde fuera del Mundo Macho. Millones y millones de seres humanos, de bestias; miles de dioses, de mitos, habían descubierto en alguna ocasión que su rostro se refleja en una pequeña pirámide de mármol donde yace, amenazadora, la fuerza de un poder que llega a esclavizar a hombres, dioses y mitos y, así, les hace ser lo que el poder quiere que sean y nada más. Millones de hombres, sí. Y, en el fondo de todo ello, siempre la gran duda.

De un salto, entré en la cámara de los espejos y, al reproducirme éstos, el cuerpo de Epsamón apareció multiplicado por todas partes: me amenazaba desde cada muro que me reflejaba, desde el techo y desde el suelo. Y tenía un rostro inexpresivo, Epsamón Divino: cetrino, dominado, y, desde todos los siglos, víctima de su propio poder y, con respecto a sí mismo, esclavo y rebelde a la vez. Pero tenía los brazos levantados, estaba a punto de cortarme la cabeza con aquella tremenda cimitarra y yo, jadeando como él, comprendí que necesitaba atravesar los espejos y salir por los pasillos del templo de Homo Demeter, en cuyas grandes terrazas todo el pueblo de Lur estaría celebrando las primeras ceremonias de las Jornadas de la Reproducción. Al otro lado de esta pesadilla, me acogería, de nuevo, a la suntuosidad litúrgica que volvería a combinar el arte, la alegría, el lujo y los perfumes de todos los dioses que imperaron sobre tantas y tantas tierras ajenas al Mundo Macho.

DUERMA USTED A GUSTO, profesor, porque ya no me importa su atención ni su consejo. Duerma su droga; digiera el vino de zanahoria; váyase a la mierda, en resumen, porque no podría dar respuesta a mi pregunta inesperada: ni usted ni nadie; y, en el fondo, cuando abandone la habitación que ha tenido usted la amabilidad de prestarme, ya no me importará ni siquiera la pregunta. Terminaré mi narración, no me preocuparé en llenar ninguna laguna, volveré a Lur y nunca olvidaré que toda explicación, incluso la que les he dado a usted y a Larry, ha sido y será siempre absurda, puesto que nadie va a creerme. Y no voy a preguntarme por qué he sido yo el elegido: ahora lo sé; lo supe desde el momento en que descubrí el rostro de Epsamón y adiviné que él, como yo, fue alguna vez un muchachito alegre que saltaba por las calles de su ciudad anónima hasta que dos atletas vestidos de negro lo ataron cabeza abajo y lo introdujeron en el compacto anillo de montañas que rodea las selvas espesas en las cuales otro Epsamón, rebelde contra aquellos que le habían convertido en mito, tenía que ser sustituido, repitiendo de este modo la historia que no ha de interrumpirse jamás.

La historia de Cobra encadenada.

Pero no era Cobra, sino Epsamón Divino quien me cerraba el paso hacia las ceremonias que yo debía presidir, al otro lado de los espejos. Me disponía a entrar en un espejo, y él avanzaba hacia mí, amenazador, llorando de rabia e impotencia, soberano contra su deseo. Después, aquel cuerpo multiplicado hasta el infinito formaba un pasadizo de Epsamones que se cerraba cuando yo me lanzaba por él, en carrera rápida. Ya me hallaba entre aquellos cuerpos, y si me agachaba para evitar el golpe de Epsamón, todas sus representaciones me imitaban; y si me levantaba, él también se levantaba; y si yo corría hacia más allá de la pared, ellos salían de los espejos. Huía de Epsamón, que me perseguía, y a continuación debía retroceder porque me encontraba ante otro Epsamón, y muchos más al lado, arriba, encima..., y era siempre yo, sí, yo Divino, yo dictador, yo ángel de la muerte y demonio de la vida, lanzándome contra mí mismo al arrojarme contra Epsamón...

... salté sobre todos los Epsamones, sobre mi horror, rasgué el último espejo, caí en un vacío inmenso, flotaba entre escombros de la más absoluta negación, nadaba entre oscuras oleadas de no-existencia, traspasé finalmente los límites de cuanto yacía en los recovecos de la eternidad mucho antes de cualquier creación.

¿Qué insólito fondo llegué a tocar? ¿Qué principio, qué fin?

De pronto, o acaso siglos más tarde, mis pies desnudos rozaron el ardor de la arena y sentí que el desierto de Egipto volvía a ofrecérseme inmenso, con los pliegues de las dunas y el azul ilimitado del cielo como únicos elementos que llenaban con algo el vacío que se desliza, inalcanzable, al otro lado de los espejos.

Al caer mi rostro sobre la arena, al recibir mi espalda el flagelo del sol, fui consciente de que me hallaba en vuestro País de la Nada. En él perdí de vista los colores. Después, las formas. Y morí.

Y ahora sé que he permanecido demasiado tiempo entre vosotros. Y mientras Larry está a punto de encontrarme, por cualquier callejón enlodado de Minia, lanzo mi grito al viento y espero que, desde algún rincón del palacio de Lur, el nuevo Astor me oiga y, de este modo, me localice y tome las riendas de mi caballo alígero para guiarme hacia mi reino, hacia mi destino, hacia las letras que fueron escritas desde el principio de todas las historias.

«¡Mundo Macho —grito—, Mundo Macho!»

Es curioso, pero aún me parece pedir ayuda desde los abismos de mi grito. Y algo en mi experiencia me asegura que es una súplica inútil. Porque nadie me ha creído, porque nadie me creerá.

FIN

Roma, primavera-invierno 1970.
Primera revisión del texto castellano: Tánger, otoño 1985.
Edición definitiva: otoño 1998.